American Psychopathological Association Series

PSYCHOPATHOLOGY IN THE AGED

American Psychopathological Association Series

Psychopathology in the Aged
Jonathan O. Cole and James E. Barrett, editors, 332 pp., 1980

Stress and Mental Disorder
James E. Barrett, editor, 310 pp., 1979

Critical Issues in Psychiatric Diagnosis
Robert L. Spitzer and Donald F. Klein, editors, 355 pp., 1978

Psychopathology and Brain Dysfunction
Charles Shagass, Samuel Gershon, and Arnold J. Friedhoff, editors, 399 pp., 1977

Hormones, Behavior, and Psychopathology
Edward J. Sachar, editor, 325 pp., 1976

American Psychopathological
Association Series

Psychopathology in the Aged

Editors

Jonathan O. Cole, M.D.
Chief
Psychopharmacology Unit
McLean Hospital
Belmont, Massachusetts

James E. Barrett, M.D.
Associate Professor of Psychiatry
Boston University
School of Medicine
Boston, Massachusetts

Raven Press ▪ New York

Raven Press, 1140 Avenue of the Americas, New York, New York 10036

The material contained in this volume was submitted as previously unpublished material, except in the instances in which credit has been given to the source from which some of the illustrative material was derived.

Great care has been taken to maintain the accuracy of the information contained in the volume. However, Raven Press cannot be held responsible for errors or for any consequences arising from the use of the information contained herein.

Library of Congress Cataloging in Publication Data

American Psychopathological Association.
  Psychopathology in the aged.

  (American Psychopathological Association Series)
  Proceedings of the 69th annual meeting of the
American Psychopathological Association.
  Includes bibliographical references and index.
  1. Geriatric psychiatry—Congresses. I. Cole,
Jonathan O. II. Barrett, James E. III. Title.
[DNLM: 1. Mental disorders—In old age—Congresses.
WT150 A513p 1979]
RC451.4.A5A53 1980   618.97′689   79–65139
ISBN 0–89004–406–6

Preface

The present volume on the Psychopathology of the Aged emerged from the Sixty-Ninth Annual Meeting of the American Psychopathological Association.

There have been many similar symposia volumes on aging published in the last few years but most of them have had a strong biological or neuropathological focus. In the present volume, our aim is to focus on clinical issues in the psychopathology of the aged and we have consciously avoided giving encyclopedic attention to biological abnormalities, only stressing those the Program Committee felt were of special current importance such as Ingvar's work on brain blood flow and Heston's work on genetics. We have tried to combine overviews of the current state of the field with reports on recent research in the area and therefore included both overview papers by Eisdorfer, Friedel, Lawton and Reisberg on, respectively the psychopathology of normal aging, pharmacotherapy of depression, psychosocial therapy of dementia and pharmacotherapy of dementia with papers pulling together extensive work by the author such as Wells' analysis of problems in differential diagnosis in the elderly and Gurland's work on epidemiology in the elderly.

New data on psychological testing in the elderly by Cohen, Miller, and Perez are included as are drug studies by Gerner and Branconnier. Growdon contributed his new work on acetylcholine precursors as a rational and innovative approach to the treatment of senile dementia.

In short, we tried to provide the reader with an overview of the current state of research in clinical geriatric psychopathology and to offer him some new data from important growth points in the field.

In particular, we are delighted to be able to have Professor Sir Martin Roth, recipient of the Association's Paul Hoch Award, present an overview of his extensive work on diagnosis and outcome in the psychiatrically impaired elderly.

Our hope is that the book will be of use both to clinicians and to investigators interested in this increasingly important area of psychopathology.

The Editors

Contents

Part I. Overview

Part II. Psychological Dysfunction in the Elderly

Part III. Depression in the Elderly

Part IV. Paul Hoch Award Lecture

Part V. Treatment of Dementia in the Elderly

Contributors

David Behar, M.D.
Resident in Psychiatry
Department of Psychiatry
University of Iowa College of Medicine
Iowa City, Iowa 52240

Roland Branconnier, M.A.
Research Director
Geriatric Psychopharmacology
Boston State Hospital
591 Morton Street
Boston, Massachusetts 02124

Donna Cohen, Ph.D.
Department of Psychiatry and
  Behavioral Sciences
University of Washington
Seattle, Washington 98195

Jonathan O. Cole, M.D.
Chief
Psychopharmacology Unit
McLean Hospital
115 Mill Street
Belmont, Massachusetts 02178

Suzanne Corkin, Ph.D.
Department of Psychology
Massachusetts Institute of Technology
Cambridge, Massachusetts 02139

Peter Cross
Research Scientist
Department of Geriatric Research
New York Psychiatric Institute
722 168th Street
New York, New York 10032

Laura Dean, M.A.
Staff Associate
Department of Psychiatry
College of Physicians and Surgeons
  of Columbia University;

Center for Geriatrics and Gerontology
New York, New York 10032

David Dunner, M.D.
Chief of Psychiatry
Harborview Medical Center
325 9th Avenue
Seattle, Washington 98104

Carl Eisdorfer, Ph.D., M.D.
Professor and Chairman
Department of Psychiatry and
  Behavioral Sciences
University of Washington
Seattle, Washington 98195

W. Estabrook, M.D.
University of California at Los Angeles
Neuropsychiatric Institute
The Center for Health Sciences
760 Westwood Plaza
Los Angeles, California 90024

Steven H. Ferris, Ph.D.
New York University Medical Center
550 First Avenue
New York, New York 10016

Robert O. Friedel, M.D.
Professor and Chairman
Department of Psychiatry
Medical College of Virginia
Virginia Commonwealth University
Richmond, Virginia 23298

Robert Gerner, M.D.
University of California at Los Angeles
Neuropsychiatric Institute
The Center for Health Sciences
760 Westwood Plaza
Los Angeles, California 90024

Samuel Gershon, M.D.
New York University Medical Center
Department of Psychiatry
550 First Avenue
New York, New York 10016

Robert R. Golden, Ph.D.
Assistant Professor
Department of Biostatistics
School of Public Health
Columbia University
New York, New York 10032

Gerald Goldstein, Ph.D.
V.A. Medical Center 645–151 R
Highland Drive
Pittsburgh, Pennsylvania 15206

John Growdon, M.D.
Department of Neurology
Tufts University
Ziegler Bldg. 646
136 Harrison Avenue
Boston, Massachusetts 02111

Barry Gurland, MRCP, MRCP Psych.
Chief
Department of Geriatric Research
New York Psychiatric Institute
722 West 168th Street
New York, New York 10032

Leonard Heston, M.D.
Professor
Psychiatric Research Unit
University of Minnesota
Mayo Box 392
Minneapolis, Minnesota 55455

David H. Ingvar, M.D.
Department of Clinical Neurophysiology
University Hospital S-221 85
Lund, Sweden

Lissy Jarvik, M.D., Ph.D.
University of California at Los Angeles
Neuropsychiatric Institute
The Center for Health Sciences
760 Westwood Plaza
Los Angeles, California 90024

P. Kakkar, M.D.
University of California at Los Angeles
Neuropsychiatric Institute
The Center for Health Sciences
760 Westwood Plaza
Los Angeles, California 90024

Walter Keckich, M.D.
Instructor
Department of Psychiatry and Behavioral Sciences
University of Washington
Seattle, Washington 98195

Donald Klein, M.D.
New York Psychiatric Institute
722 West 168th Street
New York, New York 10032

M. Powell Lawton, Ph.D.
Director Behavioral Research
Philadelphia Geriatric Center
5301 Old York Road
Philadelphia, Pennsylvania 19141

Nancy Miller, Ph.D.
Chief
Clinical Research Program
Center for Studies of the Mental Health of the Aging
National Institute of Mental Health
Rockville, Maryland 20857

Francisco I. Perez, Ph.D.
Clinical Psychologist
Baylor College of Medicine
Department of Physical Medicine and Rehabilitation
6500 Fannin—Suite 1224
Houston, Texas 77030

Barry Reisberg, M.D.
New York University Medical Center
550 First Avenue
New York, New York 10016

Professor Sir Martin Roth
Newcastle University Hospital
Queen Victoria Road
Newcastle-Upon-Tyne
NE 1 4LP England

Michael Schlesser, M.D.
Resident in Psychiatry
Department of Psychiatry
University of Iowa College of
    Medicine
Iowa City, Iowa 52240

J. Steuer, Ph.D.
University of California at Los Angeles
Neuropsychiatric Institute
The Center for Health Sciences
760 Westwood Plaza
Los Angeles, California 90024

Robert Terry, M.D.
Chairman and Professor
Department of Pathology
Albert Einstein College of
    Medicine
1300 Morris Park Avenue
Bronx, New York 10461

L. Waltuch, R.N.
University of California at Los Angeles
Neuropsychiatric Institute
The Center for Health Sciences
760 Westwood Plaza
Los Angeles, California 90024

Charles E. Wells, M.D.
Professor of Psychiatry and Neurology
School of Medicine
Vanderbilt University
Nashville, Tennessee 37232

June White, M.D.
Psychiatric Research Unit
University of Minnesota
Minneapolis, Minnesota 55455

George Winokur, M.D.
Professor and Head
Department of Psychiatry
University of Iowa College of Medicine
Iowa City, Iowa 52240

Psychopathology in the Aged, edited by
Jonathan O. Cole and James E. Barrett.
Raven Press, New York © 1980.

The Normal Psychopathology of Aging

Carl Eisdorfer and Walter Keckich

*Department of Psychiatry and Behavioral Sciences, University of Washington,
Seattle, Washington 98195*

Among the more difficult problems currently being addressed by researchers and clinicians in gerontology is the definition of normal. The title of this chapter, "Normal Psychopathology," reflects a popular though arguable concept, namely that with the passage of time aging eventuates in pathology. If this were indeed the case, then pathology could be considered part of the cost/benefit alternative of normal living. It is our contention, however, that whereas aging is a bio-psychosocial process which brings with it certain changes in structure and function, and although an increased risk of pathology is present among the aged, it is misleading to view aging itself as a pathologic process. We recognize that this posture is not without problems, both empirically and in its implication for clinical intervention, but propose that a hypothetical structure that distinguishes the process of normal aging from the definition of pathology has much to commend it at this point in the history of gerontology (and psychiatry).

Epidemiologic data indicate that the number and proportion of elderly (over 65) will grow to approximately 29,000,000 persons (more than 12% of the population) as we approach the 21st century and will continue to increase until at least the year 2020 when approximately 18–20% of the population will be 65 or older. Studies indicate that this is a population at increased risk for physical, economic and social problems (41). Such change (and growth) in the age structure underscores the importance of dealing with an accurate data base from which to identify, understand, and plan for the needs of future generations.

This chapter examines three issues: (a) the normal data base concerning the psychopathology of aging and the difficulties in establishing that data base; (b) current concepts in the bio-psychosocial spheres of aging; and (c) gerontology i.e., the study of aging itself.

THE NORMAL DATA BASE

The establishment of a normative data base for older people is plagued with problems. The degree of functional change associated with primary as contrasted with secondary aging is difficult to determine. Primary and secondary aging are concepts described by Busse (5). Basically they refer to the differences which

1

occur as a function of time versus those which are consequences of multiple events occurring during the passage of time. Because such traumata as disease or psychosocial stress are inescapable and potentially cumulative in effect (22,25) it is difficult to identify those changes which affect the person because of the sum of multiple physical and psychological stresses versus those due to the normal process of aging itself.

Interpretation of the data on aging is also affected by the research strategy employed in obtaining such data. In studies of populations using cross-sectional, longitudinal, or even cross-sequential methodologies, the data are influenced by the fact that each population subgroup has experienced a different constellation of physical, social, psychologic, historic, and educational factors which will, in all likelihood, remain persistent influences on those individuals (9). A classic example of this type of problem is illustrated by cognitive testing in the elderly. Until 5 years ago it was widely thought that there was an inverse relationship between aging postmaturity and intelligence. In 1973, however, the task force on aging of the American Psychological Association recommended that this belief be discarded because the data were based on cross-sectional studies made with tests originally designed to study young adults (19) and did not hold up for a given sample over time. Other problems in interpretation have arisen since. Those persons less able to tolerate the traumata of life die earlier. Similarly, certain personality and behavioral types may be prone to disease and death at earlier ages, thus affecting the prevalence of such persons in later life. Statistically, the variance in psychological experiments increases as a direct function of age.

If researchers are ever to develop a true normal data base, all of these and other factors must be considered, and the aged cannot simply be aggregated into one group over 60. Further, the changes in performance in the aged appear to be indistinguishable among the younger members of this group, with change becoming apparent only in the eighth decade or later. This phenomenon is aptly described by Neugarten (28) who refers to the dichotomy between the "young-old" and the "old-old."

The young-old are in many ways indistinguishable from younger adults in terms of social needs, health, and physical condition. The old-old, i.e., those 75 and above, in contrast, are characterized as having increasing difficulties with health, cognitive dysfunction, social isolation, and activities of daily living.

BIOLOGIC ASPECTS

It is well recognized that the biogenic amines, norepinephrine, serotonin, dopamine, and acetylcholine, act as neural transmitters at the central nervous system (CNS) synaptic junctions (34). Monoamine oxidase, an enzyme basic to the metabolic degradation of norepinephrine in the brain, has been shown to be increased with age in peripheral circulation in human, rhesus monkey, and mouse in a series of recent studies (34). The levels of norepinephrine and serotonin in the hypothalamus of man and rhesus monkey appear to decrease significantly with age (23), although serum levels of norepinephrine may increase (P. Prinz, J. Halter, and M. Raskind, *in preparation*). Levels of dopamine in the striata of senescent mice are also reported to be reduced. The direct consequences of these changes as they relate to behavior in the normal older person are unknown at this time. We do know, theoretically, however, that alterations in CNS norepinephrine level may be associated with depressive illness and that idiopathic Parkinson's disease is characterized by a marked decrease in dopamine concentration in the nigro-striato-pallidal system (34). Changes in monoamine metabolism can significantly lower concentrations of homovanillic acid in the brain and have been associated with senile dementia (34), and lowered acetylcholine seems to be a factor in memory.

Correlations between disease and significant decreases in certain neurotransmitters are emerging, but it remains to be demonstrated that there is any recognizable change in behavior associated with these "normal" changes in the CNS.

Neuropathologically, the brain parenchyma involving both cortex and white matter shrinks 10 to 15% among aged normals and up to 30% or more in those diagnosed as demented (39). There is also a greater relative loss of white than gray matter in the aged, leading to a dilation of the lateral cerebral ventricles. Whether this decrease is related to neuronal loss or to other factors is an area of current investigation. Although neuronal loss is certainly present, it may not be a sufficient explanation for the quantity of shrinkage of the brain. Diminished extracellular space and reduced dendritic arborization in cortical and cerebellar Purkinje cells are doubtless also involved. Indeed, reduced arborization rather than neuronal loss, *per se,* has been implicated as a major factor in dementia by Terry and Wisniewski (39). Lipofuscin, neurofibrillary tangles, and neuritic plaques are present in both the "normal" or functional aged, and the severely demented aged, although in different proportions, with the nondemented aged rarely showing a density of plaques above the average of that found among dementia victims. A study by Blessed et al., (3) showed a strong correlation between decreased psychometric ability and increased concentration of neurofibrillary tangles and neuritic plaques. Wisniewski and Soifer (44), in a recent review, have implicated a β helical protein present in the tangles (as filaments) and related it to dementia as well as to advanced age. Although this does not show a cause and effect relationship, it does raise the question of whether Alzheimer's disease is an extension of a normal aging process that has somehow become accelerated or metabolically aberrant. The failure of the organism to metabolize proteinaceous material which may accumulate in the cells may be a variation of such a continuum from the normal to the pathological. Some cellular theories of aging propose that the cumulative effects of trauma such as genetic changes, chemicals, toxins, accumulation of waste materials, and stress result in cellular dysfunction and death (22).

Recent studies of immune globulins have also yielded interesting data since poorer performance is associated with elevated IgG in some studies, and with lower serum immune globulins among patients with demonstrable dementia (8). Older persons are ill more frequently than are the young, and illness and poorer cognitive performance have been clearly related, particularly so far as cardiovascular disease is involved (22,42). Change in performance as a prodromal sign of a terminal phase has also been suggested, although the data are still equivocal (36).

In many other theories and hypotheses of aging, stress has been acknowledged as a critical element in mediating or accelerating both the primary as well as the secondary aging processes.

Holmes and Rahe (25), in their work with the Life Events Rating Scale, have reported a significant relationship between life change units and susceptibility to disease. Over 40% of the items in the rating scale can be anticipated to occur with greater frequency among the elderly. These are items such as the death of a spouse, retirement, children leaving home, financial difficulties, etc. (13).

Neugarten (28), however, suggests that life change events may not constitute as severe a stress if they occur at appropriate and anticipated times in one's life. Although the death of a spouse is a traumatic event, aged women may be more prepared for such losses than are the young. It is hypothesized that becoming widowed at 65 is, relatively speaking, less impactful than losing a spouse at 35 (22). Loneliness, fear of rejection, interpersonal relationships, finding a new mate, and sexual problems were reported as the most difficult problems faced by the elderly in a survey of letters written to "Dear Abby" (24).

Stress, whatever the cause or time in life, seems to have diverse physiologic effects. Neurochemically the effects of stress are still a matter of some conjecture, but brain chemistry is probably influenced by both the severity and duration of stress. A decrease of norepinephrine level is usually found after conditions of short-term and severe stress, whereas a more moderate crisis over a longer period of time yields an increase of norepinephrine. Stress does not appear to alter the dopamine levels of the brain, however (34). These findings are consistent with neurochemical theories related to depression and stress.

As indicated, stress is probably a precursor of an array of illnesses, and far more an ideosyncratic response than initially suspected, although the details of that theory are not completely worked out. There is also a strong belief that stress and its subjective companion, anxiety, have a significant influence on cognition. There is, of course, an experimental literature relating anxiety to poorer performance on complex tasks including learning, and Birren (2) has proposed a discontinuity hypothesis relating high stress to impaired cognitive performance. That hypothesis suggests that changes in cognitive functioning are not affected directly until a critical level of stress is reached, after which there is cognitive loss. However, since the reserve capacity of the elderly is less than that of the young, the cognitive impact would be seen earlier and more rapidly (12). The literature indicates that the relationship between autonomic arousal and behavior is such that subjective anxiety may not be a necessary mediating factor, although state anxiety has been related to poorer performance in many tasks (F. Wilkie, C. Eisdorfer, and M. Raskind, *unpublished ms.*). This can best be illustrated by an inverted U-shaped curve with autonomic arousal on the abscissa and behavioral performance on the ordinate. According to this hypothesis, too low an arousal level, as well as too high an arousal level, will produce inefficiency and impair performance. Performance and associated learning seem to be best at an intermediate level of arousal (12).

Studies of learning indicate that older men appear to have poorer learning scores compared to the young because of heightened omission errors. This is most conspicuous at rapid presentation rates, with the difference diminishing as the pace slows down (15). It has been postulated that heightened arousal in older men might account for the greater tendency toward omission errors, and there is some interesting evidence in a series of studies by Eisdorfer and his colleagues using serial rote learning and concurrent GSR and serum free fatty acid levels to monitor autonomic response (20). To test this hypothesis, a beta adrenergic blocking agent (propranolol) was used in a study of learning among older men to block the autonomic activity, and improved responses in learning performance did result (43). It has also been postulated that a fear of failure in later life results in this hyperarousal and thus a tendency in the aged to become more conservative in their strategies. This means that the aged seem to require a greater degree of probable accuracy before making a response in contrast to the young who may be more motivated by a need to achieve, and thus more likely to respond to a given stimulus. Since reinforcement gives the high responder the edge, the strategy of holding back responses is perhaps more efficient, but less productive of higher performance.

One of the long propagated myths of aging has been the hypothesis of a universal progressive loss of cognitive functioning in later life. As stated earlier, we believe that the cross-sectional strategy has contributed to the perpetuation of this myth. There are a number of additional issues in this context, however. Psychometric testing, from its inception, was basically designed to assess educational needs, school performance, occupational achievement, or lack of ability to achieve in school. Horn, (26), in his extensive factor analytic studies of psychometric strategies, proposes that there are approximately 25 distinct elements or factors of intelligence including creativity, verbal productive thinking, expressional fluency, associational fluency, general reasoning, visualization, auditory abilities, non-symbolic recognition, memory, spatial, perceptual and practical intelligence, to mention only a few. Horn has organized these factors into two compartments which are labeled crystallized intelligence and fluid intelligence. Crystallized intelligence involves primarily the ability to manipulate familiar and semantic material and its utilization, while fluid intelligence involves more synthetic, nonverbal and plasticity skills. From Horn's work it has become clear that the relationship between crystallized and fluid intelligence changes with age. Performance on crystallized intelligence tasks appears to increase throughout adult life beyond age 50, while fluid intelligence tends to increase to age 20 and then begins to drop (26).

Horn has demonstrated that by varying the number of subtests reflecting crystallized intelligence or fluid intelligence, a pattern of decline or relative intellectual stability can be demonstrated in an aged population; thus, by varying the crystallized:fluid ratio, one could support or discount the contention that intelligence declines in the elderly.

The relationship between changes in cognition and biomedical variables is also worth noting since it may generate future studies. Thus, Wilkie and Eisdorfer (42) have shown that in a group of community-based volunteers aged 60 to 69 studied longitudinally over a 10-year period there was no decline in Wechsler Adult Intelligence Scale scores for those with normal blood pressure or mild hypertension. For those aged in the sample who had diastolic pressures of 105 mm Hg or above, a significant decline in intelligence test performance was noted during the same period, i.e., from mean age 64.9 to one of approximately 74.

Jarvik and her colleagues, in a series of studies of twins, has well demonstrated the importance of genetics in influencing the course of cognitive change even in later life (27).

Memory appears to be as difficult to assess as intelligence. Primary and secondary memory are theoretical constructs which are currently being used to study the process of memory storage. Primary memory refers to material which is still being processed in the consciousness after adequate stimulation, while secondary memory is stored. Thus material in the secondary memory must be retrieved to be identified. Much of our current clinical psychological testing evaluates secondary memory. An example is "immediate recall" in which retrieval from secondary memory is necessitated in addition to reports from primary memory. When primary memory alone is analyzed, and comparisons are made between older and younger subjects, age differences in primary memory are negligible. Secondary memory is, however, relatively more impaired when comparisons are made between "normal" older and younger subjects. The current belief that long term memory remains intact in the aged is not supportable in view of these findings (14).

It was mentioned earlier that cognitive strategies used by the elderly affected intelligence testing, and this seems to be a problem in testing memory function also. Older persons tend to be less focused in their learning and to respond to more incidental cues (4). It is almost as if the younger learner is responding to the more precise directions of the task, while the older learner picks up more peripheral information, and thus absorbs less of the specific material to be learned and is more sensitive to the context (4,31). A number of theorists and experimental psychologists (10) also contend that older persons develop their associations at a more superficial level. Thus learning and memory strategies which bind new data through mnemonic association, providing a "deeper" bonding, would be productive of stronger memory in older persons.

Research in learning, memory, and intelligence is among the most active fields in gerontology, and we have only touched on a few points to raise questions which are now being actively pursued. For example, one clinical consequence of the work on intelligence is the impact of the factor-analytic strategy of Horn and his colleagues, as well as those of current cognitive theorists (7). They point out that intelligence and cognition are complex concepts and require the interaction of a number of processes. This would indicate that our clinical orientation to a problem such as senile dementia has probably been too simplistic. For example, the initial deficit in dementia may be in retrieval from secondary memory, or it may be attentional, or an executive function related to strategy of cognitive performance. The difference might have consequences for intervention and care. Supportive therapeutic strategies for patients with senile dementia could be based on the type of cognitive dysfunction identified, as well as the etiology of the disorder. To date, relatively little work has been done to develop therapeutic strategies based on the microanalytic study of cognitive dysfunction. One of the primary limiting factors continues to be the absence of adequate psychometric evaluation in this sphere, as well as our therapeutic nihilism which has caused us to ignore the development of such techniques.

SOCIAL ASPECTS

If it is difficult to define "normal" in cognitive and biobehavioral studies, it is perhaps more difficult to attempt the establishment of behavioral normalcy in terms of the social milieu. The "agism" (6) of our culture stereotypes the elderly. The inevitability of aging is undeniable (and indeed much to be preferred given the alternative), but concomitant with that fact, it seems to be the belief that depression, isolation, and the loneliness of institutional life will occur unless we, fortunately, die from some other cause first. In actual fact, this view is misinformed. The family relationships and lifestyle patterns of the elderly are as diverse as those of their younger cohorts and indeed, perhaps more diverse.

At present, only approximately 4% of the population over 65 is institutionalized. Although this is a large percentage when compared to that of the younger population, it certainly negates the myth of inevitability: 79% of men and 59% of women live in some type of family situation in their own homes. Most of the rest exist independently as widowers or divorcees in solo living situations (38). Ninety percent of the aged have had contact with at least one significant outside family member each week, and indeed the number of children is an excellent predictor of whether the elderly person will exist in isolation. The relationship between the elderly and their children in this society is characterized by "intimacy at a distance." Children and parents tend to live apart but in close communication (35) with the children acting as intermediaries between the parent and the larger bureaucratic organizations. It has been demonstrated that children's knowledge of community resources is an excellent predictor of whether older persons enter the long-term care institution (40). Of some note in this regard is the fact that half of the residents of long-term care are childless. What this portends, given the currently higher rate of unmarried women and childless couples is, of course, yet to be appreciated. Children are, in many cases, the key to reentry to the larger society after retirement (38).

Retirement is one of the more significant social changes facing an elderly individual. The retired person must cope with systematic changes in both role and status. All previous periods of life (childhood, adolescence, parenthood) had been marked by growth with gains in competence, responsibility, rewards, and prestige (33). In retirement, however, the older person must face role attrition, status loss, and social isolation. One sees a marked decrease in institutional roles and a marked increase in tenuous and informal roles as aging progresses. Role attrition in the elderly results from loss of social identity and erosion of group integration which lead to an individual devaluation that is potentially demoralizing (33). It is interesting to note that this pattern is typical of social failure in younger cohort groups. In this regard, it should be noted that, clinically, retirement brings with it a "crisis" in only a small proportion of older individuals. Expectancy is a very significant variable in this regard. Those in the blue-collar labor force may view retirement as the cessation of a boring activity and a relief from an undesired pattern of life. On the other hand, individuals from higher socioeconomic classes may have a very different orientation, and there is some evidence (37) that individuals of higher socioeconomic status usually, after a period of adaptation, find some alternative ways to play socially satisfying roles. It is the individual in the middle, the white-collar worker, who had identified with his occupation that consequently has the most serious problems in his retirement. This is particularly the case if retirement represents "rejection" by the employer and is perceived as a reflection of the employee's inadequacy and failure to achieve the desired employment status.

The economic hazards of retirement are a significant issue, and doubtless have an impact on the psychological state of the individual, but this is a subject for consideration elsewhere.

It is widely believed that many of the social problems of the aged are related to our industrialized cultures, and it is presumed that older persons are better valued in stable, preliterate or primitive societies. While there are elements of truth in these beliefs, they are somewhat simplistic. A review of anthropologic data derived from observing patterns of aging in other largely more primitive cultures (11) yields the following hypotheses:

a. Where older persons control assets, they have a higher status and are perceived as more powerful.

b. A defined occupational role results in better treatment.

c. Higher status is accorded the elderly in more sedentary and stable cultures.

d. Higher status and better care of the aged are proportional to the affluence of the culture.

e. In migratory cultures, care is proportional to the resources available, with the aged receiving the lowest priority.

f. Affection is not necessarily linked to maintenance of the aged, and thus resources may be denied if scarce, even to the beloved parent.

g. Older persons are expected to leave the group for the (residual) common good in times of economic hardship.

h. The treatment of the aged is related directly to their social utility or potential social utility, e.g., as teachers and story tellers.

i. Knowledge, which has social utility and is valued, means power and influence for the older person who has such knowledge (see *h*).

j. The larger the family, the more likely the person will be protected in old age.

k. In mixed-modern cultures the support systems for the retired are inadequate, resulting in the need for supplementary charity and pauper status for many aged without families.

l. Senile older persons are highly vulnerable, and support systems are inadequate or absent in marginal economic circumstances.

m. In instances where the elderly are perceived to be closer to God and/or revered ancestors, to deny them resources is to risk the wrath of the divinity.

n. The culture may allocate a socially important role to the elderly by defining them as priests, witches, mystics, or transmitters of religious knowledge.

o. If the aged have high power and status, the young may be kept out of direct competition through "rites of passage." Typically this process will involve a hierarchical tradition which includes initiation rites and special educational (or mystical) experiences leading to advanced status (while, of course, the individual gets older).

p. In stable, property-oriented cultures, where older individuals may increase their economic control through ownership of resources, their social, political, and spiritual power may also increase. In such cultures power increases with age (and ownership), and thus the appropriately endowed older persons are properly nurtured by their descendants (11).

Thus the "normal" or "deviant" condition of aging and the aged is very much a function of the social, cultural and economic context. It is clear too that with current change in age demography and world culture, we may anticipate a period of social strain in which expectancies and behaviors will be in a process of flux.

PHASES OF GERONTOLOGY

The focus of this chapter can be better appreciated in the context of understanding the field of gerontology, that is, the scientific study of aging and the aged. Gerontology has been struggling with myths and realities of aging, including some which have been discussed above. Indeed, the first phases in the development of gerontology were the overcoming or debunking of myths and the dealing with nihilistic attitudes toward the elderly.

An individual entering the field of gerontology must often undergo a personal process of change in order to deal with his or her own nihilism and belief system. Society as a whole is only now beginning to understand this, and it is a critical role of gerontologists to help society deal with this realization. A later, clinical phase of the gerontologist's development consists of an attempt to understand, and perhaps to mediate, problems of the elderly on either an individual or social-political level, i.e., aging as a disease. It is to this stage that many applied gerontologists have devoted a great deal of energy in the past few years. The establishment of a base of normative data has been actively pursued, and therapeutic treatment of diseases of the elderly is one consequence of this primary goal. Senile dementias, pseudodementias, cardiovascular illness, and hypothermia are currently the focus of a great deal of research and active intervention in dealing with elderly patients. There is a basic philosophic problem, however, with this phase. It is based on a pathologic model—that is, the basic assumption that the elderly have diseases and that we must attempt to palliate those diseases.

The next phase lies in the future—one that we are just beginning to address. In this phase we begin to become aware that the aged are people who happen to be old, some of whom have pathology. This may necessitate that we rethink our concept of pathology. It strikes at a central premise of our social and professional belief-system, since deviance is often labeled as psychopathology. A recent meeting of the World Psychiatric Association presented cogent examples of the effect of labeling deviance as psychopathology, particularly focusing on the role of psychiatry in politics. Clearly, in some instances, if one deviated from the norms of society, even politically, one could be labeled as psychiatrically ill.

In clinical care, this concept has a number of simple if not simplistic parallels which should help identify the issue further. We know from studies of sleep and EEG that it is normal for many older persons to require less nocturnal sleep as they grow older, although too little Stage 4 or REM sleep is associated with cognitive difficulties. In most nursing homes, and indeed in many hospitals across the country, there is an enforced bedtime, and no heed is paid to the fact that an individual may never have gone to bed prior to midnight for the last 50 or so years of his or her life, or that, with increasing years, he or she requires less nocturnal sleep. If one cannot sleep at the assigned time, this is labeled as a sleep disturbance, and an appropriate sedative may be ordered by the physician at the urging of the nursing home staff. Indeed, the p.r.n. medication may be the physician's gift to the staff. The potential toxic side effects of this practice have been well discussed elsewhere (18,32). Nocturnal therapy and activity programs would be far better alternatives than enforced sleep but are almost never employed.

Clearly it would be an improvement to view sleep pattern variation of older persons as normal rather than as pathological. To allow the older person to read, do sculpture, or even watch TV seems far more appropriate than to pass out sleeping pills, yet, somehow, it seems easier to label the older person's behavior as pathologic and "treat it" than it is to try to change the social network of the institution and staff. By pathologizing, we can avoid a central issue: requiring the individual to conform to institutional demands.

The process of pathologizing may also involve a struggle for power in which older persons are perceived as patients and inevitably as the losers. Another interesting aspect of this problem is that often "pathology" does become the statistical norm, thereby creating confusion about what is normal and what is pathologic so that everything becomes pathologic, and therefore inevitable.

In the mental health network, the impaired older individual often meets, first, a clinical nihilism in which there is reluctance even to explore the cause of the problem. Diagnostic nihilism is fed by therapeutic nihilism. If the professional believes that there is nothing that can be done for an older patient, then it is a pointless exercise to diagnose accurately. Thus in the case of a difficulty such as dementia, potentially reversible causes are overlooked because of lack of interest in pursuing the diagnosis. Even when a proper diagnosis is obtained, and that diagnosis is nonreversible dementia, it is not uncommon to institute no therapeutic interventions for either the individual or the family involved. In this regard, a complicating issue resides in our dichotomization of psychiatric disorders into functional and organic. This concept, which emerged during an earlier stage of psychiatry, in which individual (or group) psychotherapies were the only available alternatives to institutionalization, has its vestigial effects in the attitude that the organically impaired patient is not an appropriate focus for psychiatric treatment efforts. Current data unequivocally support the value of a variety of psychosocial therapies for older cognitively impaired patients and their families (17,21).

Pathologizing allows us to categorize loneliness as depression and to deal with it at a distance, if at all. Certainly it is appropriate to be lonely when one leaves a wife, daughter, or family members to enter a hospital or nursing home. It is normal to be lonely when a spouse or friend dies or is lost to us. While we may all be quite willing to treat the patient who walks into our office suffering from a depression, are we willing to deal with the social and psychosocial events that cause the loneliness and isolation that many of the elderly feel as a result of institutional and social customs? The work of Abramson et al. (1) on models of learned helplessness and locus of control indicates that affective behavior may be a direct consequence of the loss of mastery that characterizes the life style of many older persons with diminished physical, economic, or psychosocial resources.

An abreaction to normalization, of course, leads to the opposite pattern, i.e., the tendency to ignore depression in its various forms since all older persons are supposed to be sad and lonely. This attitude is, in part, a basis for avoiding contact with aged patients, since the professional feels impotent in the face of this "normal" depression.

Obviously neither extreme of orientation is appropriate to clinical care. Rather, a careful evaluation of the individual is warranted, and the decision for treatment must be reached on the basis of careful consideration of alternatives. Elevated MAO levels and an increased probability of losses would put older persons at heightened risk for depression, but such patients are also at a high risk for reminiscence and existential sadness, reasonable states requiring understanding and support rather than medication. The clinician has a responsibility to understand the difference and to deal with his or her patient in accordance with that difference.

Paranoia in the elderly is usually treated with neuroleptic medication. Yet that paranoia may be the result of recent loss, isolation, and communication deficit. Undiagnosed hearing loss or a malfunctioning hearing aid can be significant factors associated with suspicion and paranoia in older persons.

Post (29) has described the transient paranoid reaction—a syndrome involving older persons living alone, principally women, many of whom have hearing loss, have recently moved, and are devoid of interpersonal contact apart from rent collectors. Such persons may retreat even further, driven inward by their fear and paranoia and become unable to shop or leave their apartments for fear of harm.

If we can look beyond the pathology and the wrinkled lines in the face and see an individual struggling with loneliness, isolation, sensory loss, role attrition, financial concerns, and status loss, then we can begin to see the aged as people like ourselves who happen to be old and subject to the vicissitudes of a nonsupportive environment.

We must not ignore the potential assets of the patient as a person. Focusing on cognitive impairment of older persons ignores the existence of specific skills, and thus programs which could increase productivity by upgrading skills or educational level are denied to older persons. Rehabilitation programs are restricted to the more youthful, and the result is a reinforced tendency to make older persons relatively obsolete in contrast to younger, more recently educated individuals.

This pattern exists in the face of the knowledge that there are great advantages to maintaining and exercising one's learning skills, that old people can learn new skills, and that most professions and occupations have changing data bases. We thus have a self-fulfilling prophesy. Old people become obsolete because society restricts new learning opportunities.

On a clinical level, we know from numerous studies that older people with dementia respond to social contact and stimulation with an increase in cognitive performance. Medications which are used for behavioral or sleep management often yield daytime sedation and decreased cognitive functioning as side effects. Because medication is used as a substitute for personal contact, the lack of social stimulation and isolation is cumulative, and results in a further decrease in cognitive functioning. A significant number of such patients could and do respond to long-term contingency therapies if released from pharmacologic constraints. Unfortunately, it is easier to abdicate care to an untrained nurse at 2:00 in the morning by the use of a range of medications than to carefully mediate patient care.

What are some of the potential solutions to the problems this chapter has presented? One possible solution is to revert to a more primitive era. Eskimo hunters, when they could no longer provide for themselves, did not return from the hunt unless they had meat. In the arctic winter this often meant not at all. Older Japanese would walk up to the mountain tops, and everyone would pray for snow. American Indian tribes would leave the infirm behind as they moved to better hunting grounds.

A much more difficult solution is to plan for a constructive approach to the integration of aging into the larger society. We can do this first by reinvesting in older people. This reinvestment is not only to increase their self-worth and cognitive abilities, but to benefit society as a whole. The alternative is, of course, to maintain a growing cadre of retired and economically indigent elderly who retain the power to vote but little else. Support of the aged should be perceived as healthy for the economy, not as charity. But in order to achieve this goal, the investment must promote social participation, not merely marginal viability.

Programs for reeducation of the elderly would also promote reinvestment of energies and resources. The elderly are capable of learning new careers and new technologies. This would again serve the dual purpose of increasing self-worth, while generating potentially enormous advantages to society. Perhaps new careers for the elderly should be explored to avoid obstructing the upward mobility of youth.

Technology can be used to compensate for physiologic declines in much the same way technology allows quadriplegics to lead useful lives. Improved lighting, larger lettering in phone booths, and signs of distinguishing colors on nursing home rooms and hallways, barrier-free environments, places to take long, safe walks—all of these have been empirically demonstrated to be helpful to older persons, yet often, they are absent in the proximal environment. Teaming an older person with a younger person in some occupations might provide the balance between experience and physiologic limitations. A matrix system rather than a ladder system of promotion would allow the older person to step across to a different job. This would involve a basic reeducation in the spheres of achievement and competitiveness. A redefinition of what is socially valuable is needed as well as a redefinition of the limitations of old age.

For those older persons who do have impairment and need some sort of supportive care, alternative support systems need to be designed. Subsidization of families who care for older, impaired relatives may be far more economic than our current nursing home placement system and might lead to less pathologic behavior. In England, it is possible to hospitalize an older parent for two weeks so the custodial family can take a vacation. In this country, we are horrified at such a waste of money, but then proceed to institutionalize the older parent for 52 weeks of the year, since the family can no longer cope without that vacation.

We recognize that in this chapter we have gone far beyond the scope of our mandate, but trust it was purposeful. A series of articles, handbooks, and chapters are available to study the specific bio-psycho-social changes which characterize the aged. Aging is, however, a dynamic process, and the aged change in ways which are interactive with society, as well as those mediated by internal biology and psychology. Social hypotheses tend to be self-fulfilling, and the latter part of the chapter addresses the pathology of our social attitude toward changes in the aged. For scientists and clinicians, the challenge of aging is a striking one. Not to meet the challenge would be unfortunate—for us not to attempt to meet it—tragic.

REFERENCES

1. Abramson, L. Y., Seligman, M. E. P. and Teasdale, J. D. (1978): Learned helplessness in humans: Critique and reformulation. *J. Abnorm. Psychol.,* 87(1):49–74.
2. Birren, J. E. (1964): *The Psychology of Aging.* Prentice Hall, Englewood Cliffs.
3. Blessed, G. (1968): Tomlinson, B. E., and Roth, M. The association between quantitative measures of dementia and of senile change in the cerebral grey matter of elderly subjects. *Br. J. Psychiatry,* 114:797–811.
4. Boyarsky, R. E., and Eisdorfer, C. (1972): Forgetting in older persons. *J. Gerontol.* 27:254–258.
5. Busse, E. W. (1969): Theories of aging. In: *Behavior and Adaptation in Late Life.* edited by E. W. Busse and E. Pfeiffer. Little, Brown, Boston, pp. 11–32.
6. Butler, R. (1975): *Why Survive? Being Old in America.* Harper and Row, New York.
7. Cohen, D. and Eisdorfer, C. (1979): Cognitive theory and the assessment of change in the elderly. In: *Psychiatric Symptoms and Cognitive Dysfunction in the Elderly: Measurement and Assessment.* edited by A. Raskin and L. F. Jarvik. Hemisphere Publishing, Washington *(in press).*
8. Cohen, D. and Eisdorfer, C. (1979): Serum immunoglobulins and cognitive status in the elderly. I. A Population Study. *Br. J. Psychiat. (in press).*
9. Cohen, D. and Wilkie, F. (1979): Sex differences in cognition. In: M. Wittig and A. Peterson (eds.) *Determinants of Sex Related Differences in Cognitive Functioning.* New York: Academic Press.
10. Craik, F. I. M. (1977): Age differences in human memory. In: *Handbook of the Psychology of Aging.* edited by J. E. Birren and K. W. Schaie. Van Nostrand Reinhold, New York, pp. 384–420.
11. Eisdorfer, C. (1979): The implications for public policy of other ways of growing old—The afterword. In: *Other Ways of Growing Old,* edited by P. Amoss and S. Harrell. Stanford University Press, Stanford.
12. Eisdorfer, C. (1977): Intelligence and cognition in the aged. In: *Behavior and Adaptation in Late Life.* edited by E. Busse and E. Pfeiffer. Little, Brown, Boston, pp. 212–226.
13. Eisdorfer, C. (1977): Stress, disease and cognitive change in the aged. In: *Cognitive and Emotional Disturbance in the Elderly: Clinical Issues.* edited by C. Eisdorfer and R. Friedel. Year Book Medical Publishers, Chicago, pp. 27–44.

14. Eisdorfer, C. (1978): Psychophysiologic and cognitive studies in the aged. In: *Aging: The Process and the People.* edited by G. Usdin and C. J. Hofling. Brunner/Mazel, New York, pp. 96–129.
15. Eisdorfer, C., Axelrod, S., and Wilkie, F. (1963): Stimulus exposure time as a factor in serial learning in an aged population. *J. Abnorm. Psychol.* 67:594–600.
16. Eisdorfer, C. and Cohen, D. (1980): Immunologic-behavioral relationships in the cognitively impaired elderly. *Br. J. Psychiat. (in press).*
17. Eisdorfer, C., Cohen, D. and Preston, C. (1979): Behavioral and psychological therapies for the older patient with cognitive impairment. In: *The Clinical Aspects of Alzheimer's Disease and Senile Dementia.* edited by G. Cohen and N. Miller, Raven Press, New York *(in press).*
18. Eisdorfer, C. and Friedel, R. O. (1977): Psychotherapeutic drugs in aging. In: *Psychopharmacology in the Practice of Medicine.* edited by M. Jarvik. Appleton-Century-Crofts, New York, pp. 361–374.
19. Eisdorfer, C. and Lawton, M. P. (eds.) (1973): *The Psychology of Adult Development and Aging.* The American Psychological Association, Washington.
20. Eisdorfer, C., Nowlin, J. and Wilkie, F. (1970): Improvement of learning in the aged by modification of autonomic nervous system activity. *Science,* 170:1327–1329.
21. Eisdorfer, C. and Stotsky, B. A. (1977): Intervention, treatment and rehabilitation of psychiatric disorders. In: *Handbook of the Psychology of Aging.* edited by J. E. Birren and K. W. Schaie. Van Nostrand Reinhold, New York, pp. 724–748.
22. Eisdorfer, C. and Wilkie, F. (1977): Stress, disease, aging and behavior. In: *Handbook of the Psychology of Aging.* edited by J. Birren and W. Schaic. Van Nostrand Reinhold, New York, pp. 251–275.
23. Finch, C. E. (1977): Neuroendocrine and autonomic aspects of aging. In: *Handbook of the Biology of Aging.* edited by C. E. Finch and L. Hayflick. Van Nostrand Reinhold, New York, pp. 262–280.
24. Gaitz, C. M. and Scott, I. (1975): Analysis of letters to 'Dear Abby' concerning old age. *Gerontologist,* 15(1):47–51.
25. Holmes, T. H. and Rahe, R. H. (1967): The social readjustment rating scale. *J. Psychosom. Res.* 11:213–218.
26. Horn, J. L. (1975): Psychometric studies of aging and intelligence. In: *Aging. Volume 2: Genesis and Treatment of Psychologic Disorders in the Elderly.* edited by S. Gershon and A. Raskin. Raven Press, New York, pp. 19–43.
27. Jarvik, L. and Cohen, D. (1973): A biobehavioral approach to intellectual changes with aging. In: *The Psychology of Adult Development and Aging.* edited by C. Eisdorfer and M. P. Lawton. The American Psychological Assn., Washington, pp. 220–280.
28. Neugarten, B. (1978): The future and the young-old. In: *Aging into th 21st Century. Middle Agers Today.* edited by L. F. Jarvik. Gardner Press, New York, pp. 137–152.
29. Post, F. (1973): Paranoid disorders in the elderly. *Postgrad. Med.* 53(4):52.
30. Prinz, P., Halter, J., and Raskind, M. (1980): Diurnal catecholamine variations in young and old men. *J. Clin. Endocrinol. Metab. (submitted).*
31. Rabbitt, P. (1977): Changes in problem solving ability in old age. In: *Handbook of the Psychology of Aging.* edited by J. E. Birren and K. W. Schaie. Van Nostrand Reinhold, New York, pp. 606–625.
32. Raskind, M. and Eisdorfer, C. (1977): When elderly patients can't sleep. *Drug Ther.,* 7(8):44–50.
33. Rosow, I. (1976): Status and role change through the lifespan. In: *Handbook of Aging and the Social Sciences.* edited by R. H. Binstock and E. Shanas. Van Nostrand Reinhold, New York, pp. 451–482.
34. Samorajski, T. (1975): Age-related changes in brain biogenic amines. In: *Aging. Volume 1: Clinical, Morphologic and Neurochemical Aspects in the Aging Central Nervous System.* edited by H. Brody, D. Harman, and J. M. Ordy. Raven Press, New York, pp. 199–214.
35. Shanas, E. (1962): *The Health of Older People: A Social Survey.* Harvard University Press, Cambridge.
36. Siegler, I. C. (1975): The terminal drop hypothesis: Fact or artifact. *Exp. Aging Res.* 1:168–185.
37. Simpson, I. H., Back, K. W. and McKinney, J. C. (1966): Attributes of work involvement in society and self-evaluation in retirement. In: *Social Aspects of Aging.* edited by I. H. Simpson and J. C. McKinney. Duke University Press, Durham, pp. 55–74.

38. Sussman, M. (1976): The family life of old people. In: *Handbook of Aging and the Social Sciences.* edited by R. H. Binstock and E. Shanas. Van Nostrand Reinhold, New York, pp. 218–243.
39. Terry, R. D. and Wisniewski, H. M. (1975): Structural and chemical changes of the aged human brain. In: *Aging, Volume 2: Genesis and Treatment of Psychologic Disorders in the Elderly.* edited by S. Gershon and A. Raskin. Raven Press, New York, pp. 127–142.
40. Tobin, S. S. and Kulys, R. (1979): The family and services. In: *Annual Review of Gerontology and Geriatrics.* edited by C. Eisdorfer. Springer, New York *(in press).*
41. U. S. Department of Commerce, Series P23, No. 43, February, 1973. Some demographic aspects of aging in the U.S.
42. Wilkie, F. and Eisdorfer, C. (1971): Intelligence and blood pressure in the aged. *Science.* 172:959–962.
43. Wilkie, F., Eisdorfer, C. and Nowlin, J. B. (1976): Memory and blood pressure in the aged. *Exp. Aging Res.* 2(1):3–16.
44. Wisniewski, H. M. and Soifer, D. (1979): Neurofibrillary pathology: current status and research perspectives. *Mech. Aging Dev.* 9:119–142.

OPEN DISCUSSION

Dr. Robert Spitzer: It is not clear to me what you mean when you say we have to reevaluate our attitude toward what is psychopathological. For example, do you feel that the intellectual decline associated with aging should be regarded as pathological?

Dr. Keckich: My view is that we cannot say at this time that intellectual decline is primarily a normal part of aging. The data base is too confused because of cohort problems and problems of data interpretation. We don't know at this point whether such decline is a normal part of aging or whether it is related to the secondary aspects of aging such as stress, illness, or trauma.

Dr. Robert Spitzer: It strikes me that what is called normal really is often a function of whether a condition is treatable. Very often we regard something as normal if we think it is inevitable, but that may only mean that we do not have a treatment yet.

Dr. Keckich: I am uncomfortable with an operational definition of pathology or normalcy that is tied directly to the ability to change or intervene in a process. Sleep in the elderly is an example. We can intervene and cause older persons to sleep by use of medications, and yet this does not answer the question of pathology versus normalcy. In fact, in the case of sleep, we have an example where something normal has been labeled pathological many times. Studies show the elderly need less sleep, and medications are used regularly to "cure" that supposed pathology. We should not let the fact of normalcy or pathology influence the stimulation of research and intervention in an area. We can many times change what nature intended to be "normal."

Dr. Robert Spitzer: The sleep problem is really quite different. If somebody only needs 4 hr of sleep instead of 8, so much the better. I don't see how that is in any way dysfunctional. On the other hand, if somebody has a detriment in intellectual function, that is undesirable, and then the issue is what kind of things that are undesirable do we want to consider pathological as well?

Dr. Keckich: I am not saying that to sleep less is dysfunctional or pathologic but, rather, the contrary in a healthy elderly person. What is pathologic, however, is society's response to decreased sleep in the elderly, which is to sedate the elderly. Undesirable aspects are often labeled pathologic, and this is a major clinical problem. In nursing homes, one commonly sees vicious circles of oversedation, yielding decreased cognitive functioning and leading to agitation and thus more subsequent oversedation.

Dr. Jarvik: I should like to raise two issues. One is a problem of definition. What do we mean by intellectual decline? I do not think we can simply speak of intellectual decline as such unless we very carefully define it. I think we do know that certain cognitive functions do not seem to decline with age in a population without psychopathology, while other functions do show a decline with age. For that reason, I think we need to be far more specific.

Secondly, I think sleep is very important, and I do not believe that old people need less sleep than younger adults. Even though sleep studies have shown that Stage 3 and Stage 4 sleep are markedly reduced in the elderly, I think that some of the psychopathology we see with aging may result from sleep deprivation as may some of the age-associated cognitive decline. We know that sleep deprivation in the young is associated with impaired cognitive functioning.

It would be very helpful if somebody were to keep sleep records on older people. Reports from our own twin studies show that there are people in their 80s and 90s who tell us that they sleep 10 hr a night, although they may get up to go to the bathroom and then go back to sleep again. I have a personal observation of an 89-year-old and a 91-year-old, each of whom sleeps approximately 10 hr a night, and both are functioning very well intellectually. We cannot dismiss these types of observations. We need to look into these areas.

Dr. Keckich: I would agree that we need to investigate both aspects. Your data that older people do not need less sleep is an example of the disagreement over interpretation of data present in this field, and it exemplifies the difficulties of establishing a normative data base.

Dr. Jonathan Cole: Mr. Branconnier and I have been studying a large number of symptomatic volunteers who come from the community, are over 65, and respond to advertisements seeking older people who have memory problems. We have declared them to be suffering from Senile Organic Brain States and have been running various tests on them. It would be very easy for us to say the subjects we study are, for example, in the bottom 50% of individuals studied on Test No. 17. But does that mean that they have senile dementia or that they are impaired? I wish there were some system of categorizing such people as normal or abnormal. Is there any solution to our problem? Is there a master test we can give which will tell us whether such subjects are normal or abnormal?

Dr. Keckich: There is no master test at this time that is reliable. This is an area which needs development. We need a reliable test of all aspects of cognitive functioning (fluid and dynamic) that is standardized in a way that would eliminate cohort problems.

Dr. Zubin: The controversy that arose between Dr. Spitzer and Dr. Jarvik really raises a fundamental question with regard to the aging problem. There are two components to be considered: there is senescence, normal aging, and there is deterioration. We must distinguish between the two. Everybody senesces. Things change as a person develops. We lose our Babinski reflex at 3 months, and that is hardly deterioration. Blood pressure increases after a certain age, but does this mean that we are deteriorating?

There are certain functions that man is characterized by which do change with age. Some of them do not change so rapidly and dramatically that we consider them diseases or degenerative changes. Yet we have not been able to determine the borderline between these two kinds of conditions.

For this reason, it seems to me that we need to have new approaches to the investigation and measurement of senescence. Newer techniques such as information processing are required. An analysis based on information processing does not merely determine that a difference exists between the old and the young. It determines where in the course of information processing the deviation occurs. We might then conclude that, up to a certain point, the aged person is as functional as his younger counterpart. At this particular point, he may begin to differ, and the difference may not be a matter of disorder. It may be simply a quantitative difference because he is slowing down a bit.

Furthermore, introducing methods such as signal detection theory techniques which can distinguish the sensitivity of a person from his attitudes, from his willingness to take a risk, etc., will prove invaluable aids in defining normal and pathological changes. We need to know if there is really a loss in sensitivity, or is there simply a loss in the degree to which a person is willing to take risks in answering certain questions?

It would appear that in order to answer the question which Dr. Spitzer raised, we must begin our investigations over again with the newer techniques available to us so that we may determine whether there is actual cognitive loss or not.

Psychopathology in the Aged, edited by
Jonathan O. Cole and James E. Barrett.
Raven Press, New York © 1980.

The Differential Diagnosis of Psychiatric Disorders in the Elderly

Charles E. Wells

*Departments of Psychiatry and Neurology, Vanderbilt University School of Medicine,
Nashville, Tennessee 37232*

In 1955, Sir Martin Roth published an article (28) on the natural history
of mental disorders in old age. Little can be added even now to his classic
description. In this chapter, I propose not to survey the field but rather to
look at a circumscribed problem facing all psychiatrists whenever they commence
the differential diagnostic process, and especially when they attempt the difficult
differential diagnosis of psychiatric disorders in the elderly. The problem may
be stated: *Is there evidence of organic impairment? If so, what role does organic
impairment play in the patient's clinical dysfunction?* First, I shall discuss some
of the problems involved in trying to answer these two questions in the elderly;
then I shall look critically at those diagnostic measures currently at the clinician's
disposal to assist in achieving an answer to these questions.

The task of identifying organicity and assaying its role and importance is
made difficult because virtually all diagnostic instruments in use today to help
establish the integrity of the central nervous system or to demonstrate its disinte-
gration change with advancing years. Thus, if almost any measurement of central
nervous system function, structure, or performance is plotted against age, a
graph is obtained which looks something like that shown in Fig. 1. Furthermore,
the boundaries of "normality" become increasingly blurred as the organism
ages, so that it becomes increasingly difficult to distinguish between that change
(usually a decline in function) acceptable as a normal aspect of aging *per se*
and that which can only result from the chemical and structural deviations of
disease. As Butler (2) so clearly expressed it ". . . there are wider differences,
both physiological and psychological, between two older persons of the same
age than between two 20-year-olds." In other words, as patients age, it is often
impossible to know whether a given change should be regarded as normal or
abnormal. The development of norms for aging populations is of some, but
only limited, assistance, and often the clinician is left in a gray zone, not knowing
how an observation should be interpreted. Thus, the precision of most of our
diagnostic instruments decreases as a function of age, as shown in Fig. 2.

In this chapter, I shall look critically at those diagnostic instruments that
are commonly used in clinical practice to help evaluate the role that organic

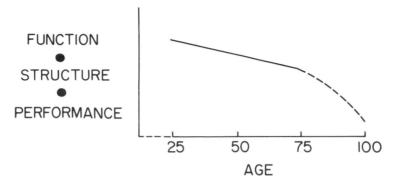

FIG. 1. Relationship of brain function, brain structure, and neurally dependent performance to age.

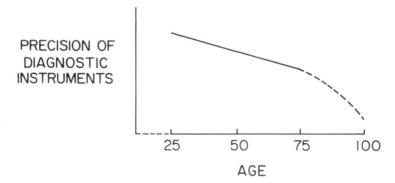

FIG. 2. Relationship between the precision of ancillary diagnostic instruments and age.

dysfunction plays in the psychiatric disorders encountered in elderly patients. In practice, one often observes an ill-considered tendency to regard individual instruments of observation and measurement as *exact* diagnostic instruments, that is, a test interpreted as "abnormal" or "consistent with organicity" too often is considered to establish the dysfunction as organic in origin. I shall examine, then, those diagnostic instruments used commonly in clinical evaluation to consider just how certain are the diagnostic conclusions based on the individual tests alone. The diagnostic instruments to be considered are listed in Table 1.

In exploring the available diagnostic tools with this objective in mind, one is chagrined to discover how little is known about the effectiveness of the individual diagnostic instruments that clinicians use every day. Clinical investigators usually approach the subject from the other direction, that is, they assemble a group of patients with an established diagnosis (for example, epilepsy or senile dementia), carry out some specific diagnostic procedure on each patient, and publish the study as "The EEG in Epilepsy" or "The CT-Scan in Senile Dementia." Such studies are useful and are not to be disparaged. They fail, however,

TABLE 1. *Estimated efficiency of ancillary diagnostic techniques in the identification of organic brain disease*

Test	False positives [b]	False negatives [b]
Neurologic examination	**	***
Skull radiographs	*	****
Electroencephalogram [a]	*	***
Computed cranial tomography	***	***
Psychological testing	***	*
Cerebrospinal fluid	*	****
Amobarbital interview	**	***

[a] Using strict criteria for identification of abnormalities in the elderly.
[b] Scale: * to ****

to tell much about *how* useful the EEG or the CT-scan *per se* is in the evaluation of the patient whose diagnosis is uncertain, especially when there is uncertainty whether or not an organic disease process exists. This is true even if one searches for figures as to the accuracy of specific diagnostic measures in the young adult; studies examining the efficiency of these instruments in the aged are even rarer. Much of what I shall bring to attention in this chapter then is a statement about what is not known rather than an appreciative summary of what is known.

NEUROLOGIC EXAMINATION

Let us turn to the specific diagnostic instruments listed in Table 1 and look first at the neurologic examination, the pride of neurologists and often the bane of other medical specialists. Surprisingly, so far as I have been able to discover, studies specifically assessing the diagnostic accuracy of the traditional neurologic examination are virtually nonexistent. I have found only one study, that of Fisher and Gonda published in 1955 (7), that addresses this topic specifically. Of the 118 patients admitted to a neurology service for diagnostic evaluation, Fisher and Gonda reported that the neurologic examination was falsely positive (meaning that it pointed to disease that could not be established) in 41% of the cases and falsely negative (meaning that it failed to point to disease that was manifestly present) in 29%. These figures may be somewhat flawed, however, by the criteria used by the authors in separating organic from nonorganic cases which probably caused inflation of the false positive figure just quoted. In another study, Filskov and Goldstein (6) also assessed techniques used to distinguish between functional and organic brain dysfunction and stated that the basic neurologic examination was "the least valid of all the physical procedures."

In regard to the elderly specifically, much information is available about changes in the neurologic examination seen with increasing age. Critchley (3) and others (16,26,31) have reported that the following changes may be seen with normal aging and should not be regarded as evidence of disease: *(a)* small, poorly reactive pupils; *(b)* limited upward conjugate gaze; *(c)* muscular wasting, especially in the small muscles of the hands and feet; *(d)* intention or static tremor of the hands; *(e)* diminished appreciation of vibration distally in the lower extremities; *(f)* hypoactive muscle stretch reflexes (ankle jerks and superficial abdominal reflexes may even be absent); and *(g)* akinetic, hypertonic changes with a general flexion attitude, poverty and slowness of movement.

Klawans and associates (16) reported that Achilles' reflexes were absent and vibration sense lost in the distal portions of the lower extremities in more than half of a large group of apparently healthy elderly subjects. In addition, Skre (31) found atrophy of the small muscles of the feet and tremors of the hands in over half of another group of normal subjects 65 years of age and older. Obviously then, these findings cannot be accepted as evidence of neurologic disease in the elderly.

Besides these changes in the routine neurologic examination, Paulson (26) has called attention to the emergence of the so-called primitive reflexes in old age, especially in the presence of diffuse cerebral degenerative processes. These include the glabella tap reflex, snout reflex, suck reflex, jaw jerk, nuchocephalic reflex (13), palmomental reflex, hand grasp reflex, and the tonic foot response. In addition, a variety of other neurologic abnormalities have been reported to be common with diffuse cerebral degeneration, including limitations in upward and downward conjugate gaze, faulty visual tracking, motor impersistence, oculocephalic reflex, paratonia, and errors on double simultaneous stimulation.

Jenkyn and associates (12), in an excellent study, sought to elicit a number of these rather nonspecific neurologic signs in a series of patients referred for neuropsychologic evaluation in approximately equal numbers from the psychiatry, neurology, and neurosurgery services. These workers found that some signs were rarely if ever present in the absence of organic brain disease. These included the oculocephalic reflex, nuchocephalic reflex (13), limitations in upward or downward gaze, lateral gaze impersistence, abnormal visual tracking, suck reflex, paratonia, and errors on double simultaneous stimulation. While false positive responses were rare, unfortunately, the rate of false negatives tended to be high, reaching as high as 88% for the grasp reflex. These investigators separated out a group of tests in which false positives were rare and false negatives did not exceed 60%. With these selected tests only, although there was considerable overlap between those with and those without brain damage, the presence of a number of these signs correlated well with the presence of severe organic brain disease. As might have been expected, correlation was not so good in milder instances of organic dysfunction. Unfortunately too, such commonly sought signs as persistence of the glabella tap response, snout reflex, and the palmomental reflex, were associated with unacceptably frequent false positives and false negatives, a finding confirmed in large part by Villeneuve and associates (32).

Based on the evidence now available, (and it should be emphasized that the evidence is still in many respects scanty), I conclude that the value of the neurologic examination as a diagnostic instrument is significantly limited by the frequency of both false positives and false negatives (see Table 1), perhaps more so in the elderly than in younger age groups. This is true both for the conventional neurologic examination and for the extended neurologic examination described above. If we consider only focal abnormalities on the conventional neurologic examination, it is likely that the incidence of false positives is reduced, but a normal neurologic examination is still not at all unusual in the presence of focal brain disease.

SKULL RADIOGRAPHS

There is little to suggest that plain skull X-rays are or ever have been a very effective diagnostic instrument. The best that can be said is that false positives probably are rare. The converse, of course, is that false negatives are exceedingly frequent. Indeed, probably no other commonly used diagnostic instrument provides such a surfeit of false negatives (see Table 1). It is evident at once that the vast majority of diseases to which the elderly brain is prey produce no change whatsoever in the skull radiograph. Today, the skull X-ray probably is justified only *(a)* when a disorder known to produce skull X-ray changes is specifically suspected or *(b)* when other neurodiagnostic procedures are unavailable.

ELECTROENCEPHALOGRAM

Except in patients with epilepsy, the electroencephalogram (EEG) generally has provided less help diagnostically in the borderlands between psychiatry and neurology than was once foreseen. With the EEG, as with other diagnostic procedures, the chief problem lies in the overlap in observations between normal and abnormal subjects, or as Lairy (17) put it "the margin of discrepancy between the 'normal adult EEG' and the 'EEG of the normal adult.'" Kiloh et al. (15) described the situation clearly: "The so-called normal EEG patterns . . . are simply those that are most often found in people without demonstrable functional or structural cerebral abnormality. This . . . in no way precludes this occurrence in patients who are manifestly ill; nor does it preclude the occurrence of statistically abnormal findings in people who in other respects satisfy the most stringent definition of normality." In various control populations, between 5 and 20% of presumed normal subjects have EEGs which are in some aspects outside the usual bounds of normality (25).

What is true even for a young adult population is even more true for the elderly. In contrast to some other diagnostic studies, however, the EEG changes with aging have been studied extensively (1,23,24). In only about half of subjects over age 65 would the EEG be considered normal if the criteria for normality in the young adult were applied. In normal older people, there is slowing in the frequency of alpha rhythms, most frequently dropping to the slower alpha frequencies but sometimes falling into the faster theta range. In about a fourth, there are focal disturbances, most often theta activity in the left anterior temporal region. All these changes may be seen in healthy old people without significant intellectual decline. The age of the patient is often discounted in the interpretation of the EEGs in the elderly, however, and these changes, commonly reported as electroencephalographic abnormalities, add to the confusion of the unwary psychiatrist. Focal slowing outside the anterior temporal areas and diffuse slowing below 7 Hz are probably more exact evidence of cerebral dysfunction in the elderly, and limiting the interpretation of "abnormality" in the elderly to these changes would probably increase the diagnostic efficiency of the EEG. Even so, it is not at all uncommon to see an EEG which is normal by the most stringent criteria in a patient with unequivocal organic brain disease. If the strict criteria suggested above were employed for EEG interpretations in the elderly, it is likely that false positives would not be too frequent, while false negatives would probably remain relatively common (see Table 1). It is possible that studies of evoked potentials may provide more exact differentiation, but these techniques are not available for routine clinical use.

COMPUTED CRANIAL TOMOGRAPHY

The newest of our neurodiagnostic procedures, and certainly the most technologically complex, computed cranial tomography (CT-scan) offers the clinician certain obvious advantages for imaging the brain. Perhaps the clearest is that it is neither painful nor dangerous, important considerations at any age but even more so in the elderly. As a result, the CT-scan has virtually replaced pneumoencephalography as a diagnostic technique and at the same time has significantly reduced the need for cranial arteriography (18). The CT-scan is furthermore an excellent instrument for the demonstration of focal lesions. Thus, when the lesions are of sufficient size (about 1.5 cm in diameter or larger), the CT-scan can be counted on to demonstrate focal areas of infarction, and encephalomalacia, and expanding masses as well, whether they be neoplasms, abscesses, or hematomas (21).

The value of using the CT-scan in the elderly, however, especially to distinguish the normal changes of aging from the pathologic changes that occur in the aged, is not so clear. For this most important differential diagnostic task, it must be admitted, in fact, that the CT-scan is not very helpful. As Huckman et al. (11) stated: "There are many patients with radiographic signs of atrophy and no dementia and many patients with dementia and no radiographic evidence of atrophy. . . . In fact, gross atrophy is not necessarily of clinical significance." They went on to conclude that CT-scan evidence of atrophy (that is, widened sulci and enlarged ventricles) might occur with aging alone, with or without dementia. Perhaps the most useful point that can be made clinically about the CT-scan in the investigation of suspected cerebral degeneration in old age [and a point made by this group earlier (10)], is that dementia in the absence of brain atrophy should at least suggest to the clinician the diagnosis of one of the reversible causes of dementia. Regrettably, it must be concluded that in the specific area of neuropsychiatry considered in this paper, both false positives and false negatives are frequent (see Table 1).

PSYCHOLOGICAL TESTING

Methods of psychological assessment have been refined over the past three or four decades so that there is little question that neuropsychological testing now offers both sensitive and comprehensive measures of cerebral function. There is little doubt, for example, that in patients with established organic disease, neuropsychological testing performed by a competent clinical psychologist reveals changes consistent with organic dysfunction in virtually every patient. Indeed, in a group of 89 patients with organic disease reported by Filskov and Goldstein (6), the Halstead-Reitan battery revealed evidence that suggested organic dysfunction in every instance. Such findings do not, however, demonstrate, in patients whose diagnosis is uncertain, that neuropsychological testing can predictably identify which patient has organic disease and which does not. When the problem is the separation of functional from organic disease in the elderly specifically, the efficiency of psychological testing as a diagnostic tool is even less certain.

Several problems arise when the clinician seeks to use psychological testing to help make this distinction in the aged patient. First, good neuropsychological testing depends upon the patient's ability and willingness to cooperate, usually over a significant period of time. Obviously many psychotic or demented elderly are poor subjects for such a demanding task. Second, for many portions of most standard test batteries, levels of normality have not been established for the older aged population, especially for those over 75. Thus it is often difficult to state with certainty whether a given performance ought or ought not to be considered abnormal for a specific aged person. Third, many of the errors on specific psychological tests that are known to be typical of organic disease also occur with some frequency in functional disorders. Both Kiloh (14) and Post (27) have stated that psychological test performance in pseudodementia (most often in their experience associated with depressive disorders) is often indistinguishable from that in true dementia. In addition, Folstein et al. (9) showed that abnormalities on their mini-mental state examination, of the sort usually seen in organic disease, were not at all rare in depressive disorders. They also demonstrated in these patients the return of the mini-mental state examinations toward normal following effective treatment of the depression.

What is most needed by both the psychiatrist and neurologist from the clinical psychologist is help in distinguishing patients who have an organic brain disease from those who do not—help especially in those patients whose diagnosis is uncertain after careful psychiatric and neurologic assessment. Matthews et al. (20) sought to evaluate the usefulness of neuropsychological measures in a group of 32 "pseudo-neurologic" patients, i.e., patients with signs and symptoms that initially suggested organic brain disease and whose disorder was eventually diagnosed as functional in origin. These workers found that although performance on neuropsychological measures significantly distinguished between the group of 32 "pseudo-neurologic" patients and the group of 32 patients with proved neurologic disease, no single test or combination of tests could be used to predict whether the individual patient had or did not have organic brain disease. When the cutoff point for distinguishing organic from functional disorders was set at "a level sufficient to produce a meaningful percentage of correct classification of brain-damaged subjects, false positives abounded." When the cutoff point was changed to reduce the number of false positives, "correct classification of brain-damaged individuals fell to 72% (20).

In another study of patients admitted to a neurology service, Schreiber and associates (29) found neuropsychological test evidence of organic impairment in all 62 patients diagnosed as organic, but they also made false positive diagnoses in 4 of 16 subjects found not to have organic disease. Studies to date suggest that sophisticated neuropsychological testing is probably the most sensitive available ancillary diagnostic procedure for the detection of organicity (6), but the frequency of false positives limits the conclusions that can be drawn. Unfortunately, all of these studies have been performed largely on middle-aged subjects; comparable studies in the elderly are not available.

In trying, as of this moment, to estimate the efficiency of neuropsychological testing as a diagnostic instrument in the elderly (see Table 1), I suspect that false positives are common, i.e., that psychological tests often suggest a diagnosis of organicity when the disorder is primarily functional. On the other hand, false negatives probably are rare. If a subject consistently performs well on a variety of measures sampling different cognitive functions, then the likelihood of significant underlying organic disease is not too great. Indeed, the only obvious cause for a false negative result is for average function to be interpreted as normal in a person who had previously performed in the superior range.

CEREBROSPINAL FLUID EXAMINATION

Examination of the cerebrospinal fluid (CSF) is a diagnostic measure hallowed by time and tradition, but a technique whose diagnostic efficiency has unfortunately never been critically assessed. In textbook descriptions of almost every neurologic disease, there is a paragraph detailing the CSF changes that occur in that disorder. As with other diagnostic procedures, however, there is usually no mention of how frequently examination of the spinal fluid is actually helpful in reaching the correct diagnosis—or, regarding the topic considered here, just how often it helps distinguish between functional and organic cerebral disorders.

So far as diagnostic problems in the aged are concerned, there are further complexities. First, the changes in the composition of the cerebrospinal fluid itself, if any, with aging are uncertain. Although Fishman (8) and Dencker (5) stated that spinal fluid protein does not increase with age, others (4,19,22) have suggested that levels above those normal for young adults are not unusual after the age of 60. Second, the most common neurologic disorder of old age, senile dementia, is not usually associated with any significant changes in the spinal fluid. Third, there is some evidence that phenothiazines may cause elevations of spinal fluid protein (30). This might be especially confusing in the population under consideration.

I conclude, therefore, that for examination of the cerebrospinal fluid, false positives are rare, except perhaps for patients who have been receiving phenothiazines. Conversely, false negatives are exceedingly common (see Table 1). Many patients have serious cerebral disease which is never reflected by changes in the cerebrospinal fluid.

AMOBARBITAL INTERVIEWS

Recently Ward et al. (33) have revived interest in the amobarbital interview as a technique to help in the differentiation between functional and organic confusion. Over a quarter of a century earlier, Weinstein et al. (34) described increased denial of illness and 12 different patterns of disorientation in patients with organic brain disease that were not found in their control population. To my knowledge, however, they did not extend their observations to the normally functioning elderly, nor did they seek specifically to evaluate the usefulness of the amobarbital interview technique in patients in whom there was serious question of organic versus functional disease.

Ward et al. (33) sought to use the amobarbital interview as a diagnostic procedure in just such patients. They described four patients in whom the technique appeared helpful, in all of whom clearing of confusion with the barbiturate pointed toward a functional diagnosis. These workers called attention, however, to the occurrence of false positives in cases suspected of having alcohol withdrawal syndromes and of false negatives especially "in cases with a substantial component of hysteria or malingering." The estimated frequency of false positives and negatives using amobarbital interviews is presented in Table 1.

DISCUSSION

This summary is admittedly somewhat discouraging, for it points up clearly what is often acknowledged only with reluctance, i.e., the rather striking limitations in the validity of all of our currently available ancillary diagnostic techniques. No single test, nor any combination of tests, reliably differentiates between organic and functional disease, either in the young patient or in the elderly in whom these differential diagnostic problems are more frequent and often more vexing. Some procedures, skull X-rays and cerebrospinal fluid examination for example, have few false positives. They rarely point to organic disease when it is not present. Unfortunately, it is just these tests in which false negatives are most common. Other procedures, notably psychological testing, produce

TABLE 2. *Clinical features differentiating pseudodementia from dementia* [a]

Pseudodementia	Dementia
Clinical Course and History	
1. Family always aware of dysfunction and its severity	1. Family often unaware of dysfunction and its severity
2. Onset can be dated with some precision	2. Onset can be dated only within broad limits
3. Symptoms of short duration before medical help is sought	3. Symptoms usually of long duration before medical help is sought
4. Rapid progression of symptoms after onset	4. Slow progression of symptoms throughout course
5. History of previous psychiatric dysfunction common	5. History of previous psychiatric dysfunction unusual
Complaints and Clinical Behavior	
1. Patients usually complain much of cognitive loss	1. Patients usually complain little of cognitive loss
2. Patients' complaints of cognitive dysfunction usually detailed	2. Patients' complaints of cognitive dysfunction usually vague
3. Patients emphasize disability	3. Patients conceal disability
4. Patients highlight failures	4. Patients delight in accomplishments, however trivial
5. Patients make little effort to perform even simple tasks	5. Patients struggle to perform tasks
6. Patients don't try to keep up	6. Patients rely on notes, calendars, etc. to keep up
7. Patients usually communicate strong sense of distress	7. Patients often appear unconcerned
8. Affective change often pervasive	8. Affect labile and shallow
9. Loss of social skills often early and prominent	9. Social skills often retained
10. Behavior often incongruent with severity of cognitive dysfunction	10. Behavior usually compatible with severity of cognitive dysfunction
11. Nocturnal accentuation of dysfunction uncommon	11. Nocturnal accentuation of dysfunction common
Clinical Features Related to Memory, Cognitive, and Intellectual Dysfunctions	
1. Attention and concentration often well preserved	1. Attention and concentration usually faulty
2. "Don't know" answers typical	2. "Near miss" answers frequent
3. On tests of orientation, patients often give "don't know" answers	3. On tests of orientation, patients often mistake unusual for usual
4. Memory loss for recent and remote events usually equally severe	4. Memory loss for recent events usually more severe than for remote events
5. Memory gaps for specific periods or events common	5. Memory gaps for specific periods unusual [b]
6. Marked variability in performance on tasks of similar difficulty	6. Consistently poor performance on tasks of similar difficulty

[a] Modified from Wells, Ref. 35.
[b] Except when due to delirium, trauma, seizures, etc.

few false negatives. They seldom are marked by an absence of evidence suggesting organic disease when this is not the case. Unfortunately, a low incidence of false negatives is usually associated with a high incidence of false positives.

What are we to do? Certainly we can work toward a refinement in our ancillary diagnostic techniques, striving to find diagnostic procedures in which both false positives and false negatives are rare. We cannot, however, avoid our diagnostic responsibilities until these goals are achieved.

During the past several years, I have gone back to the basics of clinical observation in an effort to achieve more accuracy in separating those patients whose difficulties are primarily organic from those whose difficulties are primarily functional in origin, recognizing at the same time that the symptoms and signs presented by the elderly often are due to both organic and functional factors. Basing my clinical observations on the earlier work on pseudodementia done by Kiloh (14) and by Post (27), I have sought to build a clinical picture, a gestalt, of the syndrome of pseudodementia and to contrast that with the pattern usually seen with dementia *per se* (35). The clinical features that I have found helpful in distinguishing pseudodementia from true dementia are shown in Table 2.

It is obvious, and especially obvious in the elderly, that not every patient about whom there is some diagnostic confusion falls into one or the other of these categories. Often both organic and functional elements are important, and in such cases one would not expect clear differentiating features. Nor should it be suggested that these proposed differentiating clinical features have yet been subjected to a rigorously controlled, statistically sophisticated clinical investigation. It may well prove that this clinical diagnostic technique is no more efficient in the separation of organic from functional cases than are the ancillary diagnostic techniques discussed earlier. The possibility should at least be considered, however, that detailed and searching clinical observations may be the equal of the most advanced ancillary diagnostic procedures, and may perchance be even more sensitive, in the many patients who require an answer to the questions: *Is there evidence of organic impairment? If so, what role does organic impairment play in the patient's clinical dysfunction?*

REFERENCES

1. Busse, E. W., Barnes, R. H., Friedman, E. L., and Kelty, E. J. (1956): Psychological functioning of aged individuals with normal and abnormal electroencephalograms. I. A study of non-hospitalized community volunteers. *J. Nerv. Ment. Dis.* 124:135–141.
2. Butler, R. N. (1978): Overview on aging. In: *Aging: The Process and the People*, edited by G. Usdin and J. Hofling, pp. 1–19. Brunner/Mazel, New York.
3. Critchley, M. (1956): Neurologic changes in the aged. *J. Chronic Dis.* 3:459–477.
4. Davson, H. (1967): *Physiology of the Cerebrospinal Fluid.* Little, Brown, Boston.
5. Dencker, S. J. (1962): Variation of total cerebrospinal fluid proteins and cells with sex and age. *World Neurol.* 3:778–781.
6. Filskov, S. B., and Goldstein, S. G. (1974): Diagnostic validity of the Halstead-Reitan neuropsychological battery. *J. Consult. Clin. Psychol.* 42:382–388.

7. Fisher, J. and Gonda, T. A. (1955): Neurologic techniques and Rorschach test in detecting brain pathology. A study of comparative validities. *Arch. Neurol.* 74:117–124.
8. Fishman, R. A. (1973): Cerebrospinal fluid. In: *Clinical Neurology,* edited by A. B. Baker and L. H. Baker. Harper & Row, New York.
9. Folstein, M. F., Folstein, S. E., and McHugh, P. R. (1975): "Mini-mental state." A practical method for grading the cognitive state of patients for the clinician. *J. Psychiatr. Res.* 12:189–198.
10. Fox, J. H., Topel, J. L., and Huckman, M. S. (1975): Use of computerized tomography in senile dementia. *J. Neurol. Neurosurg. Psychiatry* 38:948–953.
11. Huckman, M. S., Fox, J. H., and Ramsey, R. G. (1977): Computed tomography in the diagnosis of degenerative diseases of the brain. *Semin. Roentgenol.* 12:63–75.
12. Jenkyn, L. R., Walsh, D. B., Culver, C. M., and Reeves, A. G. (1977): Clinical signs in diffuse cerebral dysfunction. *J. Neurol. Neurosurg. Psychiatry* 40:956–966.
13. Jenkyn, L. R., Walsh, D. B., Walsh, B. T., Culver, C. M., and Reeves, A. G. (1975): The nuchocephalic reflex. *J. Neurol. Neurosurg. Psychiatry* 38:561–566.
14. Kiloh, L. G. (1961): Pseudo-dementia. *Acta Psychiatr. Scand.* 37:336–351.
15. Kiloh, L. G., McComas, A. J., and Osselton, J. W. (1972): *Clinical Electroencephalography, 3rd ed.* Appleton-Century-Crofts, New York.
16. Klawans, H. L., Jr., Tufo, H. M., Ostfeld, A. M., Shekelle, R. B., and Kilbridge, J. A. (1971): Neurologic examination in an elderly population. *Dis. Nerv. Syst.* 32:274–279.
17. Lairy, G. C. (1976): *Preface.* In: *Handbook of Electroencephalography and Clinical Neurophysiology, Vol. 6, Part A: The EEG of the Waking Adult,* edited by G. E. Chatrain and G. C. Lairy, pp. 3–5. Elsevier Scientific Publishing Co., Amsterdam.
18. Lowry, J., Bahr, A. L., Allen, J. H., Jr., Meacham, W. F., and James, A. E., Jr. (1977): Radiological techniques in the diagnostic evaluation of dementia. In: *Dementia, 2nd ed.,* edited by C. E. Wells, pp. 223–245. F. A. Davis, Philadelphia.
19. Madonick, M. J., and Weissman, F. (1955): The total spinal fluid protein concentration in patients over 65. *Geriatrics* 10:533–535.
20. Matthews, C. G., Shaw, D. J., and Klöve, H. (1966): Psychological test performance in neurologic and "pseudo-neurologic" subjects. *Cortex* 2:244–253.
21. Mori, H., Lu, C. H., Chiu, L. C., Cancilla, P. A., and Christie, J. H. (1977): Reliability of computed tomography: Correlation with neuropathologic findings. *Am. J. Roentgenol.* 128:795–798.
22. Müller, O. H., Jaworski, A. A., Silverman, A. C., and Elwood, M. J. (1954): The effect of age on the protein concentration of cerebrospinal fluid of "normal" individuals and patients with poliomyelitis and other diseases. *Am. J. Med. Sci.* 228:510–519.
23. Obrist, W. D. (1954): The electroencephalogram of normal aged adults. *Electroencephalogr. Clin. Neurophysiol.* 6:235–244.
24. Obrist, W. D., Busse, E. W. (1965): The electroencephalogram in old age. In: *Applications of Electroencephalography in Psychiatry,* edited by W. P. Wilson, pp. 185–205. Duke University Press, Durham.
25. O'Leary, J. L., Landau, W. M., and Brooks, J. E. (1973): Electroencephalography and electromyography. In: *Clinical Neurology,* edited by A. B. Baker and L. H. Baker. Harper & Row, New York.
26. Paulson, G. W. (1977): The neurological examination in dementia. In: *Dementia, 2nd ed.,* edited by C. E. Wells, pp. 169–188. F. A. Davis, Philadelphia.
27. Post, F. (1975): Dementia, depression, and pseudodementia. In: *Psychiatric Aspects of Neurologic Disease,* edited by D. F. Benson and D. Blumer, pp. 95–120. Grune and Stratton, New York.
28. Roth, M. (1955): The natural history of mental disorder in old age. *J. Ment. Sci.* 101:281–301.
29. Schreiber, D. J., Goldman, H., Kleinman, K. M., Goldfaber, P. R., and Snow, M. Y. (1976): The relationship between independent neuropsychological and neurological detection and localization of cerebral impairment. *J. Nerv. Ment. Dis.* 162:360–365.
30. Simpson, G. M., and Cooper, T. B. (1966): The effect of phenothiazines on cerebrospinal fluid. *Int. J. Neuropsychiatr.* 2:223–226.
31. Skre, H. (1972): Neurological signs in a normal population. *Acta Neurol. Scand.* 48:575–606.
32. Villeneuve, A., Turcotte, J., Bouchard, M., Côte, J. M., and Jus, A. (1974): Release phenomena and iterative activities in psychiatric patients. *Can. Med. Assoc. J.* 110:147–153.

33. Ward, N. G., Rowlett, D. B., and Burke, P. (1978): Sodium amylobarbitone in the differential diagnosis of confusion. *Am. J. Psychiatry* 135:75–77.
34. Weinstein, E. A., Kahn, R. L., Sugarman, L. A., and Linn, L. (1953): The diagnostic use of amobarbitol sodium ("Amytal Sodium") in brain disease. *Am. J. Psychiatry* 109:889–894.
35. Wells, C. E. (1979): Pseudodementia. *Am. J. Psychiatry,* 136:895–900.

OPEN DISCUSSION

Dr. Cole: I am reminded of my recent attempt to set up criteria for diagnosis in senile dementia. After studying DSM III, I finally decided that senile dementia is simply a chronic and progressive dementia in the elderly for which no other reasonable explanation can be found, which is a rather negative criterion. If all else fails, we are left with a diagnosis of senile dementia. Are there questions? Dr. Winokur.

Dr. Winokur: I thought Dr. Wells gave a superb presentation. I think it revealed a great deal. One of the things I learned particularly was the usefulness of the plus and minuses on one of the last slides. They, in a sense, are *sine quo non*. Those types of positive findings are very useful and not commonly found. When they are, they are very meaningful.

I would like to introduce another point. In the last series of slides there was a set of criteria for pseudodementia versus true dementia. If we look at those data on pseudodementia, we find they fit patients who have conversion symptoms at times, and they also fit a lot of depressives. Who they do not correlate with is another group of people who are considered as having pseudodementia, and that group is composed of late life schizophrenics, who, in the hospital, have marked memory defects, frequently are unable to calculate, and have always been said to be impaired not because they have brain damage but, rather, because they are withdrawn and removed from things.

One of the subjects I would like Dr. Wells to address is the question "Is it possible that old age schizophrenics who have been chronically ill for a long time in fact have a real dementia?"

Dr. Cole: And if so, how would you tell?

Dr. Wells: I think the appropriate thing for me to do is to thank Dr. Winokur for his comments and to say that very obviously I do not have the answer. I wish I did, because you certainly point out something we have been concerned with recently, and that is how little we actually know about what happens in the elderly schizophrenic. I do not know how to approach that problem. You are quite correct; the elderly schizophrenic with cognitive changes does not fall into the sort of differential separation that I am trying to make.

Dr. Cole: I have seen two or three patients who were elderly and fit Dr. Winokur's criteria who, in fact, became cognitively more intact after a retrial on antipsychotic drugs to which they had previously responded. This approach is like giving an antidepressant to prove pseudodementia if the depression lifts and cognitive functions improve.

Dr. Ingvar: The question was raised concerning differences between organic dementia and the alleged schizophrenic dementia. I will show that there are indeed fundamental differences between these two forms which are reflected in the oxydative metabolism and blood flow of the brain.

Dr. Elliot D. Weitzman: I have a problem with the conceptual basis on which you based your positive and negative decision-making processes. You assume that dementia and "organic brain syndrome" constitute a disease. They are, however, primarily symptoms or a group of symptoms, and therefore it is important that we search for a better nosology of these symptoms or group of symptoms. It is not necessary to perform all these diagnostic tests and end without a definitive conclusion. I am certain you do not do that, but others might not share my opinion. We have to search for the pathophysiological basis underlying dementia.

For example, a patient with a spongiform encephalopathy who develops a progressing dementia over several months will often have unequivocal findings on the EEG and brain scan. It is therefore very important to search for these abnormalities and not to assume that we are dealing with a disease entity called "organic brain syndrome." The question which should be considered is: "Do we have a positive or negative finding, and positive or negative for what type of pathology?"

Dr. Cole: To add to that, should all people with apparent senile dementia get ECT to prove it is dementia, which is the other extreme?

Dr. Wells: Let me try to respond. I do not want to give the impression or even make the suggestion that I am advocating not evaluating patients thoroughly. I believe that all of my writings, over some 10 years, on dementia stress the importance of evaluating every patient who appears to have cognitive changes, to try to locate the correct diagnosis in hope of finding one of those which we can treat.

Today, though, I am trying to address a very small and narrow segment, the older patient whom we think may have one of these dementing diseases, but about whom we are not sure. What can help us?

I would probably use most of the tests that I have just damned with faint praise. I am trying, however, to make a point that I have observed so frequently. Someone will decide the EEG is abnormal and that, therefore, the cause must be organic. That simply is not true! We must try to evaluate our diagnostic instruments with more sensitivity.

Dr. Jarvik: I would like to add emphasis to Dr. Winokur's comments. I found your presentation, Dr. Wells, remarkably clear and should like to congratulate you on a beautifully done job.

I would like to ask you a question that concerns the differential diagnosis between pseudodementia and true dementia. We all see cases who have been misdiagnosed. I think the estimate is that, in general, perhaps 15% of cases may be misdiagnosed. In our experience, by the time patients come to us, a geriatric psychiatry service, that percentage is probably well below 5%. I wonder what your experience is, and what is the experience of others in that area.

Dr. Wells: I cannot answer the question in terms of the geriatric psychiatry service. I can tell you, however, what the figures are in patients who have been admitted for inpatient neurologic evaluation because of presumed dementia. I have just compiled data from six series involving patients who were all admitted to neurologic or neuropsychiatric services for evaluation of their dementia. Roughly, we have a total of 417 patients. About 9% of those patients were determined to be not demented after they had been observed in hospital and all of the diagnostic procedures had been done. Then, as you might expect, there are a whole group of diagnostic entities under the pseudodementia category.

Dr. Jean Endicott: I want to make two points. One is a statistical point concerning tests which produce false positives and false negatives like this. You will get a very low correlation.

However, there is a technique called Fisher's Twisted Pair, that is useful when one plots data and finds that there is one of four cells with clustering in it; the technique establishes that within that cell there is some correlation. It reflects what Dr. Jarvik and Dr. Winokur have said, that a positive finding is something to pay a great deal of attention to, and a negative finding really reveals nothing. If we only look at the issue from a correlational point of view, we can conclude that your test has no correlations with the disorder, whereas there is a positive relationship, what is called a Fisher's Twisted Pair effect. If we were to plot the data, we could see the relationship.

The other question has been touched upon. What kind of external criteria do we have for the designation of pseudodementia?

Dr. Wells: Could you define external?

Dr. Jean Endicott: Something beyond the clinical picture. For example, suppose, when you have done very good evaluations of these patients, 80 to 90% turned out to be not demented. You followed these patients over a period of time, and there was no indication that they became more demented and/or later in life develop clear organic signs. In other words, is there something outside of the description of the clinical syndrome which indicates that the designation of pseudodementia is correct.

Dr. Wells: In the small group of patients with a diagnosis of pseudodementia whom I have followed over some time, roughly half have had the disappearance of all of their symptoms after treatment. These were largely depressed patients treated with antidepressants.

There were several in whom the complaints diminished markedly but did not disappear entirely. These were largely patients with longstanding characterological problems who appeared pseudodemented, and indeed looked very demented for a while. Then the symptoms subsided and disappeared, and other symptoms came along to replace them.

I have not followed a large number of these patients, but I think the way one can eventually establish the diagnosis is that either the cognitive dysfunction disappears or it fails to follow the course of any of the dementing illnesses that we know about at present.

Dr. Jean Endicott: But there has not been a large group?

Dr. Wells: Not to my knowledge, no.

Psychopathology in the Aged, edited by
Jonathan O. Cole and James E. Barrett.
Raven Press, New York © 1980.

The Epidemiology of Depression and Dementia in the Elderly: The Use of Multiple Indicators of these Conditions

Barry Gurland, Laura Dean, Peter Cross, and Robert Golden

New York Psychiatric Institute, and Center for Geriatrics and Gerontology, Columbia University, New York, New York 10032

The prevalence rates of dementia in the senium as reported from various surveys can be seen either as reassuringly consistent or surprisingly different, depending on one's viewpoint. Figure 1, adapted from Wang (17), shows the great range of rates reported by various investigators.

Some reviewers point to such studies as those of Essen-Möller (2), Parsons (13), or Kay and his colleagues (7,8), which provide prevalence figures in the range of around 4% to 6% for definite cases of dementia in the elderly population 65 years and older. Yet, to other observers, there are striking differences between survey findings. Definite cases of dementia are reported as high as over 9% by Hagnell (6) and 7.1% by Pfeiffer (14), or as low as 3.1% by Nielsen (12) and 1.6% by Bollerup (1). Mild cases run as high as 24.7% according to Pfeiffer and as little as 2.6% as reported by Kay. Total prevalence without reference to severity peaks at 31.8% in Pfeiffer's study in North Carolina and bottoms out at 0.5% in Lin's study in China (11). Even within a single country, Sweden, almost a threefold difference in rates of definite dementia can be found among studies; the same is true for studies in Great Britain.

Those who are impressed by similarities in prevalence rates among surveys are inclined to explain away the differences by pointing to uncertainties about the techniques for case finding and the criteria used for making the diagnosis of dementia especially in the community elderly, as well as to differences in survivorship and the age structure of the populations, sampling, cultural bias in the assessment techniques, and so on. Nevertheless, were these prevalence figures to be taken seriously, then the differences between surveys would need close study to extract possible clues to the etiology of dementia. Thus, there is a pressing need to develop reliable and useful procedures for comparing rates of dementia between populations.

A corresponding situation of uncertainty exists with respect to studies reporting on the distribution of rates of depression over the age span. Silverman (15) pointed out that "the factor of age has often influenced the diagnosis of

37

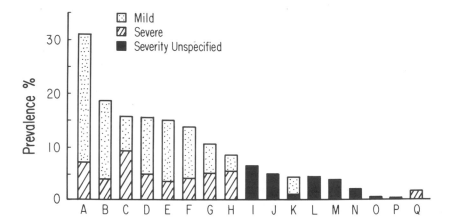

FIG. 1. Rates of dementia in the elderly as reported by various investigators.

	Author	Date	Country	Age	N
A	Pfeiffer	1975	U.S.A.	65+	925
B	Nielson	1962	Scand.	65+	978
C	Hagnell	1962	Scand.	60+	441
D	Essen-Moller	1956	Sweden	60+	443
E	Sheldon	1948	England	65+	349
F	Parsons	1965	England	65+	228
G	Kay	1964	England	65+	297
H	Kay	1970	England	65+	758
I	Kaneko	1967	Japan	65+	531

	Author	Date	Country	Age	N
J	Bentson	1970	Norway	60+	942
K	Bollerup	1975	Denmark	70+	626
L	Halgason	1973	Iceland	74–76	626
M	Primrose	1962	Scotland	74–76	222
N	Bremer	1951	Norway	60+	119
O	Akesson	1969	Sweden	65+	4198
P	Lin	1953	China	60+	1113
Q	Wang	1969	U.S.A.	65+	Nation

Adapted from Wang (17).

psychotic affective disorders and, thereby, also the reported age distribution of these illnesses." Furthermore, the age variation in rates of depression is quite different between studies that base their results on diagnosis and those that employ scale scores of depressive symptoms (3). Unfortunately, no one study reports both diagnosis and scale scores of depression, so these modes of comparison are confounded with all the other differences in procedure that distinguish one study from another.

The United States–United Kingdom Cross-National Geriatric Community Study attempted to apply a consistent set of measurement and classificatory procedures in the domains of dementia and depression (among other health and social problems) to a representative sample of elderly persons living at home in New York and London (5). Some of these procedures will be described here as will illustrative findings based on the New York data.

MAJOR METHODOLOGICAL FEATURES OF THE US-UK CROSS-NATIONAL GERIATRIC COMMUNITY STUDY

The principal aims of this study were cross-national comparisons between the elderly populations in the communities of New York and London of the prevalence of psychiatric problems and their medical and social associations, service utilization in these different health care systems, and the course and outcome of chronic disorders. Interviews were conducted with randomly selected persons over 65 years of age across the whole of New York City and Greater London. Subjects were randomly assigned to interviewers; in addition, five or more random subsamples were interviewed in successive waves spread across the year. Subjects were interviewed in their homes by specially trained project staff. All the London subjects and a random half of the New York subjects were interviewed by psychiatrists; social scientists interviewed the remainder. A 1 year follow-up interview was completed.

Over 1500 bits of information were collected on each subject by means of a reliable and valid semistructured technique, the Comprehensive Assessment and Referral Evaluation (CARE). This instrument is briefly described below.

Major Features of the CARE Technique

This instrument is designed specifically for the elderly person living in the community and is intended to assess a broad range of problems that are the concern of health and social services. A semistructured interview technique is provided to promote consistency in the order, content, phrasing, and scope of questions put to the subject. An inventory of defined and precoded items on discrete symptoms and problems is provided to promote consistency in recording of subjects' responses. In addition to the discrete items, information is recorded in a manual of global ratings and in a systematic narrative summary according to prescribed guidelines. There is comprehensive coverage of mental, physical, and social problems, and service utilization. Positive assets as well as deficits are covered. The phrasing and format of the interview questions are designed to be tactful and to reduce stress on the subject. Questions are short and straightforward. Test items are relieved by interspersed self-report items, and psychiatric by medical and social items. The length of the interview is kept as short as possible by use of header questions and cut-off rules for contingency items. The current version takes about 1 hr to administer on average; less time is required for well subjects and more for those with multiple problems.

Sources of information include self-report, observation, testing of the subject, and reports from informants. Each item is assigned a designated source of information (e.g., items on feelings must reflect only the self-report of the subject). The information gathered does not rely upon the subject's assuming the sick role, nor is it restricted to hearsay evidence of a medical label; specific symptoms are recorded to allow independent recognition of important syndromes or problems. The information elicited permits distinctions to be made among psychiatric, medical, and social problems, and among types of problems (or syndromes) within each of these domains. These distinctions can be made by global judgements, diagnosis, or statistical and algorithmic treatment of the discrete items. Specific criteria are provided for diagnosis of types of depression and dementia.

The information elicited permits comparisons of the health and social problems among individuals, or groups of individuals, or across time. Comparisons may be based on item frequencies, continuous scale scores, latent class assignments, global judgments, or diagnosis.

The present version has been the outcome of psychometric development over a period of more than 10 years, with repeated empirical and clinical modifications. The reliability of the interview ratings, latent class assignments, and global and diagnostic judgements is established across psychiatric and nonpsychiatric disciplines. A data base was established on over 800 randomly selected elderly community persons living in New York City and London and assessed at initial and 1 year follow-up. Measures of reliability, validity, and sensitivity to change, and normative standards have been derived from these data as have over thirty latent class scales. The data base has been expanded by studies on the elderly in institutions.

Multiple Indicators of Depression and Dementia

Multiple indicators of depression and dementia are utilized in the analyses that follow in this chapter. They are (a) attainment of a criterion score on the rational scales, (b) the mean score on the rational scales, (c) diagnosis, and (d) latent class assignment based on latent class scales.

The rational scales are based on previous work, our own and that of others, or on the face validity of the component items. Results on the rational scales can be related to results of previous work and to conventional constructs from the clinical arena, but they may not be as valid or internally consistent when applied to the community elderly as they were in other populations. The latent classes were developed mainly by statistical analysis of the data from the study we report here. Latent class assignments are derived from Lazarsfeld's methods for detecting taxonic structures (9, 10; R. R. Golden, J. A. Teresi, and B. Gurland, *in preparation*). The assignment is determined by the individual's pattern of responses on the items. Latent class analysis can be useful where we do not have a known infallible sign by which we can perfectly classify individuals. Latent classes are homogeneous, nonoverlapping, and relatively comprehensive in detecting distinctive patterns of symptoms and behavior when used on the data from the population from which they are derived, but they may not serve equally well for constructs found useful in other and related studies.

The items in both rational and latent class scales of both depression and dementia are listed in Appendix I. The content of the latent class scales is similar but not identical to that of the rational scales (i.e., the component items overlap).

Diagnosis was according to explicit criteria designed especially for use with the community elderly. The main features of the explicit and specific diagnostic criteria are as follows: each element in the criteria is defined, and in most instances the definition is based on a specific CARE item; the elements of the criteria can be synthesized into a diagnosis by following the guidelines; the criteria relate both to the pattern of symptoms and to their severity; subclinical as well as clinical states are defined; symptom patterns, social adjustment, positive mental health, stress, associated conditions, and course of illness are taken into account; distinctions important to the diagnosis of depression and dementia are made between symptoms of psychiatric and medical origin and among the memory disorders of dementia, depression, and normal aging. These diagnostic criteria are shown in Appendix II.

The terms *pervasive depression* and *pervasive dementia* are intended to refer to cases which are at a clinical level of severity, i.e., which require the attention of a health care professional. The diagnosis of the pervasive states is more firmly based on current or observable data than are subtype diagnoses (such as manic-depressive disorder or Alzheimer's dementia) which involve historical data and a greater degree of judgment. Both the pervasive and the subtype diagnoses were based on specific criteria.

Cases were selected for diagnostic review if they met a criterion score (6 or more) on the scales of dementia or depression, if they qualified for a latent class assignment of depression or dementia, or if they exceeded a criterion score on a global rating of psychiatric impairment. About one in three cases in each city met these criteria. These cases were then reviewed by a psychiatrist. The profile of scale scores and narrative summaries were scrutinized, and the diagnostic criteria for depression and dementia applied. The narrative summaries were written by interviewers along prescribed guidelines with special emphasis on a chronology of the illness and on a raw description of symptoms. In order to detect false negatives arising from the screening process, all cases with a psychiatrist's face-to-face provisional diagnosis of depression or dementia were added to the screened cases and reviewed even if they did not meet the screening criteria. Only 2 cases out of 86 with a final diagnosis of depression or dementia did not meet the screening criteria (both cases were finally diagnosed as depressed).

The reliability of the diagnosis of pervasive depression between pairs of raters, as indicated by *kappa,* was between .63 and .67; that of pervasive dementia was between .66 and .92. Reliability between psychiatrists and non-psychiatrists was at least as good as among psychiatrists.

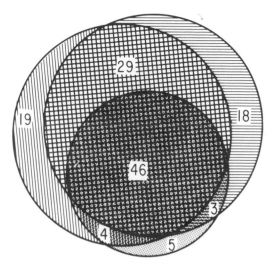

FIG. 2. Overlap in the number of cases identified as depressed by each of three methods. ⬚, latent class of depression, $n = 98$; ⬚, rational scale of depression, $n = 96$; ⬚, pervasive depression, $n = 58$.

The overlap between the cases identified by the various indicators of depression is shown in Fig. 2. The latent class of depression includes almost all the cases of pervasive depression, but the converse is not true. About a fifth of those reaching the criterion score on the rational scale of depression are excluded

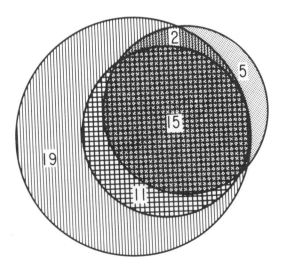

FIG. 3. Overlap in the number of cases identified as demented by each of three methods. ⬚, latent class of dementia, $n = 47$; ⬚, rational scale of dementia, $n = 26$; ⬚, pervasive dementia, $n = 22$.

from pervasive or latent class depression. Common to all three indicators are the vast majority of cases of pervasive depression but less of the other two indicators.

The overlap among the cases identified by the various indicators of dementia is shown in Fig. 3. Latent class dementia includes almost all cases identified by the other two indicators, but the converse is not true. Common to all three indicators are the majority of pervasive dementias, and cases identified by the rational scale of dementia, and about a third of the latent class dementias.

The Point Prevalence of Depression by Various Indicators

The rates of depression and dementia quoted in this chapter are point prevalence rates since the interview focused on current symptoms (at the time of the interview or during the preceding month).

Table 1 shows the prevalence rates of depression among the elderly of New York by various indicators. Depressions of a clinical level of importance amount to about 13% of the population. If one relaxes the criteria to include all those who had 6 or more symptoms from the syndrome of depression, then the prevalence rate almost doubles (to 22%) and corresponds to the latent class prevalence rate which is also 22%. On the other hand, if the cases are restricted to those resembling severe or major affective disorders then the figure we obtain is around 2.5%.

Table 2 shows the age distribution of depression by various indicators. Certain features are consistent across all indicators. Among males there is a dip in the prevalence of depression at age 70 to 74, while by far the highest rate occurs at age 80 and over. For females, the age distribution is generally flatter than for men. On almost all pairs of comparisons the female rates are markedly higher than male rates below age 75 and somewhat higher for the age group 75 to 79. However, an inconsistent finding is that female rates are much below those of males in the age group 80 and over by three indicators and about equal between the sexes for the latent class of depression. Furthermore, the prevalence rate of depression among females declines with age according to the pervasive depression indicator but rises a little with age according to the latent class indicator.

Table 3 compares the use of psychotropic medications by pervasive depressives

TABLE 1. *Point prevalence rates of depression by multiple indicators: New York City*

Criterion	Prevalence (%)
Diagnosis of pervasive depression	13.
6 or more on rational scale of depression	22.
Latent class probability over 0.90	22.
Manic-depressive-depressive disorder	2.5

TABLE 2. *Percentage depressed by age group*

Age	Number Males	Number Females	Pervasively depressed Males	Pervasively depressed Females	Rational score 6+ Males	Rational score 6+ Females	Latent class depression Males	Latent class depression Females	Mean rational score Males	Mean rational score Females
65–69	61	81	8%	21%	25%	22%	16%	25%	2.6	3.6
70–74	48	75	4%	17%	10%	28%	8%	21%	1.6	3.8
75–79	35	60	6%	10%	14%	17%	11%	27%	2.3	3.3
80+	33	50	24%	10%	39%	18%	33%	30%	5.1	3.4
Total	177	266	10%	15%	21%	22%	15%	27%	2.9	3.5

TABLE 3. *Percentage of subjects taking medication
for psychological symptoms[a]*

Pervasive Depression (N = 58)	48%
Latent Class Depression (N = 98)	38%
Latent Class Depression but not Pervasive Depression (N = 48)	20%
Not Depressed (N = 98)[b]	15%

[a] Includes all medications subject reported taking
for "insomnia," "nerves," or "depression."
[b] A random subsample of subjects who were not
depressed.

and latent class depressives. Subjects with pervasive depression use on average over three times as many psychotropic medications as do a non-depressed comparison group; almost half the pervasive depressives take such medications while less than one in six of the comparison group do so. The corresponding data for the latent class depressives show less difference from the comparison group than do the pervasive depressives. Latent class depressives who were not also pervasive depressives show only a small excess of medication usage compared with those who were not depressed.

The Point Prevalence of Dementia by Various Indicators

Table 4 shows the prevalence rates of dementia among the elderly of New York City by various indicators. Pervasive dementias amount to about 5% of the population; the majority of these belong to the category of senile or Alzheimer type dementia. The criterion score for the rational scale of dementia is achieved also by about 5% of subjects. The latent class assignments are, however, about twice as high as the estimates based on the other indicators.

Table 5 shows the age distribution of dementia by various indicators. The constant features across all indicators are as follows. For males, the lowest rates were in the age group 65 to 69, and there is no age group with a higher rate than the oldest cohort (aged 80 and older). For females, there are markedly higher rates in the oldest cohort than in any other age group, and those 75 to

TABLE 4. *Point prevalence rates of dementia by multiple indicators: New York City*

Criterion	Prevalence (%)
Clinical Diagnosis of Pervasive Dementia	4.9
6 or more on Rational Scale of Dementia	5.8
Latent Class Probability over .90	10.6
Alzheimer's (Senile) Dementia	3.9

TABLE 5. *Percentage demented by age group*

Age	Number Males	Females	Pervasively demented Males	Females	Rational score 6+ Males	Females	Latent class dementia Males	Females	Mean rational score Males	Females
65–69	61	81	2%	4%	0%	3%	2%	7%	.4	1.0
70–74	48	75	0%	3%	2%	4%	6%	5%	.5	.6
75–79	35	60	6%	7%	6%	8%	6%	17%	1.2	1.7
80+	33	50	6%	16%	9%	16%	15%	32%	2.8	3.8
Total	177	266	3%	6%	3%	7%	6%	13%	1.2	1.7

79 years of age have higher rates than those younger. In every age group on every indicator, the females have higher rates than the men; the one exception is the age group 70 to 74 on the latent class indicator. Although there are inconsistencies, the indicators show that the rates for dementia increase with age, with the largest increases occurring across the age boundaries of 75 years and 80 years, especially in women. However, the latent class shows *markedly* higher rates in the oldest age group (80 years and over) compared with all others, while the pervasive dementias show this only for females.

Table 6 shows the death rate for the pervasive and the latent class dementias over the year subsequent to the initial diagnostic interview. For the pervasive dementias there is a strikingly higher death rate than in the remainder of the population (22% versus 7%), although this discrepancy springs entirely from the age group 65 to 79 years of age (41% versus 5%). The corresponding comparisons for the latent class dementias shows much less in the way of an increased death rate.

TABLE 6. *Pervasive dementia and latent class dementia: Percentages of each dead at 1-year follow-up*

	Age 65–79	80+	Total (subjects)
Entire sample	5% (358)	15% (87)	7% (445)
Pervasive dementia	41% (12)	0% (10)	22% (22)
Latent class dementia	15% (26)	4% (21)	13% (47)

TABLE 7. *The relationship of pervasive and latent class dementia with personal time dependency*

	None		Limited home care		Adult home level		Nursing home level		Total	
	N	%	N	%	N	%	N	%	N	%
Pervasive Dementia	0	0%	1	5%	2	9%	19	86%	22	100%
Latent Class Dementia	18	38%	5	11%	8	17%	16	34%	47	100%

Table 7 shows the relationships between pervasive and latent class dementia on the one hand and personal time dependency on the other hand. Personal time dependency exists when one person must give the benefit of his personal time to another in order to help him in life-sustaining activities. This concept has been further defined and its reliability described elsewhere (4). Levels of severity are defined in terms of the institutional counterpart of the personal services received by the dependent person at home. All the pervasive dementias are dependent, the majority at the most severe level of dependency. The latent class dementias are, however, not dependent in over a third of cases and only about a third are at the most severe level of dependency.

DISCUSSION

We have demonstrated the use in geriatric epidemiology of multiple indicators of such psychiatric problems as depression and dementia. The main advantages of this approach are that (a) the various indicators may delineate groups of subjects whose differing characteristics help to determine which indicator is most relevant to the particular purpose of the epidemiological study; and (b) comparisons between groups may gain strength from convergent findings on all the indicators or gain precision from discrepancies among the indicators.

The first of the above advantages is illustrated here by the relative death rates in the groups of pervasive and latent class dementias. Insofar as dementia is defined as a progressive disorder leading to accelerated death, pervasive dementia has better predictive validity than does latent class dementia. Also, from the viewpoint of the health care services, the concept embodied in pervasive dementia turns out to be more useful than that in latent class dementia since the former is associated with higher rates of disability than is the latter. Correspondingly, pervasive depression has more powerful implications for the health services than does latent class depression since the former is more strongly associated with use of psychotropic medication than is the latter. All of this leaves open for study the question of whether the latent classes are examples of indicators which identify groups with important but as yet undetermined characteristics, possibly early dementias or situational depressions.

The second of the above advantages is illustrated by the analysis of the age distributions of the various indicators. We have convergent findings on there being, in men, a dip in the rates of depression at age 70 to 74 and a peak at age 80 and over. Explanation of age distribution in women must be more precise than that for men insofar as it must take into account the observation that compared with younger women (i.e., less than 75 years of age), the older women have lower rates of pervasive depression but higher rates of latent class depression.

The age distributions of the dementia indicators give further insight into the advantages of looking for convergent or discrepant findings. We have noted that the death rates in pervasive dementia were increased in those less than 80 years of age (the young-old) but not in those 80 years of age or older (the old-old). One possibility that arises is that the host-disease interaction differs between those two age groups; another possibility is that the same indicator identifies different kinds of conditions in the two age groups. The latter hypothesis seems the less likely one because none of the indicators of dementia used here were associated with a higher mortality in the older than in the younger age groups.

Among the indicators used here for depression, the pervasive states have the most immediate relevance to the health-care system. The need of such states for the attention of the health care system is evident from the intensity and persistence of the symptoms required to meet the criteria for this diagnosis and from the high usage of psychotropic medications by this group without apparent relief. The 13.0% point prevalence rate of pervasive depression translates into approximately 130,000 persons over 65 years of age in New York City, a substantial challenge to the capacity of the health care system. The excessively high rate (over 20%) among very old men is of particular importance because this group is suicide prone. Among the very old (80 years and over), the male rates of pervasive depression exceed those of women in contradiction of the rule that holds for almost all younger age groups.

The health care issues posed by pervasive dementia are again implicit in the criteria for diagnosis as well as in the associated death rate and chronic disability shown by the data presented above. The point prevalence rate of about 5% can be projected to approximately 50,000 elderly persons in New York City. If it is assumed that no more than half the elderly in New York City's long-term care facilities are suffering from dementia (16), then it might appear from these data that there are about three times as many demented elderly outside long-term care facilities as in them. As may be seen from the data in this chapter, the vast majority of the pervasive dementias in the community elderly are sufficiently disabled as to be eligible for a skilled nursing facility. They are being kept at home mainly through the efforts of family members

(4). Of all the community elderly who are disabled to this degree, almost half are demented. Not only is this situation of crucial importance to the home care service system but it has also been found to promote high rates of pervasive depression among family members who constitute the informal support system (4).

If the pervasive states of depression and dementia emerge in this chapter as key concerns of the health care system, it is partly because of the perspective obtained by comparing the findings on various indicators of these conditions. Nevertheless, the urgent relevance of the pervasive states should not detract from the need to examine further the characteristics of groups which do not meet the criteria for these states, but which are yet identified by other indicators as having symptoms of depression or of changes in memory and cognitive skills.

ACKNOWLEDGMENTS

Members of the United States-United Kingdom Cross-National Project who took part in the Geriatric Community Study are:

United States Team:[1] B. Gurland (U.S. Director and Principal Investigator), L. Sharpe, R. Simon, J. Kuriansky, P. Stiller, L. Dean, R. Bennett, D. Wilder, J. Teresi, R. Gurland, R. Golden, and D. Cook
United Kingdom Team:[2] J. Copeland (U.K. Director), M. J. Kelleher, J. Kellett, J. Gourlay, D. Cowan, A. Smith, A. Mann, Y. Tsegos, and B. Robinson
Main Consultants: J. Zubin, International Advisor, the late A. Goldfarb, W. E. Deming, J. Fleiss, and F. Post
Collaborating Colleagues: G. Duckworth and P. Birkett

The data for the study reported here comes from the Geriatric Community Study, funded by the National Institute of Mental Health (Grant No. 5R13MH 09191), the Administration on Aging (Grant No. 93-P-57467), and the New York State Department of Mental Hygiene.

REFERENCES

1. Bollerup, T. R. (1975): Prevalence of mental illness among 70-year-olds domiciled in nine Copenhagen suburbs. *Acta Psychiatr. Scand.,* 51:327–339.
2. Essen-Möller, E. (1956): Individual traits and morbidity in a Swedish rural population. *Acta Psychiatr. Neurol. Scand. (Suppl.),* 100:1–161.
3. Gurland, B. (1976): The comparative frequency of depression in various adult age groups. *J. Gerontol.,* 31:283–292.
4. Gurland, B., Dean, L., Gurland, R., and Cook, D. (1978): Personal time dependency in the elderly of New York City: Findings from the U.S.-U.K. Cross-National Geriatric Community

---

[1] Project staff in New York are or were members of the Center for Geriatrics and Gerontology in the Faculty of Medicine, Columbia University, and the Department of Geriatrics New York State Psychiatric Institute

[2] Project staff in London are or were members of the Institute of Psychiatry at the Maudsley Hospital.

Study in Dependency in the Elderly of New York City. Report of a Research Utilization Workshop, pp. 9–44.

5. Gurland, B., Kuriansky, J., Sharpe, L., et al (1977): The comprehensive assessment and referral evaluation (CARE) - Rationale, development and reliability. *Int. J. Aging Hum. Dev.*, 8:9–42.

6. Hagnell, O. (1970): Disease expectancy and incidence of mental illness among the aged. *Acta Psychiatr. Scand. (Suppl.)*, 219:83–89.

7. Kay, D. W. K. (1972): Epidemiological aspects of organic brain disease in the aged. In: *Aging and the Brain*, edited by C. M. Gaitz. Plenum Press, New York.

8. Kay, D. W. K., Beamish, P., and Roth, M. (1964): Old age mental disorders in Newcastle-upon-Tyne. I. A study of prevalence. *Br. J. Psychiatry*, 110:146–158.

9. Lazarsfeld, P. R. (1959): Latent structure analysis. In: *Psychology: A Study of a Science, Vol. 3, Formulations of the Person and the Social Content*, edited by S. Koch, pp. 476–543. McGraw-Hill, New York.

10. Lazarsfeld, P. R., and Henry, N. W. (1968): *Latent Structure Analysis.* Houghton Mifflin, Boston.

11. Lin, A. Y. (1953): A study of the incidence of mental disorder in Chinese and other cultures. *Psychiatry (Minneap.)*, 16:313–336.

12. Nielsen, J. (1962): Geronto-psychiatric period-prevalence investigation in a geographically delimited population. *Acta Psychiatr. Scand.*, 38:307–330.

13. Parsons, P. L. (1965): Mental health of Swansea's old folk. *Br. J. Prev. Soc. Med.*, 19:43–47.

14. Pfeiffer, E. (1975): A short portable mental status questionnaire for the assessment of organic brain deficit in elderly patients. *J. Am. Geriatr. Soc.*, 23:433–441.

15. Silverman, C. (1968): *The Epidemiology of Depression.* Johns Hopkins University Press, Baltimore.

16. Staff of the U.S. - U.K. Cross-National Institutional Study (1979): A preliminary report on a cross-national comparison of institutionalized elderly in the cities of New York and London. *Psychol. Med.* 9:781–791.

17. Wang, H. S. (1977): Dementia of old age. In: *Aging and Dementia*, edited by W. L. Smith and M. Kinsbourne, pp. 1–24. Spectrum Press, New York.

APPENDIX I. *Items in the "rational" and "latent class" scales*

Depression Scale Items

Worries a lot about one or two things[a]
Is a worrier or worries about almost everything
Worrying is bothersome[a]
Cannot stop worrying[a]
Depressed mood[a]
Has cried
Has felt like crying
Depressed mood lasts longer than an occasional few hours
Depression is worse at particular time of day
Has felt life wasn't worth living
Minor depressive feelings[a]
Pessimism about the future[a]
Future seems bleak or unbearable
Has ever felt suicidal or wished to be dead[b]
Has wished to be dead but has rejected suicide
Has fleeting suicidal thoughts
Has considered a method of suicide
Has attempted suicide[b]

Does not mention feeling happy in past month[b]
Unrealistic self-deprecation[a]
Keeps referring to physical shortcoming or handicap[b]
Feels worthless[a]
Keeps blaming self for harmful affects on others
Obvious self-blame over past or present pecadilloes
Mentions regrets about past[b]
Looks sad, mournful or depressed[a]
Sounds gloomy or mournful[a]
Going out less than seven days a week causes loneliness, boredom, or frustration[b]
Is bothered by current loneliness[b]
Wants to stay away from people[a]
Is more irritable lately
Gets angry with self
Poor appetite in absence of known medical cause or nausea[b]
Sleep difficulty due to altered moods, thoughts or tension[b]
Awakes more than 2 hours early and cannot get back to sleep[a]
Has difficulty relaxing[a]
Admits to being restless[a]
Is doing less than usual[b]
Slowness or anergia is worst in morning[b]
Sits or lies around due to lack of energy[b]
Describes any headaches[b]
Subjectively slowed down in movements[b]
Has aches and pains without identifiable organic basis[a]
Numerous aches and pains without identifiable organic basis[a]
Undue preoccupation with physical complaints and conditions[a]
Almost nothing is enjoyed
Less enjoyment or interest in activities than previously[b]
Loss of enjoyment or of interest due to 'depression' or 'nervousness'[b]
Has been seriously depressed prior to past month[b]
Is not very happy
Retarded speech[a]
Is worried or pessimistic about future[b]

Dementia Items

Cannot spell name[a]
Cannot repeat rater's name[a]
Doesn't know age
Doesn't know year of birth
Uncertain about age and birthdate[b]
Discrepancy between age and birthdate is not corrected by subject
Either age or birthdate is obviously wrong
Doesn't know how long he's lived in area[b]

Doesn't know year he's lived at this address
Doesn't know year which he moved to this address
Discrepancy between reported year of move to this address and years at this address
Gives incorrect or incomplete home address
States he doesn't know home address
Does not recall name of President
Does not recall name of previous President
Does not recall interviewer's name[b]
States he doesn't know day[a]
Gives wrong day[a]
States he doesn't know month
Gives wrong month
States he doesn't know year
Gives wrong year[b]
Doesn't recall interviewer's name (2nd try)
Knee-hand-ear test[b]
Hesitancy on multiple attempts on knee-hand-ear test[b]
Perseverates during interview[a]
Number of years in error in stating present year[a]

APPENDIX II. *Diagnostic criteria for depression and dementia*

CLASSIFICATION OF DEPRESSION

1. SEVERITY CRITERIA:
   A = Level 1
   B = Level 2
   B + (C or D) = Level 3
   B + C + D = Level 4
   B + E = Level 5
2. CLASSIFICATION:
   A = Limited Depression
   B in any combination = Pervasive Depression
   C in the absence of B = Masked Depression
3. SUBCLASSIFICATION OF PERVASIVE DEPRESSION:
   B + (C or D or E) = Clinical Pervasive Depression

   B + Irrelevant Stress = Free-floating Depression
   B + Sufficient Stress = Reactive Depression
   B + Necessary Stress = Aggravated Depression

---

[a] Appears only in rational scales.
[b] Appears only in latent class scales.

B + Subsequent Stress = Subsequent Depression
B + Concurrent Stress = Concurrent Depression

4. TRANSLATION INTO CONVENTIONAL DIAGNOSTIC LABELS:
Manic-depressive - depressive disorder is operationally defined as (B) pervasive depression + (C) vegetative symptoms + insufficient stress (i.e., other than sufficient) + episodes (present or past).

Rules for Rating-Criteria for Diagnosis and Severity of Depression

General

Rating form is shown in Fig. Appendix 1.

In making the ratings, take into account all information in the summary (with only the explicit psychiatric diagnosis expurgated) and the profile of rational scores. Where inadequate information is provided in a summary, the following note should be applied: A high score on depression (11+) and a quota score on Section B allows one to add one point assigned to any item in Section C (thus the C quota may be fulfilled in this way).

Not to be considered in making ratings (even where known) are the following: treatment received, self-labeling, symptoms which are "suspected" rather than reported or observed, or the diagnosis of the rater who wrote the summary.

Time

Rate only symptoms that occurred in past month (unless otherwise specified). Example: If two months ago the subject had a pervasive depression but over the past month it was a limited depression (at worst) then it qualifies as a limited depression. If symptoms fluctuated over past month, then rate them at their worst, except that the depression must occur in more than 1 week of the month to qualify as limited and in more than 2 weeks to qualify as pervasive.

Positive mood is rated at best in past month.

Transient situational neuroses can qualify as limited depression if they last over week or more.

Don't count habitual constipation preceeding the depression.

Limited depression. As defined in the criteria. In general it refers to depression which is transient or can be self-suppressed so that a substantial part of life is free of depression. The severity of depression while it lasts is *not* an issue, nor is the response of the person to antidepressant medication, nor past history.

By definition, vegetative signs and attempted suicide (for example) may occur in limited depression. Where there is difficulty in deciding between limited and pervasive depression, the presence of positive mood sways the diagnosis toward the former diagnosis; so does a low depression score (<6) or the presence of good life satisfaction or a self-rating of being very happy. The low score and

CASE #_____   APPENDIX II
                               RATER:_____   DATE:_____

CRITERIA FOR DIAGNOSIS AND SEVERITY OF DEPRESSION		✓IF QUOTA FILLED	
A. LIMITED DEPRESSION	✓IF PRESENT	1	2

A. LIMITED DEPRESSION

1 Depression lasts only a few hours - can snap out of it	1 { }	
2 Occasional low days	2 { }	
3 Worried about specific problem - can turn mind to other things	3 { }	
4 Cries only when a particular event or situation is discussed	4 { }	
5 Future looks empty	5 { }	

B. PERVASIVE DEPRESSION

1 Depression lasts whole day or longer	1 { }	
2 Crys or feels like crying, often	2 { }	
3 Depression is bothersome and not easily shaken off	3 { }	
4 Future looks bleak or unbearable	4 { }	
5 Can't stop worrying - worry is disproportionate to cause	5 { }	
6 Looks depressed through much of interview	6 { }	

C. VEGETATIVE SYMPTOMS (Not accounted for by physical disease)

1 Palpitations	1 { }	
2 Trembling	2 { }	
3 Dizziness	3 { }	
4 Poor appetite	4 { }	
5 Constipation	5 { }	
6 Loss of weight	6 { }	
7 Sleep disturbance	7 { }	
8 Poor concentration	8 { }	
9 Early morning wakening	9 { }	
10 Lies awake with anxious or depressing thoughts	10 { }	
11 Depression worst in mornings	11 { }	
12 Weak or tired	12 { }	
13 Slowed in speech or movement	13 { }	
14 Unexplained aches and pains	14 { }	
15 Subjective complaints of impaired memory	15 { }	

D. SELF-DEPRECIATION

1 Self-conscious in public	1 { }	
2 Feels a failure	2 { }	
3 Feels guilty	3 { }	

E. SUICIDAL OR PSYCHOTIC (Not accounted for by a non-depressive state)

1 Actively suicidal (strong impulse, preparations, or attempt)	1 { }	
2 Deluded or hallucinated with a depressive content	2 { }	
3 Mute or immobile	3 { }	
4 Serious injury or ill effect following suicidal attempt	4 { }	
5 Starvation or intercurrent infection	5 { }	
6 Homicidal behavior	6 { }	

F. OTHER FEATURES

1 Stress: a. Irrelevant{ }
          b. Necessary { } or Sufficient { }
                          c. Concurrent { } or Subsequent { }
2 Current or Past Excitement: Yes { }   No { }
3 Present Episode: Yes { } No { }
4 Past Episode: Yes { } No { }
5 Positive Mood: Yes { } No { }

(Continued on page 54.)

DEMENTIA CRITERIA (Continued)

```
F.   OTHER FEATURES                                                          YES  NO

     1  Positive Cognition                                                 { } { }
     2  Supervision Required                                               { } { }
     3  Progressive Over Last Five Years                                   { } { }
     4  Duration:  Over Five Years                                         { } { }
     5            Six Months to Five Years                            or  { } { }
     6            Less than Six Months                                     { } { }
     7  MSQ:  Moderately Impaired                                          { } { }
     8        Grossly Impaired                                        or  { } { }
     9  Lucid Intervals During Past Six Months                            { } { }
    10                Last Less than One Week                            { } { }
    11                Last One Week or More                              { } { }
    12  Evidence of Arteriosclerosis                                      { } { }
    13  Episodes Occur in Last Five Years                                 { } { }
    14  Episodes Coincide:  With General Illness or Medication            { } { }
    15                      With Relocation or Other Stress               { } { }
    16  Misperceptions or Hallucinations                                  { } { }
    17  Marked Tremor or Stiffness or Other Parkinsonian Feature          { } { }
    18         Preceded Onset of Cognitive Disturbance by Three Years or More { } { }
```

self-ratings may also decide the diagnosis against even limited depression in cases of doubt. Conversely, it may be borne in mind that many cases with a score of 6 or more on depression (rational scales) have either limited or pervasive depression.

Pervasive depression. As defined in the criteria. In general it refers to depression that pervades most aspects of life.

Depression that occurs regularly each day for a large portion of the day and at the same time of day (e.g., morning) is regarded as qualifying for B3—"Depression is bothersome and not easily shaken off."

If several (four or more) symptoms are rated in Sections B through E, with only one occurring in B then pervasive depression should be rated nonetheless.

Vegetative symptoms. A judgment must be made whether the symptoms germane to this area result from psychiatric or medical causes. The latter do not qualify, whereas the former do. A note on memory appears below. With respect to the other vegetative symptoms, bear in mind that vegetative symptoms are likely to be psychiatric if: (a) there is no accompanying physical illness, (b) the symptoms are undiagnosed or are diagnosed as "due to nerves," etc., (c) the symptoms are preceded by a feeling of anxiety, (d) wakefulness (i.e., sleep disturbance) is accompanied by depressing or anxious thoughts rather than pain, etc., or (e) early morning wakening occurs (wakes 2 or more hours before usual time and wants to go back to sleep but cannot).

On the other hand, tiredness occurring as a result of long hours at work or unusual effort is not rated as psychiatric; nor are weight loss from dieting, symptoms caused by medications, shortened sleep hours without difficulty in falling asleep, or tiredness on wakening.

Sleep disturbance. Sleep disturbance with the distinctive pattern of depression (see d and e above) rates in two places (Sections C7 and C9 or C10). Early morning wakening should not be rated unless the subject wants to go back to sleep (feels the need for more sleep) and yet cannot. Under these circumstances early morning wakening also counts as sleep disturbance (i.e., picks up 2 points).

Memory. Subjective complaints of impaired memory refers to the subject's report; never to the rater's observations or tests. The performance testing of memory shows little or no impairment. Typically, the subject complains of difficulty in remembering names (but *not* of close friends or family), misplacing possessions, being muddled about appointments, forgetting what he was intending to do, forgetting something just seen or heard, and having difficulty in recalling the right word to use in phrasing a thought, or getting thoughts confused.

Self-depreciation. As defined in criteria.

Suicidal or psychotic. As defined in criteria.

Other features. Stress is *irrelevant* if it does not appear to explain the depression (see below); *necessary* if it has played a substantial part in causing the depression but is not overwhelming (i.e., many people are not depressed in those circumstances); *sufficient* if it is overwhelming and would cause depression in most people. An example of sufficient stress would be a recent bereavement or a previously active and energetic person being rendered severely handicapped in a relatively short period of time.

If stress is necessary or sufficient, then it must be classified as *subsequent* when it follows the stress and *concurrent,* if it is accompanied by ongoing stress. Bereavement is regarded as a subsequent depression. Depression associated with disability or environmental deprivation is concurrent. A judgment must be made in other cases as to whether it is an event or its consequences that is the stress (the former is subsequent and the latter is concurrent), where this is difficult to judge the following arbitrary rule should be used: Depression which outlasts an event by 1 year becomes concurrent—by 5 years is free-floating.

Irrelevant stress is to be rated when there is no apparent stress to account for the depression, or when the stress that is suggested by the subject is implausible (e.g. trivial), or when there have been a series of depressions each with a different cause attributed to it (i.e., almost anything triggers the depression), or when a variety of events such as past bereavements, relocations and retirement have changed the subject's life style to one which, though not acutely deprived, is viewed negatively by the subject.

Excitement refers to an episode of unusual and inexplicable happiness (elation), overactivity (starting new activities, working extended hours, overdoing things), overtalkativeness, overconfidence, or impetuous behavior. Irritability, boasting, and grandiose psychotic behavior may accompany this syndrome.

A present episode is occurring when the current state of depression is distinctly worse than the best state enjoyed over the past 2 years. For example the best evidence of a present episode is a relatively clear-cut and rapid onset to the depression (occurring in the past 2 years).

A past episode is a previous state of depression separated from the present state by a distinctly less depressed phase of at least 2 months. Example—Received ECT or antidepressants for depression in the past and recovered to a greater or lesser extent.

Positive mood refers to evidence of a mood state that is surprising to find in a depressed person, e.g., a bright, engaging manner at interview; involvement in social and leisure activities; reporting an enjoyable event; exciting plans for the future; taking an interest in one's appearance. Struggling along and managing to cope is *not* a sign of positive mood; nor is engagement in desultory activities.

CLASSIFICATION OF DEMENTIA

1. SEVERITY CRITERIA:
   A = Level 1
   B = Level 2
   B* + C = Level 3
   (B* or C) + D = Level 4
   (B* or C) + E = Level 5
   *If the subject is too sick to test B, then Level 3–5 must be based either on a history of B or on C, D, or E alone
2. CLASSIFICATION:
   Limited cognitive disturbance = Level 1; or Level 2 + Positive cognition
   Pervasive dementia = Level 2 without positive cognition or Level 3–5.
3. SUBCLASSIFICATION OF PERVASIVE DEMENTIA:
   i. Arteriosclerotic dementia—evidence of arteriosclerosis as defined elsewhere
   ii. Acute confusional state—no evidence of arteriosclerosis.
       Episodes coincide with general illness or medication.
       Lucid intervals
       Duration less than six months.
       Misperception or hallucinations.
   iii. Secondary dementia—no evidence of above states (i) and (ii).
        Onset preceded immediately by insult to brain, or
        Evidence of Parkinson's disease preceeding cognitive disturbance by three or more years.
   iv. Senile (Alzheimer's) dementia—no evidence of above states, (i–iii).
       Duration less than 10 years.
       Visible progress over past 5 years.
       No lucid interval lasting over 1 week, in past 6 months.
       Marked fluctuations do not occur unless the episodes of deterioration occur with illness, medication, relocation or stress.
   v. Unclassified: the residual cases of pervasive dementia.

Rules for Rating Criteria for Diagnosis and Severity of Dementia

General

Rating form is shown in Fig. Appendix 2.

In making the ratings take into account all information in the case summary (with only the explicit psychiatric diagnosis expurgated), and the profile of rational or homogeneous scores.

CASE #_____ RATER:_____ DATE:_____

CRITERIA FOR DIAGNOSIS AND SEVERITY OF DEMENTIA

		✓ IF PRESENT	✓ IF QUOTA FILLED 1 2
A. LIMITED COGNITIVE DISTURBANCE			
1	Reports a decline in memory	1 { }	
2	Increased reliance on notes as reminders	2 { }	
3	Occasionally (less than once a week) forgets names of acquaintances, or forgets appointments or misplaces objects	3 { }	
4	Occasionally (less than once a month) has destructive or dangerous memory lapses such as burning cooking or leaving on gas tap	4 { }	
5	One or two errors on cognitive testing: forgets current or past president, exact date, phone number, zip code, dates of marriage or moving to present location; can't remember interviewer's name even on third challenge	5 { }	
B. PERVASIVE DEMENTIA			
1	Frequently shows lapses in A3	1 { }	
2	More than two errors in A5	2 { }	
3	Keeps forgetting important or recent events even after repeated reminders	3 { }	
4	Forgets name of close friends or family or other frequent contacts and cannot soon correct self	4 { }	
5	Has at least once in past month forgotten the way home from a point in neighborhood	5 { }	
6	Several years out in age, birth or present year	6 { }	
C. DEPENDENT			
1	Frequently (at least once a week) forgets familiar contexts i.e. acts if he is in a different context (as at work), at a different age (still a young person), or with a different person (misidentifies interviewer as close family member and does not correct self)	1 { }	
2	Wanders; gets lost frequently (at least once a month) or is restricted or escorted because of wandering	2 { }	
3	Shows indiscreet behavior (e.g. undresses in public, lights fires, steals)	3 { }	
4	Panics if alone	4 { }	
5	Puttering about most of the night	5 { }	
6	Apathetic and largely inactive during day	6 { }	
7	Requires supervision for administration of medication	7 { }	
8	Requires supervision for bathing and eating	8 { }	
D. REGRESSED (Not accounted for by other physical disorder)			
1	Incontinent (less than once a month) of feces or urine	1 { }	
2	Has to be taken to toilet regularly to avoid accidents	2 { }	
3	Only communication is of basic needs or empty social forms	3 { }	
4	Irrelevant or stock answers to fairly simple questions	4 { }	
5	Requires to be dressed, washed or groomed	5 { }	
6	Requires to be fed	6 { }	
E. DETERIORATED (Not accounted for by a physical disorder)			
1	Bed or chairbound or cannot move wheelchair	1 { }	
2	Has to be transferred	2 { }	
3	Doubly and frequently incontinent or on catheter	3 { }	
4	Utterances are unintelligible	4 { }	
5	Doesn't communicate needs	5 { }	
6	Unresponsive	6 { }	
7	Has to be tube fed	7 { }	

Time

Rate only symptoms in past month (unless otherwise specified). If symptoms fluctuated during the past month then rate at worst, except positive cognition is rated at best in past month.

Limited cognitive disturbance. As defined in the criteria. Refers usually to an impairment of memory but with substantial aspects of living adequately performed, e.g., memory lapses but positive cognition as well or memory lapses but largely independent (requiring little or no supervision).

Pervasive dementia. As defined in the criteria. Refers usually to an impairment of memory which renders the subject incapable of certain task performance (ADL-IADL) and renders it necessary for the subject to be supervised (see Supervision).

Dependent. As defined in the criteria.

Regressed. As defined in the criteria.

Deteriorated. As defined in the criteria.

Other features. Positive cognition refers to a capacity which would be surprising to find in one who is demented such as the following:

Able to go out alone and beyond immediate neighborhood (e.g. to church, cinema), and finds way back safely. Can use public transportation alone. Able to stay in unfamiliar accomodation without resulting confusion.

Shops or cooks without aid (or performs other complicated task).

Lives alone.

Able to conduct a rich and varied and responsive conversation which is full of accurate facts—can relate an internally consistent and complicated chronology of recent events such as operations, relocations, (sequence correct even if dates are imprecise)—can discuss current events and abstract a conclusion from them—can relate the story of a recent book read or film seen.

Takes an active interest in a social network and keeps track of those in it. (Not merely being cheerful and putting on a good social manner, which is positive for mood).

Can describe a complicated personal situation (e.g. dealings with a public agency, the course and treatment of an illness, details of medication, etc.).

Looking after a sick spouse.

Involved in hobbies which require ability and the capacity to follow written instructions.

Anticipatory knowledge of an imminent future event not of a routine nature (e.g., a visit or excursion).

Able to carry on a written correspondence without help.

Supervision refers to the need for someone to supervise, assist or substitute for subject in performing tasks under cognitive control. These are continence, housekeeping, cooking, dressing, handling money and business, shopping, initiative and planning, and needing to be accompanied on excursions to avoid wandering, etc. If there is a physical disability requiring personal intervention the latter does not count as supervision. If it is not clear whether the need for supervision is physical or cognitive, then 'supervision' *is* rated positive. Do *not* include assistance or supervision in response to the subject's anxiety about excursions (agoraphobia).

Certain deficits in the subject are specifically suggestive of poor cognitive control: incontinence without awareness, wandering, *loss* of ability to manage cash, forgetting what to buy when in shop, etc. Certain other deficits are suggestive of non-cognitive causes: inability to do heavy chores, carry heavy parcels, etc.

Supervision is most clearly seen when someone has made special arrangements to provide it (e.g., a formal service, given up job to do so, moved in with subject, given up going out so as not to leave subject alone, etc.).

Progressive means that there has been a dramatic degeneration visible at least over a five year or lesser period.

Moderate versus gross MSQ errors refers to a set of items constituting the majority of the scale of cognitive impairment. Gross errors are (a) total disorientation for time (not even approximately right in day, month, year, age) (b) high MSQ score (8+ on rational scale of cognitive impairment).

Moderate includes (a) giving an incorrect answer on MSQ but correcting it either spontaneously or on challenge or (b) a low score on MSQ (2–4), or (c) an intermediate score on MSQ (5 7) but in a person with poor education or (d) an error-free MSQ score (0–1) but with errors in giving other facts and dates (e.g., date of marriage).

Lucid intervals are periods of apparent return to normal cognition.

Evidence of arteriosclerosis should be rated when the subject with pervasive memory disturbance (a) has hypertension and a series of 'blackouts' (but *not* if the blackouts only occur on rising from sitting or lying to a standing position, and *not* if hypertension alone nor blackouts alone, and not dizziness); (b) has a series of falls not explained by weakness or tripping (and not dizziness alone); or (c) has episodes of time in which speech is lost or disrupted, or there is dysarthria, slurred speech, weakness or paralysis on one side (stroke), or incoordination, especially if an episode or series of episodes precede the memory disturbance.

Do *not* include a diagnosis by a doctor of hardening of the arteries or arteriosclerosis.

Do *not* include leg cramps on walking (intermittent claudication), tremors, or dysphasia (difficulty with naming objects). When in doubt between arteriosclerosis and senile dementia, diagnose the latter.

Episodes refers to cases where the symptoms described for dementia have had at least one distinct onset *and* termination during the past 5 years.

Coinciding with general illness or medication refers to episodes of cognitive disturbances which appear to have an onset and termination related to an acute illness (e.g., infection, dehydration, acute cardiac failure) or a potent medication (e.g., barbiturate, antidepressant).

Misperceptions or hallucinations are described when subject has visual hallucinations (i.e, sees objects that aren't there) or misperceptions (i.e., sees stable objects moving). These misperceptions or hallucinations are not considered if they occur only when the person is falling asleep.

Onset preceded by insult to brain is considered when, immediately before the onset of the cognitive disturbance, there was some injury to the brain due to accident, lack of oxygen (e.g., cardiac arrest), infection (e.g., encephalitis), or spread of cancer, etc. Stroke is excluded as this is rated under arteriosclerosis.

Parkinsonian features include marked tremor of hands and a stiff shuffling gait sufficient to disable the subject to some extent *or* treatment with L-DOPA or other antiparkinsonian drug (e.g., Cogentin). Exclude side effects of major tranquilizers.

OPEN DISCUSSION

Dr. Zubin: I wonder whether Dr. Gurland would say something about the difference in the female rate and the male rate for dementia in terms of selection resulting from survival in the two groups.

Dr. Gurland: One of the hypotheses available to explain the higher rates of dementia among the females than among the males is that female dements survive for longer than do male dements. Another is that male dements are removed from a community sample by institutional admission sooner than are female dements. It is also possible that there is a higher incidence of dementia among females than among males.

Dr. Kramer: I would like to emphasize several points that must be kept in mind when comparing prevalence rates of mental disorders between countries, such as those just shown by Dr. Gurland.

It is important to be aware of the many factors that can account for differences in prevalence, even when the case-finding and diagnostic procedures are standardized. There are two commonly used prevalence rates: (a) the point prevalence rate, which provides a measure of persons in a population with a disease or disorder as of a given day; and (b) the interval prevalence rate, which provides a measure of the number of persons with a disease or disorder in a population during an interval of time, e.g., 1 year. The following comments apply to the point prevalence rate since it is the simpler one to describe.

The point prevalence rate varies as the product of the incidence rate (i.e., the rate at which a disorder occurs) and its duration. The various levels of mortality in different countries must be taken into account when interpreting differences in the point prevalence rates reported for mental disorders, particularly for persons in the age groups 65 years and over. In countries that have a high fatality rate for a specific disorder of the aged (e.g., chronic brain syndrome with cerebral arteriosclerosis), the prevalence rates may be low, although the incidence rates (i.e., the number of new cases occurring during a year) may be quite high.

The point prevalence rate can be affected not only by differential mortality rates but by differential institutionalization rates; for example, number of persons in mental institutions and nursing homes. In the United States, the number of persons in nursing homes in some age groups, particularly those 65 years and over, is quite large. The percent of the total population in the age groups 80 to 84 and 85 years and over who were in nursing homes in the United States in 1974 illustrate this point. About 11% of all white females in the 80 to 84 year age group and 30% of those in the 85 years and over group were in nursing homes. For black females, the corresponding proportions were considerably lower, 4% in the age group 80 to 84 years, and 9% in the 85-years-and-over group. For white males, the corresponding proportions were 6% for the age group 80 to 84 years and 19% for the age group 85 years and over; for black males, about 3% for the age group 80 to 84 and 8% for those 85 years and over.

A high proportion of the persons in nursing homes have a mental disorder. According to the profile of chronic illness in nursing homes in 1974, published by the National Center for Health Statistics, mental disorders were the fourth most frequently reported condition among the 1.1 million residents of these homes, being reported for 18% of these residents. This is undoubtedly a conservative estimate since it excluded the diagnosis of senility which was the most frequently reported, for 627,000, or about 58%, of these residents. Thus, prevalence rates that are based on the noninstitutional population can provide a misleadingly low estimate of the prevalence of a condition in a population if the number of persons with the condition in institutions is not taken into account.

Deinstitutionalization practices must also be taken into account, since this process can affect the prevalence rate of such disorders as schizophrenia in the surveys of the noninstitutional population. A community can find that there has been a sudden large increase in the prevalence rate of schizophrenia in the noninstitutional population merely because of a sudden release of large numbers of such patients from the mental hospital to the community.

To summarize, it is important to be aware of the many factors that can affect the level of the point prevalence rates reported for specific mental disorders based on the noninstitutional population. These include not only the diagnostic and case-finding procedures used in these surveys but a series of factors that determine the number of cases of a specific disorder that will be found in the noninstitutional population at a given moment in time. These include the rates of institutionalization and deinstitutionalization, the fatality rates of persons with the disorder, and the general level of mortality of the population in which the surveys are carried out.

Comparisons of the period (interval) prevalence rate are far more difficult to interpret since this rate is a combination of point prevalence rates, incidence rates, and relapse rates. Thus, any or all of the factors that affects its component parts can produce differences in the period prevalence rate.

Psychopathology in the Aged, edited by
Jonathan O. Cole and James E. Barrett.
Raven Press, New York © 1980.

A Family Study of Alzheimer's Disease and Senile Dementia: An Interim Report

Leonard L. Heston and June White

Psychiatry Research Unit, University of Minnesota, Minneapolis, Minnesota 55455

This chapter describes the current status of an ongoing genetic study of dementing illness. It will focus on dementia associated with Alzheimer's neuropathological changes, chiefly neurofibrillary tangles and senile plaques. The study has been done in two stages. A first group of probands had classical Alzheimer's disease, defined as dementing illness with onset before age 65 coupled with Alzheimer's neuropathology. A second group of probands had senile dementia, also defined by dementia and Alzheimer's neuropathology, but by convention the age of onset is over 65. Alzheimer's disease and senile dementia have often been regarded as the same illness. One aim of this chapter is to examine the two entities together from a genetic perspective in the hope that our understanding of either or both might be increased.

The older and younger onset groups combined totaled 115 probands, and a first round of field work has been completed on all families except for 12 whose probands are from the older onset group. This is, therefore, a progress report, and conclusions will be tentative both because of the 12 unstudied families and, more importantly, because of our conviction that the only way to obtain satisfying evidence on some genetic parameters is to follow closely an entire generation through its lifetime.

METHODS

Probands came from a series of autopsies done between 1952 and 1972 in Minnesota State Hospitals. General autopsies were performed at the hospitals where the patients had died, and the brains in formalin were sent to Anoka State Hospital where a neuropathological laboratory had been established. There, the brains were sectioned, slides were prepared, and neuropathological diagnoses made. The starting point for this project was the record of 2,204 autopsies compiled by the laboratory. There were 30 cases diagnosed as Alzheimer's disease and 191 diagnosed as senile dementia. After the families of the 30 Alzheimer's cases had been studied, the first 85 probands who had been diagnosed as suffering senile dementia were analyzed. Nearly all diagnoses were reviewed by one neuropathologist (Dr. Angeline R. Mastri) using both the original slides and new

TABLE 1. *Probands' ages of onset and death*

	Males	Females
N	55	60
Mean Age Onset	69.25 ± 1.2	66.59 ± 1.2
Mean Age Death	75.08 ± 1.3	73.75 ± 1.3

ones prepared from tissue in paraffin blocks. The complete hospital records of all subjects were reviewed, and, during this process and subsequent field work, the ages of onset were reestimated in some cases, generally in a downward direction, with the final result that 47 probands are now regarded as having had an onset of dementia before age 65. Some features of the proband group can be seen in Table 1. The mean ages of onset and death are nearly the same for males and females. There was no consistent difference between the sexes in regard to severity of illness. Females are affected a little earlier in life but survive a bit longer. The correlations between age at onset and age at death are 0.87 and 0.88, respectively, for males and females. Evidently, no matter when the illness becomes apparent, there is a fairly consistent period of life remaining. However, there is a small, but definite tendency for earlier onset to be associated with shortened life, at least in probands with onsets before age 70. Until age 70, the earlier the onset, the shorter was the course, presumably because the cases with earliest onset were the most severe. After age 70, other illnesses cause significant mortality and, on the average, mask this trend. However, there are individuals having onset of illness after age 70 who have lived on as long as 18 years. Since the longest survival among cases with onset before age 55 was 8 years, the data as a whole are consistent with a rather sharp gradation in severity, with early onset being associated with severe, rapidly fatal illness, and late onset with slow progression.

The distribution of age of onset can be seen in Table 2. It is noticeable that few probands had onset before age 55, although these cases are probably very significant.

It should be mentioned at this point that it is often difficult to estimate the age of onset, which we have operationally defined as that age when loss of short-term memory became evident. We originally used age at death as our parameter but were surprised to find that analyses based on age of onset gave

TABLE 2. *Distribution of age of onset of probands' illness*

Age interval	Males	Females
40–54	2	9
55–69	28	26
>70	25	25

similar results. Since age of onset seems to be the more appropriate parameter, we have chosen to use it.

At least one and more often two or three close relatives of each proband were interviewed with the aim of obtaining a complete medical history of each first- and second-degree relative. Death certificates were obtained for nearly all deceased relatives, as were all available medical records. Additional details have been published previously (3).

Secondary cases

We found 67 secondary cases, 29 males and 38 females. We regard the excess of females as statistically reflecting the fact that more females survive to, and through, the risk period. Diagnoses were based on autopsy in only 14 cases, a major weakness in this and similar studies. Autopsies were obtained on all persons who were living at the time we contacted their families and who later died of dementing illness. Only six autopsy records were obtained from persons who died before our study began. Only prospective study of families can insure the availability of medical and autopsy records. When there had been no autopsy, our diagnosis required a history of steadily progressive intellectual decline, especially failure of recent memory, in the absence of evidence of toxic, vascular, or systemic disease capable of explaining the decline.

RESULTS

Dementia

Recurrence risks of first-degree relatives for dementing illness can be seen in Table 3. However, these risks cannot be interpreted until severity of illness is taken into account. First, the onset of illness averaged 4.9 years later for secondary cases than for the proband through whom the family was located. This is a common finding in medical genetics where probands tend strongly to have more severe illness and hence earlier onset. It was also found in families with Pick's disease (2). Of course, severity of illness is also directly related to recurrence risk, with greater risk found to accrue to relatives of the most severely ill probands. Table 4 shows this tendency very clearly for relatives of female probands where there are dramatic stepwise decreases in risk. However, it is not true of relatives of male probands, a result which is disquieting. Most likely,

TABLE 3. *Recurrence risk for dementing illness*

Relation	Risk[a]
Siblings	7.4 ± 2.4%
Parents	14.6 ± 4.3%

[a] Weinberg mortality method (9).

TABLE 4. *Recurrence risk to first degree relatives according to probands' age of onset*

Probands age of onset	Risk to relatives[a] of male probands	Risk to relatives[a] of female probands [
40–54	1%	21%
55–69	27%	9%
>70	1%	2%

[a] Weinberg mortality method (9).

the results for males are an anomalous blip in an otherwise consistent data set since there were only two male probands in the age 40 to 59 group. Future data from the families as yet unstudied may smooth out the findings or suggest different analyses. Meanwhile, we can tentatively accept the results for female probands as being more representative.

Down's Syndrome

One of the important findings from the first study of the families of 30 early onset (< age 65) probands was a highly significant excess of relatives afflicted with Down's syndrome. This was regarded as having biological plausibility because the neurofibrillary tangle appears to involve microtubules and microfilaments (4). These structures constitute the spindle which orients and separates chromatids during cell division. Thus, there is a plausible organelle common to Down's syndrome and Alzheimer's dementia. Also, it appears that most Down's, perhaps all of them, develop Alzheimer's dementia in their middle years; it seems reasonable, therefore, to posit some sort of connection (1). Table 5 shows the Down's cases so far discovered. A significant feature is the extreme concentration of risk among relatives of the probands with earliest onset. This result, 1/66 for relatives of the earliest onset group compared to 1/700 for a general population, verges on the unbelievable. Also, we consider it certain that we have found only a fraction of the actual Down's cases. The proband

TABLE 5. *Down's cases among relatives by probands' age of onset*

Probands' age of onset	At[a] risk	Observed Down's	Rate	Expected[b] Down's	Relative risk compared to general population	Probability (Poisson)
40–54	331	5	1/66	.47	10.61	<.001
55–69	1615	4	1/403	2.33	1.73	NS
>70	1305	2	1/652	1.86	1.07	NS
All	3251	11		4.66	2.58	<.01

[a] All relatives ever born, including 3rd degree descendants, but excluding parents of probands.
[b] At an estimated risk of 1/700 in the population.

generation was born between 1860 and 1910, and their children were nearly all born before 1935. No Down's cases were found in the proband generation, and only three were among the generation of the probands' children, although members of these generations comprise about half of those considered at risk. We think it is reasonable to assume that Down's cases were present in those generations, but they have not been discovered by us because of inadequate records and because informants, who were nearly all of the generation of the probands' children, simply did not know about deaths in childhood among members of earlier generations. The mothers of the Down's cases averaged 32.4 years old at the birth of the affected child, and the two oldest mothers were both age 40. It may be especially notable that for 10 of the 11 Down's cases, the genealogical connection to the proband was through the mother of the Down's case.

Hematologic Cancer

The first study of families of probands also discovered a significant excess of hematologic cancers, especially those in the immunocytic series. This was considered biologically plausible because microtubules are critical to the function of membrane receptors. Also, there is a large excess of hematologic malignancies among Down's cases (6). However, the additional probands now included remove the total of hematological malignancies from statistical significance. Table 6 shows relationships very similar to those seen for Down's syndrome. The cancers are concentrated among relatives of early onset probands. There is also reason to suspect that hematologic malignancies may be significantly increased overall. First, Table 6 shows only first-degree relatives of probands. Among their second-degree relatives, only 7 cases were discovered, although 14 would be expected on the basis of national age-specific risks (7). The difference between first- and second-degree relatives is consistent with the degree of genetic relationship, and the difference between observed and expected numbers suggests that many cases are being lost. During the earlier generations, many persons died of cancers of undetermined type. Again, prospective study is needed.

TABLE 6. *Hematologic malignancies in first degree relatives by sex and probands' age of onset*

Age interval	Females		Males		Combined		
	Expected malignancies	Observed malignancies	Expected malignancies	Observed malignancies	Expected malignancies	Observed malignancies	*p*
40–54	1.08	2	.44	3	1.52	5	<.01
55–70	4.75	6	3.69	4	8.44	10	—
>70	4.35	1	2.90	3	7.25	4	—
All	10.18	9	7.05	10	17.23	19	—

CONCLUSION

We attempted to increase or decrease the likelihood that Alzheimer's disease and senile dementia, the forms of dementia having Alzheimer's neuropathological changes in common, are the same disease. The evidence seems to be fairly strong that the two are the same disease, but severity of illness is so strong an influence that it dominates the genetic picture. In this series, overlap between the two illnesses is clearly present simply because the age of onset for secondary cases was nearly 5 years greater than the age of onset for probands. As a result, probands with Alzheimer's disease tended to have relatives with senile dementia. Overlap in the other direction was rare. In only 1 family was there a proband over age 65 when the disease began (he was 67) coupled with a secondary case with onset before age 65. However, the pattern of recurrence of illness within families suggests one illness, not two. Because of the concentration of Down's and hematologic cancer among the relatives of the first group of early-onset probands, the same phenomena could be anticipated among relatives of the second group of probands if, in fact, they had the same illness. No such excess was found, but there was also greatly decreased frequency of dementing illness itself amongst those relatives which makes the whole of the evidence quite consistent with decreasing pathology of all kinds associated with decreasing severity of the probands' illnesses. The results obtained with respect to the transmission of dementing illness are reasonably close to those of Sjögren and his group (5,8). Of course, heterogeneity is not excluded, and, indeed, the history of medical genetics suggests that it should be expected. However, at this time, there is simply insufficient evidence to support a division of dementia of the Alzheimer's type into two or more etiologically distinct entities.

Severity of illness does, however, force subdivision for many practical purposes. Clearly, the risk level that must be considered in genetic counseling varies greatly among the 15-year subdivisions of onset of illness used in this paper. If the numbers of subjects could support finer subdivision, we suspect that each 5-year interval would be associated with substantially different risks. Similarly, quantification of severity would clearly be important to researchers whose best strategy would be to concentrate their efforts on members of severely affected families.

REFERENCES

1. Ellis, W. G., McCulloch, J. R. and Cooley, C. L. (1974): Presenile dementia in Down's syndrome: Ultrastructural identity with Alzheimer's disease, *Neurology,* 24:101–106.
2. Heston, L. L. (1978): The clinical genetics of Pick's disease, *Acta Psychiatr. Scand.* 57:202–206.
3. Heston, L. L., and Mastri, A. R. (1977): The genetics of Alzheimer's disease: Associations with hematologic malignancy and Down's syndrome, *Arch. Gen. Psychiatry* 34:976–981.
4. Iqbal, K., Grundke-Iqbal, I., Wisniewski, H. M. and Terry, R. D. (1978): Chemical relationship of the paired helical filaments of Alzheimer's dementia to normal human neurofilaments and neurotubules, *Brain Res.* 142:321–332.

5. Larsson, T., Sjögren, T. and Jacobson, G. (1963): Senile dementia: A clinical, sociomedical and genetic study, *Acta Psychiatr. Scand.* [*Suppl.*] 167.
6. Lillenfeld, A. M. (1969): *Epidemiology of Mongolism,* Johns Hopkins Press, Baltimore.
7. National Cancer Institute (1975): *Third National Cancer Survey: Incidence Data.* Monograph 41, Washington, D.C.
8. Sjögren, T., Sjögren, H., and Lundgren, A. G. H. (1952): Morbus Alzheimer and morbus Pick: A genetic clinical and ratio-anatomical study, *Acta Psychiatr. Neurol. Scand.,* [*Suppl.*] 82.
9. Slater, E. and Cowie, J. (1971): *The Genetics of Mental Disorder,* Appx. D. Oxford University Press, London.

OPEN DISCUSSION

Dr. Cole: Is there any relationship between chronic dyspepsia and your disease? I have a suspicion that an aluminum-containing antacid might be involved.

Dr. Heston: Aluminum does not produce the same lesion. It is different. I supplied a tissue to two chemists who tried to replicate those experiments. The problem is that one is operating at the extreme limits of sensitivity of any available instrument. So the findings of aluminum in Alzheimer's disease will have nearly the same range as that found in normal controls; a large number of cases must be averaged to detect the tiny difference between the Alzheimer's disease cases and the controls.

So I am equivocal about those results. I think it is of interest that, as far as I am aware, only in humans are the neurofibrillary tangle and the senile plaque observed. They are not observed in any animal.

Dr. Robert Cloninger: Would you comment on your findings of the discrepancy between siblings and parents? I was surprised to see the risk was so much higher in parents. I wonder if you thought that was caused by a defect in the age correction.

Dr. Heston: I think that the discrepancy is probably caused by selective loss of siblings to Down's syndrome, a disease for which parents were not at risk, and to hematologic malignancies for which parents were at reduced risk.

Dr. Zubin: Is it possible that some of this difference may result from generational differences caused by the outbreak of certain infectious diseases, for example, the 1917 influenza epidemic?

Dr. Heston: Yes. Of course, none of this excludes a partial viral etiology. The current view is that genetic differences in membranes make cells more or less liable to viral infections.

Dr. Jean Endicott: You mentioned the need for longitudinal studies several times. Could you indicate what kind of studies you would suggest?

Dr. Heston: I think one would have to get a series such as this one, establish relationships with the family, keep in contact with them through a lifetime, and turn the project over to someone else who could maintain contact and collect data until a complete generation had been observed.

Dr. Chester Swett: A few years ago there was a report in the *British Journal of Psychiatry* that indicated an excess frequency of a haptoglobin phenotype in senile dementia. I wonder if you investigated that finding, or, if not, whether you could in future studies.

Dr. Heston: It could certainly be looked at. I have not followed up that type of finding. By association, I think one could make a case for studying HLA antigens in these cases. The reason I have not is that the result of such a study would be just another number. I do not see that it would be very helpful.

Dr. Winokur: The thing that I find intriguing is that Dr. Heston has given two explanations for the set of findings which are related to age. One possibility is that there is polygenic transmission. The younger patients have more genes, the older patients less, and consequently by virtue of the early age of onset, the younger ones have more severe illness.

The other possibility is that of heterogeneity, that there is more than one disease in a study group. Currently, most people seem to think that it is the same illness and that it is a polygenically transmitted illness. It seems to me Dr. Heston's data indicate that the better hypothesis is heterogeneity. One, we not only have a difference in family history and a difference in age of onset for the particular illness being studied, i.e., senile dementia, but we also have a difference in the Down's syndrome and in the male/female ratio, with the very young Alzheimer's patients having 4.5 to 1 ratio of female to male.

The question is, besides the fact that the pathology looks rather similar, is it possible that, in addition to the family history material and the sex differential, there are other differences between the early onset and the late onset groups?

Dr. Heston: Yes, I have every expectation that there will be as this analysis proceeds.

Dr. Ralph A. O'Connell: I have made a clinical observation over the years which I discounted. You are relating Down's syndrome and neurofibrillary changes. I have observed several patients who had simultaneous onset of cataracts and Alzheimer's disease. I wonder if you have observed this.

Dr. Heston: I don't know the answer to that. I personally have not noticed any association.

Dr. Gershon: I have two questions about this excellent study. The first is could the absence of ill siblings be accounted for by *in utero* mortality or accidental death that escaped your statistics?

The second is how is it possible that you have these very fine statistics on parents, particularly since, if I understood you correctly, the probands were born between 1860 and 1910?

Dr. Heston: I should have commented on that. One possible explanation, of course, is if in fact we are losing a lot of siblings to disorders such as cancer and Down's syndrome, they would not be at risk for Alzheimer's disease. That may account for part of the discrepant risk for siblings as compared to parents.

As for your second question, one can obtain reliable oral histories from Minnesota farmers. They know what has happened. Not in all cases, of course. Some relatives can not be counted because there are no observations at all. Many died in Europe. But from those who immigrated here and lived out their lives in Minnesota, we have gotten reliable information.

Dr. Cole: I have heard it said that epileptic seizures are more common in presenile dementia than senile dementia. Is this true?

Dr. Heston: I say no. Dr. Wells?

Dr. Wells: I would say no, also.

Psychopathology in the Aged, edited by
Jonathan O. Cole and James E. Barrett.
Raven Press, New York © 1980.

Regional Cerebral Blood Flow and Psychopathology

David H. Ingvar

Department of Clinical Neurophysiology, University Hospital, S-221 85 Lund, Sweden

By means of multiregional cerebral blood flow measurements, two-dimensional maps of the distribution of function in the cerebral hemispheres can be obtained. This is possible because the cerebral blood flow is ultimately controlled by neuronal activity and the metabolic changes coupled thereto (11). In this chapter some principal findings on the distribution of function in the brain in psychopathological states will be discussed. Main emphasis will be given to organic dementia and chronic schizophrenia.

METHODS

Our studies are based on multiregional measurements of the cerebral blood flow with the intraarterial [133]xenon technique (18). A bolus of saline containing the isotope is injected into the internal carotid artery in conjunction with cerebral angiography. A battery of detectors placed at the side of the head records the arrival and subsequent clearance of the isotope. The clearance curve is a function of the blood flow in the region seen by each detector. Multi-detector devices have been designed to yield "functional landscapes" of the injected hemisphere. The flow values represent the levels of function in different regions of the cerebral cortex. With the aid of computers, mean landscapes can be calculated which depict the average distribution of function in normal subjects as well as in patients in different diagnostic groups.

THE NORMAL STATE

In a series of studies from our laboratory and by Dr. N. A. Lassen and his collaborators in the Department of Clinical Physiology at the Bispebjerg Hospital in Copenhagen, observations have been made in about 80 patients with normal neurological findings and without evidence of psychiatric disease (20). Findings in this group have been used to compare with observations in patients with neurologic and psychiatric disorders.

In the normal, conscious resting state, the distribution of flow/function in both hemispheres is very typical. The blood flow in frontal and precentral parts of the hemisphere cortex is significantly higher than in postcentral parts in parietal, occipital, and temporal regions (6,13). The difference in some regions is about 1 to 2. We have interpreted this pattern to show that the conscious state of awareness implies a high activity in efferent parts of the cortex which are responsible for programming our behavior. The low activity in post-central ("afferent") parts of the cortex indicates that in the conscious resting state, the afferent sensory input might be inhibited. This appears to agree with intro-spective data: while awake and resting in silence, one is not continuously aware of sensory input; at the same time, the conscious mind is busy "producing" thoughts, including plans for the future based upon previous experience. There is much evidence both from normals and from patients with neurological and psychiatric disease to support this general notion (7).

An augmentation of the sensory input in the form of cutaneous stimulation (14), auditory impulses, or visual stimulation increases brain activity and, hence, also cerebral blood flow. The increase is most marked in the primary projection area of the sensory modality stimulated, but there usually is also an increase in blood flow in the frontal parts of the brain. Possibly, the frontal activation is an integrative part of the brain activity involved in perception. For example, stimulation with white noise mainly activates the primary auditory regions, while stimulation with a meaningful noise, music or spoken words, activates the frontal lobes as well.

Voluntary motor activity activates the respective parts of the Rolandic area according to the somatotopic map. The increase in blood flow to contralateral cortical hand area during one-sided hand movements is substantial, sometimes more than 100% (6, 21). Indeed, specific pure motor ideation without visible movement, is accompanied by cortical activation including a frontal blood flow increase (12).

Speech and reading activate the classically well-known speech centers of Broca, Wernicke, and Penfield in the lower frontal lobe, the posterior temporal lobe, and the supplementary motor area, respectively (15,16). Additional centers are activated by reading aloud or even silently (19). In the latter case, the mouth region and the auditory cortex are not activated.

Problem solving in normals activates the frontal lobes and also one or more of the postcentral regions depending upon which sensory modality is required for the solution of the problem (23). Repeated tests show signs of habituation (24).

ORGANIC DEMENTIA

It is well-known that several types of brain disorders causing structural damage and neuron loss will also reduce the intellectual faculties. In posttraumatic de-mentia caused by severe head injuries following traffic accidents, etc., very low blood flows are recorded in the hemisphere with the lesion. Often blood flows as low as those of normal white matter are recorded in certain cortical regions in such cases, indicating that the neurons have succumbed completely, and the flow recorded only pertains to a gliotic scar. In such patients, who often may be stuporous, aphasic, and more or less unresponsive, it is difficult or impossible to induce the activation patterns found normally as described above (10). The ultimate state of organic dementia is exemplified by the apallic state which may develop following severe brain anoxia resulting from cardiac arrest (8). Such patients have lost the cerebral cortex almost entirely and may survive with a functioning brain stem and spinal cord for months or years. They show no higher functions; the blood flows recorded over the brain are extremely low (10 to 20% of the normal), and activation patterns are absent.

In investigating senile dementia of Alzheimer's type, we have systematically studied larger groups of patients with clinical, psychometric, and neuroradiological methods, and have also measured regional cerebral blood flows. Our main findings can be summarized thus:

(a) The hemisphere mean blood flow in senile dementia of Alzheimer's type is reduced commensurate with the intellectual deficit.

(b) Regional blood flow reductions correlate in a meaningful way with the psychometric defects. Thus, memory defects correlate with a low blood flow in temporal regions; gnostic disturbances, confusion, etc., show parieto-occipito-temporal flow decreases. The most marked defects are found in patients in whom the reduction also involves the frontal lobes (5).

(c) Observations with inhalation technique indicate that specific blood flow patterns accompany both Alzheimer's disease and Pick's disorder. In the latter case, the flow reduction is more pronounced in frontal and temporal regions, while in Alzheimer's disease, the lowest flows are recorded postcentrally in parieto-occipito-temporal regions (22).

(d) Speech disturbances recorded in patients with presenile dementia also correlate with blood flow abnormalities. Anterior flow reductions show more expressive aphasia defects, while posterior reductions may show symptoms of impressive aphasia. If the flow is reduced generally, the language ability may be completely lost or highly disorganized (4).

(e) A comparison with autopsy findings demonstrates a clear relationship between regions of low flow and regions with a marked neuron loss (1). However, the autopsy findings show that mesial brain structures, especially the hippocampus, may be heavily involved in Alzheimer's disease. These structures are not seen by the blood flow technique which mainly records the flow in lateral aspects of the hemisphere.

CHRONIC SCHIZOPHRENIA

Forty patients with chronic schizophrenia have been studied with the cerebral blood flow method. This series includes both early cases with moderate symptoms and highly deteriorated patients with illness of several decades' duration. Some of the deteriorated patients show marked signs of what has been termed schizophrenic dementia.

Several major differences have been found between patients with organic dementia and those with schizophrenic dementia. In the schizophrenics, it has been confirmed that the mean cerebral blood flow is within the normal range, a finding made earlier with Kety's nitrous oxide technique (16). However, in deteriorated schizophrenics, we often found an abnormal resting flow distribution. The flow in frontal regions is relatively low, and the flow in postcentral parieto-temporal regions relatively high. This hypofrontal pattern thus differs from the hyperfrontal pattern seen in normals (9).

Detailed correlations with the symptoms of the schizophrenic patients as measured by conventional rating scales show that the lower the blood flow is in frontal structures, the more inactive, autistic, and mute is the patient. The higher the flow in postcentral structures, the more evidence there is of a cognitive disturbance. Emotional symptoms rated in the patients do not show any correlation to the flow measurements (2). The findings in patients with schizophrenia demonstrate that the defect in this disorder is of a fundamentally different character than that in organic dementia. In organic dementia, the intellectual deficits correlate distinctly to the loss of neurons as well as to the distribution of this loss.

In deteriorated, chronic schizophrenics, on the other hand, the mean cerebral blood flow, i.e., mean cerebral functional level, is within the normal range. What is abnormal is the *distribution of activity* as reflected in the hypofrontal flow pattern. This abnormal distribution may be related to the cognitive and perceptual disturbances which characterize the disease. It is well-known that sensory impulses from all modalities reach the cerebral cortex in a normal fashion in chronic schizophrenia, but that there they give rise to abnormal perceptual experiences, often of intense, threatening, and agonizing types. These perceptions might well be related to the high flow activity in postcentral afferent-gnostic areas of the cortex. On the other hand, in deteriorated chronic schizophrenics, sensory input does not give rise to an adequate goal-directed behavior as it does in normals. Instead, chronic schizophrenia is often characterized by autism, inactivity and, in some cases, a completely mute, catatonic state. This general lack of behavioral response to one's surroundings may be related to the low activity level found in those regions of the brain responsible for the synthesis of goal-directed behavior, namely, the precentral parts of the hemispheres, the frontal lobes.

ACTIVATION PROCEDURES

It is possible to study not only resting brains, but also brains being activated by augmented sensory input, by voluntary motor activity, and by psychological testing. Our limited experience with patients suffering organic dementia has shown that highly abnormal activation patterns are recorded in such patients.

Often the abnormalities show a clear relationship to the underlying focal or diffuse cortical disorder.

In chronic schizophrenics, activation testing shows that such patients do not activate their frontal lobes in the same manner as do normals when exposed to intense cutaneous stimulation of mildly painful character (3). This finding agrees with the interpretation, summarized above, that schizophrenia involves a defective "translation" of the sensory input into meaningful, goal-directed behavior. It is well known that many chronic schizophrenics show a marked indifference to the outer world and even to painful stimulation.

CONCLUSION

With multidetector measurements of the regional cerebral blood flow, two-dimensional maps can be obtained of the distribution of functional activity in the cerebral cortex. Patients with organic dementia and chronic schizophrenia have so far been studied with these techniques. In both groups, deviations from the normal patterns have been found, both in the resting state and following activation procedures. Focal features of these deviations relate in a meaningful way to symptoms of the disorders in question. It seems a distinct possibility that regional cerebral blood flow measurements when applied with atraumatic (inhalation) techniques can be used in clinical diagnosis and to evaluate various forms of therapy.

At present, three-dimensional techniques based upon emission tomography are being developed to measure regional cerebral blood flow and metabolism. Some of the findings briefly summarized in this chapter for normals as well as for patients with neurologic and psychiatric disease, have been confirmed with the new techniques, and, most likely, they will in a few years immensely augment our knowledge of cerebral events underlying both normal mentation and various psychopathological states.

ACKNOWLEDGMENTS

The author was aided by grants from the Swedish Medical Research Council, the Wallenberg and the Thuring Foundations.

REFERENCES

1. Brun, A., Gustafson, L., and Ingvar, D. H. (1975): Neuropathological findings related to neuro-psychiatric symptoms and regional cerebral blood flow in presenile dementia. Proceedings VII Int. Congress Neuropathology, Budapest, September, 1974. Excerpta Medica, Amsterdam, pp. 101–105.
2. Franzén, G., and Ingvar, D. H. (1975): Abnormal distribution of cerebral activity in chronic schizophrenia. *J. Psychiatr. Res.* 12:199–214.
3. Franzén, G., and Ingvar, D. H. (1975): Absence of activation in frontal structures during psychological testing of chronic schizophrenics. *J. Neurol. Neurosurg. Psychiatry* 38:1027–1032.
4. Gustafson, L., Hagberg, B., and Ingvar, D. H. (1978): Speech disturbances in presenile dementia

related to local cerebral blood flow abnormalities in the dominant hemisphere. *Brain Lang.* 5:103–118.

5. Hagberg, B., and Ingvar, D. H. (1976): Cognitive reduction in presenile dementia related to regional abnormalities of the cerebral blood flow. *Brit. J. Psychiatry* 128:209–222.

6. Ingvar, D. H. (1977): Patterns of brain activity revealed by measurements of regional cerebral blood flow. In: *Brain Work,* edited by D. H. Ingvar and N. A. Lassen, pp. 397–413. Munksgaard, Copenhagen.

7. Ingvar, D. H. (1979): Hyperfrontal distribution of the gray matter blood flow in the resting conscious rate. *Acta Neurol. Scand. (in press).*

8. Ingvar, D. H., Brun, A., Johannson, L., and Samuelson, S. M. (1978): Survival after severe cerebral anoxia with destruction of the cerebral cortex: The apallic syndrome. *Ann. N.Y. Acad. Sci.* 315:184–208.

9. Ingvar, D. H., and Franzén, G. (1974): Abnormalities of cerebral blood flow distribution in patients with chronic schizophrenia. *Acta Psychiatr. Scand.* 50:425–462.

10. Ingvar, D. H., and Gadea-Ciria, M. (1975): Assessment of severe damage to the brain by multiregional measurements of cerebral blood flow. In: *Outcome of Severe Damage to the Central Nervous System,* Ciba Foundation Symposium 34, edited by B. Jennett and F. Plum. Elsevier, Amsterdam.

11. Ingvar, D. H., and Lassen, N. A. (1975): *Brain Work.* Munksgaard, Copenhagen.

12. Ingvar, D. H., and Philipson, L. (1977): Distribution of cerebral blood flow in the dominant hemisphere during motor ideation and motor performance. *Ann. Neurol.* 2:230–237.

13. Ingvar, D. H., and Risberg, J. (1967): Increase of regional cerebral blood flow during mental effort in normals and in patients with focal brain disorders. *Exp. Brain Res.* 3:195–211.

14. Ingvar, D. H., Rosen, I., Eriksson, M., and Elmqvist, D. (1976): Activation patterns induced in the dominant hemisphere by skin stimulation. In: *Sensory Functions of the Skin,* edited by Y. Zotterman, pp. 549–557. Pergamon Press, New York.

15. Ingvar, D. H., and Schwartz, M. S. (1974): Blood flow patterns induced in the dominant hemisphere by speech and reading. *Brain* 96:274–288.

16. Kety, S. S. and Schmidt, C. F. (1945): The determination of cerebral blood flow in man by the use of nitrous oxide in low concentrations. *Am. J. Physiol.,* 143:53.

17. Larsen, B., Skinhøj, E., and Lassen, N. A. (1978): Variations in regional cortical blood flow in the right and left hemispheres during automatic speech. *Brain* 101:193–209.

18. Lassen, N. A., and Ingvar, D. H. (1972): Radiosotopic assessment of regional cerebral blood flow. *Prog. Nucl. Med.* 1:376–409.

19. Lassen, N. A., Ingvar, D. H., and Skinhøj, E. (1978): Brain function and blood flow. *Sci. Am.* 239:62–71.

20. Lassen, N. A., Roland, P. E., Larsen, B., Melamed, E., and Soh, K. (1977): Mapping of human cerebral functions. In: *Cerebral Function, Metabolism, and Circulation,* edited by D. H. Ingvar and N. A. Lassen, pp. 262–263. Munksgaard, Copenhagen.

21. Olesen, J. (1971): Contralateral focal increase of cerebral blood flow in man during arm work. *Brain* 94:635–646.

22. Risberg, J. (1979): Regional cerebral blood flow measurements by 133 Xe-inhalation: Methodology and applications in neuropsychology and psychiatry. *Brain and Language (in press.)*

23. Risberg, J., and Ingvar, D. H. (1973): Patterns of activation in the gray matter of the dominant hemisphere during memorization and reasoning. *Brain* 96:737–757.

24. Risberg, J., Maximilian, A. V., and Prohovnik, J. (1977): Changes of cerebral activation patterns during habituation to mental testing. *Acta Neurol. Scand. [Suppl.]* 64:266–267.

OPEN DISCUSSION

Dr. Robert Cloninger: You told us the mean blood flow level. Can you now tell us something about the variability in different populations? You told us about a normal picture in schizophrenics, and vice versa. How much variability is there?

Dr. Ingvar: The variability is small. It is about 5 to 7% in repeated determinations at rest in the same region. Changes of more than 15% during activation are considered significant.

Dr. Robert Cloninger: Would a schizophrenic ever show a normal pattern?

Dr. Ingvar: Yes, some of them did in our 40 patients. Some of the younger ones had a normal type of pattern, especially those who had a productive type of psychosis. But we also saw some young patients with a more hypofrontal pattern. They were more of the *dementia praecox* type.

Dr. Robert Cloninger: Could you comment on the stability of the pictures over time?

Dr. Ingvar: We have 7 patients who were studied twice with an interval of 3 years. There was an amazing constancy as to flow level and the flow distribution.

Dr. Elliot D. Weitzman: This is really a brave new world that we are beginning to see, and I think it is very exciting.

I have two questions for Dr. Ingvar. I notice on your slide you used the term Alzheimer's disease, suggesting that you did want to differentiate it from Pick's disease. It seems to me that this regional flow technique, with what we know about the pathology of these conditions, should differentiate the two.

Dr. Ingvar: I think there are certain possibilities to use flow studies for differential diagnosis. For Alzheimer patients there is, as also shown by Risberg et al., a frontal/temporal flow decrease. For Pick's disease there is a much more frontal decrease.

Dr. Elliot D. Weitzman: The second question relates to patients who have a cerebral infarction, where you show an abnormal flow associated with the neurological deficit. When the neurological deficit improves, does the regional blood flow improve or does it remain abnormal in that area?

Dr. Ingvar: This is difficult to answer with the two-dimensional cerebral blood flow technique. We have a feeling it may improve, but this improvement may be so subtle and so localized that we cannot see it with our technique. With three-dimensional techniques you can see, for example, that if you put an anastomosis into the brain, the flow increases locally, and the symptoms disappear at the same time.

Dr. Klein: I was concerned about the causal arrow in schizophrenics. Do their peculiar neurophysiological patterns lead to the odd cerebral vascular flow patterns, or is it the other way around?

One possible way of looking at that is to take a look at the blood flow patterns while they are asleep. Do the schizophrenics' brain flow patterns differ while they are asleep from that of normal flow?

Dr. Ingvar: In answer to your first question, it must be stated again that the flow changes are secondary to metabolic events.

Your second question concerned sleep. We have done only a few sleep measurements. It is very difficult to have people sleep during flow studies, as it appears that sleep gives a reduction of flow in the frontal lobe.

Dr. Charles Shagass: We have been very excited about Dr. Ingvar's findings because of our own initial results that provided evidence of a posterior displacement of somatosensory evoked potentials in chronic schizophrenics. This seems to be in pretty good agreement with at least the direction of the findings on regional blood flow.

As we are understandably reluctant to apply an invasive technique to schizophrenics, we have been looking at noninvasive methods. Dr. Jacquy in Charleroi, Belgium, has published findings, using the noninvasive technique of rheoencephalography, which appear to be very much in line with the results obtained by Dr. Ingvar. However, the degree of resolution is far less. I have talked to Dr. Ingvar briefly about the rheoencephalographic method, and I wonder if he would care to comment about its status. We have been trying to get the method going in our laboratory. So far we have not been able to test it properly.

Dr. Ingvar: I would like to stress that the phenomena shown in my slides have a neurophysiological background. Your posterior displacement is in line with our flow findings.

The second point about atraumatic techniques is important. Dr. Risberg of Lund, Sweden, has developed an atraumatic inhalation technique and so have other workers in this country. This technique does not have the same resolution as the intra-arterial, but improvements are on the way. There are also atraumatic three-dimensional techniques coming.

Concerning rheoencephalography, not all workers have been so successful as the group in Belgium which showed a good correlation between cerebral blood flow and the rheo parameters.

Dr. Allen Willner: You mentioned there is a reduced blood flow for Alzheimer dementia. I think you are saying that is a secondary reaction to abnormal activity rather than being its cause.

I wonder if you would clarify whether I am correct in understanding that or not.

Dr. Ingvar: You have understood that quite correctly. The neurons degenerate, and because of that the metabolism goes down. That is why not so much flow is needed. The flow reduction then is secondary to the neuronal degeneration.

Dr. Allen Willner: In schizophrenia, you mentioned the reduced blood flow sometimes found in chronic schizophrenic patients.

There have been various studies originating with Bruetsch about 20 years ago that found one type of schizophrenia that arises in people who have rheumatic heart disease where there seem to be blockages in the small cerebral vessels. I wonder if there might be any indication of a history of rheumatic fever or rheumatic heart disease in the schizophrenic patients that you were examining.

Dr. Ingvar: There was no history of rheumatic disease in our patients.

Dr. Jarvik: I have two questions. One, you mention that in 20 out of your 60 patients you have excellent correlations between the topography of cerebral blood flow and behavior. I wonder about the other 40.

Dr. Ingvar: If the patient had just a memory disturbance, the flow would be reduced just in the temporal lobe. If there were symptoms of agnosia, the flow was low in the parietal region. So subsymptoms of the syndrome of dementia correlate with various regional decreases.

Dr. Jarvik: The second question is, how does the observation that the patients cannot compensate for the deficit in cerebral blood flow relate to Luria's training patients to compensate for deficits? And, in a brave new world, could your technique, or a less invasive technique, be used as a guide to therapy in such patients?

Dr. Ingvar: I discussed this with Alexander Romanovich Luria a short time before he passed away. I think he has been misunderstood concerning senile and presenile dementia. There does not seem to exist any reparatory processes in the remaining brain tissue which undergoes a slow further degeneration. When it comes to vascular and other focal lesions, the recovery phase can be quite long. Luria emphasized that a humane and very active attitude towards these patients may enhance the restitution.

Dr. Winokur: Is there any correlation between increasing years of chronicity and abnormal findings? Are older patients more likely to have abnormalities than younger patients?

Dr. Ingvar: No, not if they do not have brain diseases.

Psychopathology in the Aged, edited by
Jonathan O. Cole and James E. Barrett.
Raven Press, New York © 1980.

Behavioral Studies of Dementia: Methods of Investigation and Analysis

Francisco I. Perez

*Department of Physical Medicine and Rehabilitation, Baylor College of Medicine, and
Behavioral Medicine Consultants of Houston, Houston, Texas 77030*

Dementia is a disruption of behavior with impairment in the ability to learn new responses and adapt to a changing environment. By testing the ability of a subject to adapt to new environmental input, we can discover more about the capacity and health of the subject than by observing him in an already adapted state (2). Psychological tests and behavioral tasks which force the individual to learn new material, i.e., adapt, much more readily uncover a reduced capacity to handle information than do observations or tests of the person's preexisting knowledge. In measuring the adaptive capacity of a system, we are interested not only in whether or not the system adapts but also in the speed with which this adaptation takes place. It is the present hypothesis that unless there is some serious neurological deficit, most elderly individuals eventually respond in discrimination and reaction time task and can eventually learn some new material. What differentiates the healthy elderly individual from the patient suffering from dementia is his adaptive behavioral capacity.

The evaluation of the behavioral changes associated with dementia has been accomplished by way of neuropsychological test batteries which, unfortunately, suffer from a number of methodological as well as practical problems (4,5,7,8). These include: imprecise or nonspecific measures which do not differentiate kinds of dysfunction, i.e., do not complement structural etiology; insensitive tests which do not detect instances of disability or accurately reflect the degree of impairment; procedures which do not adequately control for differences in motivational states between individuals, thereby confounding observed differences; test environments which promote extraneous patient-clinician interactions that subsequently bias test results; test material which is prejudiced, biased, or irrelevant to the problem being diagnosed, i.e., material that is dependent on the patient's particular social and educational background. In order to achieve accurate behavioral diagnoses and to facilitate the evaluation of the effectiveness of therapeutic interventions in dementia, it is necessary to develop procedures and measures which avoid these problems.

BEHAVIORAL CONCEPTS

Behavior is action. It is observable, countable movement. A movement cycle refers to a completed unit of a behavior. A cycle begins with the start of the behavior and ends when the person is in a position to repeat the behavior. Frequency, incorporating numbers of behaviors observed over a unit of time, is the universal measure of behavior. There are essentially three categories of behavior frequency: behavioral excess—too much behavior; behavioral deficit—too little behavior; behavioral asset—adaptive behavior. This simple categorization of behavior emphasizes that the frequency of a given behavior determines the adaptability of an individual.

The future probability of a given movement cycle or behavior is influenced by its consequences. A description of the interaction between an individual and his environment must always specify three things: the occasion upon which a response occurs, the response itself, and the reinforcing consequences (12). All of us are engaged in social-environmental transactions throughout our lives. In the course of our development, however, there are marked changes in the stimulus and response complexes that make up the transactions, in those with whom we transact, and in the physical-environmental setting in which the transactions occur. In other words, we are continuously adapting because of these transactions. The physiological state of the organism, i.e., the central nervous system, interacts with the environmental determinants of behavior to establish and maintain a given behavior. A breakdown in behavior can be due to changes in the environmental determinants or the physiological (i.e., health) state of the individual.

The following behavior sequence allows us to conceptualize the interactions of the environmental and central nervous system variables determining a given behavioral act: (a) antecedent events, both past and present, are (b) registered and (c) organized by the central nervous system and are (d) integrated with prior experiences; the central nervous system then (e) initiates behavior which, in turn, leads to (f) subsequent events.

Behavior is a continuous process in time. However, this behavior sequence allows us to analyze the molecular aspects of behavior. A comprehensive analysis of behavior must include all six variables. Variable (e), behavior, is the dependent variable. Variables (a) and (f), antecedent events and subsequent events, are independent environmental variables. Variables (b) through (d) are intervening physiological variables. The following are descriptions of each of these important components of the behavior sequence.

Antecedent Events

These are the stimulus conditions preceding a given behavior. There are two essential ingredients to antecedent events. The historical events are the accumulated environmental interactions which have determined that a given behavioral movement cycle will occur when a given set of stimulus conditions is present.

We are products of our history. The behavioral history will determine the likelihood that a given stimulus will set the conditions for a given response to occur. The present events are those which are current when the given observable behavioral act is initiated. If a given behavior is reinforced in the presence of a given antecedent event, the likelihood that a given behavior will occur in the future increases, and the present event becomes part of our history.

Registered

The present antecedent event is registered by our sense organs. This is the beginning of the interaction of the environment and the physiological variables.

Organized and Integrated

These are inferential terms. The actual events occurring are physiological in nature, including neurochemical and neurophysiological transactions within the central nervous system.

Behavior

This is the observed and measurable action.

Subsequent Event

This identifies the environmental consequences of a given behavior. There are two types of subsequent events, those which increase the future probability (frequency) of a given behavior and those which decrease the future frequency of a given behavior. Subsequent events interact with the present antecedent events to set the stimulus conditions under which a given behavioral response will be made in the future. It is important to note that when an individual is exposed to a set of contingencies of reinforcement, is modified by them, and, as a result, behaves in a different way in the future, we do not need to say that he "stores" the contingencies. What is "stored" is a modified individual, not a record of the modifying variables (12). The ultimate explanation of memory will rest with the molecular analysis of behavior and the neurochemical and neurophysiological changes memory produces within the central nervous system.

BEHAVIORAL CONCEPTS OF DEMENTIA

Now we are in a position to analyze and conceptualize dementia. Dementia was previously defined as a disruption of behavior with impairment in the ability to learn new responses and adapt to a changing environment. The behavior sequence presented above conceptualizes a breakdown in behavior when the interaction of antecedent and subsequent events are no longer reinforcing, or when there is a breakdown in the central nervous system affecting the registration, organization, or integration of antecedent and subsequent events. For example, pseudodementia or depression can be conceptualized as a breakdown in behavior because the environmental determinants are no longer reinforcing and therefore are producing a decrement-deficit in a given adaptive behavioral repertoire. A case in point is retirement. Abruptly we change and eliminate many of the reinforcing environmental determinants and require a drastic behavioral change in an individual who has a limited repertoire of nonwork behavior. Neurological disease produces a breakdown in behavior by affecting the intervening central nervous system variables and therefore affecting the stimulus-response interaction.

STIMULUS-RESPONSE INTERACTION IN DEMENTIA

It is known that a single stimulus controls many responses, and a single response is controlled by many stimuli. A response usually produces reinforcement only when a particular stimulus is present. The individual's experience with the stimulus-response relations being studied, physical and social features of the environment, and the instructions he receives, will influence his performance. Such factors modulate stimulus control. Since a modulating factor controls many stimulus-response relations, a cerebral disorder that changes the influence of such factors will cause widespread deficits in stimulus control. A specific central nervous system dysfunction, however, need not break down all relations in which a particular stimulus-response participates. For example, the stimulus may be a printed word that controls all reading (S-R$_1$), copying (S-R$_2$), and pointing to a picture (S-R$_3$). A cerebral lesion that destroys (S-R$_3$), but leaves the other S-R relations intact is often said to leave the patient able to read the words without knowing their significance. The basic observations in dementia are deficient stimulus-response relations. Different stimuli, responses, and stimulus-response relations may be affected by different variables, and in quantitatively differing ways by the same variables. To clarify the factors responsible for such variability, tests must hold modulating variables constant, thus maintaining stimulus-response relations constant while varying stimuli. The present methodological approach emphasizes a functional analysis of behavior in individual patients with dementia. The primary objective of the proposed analysis is to show that we can identify a large sequence of adaptive behaviors simply in terms of stimulus-response relations.

THE AUTOMATED BEHAVIORAL ASSESSMENT SYSTEM (ABAS)

Knowledge about the behavioral status of the aged has been gained as a result of the development of experimental methods of assessment and the application of more precise conceptualization in the field of behavioral gerontology. Birren (1) proposes that laboratory research on the psychology of aging is a potential friend of the aging adult and that we ought to utilize the precise findings of the laboratory for the benefit of the aging population. However, in the behavioral study of dementia, some uncontrolled variables may lie outside the boundaries of immediate measurement and control in the clinical setting and may not be identifiable or measurable with current psychometric procedures. This is an important issue since the ultimate criterion of the success or failure of a specific treatment approach, including use of pharmacological agents, in the organic dementias is behavioral in nature. Effective research on the treatment of demented patients is dependent on the existence of precise behavioral methods of assessing the effects of proposed new forms of treatment. It is particularly important to be able to detect small but significant improvements in a patient's condition so that potentially useful forms of treatment are not abandoned prematurely. In addition, correlations of morphologic brain changes and behavioral performance are exercises in futility if either set of observations is improperly controlled. The behavioral assessment must be as rigorous as the anatomic if the correlation is to be meaningful.

Behavioral Medicine Consultants of Houston have been developing a computerized Automated Behavioral Assessment System (ABAS) (3,6). The primary objective is to develop a precise and direct behavioral measurement system that is sensitive to small changes in behavioral functioning of the healthy and demented aged individual. Characteristics of this system include control of the assessment environment, intensive study of individual subjects, continuous observation and recording of behavior, and automatic recording and programming.

The testing milieu or environment is of primary importance. A factor which introduces substantial variability into the evaluation of human functioning is the interaction between subject and examiner. One way to avoid this problem is to automate, as far as possible, the testing environment. Automated testing has long been a tradition in the operant and behavioral pharmacological research laboratories where experimental control is a high priority. The experimental analysis of behavior is concerned with accounting for and controlling all significant variables in a test situation in order to evaluate the contribution of the variables of interest. The emphasis on precise control follows an established tradition in science. This strategy has proven to be extremely valuable in the analysis of behavior and the development of an applied technology of behavior. This approach can be contrasted to the typical clinical testing environment where little care is taken to control for social, motivational, and educational variables.

Technical Developments

The development of ABAS requires considerable technical as well as methodological innovation. Indeed, a great deal of time and resources have been devoted to the instrumentation aspects of the system. The original apparatus consisted of the Human Test System (HTS) under the control of digi-bit (BRS-LVE) logic control modules. This particular configuration was adequate for operating a single basic procedure (i.e., DMTS) and collecting some other kinds of data. In order to accommodate demands for greater flexibility and more detailed data collection, the system was upgraded with the acquisition of an IMSAI 8080 microcomputer. Microcomputers are finding extensive application in a wide variety of settings because they are flexible, cost effective, and increasingly powerful. This technology allows for intelligent, on-line control of tasks, sophisticated data analysis, and convenient storage of records of the patient's moment-to-moment performance. Automated systems, especially computer systems, can be very efficient and cost effective once they are developed. However, the advantages of such a system have a price; over 2 years have been spent programming and interfacing the components of the system. The following is a description of the current ABAS in use.

The Human Test System

Figure 1 shows the Human Test System (HTS) that has been used in the initial development of the ABAS. The HTS is the interactive terminal for the assessment of the stimulus-response interaction performance for each patient. It consists of a square matrix of four translucent rearview projection windows, each 2 inches square. Below this matrix is a three-window LED matrix. The visual material is projected onto the four-window matrix by a random access programmable 35 mm slide projector. Audio is provided by a two-channel tape

FIG. 1. Human test system.

recorder which can be programmed to give verbal commands or present auditory stimuli to the patient via stereo headphones. A voice-activated microphone tape recorder can be programmed to record on-line specific verbal responses of the patient to specific stimuli, as well as any spontaneous speech occurring during the session. A coin dispenser, a speaker, and a LED display as part of the HTS deliver specific visual, auditory, and tangible reinforcers plus feedback to the patient for his correct response. Using the HTS it is possible to select in any one test: true-false, multiple choice, advance on machine command, advance on correct response, advance or backtrack on incorrect response, advance on any response, advance on subject command, advance on experimenter command, advance on time, record or not record reaction time, record inter-response time, changes in intertrial interval, and many other parameters. The logic, programming, and recording functions of the HTS are controlled by the IMSAI 8080 microcomputer.

Automated Behavioral Evaluator

Figure 2 shows the current configuration. It consists of an IMSAI 8080 microcomputer with 64K 8-bit memory, a Texas Instrument Silent 700® terminal for hard copy, a CRT terminal for video display, an ICOM dual drive floppy disk system for program development, data storage, and component interfacing. One recent addition is a TEAC reel-to-reel tape recorder which is under computer control. The task instructions are recorded in a programmed instruction format. By interfacing the tape recorder to the computer, verbal prompts may be given which require that the subject make some response to demonstrate he understands the instruction. The responses are similar to those he must make in the actual test. Subjects are often hesitant about asking questions of the examiner

FIG. 2. Microcomputer configuration.

because they don't want to admit they haven't understood. At other times they may "think" they understand the task, but this is not the same as having to emit the appropriate responses. If the subject makes an error, the instruction is repeated until he performs correctly. This ensures that all subjects have reached a criterion of instruction competence before proceeding on the actual task.

The system as it stands is a reliable, efficient, and fully automated behavioral evaluator. The microcomputer is the key to the system's versatility. One problem which has not been overcome by the addition of the microcomputer is the relative inflexibility of the Human Test System (HTS) for implementing promising new procedures. This apparatus relies on a 35 mm projector for stimulus generation. For the basic delayed matching-to-sample (DMTS) procedure this is adequate. The four-panel response window allows a maximum of four responses: one for the sample and three for choices. One must consider that a subject has a 0.33 chance of guessing correctly under these circumstances. The slide projector naturally restricts the sequence and speed at which stimuli may be presented. The HTS is structurally and functionally limited.

Interactive Graphics Computer Terminal

Ideally one would want an apparatus that is highly interactive, flexible both structurally and functionally, and able to accommodate a wide range of procedures. These features are contained in a cost-effective manner in the interactive computer graphics terminal (Fig. 3). To begin, the packaging is very compact. The system is portable and can be wheeled to the patient's bedside for inpatient testing, eliminating the need to move the patient to a special testing room. The use of the cathode ray tube (CRT) as a stimulus display unit greatly enhances our capability for creating novel and stimulating test paradigms. Here is a tool

FIG. 3. Interactive computer graphics terminal.

for establishing and maintaining substantial motivational control. The fascination with electronic video games attests to this. In addition to being visually exciting, the apparatus is as familiar as the home television. Two basic tenets of effective behavioral testing are to eliminate distracting or confounding variables and to insure maximum motivation. The two are interdependent. Individual differences in motivation reduce the sensitivity of test baselines and increase variability in dependent measures. It is not uncommon to find subjects who "don't try" or even deliberately do poorly. Automated testing, we have discovered, increases subject interest, thereby minimizing extraneous variables due to attitude and other distracting aspects of the test setting unrelated to the task. If the subject understands the task and does his best, then any deficits in performance are likely to be due to physiological-neurological impairment.

There are other advantages to the interactive graphics computer terminal approach. Tests may be arranged in order of increasing complexity from simple sensory-motor (i.e., pointing) to more complex language, memory, and learning tasks. Depending on the patient's performance, the system can dynamically adjust to his progress, presenting more complicated material as competency is demonstrated. The system can have total access to all procedures and stimulus materials from computer memory or disk storage. In addition, the generation of new stimuli would simply involve programming (not photography), and the potential number and complexity of stimuli that could be presented on the screen at one time would be considerable. An obvious advantage for the DMTS procedure is that it allows more choices.

It might be appropriate to consider how the subject actually interacts with the CRT terminal. Several devices have been developed which allow the graphics terminal user to interact directly with the screen display without having to type messages in from a keyboard (i.e., light pen, trackball, digitizing tablet, joystick, touch tablet). The most direct system involves the touch tablet which is a clear plastic sheet which fits over the display screen and is sensitive to finger touch. A patient can respond simply by touching the screen where his choice is displayed. The coordinates of the touch are automatically evaluated by the computer and compared to the coordinates of the correct answer. Some of the other devices are slightly less direct, but they could be useful nonetheless. For example, a "joystick" is a metal rod mounted vertically which can be moved in any direction in the plane perpendicular to it. Its movement directs a spot of light or "cursor" on the two-dimensional display screen. Conceivably a sensory-motor task might be designed in which the patient would direct the cursor through a maze or perhaps chase another spot of light by manipulating the joystick. One might point out that other kinds of pursuit tasks are already available (i.e., Trail-Making Test of the Halstead-Reitan Neuropsychological Battery). The virtue of the computer-based task is that all aspects of the tracking response may be quantified precisely. It is possible that certain subtle characteristics of response topography may be diagnostic. Further, the dynamic nature of the display would allow many variations of the task. Some would challenge the most healthy individuals while others would allow quantification of performance in patients with even severe dementia and behavioral deficits. The number of different kinds of manipulanda or interactive peripheral devices that can be interfaced to a computer graphics system is practically unlimited. This feature makes for a most versatile research and, eventually, clinical tool.

From a clinical point of view, the graphics system could provide a comprehensive behavioral assessment system within a single cost-effective portable package. The promise of such a system depends not only on hardware, however. Suitable tasks must be developed and validated. We have recently initiated a research program aimed at developing such a portable system in order to quantify more precisely the behavioral adaptive abilities of patients with dementing disorders. Figure 3 shows our interactive graphics computer terminal. A Chromatics microprocessor color graphics system is used. We are currently developing behavioral tasks using this system in order to assess the effects of papaverine (Pavabid-HP®, Marion) in the behavioral functioning of patients with multi-infarct dementia.

PRELIMINARY FINDINGS

The clinical studies in our laboratory have demonstrated that memory deficits are the logical focal point for behavioral analysis in the dementias (7). Therefore, our initial efforts in the development of the ABAS have been concerned with short-term recognition memory in demented patients. The delayed matching-to-sample (DMTS) procedure has proved to be a valuable tool for the study of short-term memory in the animal laboratory (10). The technique is a variation of the matching-to-sample (MTS) procedure where a time delay is interpolated between the sample and choice stimuli. Sidman, Stoddard, Mohr, and Leicester (11) have used MTS and DMTS to investigate aphasia. The DMTS procedure has been applied to the analysis of memory in patients with right and left CVAs (9), dementing disorders (3,6), and traumatic head injuries. These studies used a variation of the DMTS procedure where the delayed time was adjusted or titrated depending on performance. The patient sat in front of a Human Test System Apparatus with a display screen. This screen, a rear-view projection window, was divided into four (two by two matrix) independent response panels each 3 inches by 2 inches. A sample item was displayed on the upper left response panel. When the patient pressed this window, three choice items were displayed after some delay. If the response was correct, the delay interval increased by 10 sec on the next trial. If the response was incorrect, the sample-to-choice delay was decreased by 10 sec. In this way, the delay time was adjusted or titrated up and down depending on performance. During the delay interval, the patient performed a simple simultaneous color matching task (MTS).

Two tasks were devised using this basic paradigm. The stimuli in the first task were random shapes and, in the second, nonsense trigrams. The former stimuli were thought to be relevant to spatial memory, and the latter to verbal memory. It was found that the spatial task was sensitive to right hemisphere CVAs, and the verbal task to left hemisphere CVAs. These initial investigations using ABAS have demonstrated the sensitivity of the automatic procedure to neurological disorders. This suggests that the ABAS methodology has potential for providing the precision required for the accurate assessment of molar and molecular behavioral changes associated with structural changes in the central nervous system.

The following reports are of the individualized performance of three patients using the DMTS procedure.

Patient DAT 23 is a 64-year-old right-handed female with a 2-year history of progressive changes in memory performance. The CT scan showed a moderate degree of diffuse atrophy. The neurological work-up indicated a diagnosis of Alzheimer's disease. On the neuropsychological testing, the patient obtained a Wechsler Adult Intelligence Scale (WAIS) Full IQ of 110 (Verbal IQ = 106; Performance IQ = 113). On the Wechsler Memory Scale (WMS) she obtained a Memory Quotient (MQ) of 81. Figure 4 shows the DMTS performance. The results indicate a severe disorder of memory with the maximum delayed interval

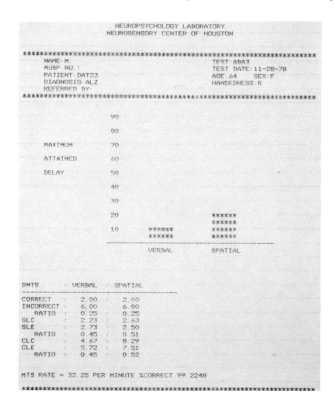

FIG. 4. Patient DAT-23 memory titration.

obtained for the verbal task being 10 sec and for the spatial task of 20 sec. The percentage (ratio) correct for both tasks was 25%. The stimulus latency correct (SLC) and the stimulus latency error (SLE) are shown. These are reaction time measures primarily indicating scanning time for the sample stimuli. The choice latency correct (CLC) and the choice latency error (CLE) are also shown. These are reaction time measures indicating the discrimination time for the choice response. Basically there was no difference between the ratio of correct to incorrect reaction time responding. The matching-to-sample (MTS) measure is the frequency of simultaneous color matching responding and the percentage of correct responses. No significant problems were noted on MTS.

Patient DAT 19 is a 69-year-old right-handed male with 1 year of college education. He is diagnosed as suffering from vertebrobasilar insufficiency (VBI). The Full WAIS IQ was 102 (Verbal IQ = 103; Performance IQ = 99). The MQ was 92. Figure 5 shows this patient's DMTS results. Significant spatial memory deficits are noted in the presence of good performance on the verbal task. The MTS shows a slower rate of responding with 94% accuracy.

Patient DAT 13 is a 70-year-old right-handed female who 3 weeks prior to the evaluation, had a sudden onset of a nonfluent aphasia with considerable difficulties in expressing herself. No formal WAIS IQ or WMS scores were

```
*******************************************************************
  NAME:                              TEST: ABA3
  HOSP  NO. :                        TEST  DATE: 11-21-78
  PATIENT: DAT19                     AGE: 69     SEX: M
  DIAGNOSIS: VBI                     HANDEDNESS: R
  REFERRED  BY:
*******************************************************************


                    90        ******
                              ******
                    80        ******
                              ******
  MAXIMUM           70        ******
                              ******
  ATTAINED          60        ******
                              ******
  DELAY             50        ******
                              ******
                    40        ******
                              ******
                    30        ******
                              ******
                    20        ******
                              ******
                    10        ******     ******
                              ******     ******
       -------------------------------------------------
                              VERBAL     SPATIAL



  DMTS       :  VERBAL  :  SPATIAL
  --------------------------------------
  CORRECT    :    5.00  :    1.00
  INCORRECT  :    0.00  :    6.00
      RATIO  :    1.00  :    0.14
  SLC        :   10.45  :   33.08
  SLE        :    0.00  :    9.92
      RATIO  :    1.00  :    0.77
  CLC        :    9.69  :   14.90
  CLE        :    0.00  :    9.07
      RATIO  :    1.00  :    0.62

  MTS RATE = 27.0909 PER MINUTE          %CORRECT 93.9597
*******************************************************************
```

FIG. 5. Patient DAT-19 memory titration.

```
                    NEUROPSYCHOLOGY LABORATORY
                  NEUROSENSORY CENTER OF HOUSTON

*********************************************************************
   NAME:                               TEST:  ABA3
   HOSP NO.:                           TEST DATE: 11-7-78
   PATIENT: DAT13                      AGE: 70 · SEX: F
   DIAGNOSIS: LCVA-APHASIA             HANDEDNESS: R
   REFERRED BY:
*********************************************************************


                       90

                       80

   MAXIMUM             70

   ATTAINED            60

   DELAY               50                        ******
                                                 ******
                       40                        ******
                                                 ******
                       30         ******         ******
                                  ******         ******
                       20         ******         ******
                                  ******         ******
                       10         ******         ******
                                  ******         ******
                                  ******         ******
                       -----------------------------------
                                  VERBAL         SPATIAL


   DMTS        : VERBAL    SPATIAL
   ------------------------------------
   CORRECT     :  4.00   :   6.00
   INCORRECT   :  4.00   :   3.00
       RATIO   :  0.50   :   0.67
   SLC         : 23.52   :  17.43
   SLE         : 26.17   :  12.07
       RATIO   :  0.47   :   0.59
   CLC         : 39.49   :  25.91
   CLE         : 31.36   :  20.72
       RATIO   :  0.56   :   0.56

   MTS RATE = 6.81081 PER MINUTE        %CORRECT 97.6191
```

FIG. 6. Patient DAT-13 memory titration.

obtained because of the language problems. She had suffered a left middle cerebral artery stroke. Figure 6 shows the DMTS results. The maximum delayed interval for verbal was 30 sec and 50 sec for spatial tasks. The percentage correct was 50% for verbal and 67% for spatial. The reaction time response was quite slow. The MTS rate was extremely slow (6.8 responses per min) but quite accurate (97.6%).

The DMTS results of these three cases are quite encouraging. We have been able to individually titrate the memory performance of each patient and to obtain measures regarding speed of responding. Patient DAT 23 is the case of a patient with Alzheimer's dementia who has fairly well preserved cognitive functioning but marked deficits in memory. The DMTS procedure was quite sensitive. Patient DAT 19's findings are consistent with our series of patients with VBI showing selective impairment for spatial memory in the presence of good verbal memory. Patient DAT 13's results indicate that the computerized automated behavioral approach can be used to evaluate memory and cognitive performance in the presence of marked expressive language deficits. The WAIS and WMS failed to assess the ability of this patient. The ABAS procedure provided an interactive environment for effective behavioral evaluation.

PROSTHETIC ENVIRONMENTS FOR THE BEHAVIORAL MANAGEMENT OF DEMENTIA

Human behavior is a functional relationship between a person and a specific social environment. If the behavior is deficient, we can either alter the individual or the environment in order to produce effective behavior. Most attempts to restore or improve behavioral efficiency in dementia have focused on medical-pharmacological treatment of the deficient individual. This medical approach assumes that there are ordinarily no deficient environments. To prolong health, physicians offer aging persons with dementia a wide range of physiological prosthetics from vitamins and drugs to increased oxygen utilization for their internal physiological environment. However, little is done to modify and program the external mechanical and social environments of the demented. They are usually sent to a nursing home environment where custodial care is the rule with no emphasis on attempting to restore or improve behavioral efficiency. The nursing home environment usually creates dependent behavior since this type of behavior requires less effort from the staff and is "easier to manage." Attention should be shifted to focus on the environmental side of deficient behavior functions of the demented individual and on the design of individualized prosthetic environments to restore and maintain competent independent performance.

The methods of investigation and analysis presently proposed are suited for behavioral geriatrics for several reasons. With respect to motivational aspects or consequences of behavior, the immediate environment can be altered to generate and maintain behavior. The sensitivity of the ABAS methods to subtle changes in such aspects of the individual's performance as response rate and latency, efficiency, and perseverance, makes these methods appropriate to the study of single individuals. Because the sensitivity does not decrease with very long periods of application with the same individual, reliable longitudinal studies are possible. Behavioral methods for the analysis of functional and dynamic relationships between individuals and their environments can produce separate measures of mechanical dexterity, intellectual functioning, and social adjustment. A laboratory behavioral description, prognosis, and evaluation can be produced that can help us in the design of prosthetic environments and in the development of an individualized prosthetic prescription for the behavioral management of dementia. Until behavioral medicine technology in the dementias catches up with organic medicine, terminal boredom will fall to those unfortunates who live beyond their environment.

ACKNOWLEDGMENTS

This work was supported by Grants NS09287–07–08 and NS13708–01–02 from the National Institute of Neurological and Communicative Disorders and Stroke, National Institutes of Health, and a grant from Marion Pharmaceutical Laboratories, Kansas City, Missouri.

REFERENCES

1. Birren, J. R. (1964): *The Psychology of Aging.* Prentice Hall, Englewood Cliffs.
2. Perez, F. I., Brown, G. A., and Rivera, V. M. (1979): Individualized assessment of memory scanning in dementia. *Exp. Aging Res. (in press).*
3. Perez, F. I., Gay, J. R. A., and Cooke, N. A. (1978): Neuropsychological aspects of Alzheimer's disease and multi-infarct dementia. In: *Senile Dementia: A Biochemical Approach,* edited by K. Nandy, pp. 185–199. Elsevier-North Holland, New York.
4. Perez, F. I., Gay, J. R. A., and Taylor, R. L. (1976): WAIS performance in the neurologically impaired aged. *Psychol. Rep.,* 38:35–39.
5. Perez, F. I., Gay, J. R. A., Taylor, R. L., and Rivera, V. M. (1975): Patterns of memory performance in the neurologically impaired aged. *Can. J. Neurol. Sci.,* 2:347–355.
6. Perez, F. I., Hruska, N. A., Stell, R. L., and Rivera, V. M. (1978): Computerized assessment of memory performance in dementia. *Can. J. Neurol. Sci.,* 5:307–312.
7. Perez, F. I., Rivera, V. M., Meyer, J. S., Gay, J. R. A., Taylor, R. L., and Mathew, N. T. (1975): Analysis of intellectual and cognitive performance in patient with multi-infarct dementia, vertebrobasilar insufficiency with dementia and Alzheimer's disease. *J. Neurol. Neurosurg. Psychiatry,* 38:533–540.
8. Perez, F. I., Stump, D. A., Gay, J. R. A., and Hart, V. R. (1976): Intellectual performance in multi-infarct dementia and Alzheimer's disease: A replication study. *Can. J. Neurol. Sci.,* 3:181–187.
9. Perez, F. I., Stump, D. A., Wray, R. E., Gay, J. R. A., Dannon, M. R., and Meyer, J. S. (1977): Automated behavioral assessment system: Precise measurement of memory performance in cerebrovascular disease. Paper presented at the Cerebrovascular Clinical Research Center Workshop, February 23 and 24, 1977.
10. Shimp, C. P., and Moffitt, M. (1974): Short-term memory in the pigeon: Stimulus response association. *J. Exp. Anal. Behav.,* 22:507–512.
11. Sidman, M., Stoddard, J. T., Mohr, J. P., and Leicester, J. (1971): Behavioral studies of aphasia. Methods of investigation and analysis. *Neuropsychologia,* 9:119–140.
12. Skinner, B. F. (1969): *Contingencies of Reinforcement: A Theoretical Analysis.* Meredith Corporation, New York.

Psychopathology in the Aged, edited by
Jonathan O. Cole and James E. Barrett.
Raven Press, New York © 1980.

The Measurement of Mood in Senile Brain Disease: Examiner Ratings and Self-Reports

Nancy E. Miller

*Center for Studies of the Mental Health of the Aging, National Institute of Mental Health,
Rockville, Maryland 20857*

The borderlands between the functional and organic psychiatric disorders in man have come under increasing scrutiny in recent years. While difficulties in cognitive function have been traditionally viewed as behavioral markers of acute or chronic organic brain pathology, growing evidence has begun to suggest that disorders of learning and memory are also implicated in states of major affective disorder. The nature and etiology of these deficits are not well understood, but they have been reliably identified across a wide age range of depressed patients. (6,17,24,34). Prior to the current flurry of interest and research activity in this area, the clinical presentation of forgetfulness in the context of a depressive symptom picture would most often be found in case reports of patients who were elderly. In a certain percentage of these cases, elderly persons would present with symptoms of memory deficit and intellectual decline so severe as to be indistinguishable from states of diffuse, progressive brain impairment. Yet, following treatment with ECT or antidepressant medication, there would occur a complete remission of cognitive symptoms, and the patient would be diagnosed *post hoc* as having had a "pseudodementia."

The terms "pseudodementia" (20) or "dementia syndrome of depression" imply that while to all extents and purposes the patient appeared to have a chronic organic brain syndrome, actually he was suffering from a depression which presented in a disguised and highly atypical form. The retrospective nature of this particular diagnostic entity remains conceptually and methodologically problematic, and even when the formulation is made prospectively, the risks of misdiagnosis remain very high, especially in the absence of an adequate history. The presence of this substantial overlap of functional with organic symptomatology, which occurs with increasing frequency as chronological age advances, poses basic and immediate questions about the nature and complex interplay of brain function, mood, and behavior in senescent psychopathological states.

Perhaps by reconsidering this issue a new perspective, fresh insights may be gained. Accordingly, rather than examining aspects of the intellectual deficit which often accompanies states of psychotic depression in older persons, this chapter will focus on the questions of whether, and to what extent, depressive symptomatology is manifested by elderly individuals with cognitive failure who are positive for dementia.

Given that the differential diagnosis between depression and dementia in an older person is considered one of the most difficult in psychiatry, it is somewhat surprising that the majority of investigators in gerontology often fail to assess the affective status of their respondents in any structured and systematic way. There are, however, a number of impressionistic accounts in the literature which tend to fall into one or the other of two broad categories. A number of anecdotal reports, for example, express the view that the dysphorias seen to accompany states of diffuse brain disease in late life are not "true depressions," but rather constitute highly labile and fragmentary episodes which present only during the initial stages of impairment (33).

While there is minimal empirical evidence either to support or deny such contentions, these views can be matched by clinical case impressions which report just the reverse. Post (28) has drawn attention to the frequency with which organic patients exhibit deep and apparently genuine depressions. Characteristic disturbances of mood in both early and intermediate phases of the dementing course have also been cited in the older literature (8), and more recent reports confirm the presence of variable severity in the affective symptom pictures of elderly dements (32). In the context of some follow-up studies of depressed and organic elderly, Post (28) commented that "serious suicidal tendencies and profound as well as convincingly communicated depressions were as common in the organic affectives as in those who were and remained cerebrally intact." Not only was it found that affective symptomatology in organic patients was indistinguishable from, and as severe as, that seen in cerebrally intact patients, but it was also reported that suicidal risk was equally high in individuals with altered brain function as it was in those with serious depressive disorders. In Post's study, almost half of the subjects who attempted suicide during the course of the investigation were found to have dementia. The number of subjects reported in his study, however, was relatively small, thus making generalization from the results somewhat problematic. The earlier clinical report of O'Neal (26) similarly found that over 50% of patients 60 years of age or older who attempted suicide were suffering from chronic or acute brain syndromes. Here too, however, sample size was quite small.

More recently, Ernst et al. (10) compared the frequency and variety of cognitive and affective symptoms in both institutionalized and community-residing groups aged 60 and up, and a significant number of affective symptoms were identified in individuals with chronic organic brain syndrome. Complaints of dysphoria were as prevalent in the institutionalized population as they were in the community-dwelling group, and over half of the respondents with altered brain function were found to show moderate to severe degrees of depression, regardless of severity of cognitive dysfunction. Cawley et al. (5) also reported that at least 50% of their demented group manifested depressive symptomatology.

In none of these investigations, however, was the level of affective morbidity quantified, nor was the patient himself asked in a systematic way to describe his internal mood subjectively. For these reasons, we were prompted to study the emotional symptoms of patients with dementia and to compare them with symptoms of mood in elderly patients with primary affective disorder. The purpose of this investigation was twofold. First, it was to contrast self-report measures of depression in demented patients with examiner-rated assessments of mood. Second, its aim was to determine whether the relationship between subjective and objective depression measures in the organic group was analogous to the relationship between these measures in a clinically depressed group.

The data to be presented are culled from a larger study of memory in late life, and the results to be described represent only the initial findings from a yet ongoing piece of work.

SAMPLING PROCEDURES

The subject sample consisted of 108 consecutive patients and collaterals aged 50 and up who were referred for psychiatric evaluation in a university hospital. The mean age of the group was 65.66 years, and the mean number of years of education was 10.71. The sample included 67 women and 41 men, of whom 70 were white and 38 black. A 90 min structured clinical interview was administered to each subject. The interview concentrated on exploration of clinical mood state, cognitive status, somatic symptomatology, and psychiatric history. In addition to the structured interview, subjects were also assisted in completing two self-report inventories of mood and were administered two brief tests of cortical integrity. After the nature of the procedures had been fully explained, informed consent was obtained from all subjects. Immediately following the completion of the interview, and on the basis of its contents, the examiner filled out a Hamilton Psychiatric Rating Scale for Depression on each subject. Following the completion of this interview, the patient was independently reexamined by a second clinician who evaluated him for presence of mood dysfunction and brain impairment. This clinician also completed a psychiatric rating scale describing the patient's affective status immediately following the close of the second interview. Inter-rater reliabilities were computed for the examiner-rated scale of depression.

DESCRIPTION AND SCORING OF DIAGNOSTIC MEASURES

To enhance diagnostic reliability, subjects were classified for this study on the basis of operational definitions based on quantitative scores derived from standardized instruments. Behavioral measures of brain function will be presented first, to be followed by a description of indices of mood state.

Measures of Cortical Integrity

Cerebral dysfunction was evaluated by two procedures, the Mental Status Questionnaire (MSQ) and the Face-Hand Test (FHT). These instruments were selected because they are brief, objective, easily administered, and are valid indicators of impaired mental function in older persons (18). In addition, these tests are less likely than traditional psychometric batteries to show false positives with depression, cultural deprivation, or with age. Subjects who manifested positive scores on both the Face-Hand Test and the Mental Status Questionnaire were delegated to membership in the Organic Group regardless of their affective status. Scoring considerations and administration of the procedures used to measure cognitive impairment are briefly described below.

The Mental Status Questionnaire is a widely used measure of orientation and memory which correlates highly with the clinical diagnosis of chronic brain syndrome. It consists of five general information questions and five questions testing orientation for place and time. Each item is scored as either right or wrong, so that a failure to answer a question is scored incorrect. The total score ranges from 0 to 10, based on number of errors. Since it was observed during validation of the test in older populations that some persons with questionable organic impairment might still make one or more errors (most commonly missing the correct day of the month or the name of the previous President), the following rating system was used: 0 to 2 errors = no or mild brain dysfunction; 3 to 8 errors = moderate dysfunction; 9 to 10 errors = severe dysfunction. The test thus makes dichotomous differentiation of presence or absence of brain dysfunction using three errors as the cut-off point for a positive result, while the absolute number of errors can provide an index of the relative severity which can be useful in making more refined correlations with other data. For the purposes of this study, subjects positive on the Face-Hand Test and making three or more errors on the MSQ were assigned to the Organic Group, regardless of their scores on other affective measures.

The Face-Hand Test is an empirically useful test of intellectual impairment that adds to diagnostic effectiveness. This scale includes 2 series of 10 trials each, 1 with eyes closed and 1 with eyes open. Each series includes 8 asymmetric combinations of face and hand, 4 contralateral and 4 ipsilateral, and 2 trials of symmetric stimuli, face-face and hand-hand. The subject sits facing the examiner with his hands on his knees and is told by the examiner, "I am going to touch you. I want you to point to where I touch you." The instructions regarding how to respond are made very explicitly, because it is occasionally the case that subjects will make the correct verbal response while simultaneously pointing to a different body region. When discrepancies arise between the subject's physical and verbal responses, the physical response always takes precedence in determining the accuracy of that particular trial. After it is certain that the subject understands the directions, he is then touched with one or two brisk strokes on the cheek and dorsum of the hand. The most common error is extinction, in which one of the stimuli is not perceived, almost always the hand. If this type of response is made on any of the first four trials, the subject is asked, "Anywhere else?" in order to remind him to consider the possibility of more than one stimuli. The concept of twoness is also reinforced by the symmetric stimuli trials which must be perceived correctly for the procedure to be a valid test of mental status. If errors are committed on these trials, it indicates that either the subject has a sensory impairment or that he is incapable of following directions. Subjects making these errors were excluded from the study at the outset. The second most common error, and one indicative of more severe pathology, is displacement, in which one stimulus is displaced to another part of the body, most often the hand stimulus being displaced to the opposite cheek. The most severe form of error, termed exosomesthesia, occurs when a stimulus is displaced outside the subject's body (12,31). If the subject continues to make errors with eyes closed, the procedure is repeated with eyes open, with the subject instructed to carefully watch where he is being touched. The Face-Hand Test cut-off criterion for admission to the Organic Group consisted of any error committed after the sixth trial with eyes closed. Subjects receiving positive scores on both the Face-Hand Test and MSQ were delegated to the Organic Group. If errors continue to be made with eyes open, a more severe cognitive impairment is indicated. Thus, like the MSQ, the Face-Hand Test also provides a continuum of dysfunction in addition to a dichotomous differentiation of organic disease.

Measures of Affective Status

Mood state was evaluated in all subjects on the basis of three measures, including one examiner-rated scale and two self-report questionnaires. Subjects with normal brain function (e.g., those with negative scores on both the Face-Hand Test and Mental Status Questionnaire) were assigned to the Depressed Group on the basis of having above median scores on the examiner-rated Hamilton Psychiatric Rating Scale for Depression (16). The Hamilton has been one of the best received and widely used rating scales in psychiatry, and a good deal of research has been generated which has demonstrated the validity and sensitivity of this instrument. It has been shown to differentiate competently psychiatric inpatients from day hospital and general practice patients, and to correlate significantly with psychiatrists' global ratings (4). The Hamilton consists of a 17-item list of symptoms to be marked for severity by a clinician on the basis of a clinical interview with the patient. Equal weight is given both to frequency and intensity of symptoms, with overall severity of depression being indicated by the summed score across items. Among the 17 items listed in the scale are depressed mood, suicidal ideation, varieties of insomnia, psychomotor retardation, hypochondriasis, and somatic symptoms. Operational definitions of each item are provided. In order to guard against individual idiosyncratic bias in examiner-ratings in the present study, each subject was independently evaluated by two skilled clinicians. The computed inter-rater reliability for the Hamilton across all subjects in this study was 0.95 ($p < 0.001$).

Two self-report measures of affect were administered to each subject, the Beck Depression Inventory (2) and an abbreviated form of an Adjective Mood

Checklist derived from McNair and Lorr (22) which has been used successfully with the elderly (19). The Beck Inventory is a self-rating scale which consists of 21 sets of statements. Each set contains four or five sentences, and the subject is asked to select the one he feels is most applicable to him. Beck has advised that patients be assisted with the completion of the questionnaire by an examiner who reads through each group of statements with them. This approach was used in the present investigation and found to be quite useful in reducing anxiety about taking a paper and pencil "test," in solidifying rapport between subject and examiner, and in providing stimuli for further elaboration of affect-laden content. The Depression Inventory has been successfully used for the detection of depression in groups of unselected psychiatric patients and among medical inpatients (2). The results of factor analyses of the Beck reveal, in addition to a general depressive factor, factors reflecting self-debasement, vegetative symptomatology (e.g., loss of sleep, appetite, and libido), inhibition, fatiguability, and hopelessness. There is reliable support for the concurrent validity of the inventory, ranging from 0.67 to 0.75 when compared with various symptom checklists (3) and with the Hamilton Scale (30). The last of the mood indices was comprised of a series of adjectives which are descriptive of pleasant and dysphoric mood states. The words were read aloud by the examiner, and the subject was to indicate whether he had felt that way in the past week (e.g., helpless, miserable, lonely, cheerful, alert, etc.). If the subject responded positively, he was asked to evaluate the severity of affective response on a two-point scale, with a score of one, if he had "felt that way a little," and a score of two if he had "felt that way a lot." Raw scores constituted the total number of positive responses reported. Previous clinical experience with these self-report measures suggests that elderly persons attain lower mean scores than do younger individuals with similar degrees of symptom severity.

Delineation of Subject Groups

The subject groups were determined as follows. Subjects were first differentiated by brain function. Individuals who had shown signs of progressive cognitive impairment for 6 months and who were positive on both measures of altered brain function were assigned to the organic group. Second, subjects with intact cortical function, as measured by the MSQ and FHT, were subdivided into depressed and normal groups on the basis of a median score on the Hamilton Psychiatric Rating Scale for Depression. No self-report measures were involved in the assignment of patients to groups. On the basis of the brain function measures and the Hamilton, the 108 subjects were classified into 3 groups, with 33 normal brain function subjects manifesting low levels of affective disorder (normals); 40 normal brain function subjects showing high levels of depressive symptomatology (depressed), and 35 subjects presenting positively for organic brain syndrome, but undifferentiated with regard to depression.

The depressed group in this study was judged as suffering from moderate-to-moderately severe major affective disorder. A substantial number of these subjects were subsequently hospitalized for depression in the hospital's acute psychiatric inpatient unit. The organic group, on the other hand, was characterized as having mild-to-moderate, rather than severe cognitive impairment. Although all organic patients required some degree of caretaking by informal and/or formal support networks because of their tendency to wander, their attentional lapses, and their confusion, none were doubly incontinent or aphasic. All patients with altered brain function were living in the community at time of testing.

For purposes of this discussion, the terms chronic brain syndrome, dementia, and altered brain function will be used interchangeably to designate what we suspect—but cannot definitively verify until post-mortem examination—is senile dementia of the Alzheimer's type (35). This disorder is characterized by a range of signs and symptoms which include progressive memory impairment, disorientation, and failure of new learning. In order to minimize the inclusion of patients with multi-infarct dementia, persons presenting with focal neurological signs or with past histories of cerebrovascular accidents were excluded. Similarly, individuals with diagnoses of parkinsonism, epilepsy, or alcoholism were not included in this study. Patients were encouraged to undergo physical examinations in order to rule out the presence of underlying infection, toxicity, electrolyte disturbance, or major systemic disease which could conceivably contribute to the presentation of an organic symptom picture.

To control somewhat for those depressive states which sometimes masquerade as progressive dementing disease, those patients with histories of recurrent episodes of affective disorder and those with an abrupt onset of impairment were not admitted into the study sample.

RESULTS

Unadjusted mean brain function and mood state scores broken down by diagnostic group are presented in Table 1.

Brain Function

The mean score across all subjects on the MSQ was 1.23 points (out of a possible score of 10). The threshold for a positive diagnosis of organicity is a score of 3. Normal subjects earned the lowest scores (0.18), followed by depressives (0.45), and finally by organics who, by definition, manifested above-threshold numbers of errors (3.11). The overall mean on the Face-Hand Test across all subjects was 2.3 errors. (A score of 1 on this index reflects errorless performance, while a score of 2 means that 1 error has been made). Table 1 reveals that normals manifested the lowest scores ($\bar{x} = 1.2$), and as on the MSQ, the depressed group had scores only slightly higher ($\bar{x} = 1.5$). Again, organics made significantly more errors than either of the other 2 diagnostic groups

TABLE 1. *Mean brain function and mood state scores by diagnostic group*

	N =	Normal (33)	Depressed (40)	Organic (35)
MSQ	x̄	0.18	0.45	3.11
	s.d.	0.46	0.55	2.48
FHT	x̄	1.27	1.50	4.37
	s.d.	0.62	0.74	1.53
Hamilton	x̄	4.97	25.98	16.66
	s.d.	3.30	7.67	8.24
Adjective vitality	x̄	6.85	3.08	4.26
	s.d.	2.72	3.15	3.57
Adjective depression	x̄	2.67	8.90	6.66
	s.d.	3.30	5.12	5.09
Beck	x̄	2.90	11.43	9.74
	s.d.	2.79	8.13	8.82

($\bar{x} = 4.37$). The cut-off scores for determination of altered brain function of the FHT was 4. As with performance on the MSQ, differences by sex or race were not statistically significant.

Memory and Speed

Before moving on to a discussion of the measurement of mood and affect, it may be useful at this juncture to provide the reader with a very brief indication of the level of intellectual and motor performance manifested by those individuals in the study classified as having altered brain function. In essence, the findings from a series of experiments were consistent in demonstrating that the organic subjects performed very poorly on all measures of psychomotor and cognitive skill. Figures 1 and 2, for example, show that the latencies of the brain-impaired subjects on both simple and choice reaction time procedures were significantly longer than those of depressed or normal controls.

Patients with senescent brain dysfunction also showed disproportionately high rates of error on a perceptual matching procedure and on an analogous short-term memory scanning task. Figure 3 is a composite summary of the accuracy rates by group across analogous choice reaction time matching tasks. The data reveal that subjects in the organic group show serious intellectual deficits in relation to both age-matched controls and clinically depressed elderly. The specifics of these experiments are detailed at greater length elsewhere (23). This brief overview is only meant to suggest the very serious nature of the difficulties experienced by these patients in attempting to respond quickly, accurately, and efficiently to simple and complex stimuli, and in trying to retrieve overlearned information from short-term storage.

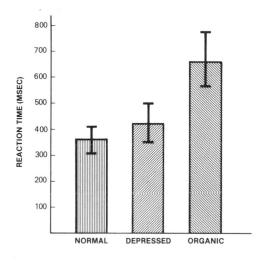

FIG. 1. Mean (liftoff) reaction time by diagnostic group.

Mood State

The measures of affective dysfunction included one examiner-rated instrument, the Hamilton Psychiatric Rating Scale for Depression, and two indices of self-report, the Beck Depression Inventory and the Lorr McNair Adjective Mood Checklist. (The scores for the latter test are divided into two categories, one, a measure of dysphoria, and the other, a measure of vitality.)

Examiner-Ratings of Depression

The grand mean on the Hamilton across all subjects was 16.5. This average was higher than anticipated and was in no small measure contributed to by the surprisingly elevated values in the organic subjects (Table 1). The normal

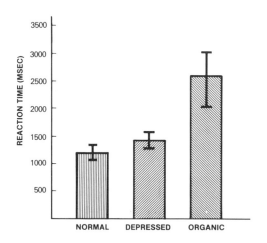

FIG. 2. Mean choice reaction time by diagnostic group across procedures.

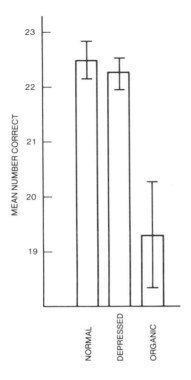

FIG. 3. Mean number correct by diagnostic group.

group, on the other hand, scored lower than expected, with a mean of 4.97. Although, according to criteria cited by Mowbray (25), these scores would be well within the range of normal affect, there has recently been some reference in the literature to the fact that with advancing chronological age, baseline scores of depression in normal populations tend to rise (9,14). Moreover, considering that both anecdotal evidence and empirical studies indicate that older persons tend to express higher levels of somatic complaint than do other age groups, and considering that the Hamilton is more heavily weighted than most scales with somatic items, the low mean score manifested by the normal subjects, whose mean age is over 65, appears curiously deflated. As would be expected, the depressed group earned the highest scores, with a mean of 25.9 on the Hamilton Scale (Fig. 4). These scores would place the depressed group in the moderately-to-severely-depressed range.

The mean score of the organic group ($\bar{x} = 16.6$) fell in the mild-to-moderately depressed range, and its size was wholly unexpected. There are a substantial number of case reports in the psychiatric literature which maintain that while depressive affect is either a common precursor of organic brain impairment or a concomitant of it at early subclinical stages, once the dementia has progressed to a diagnosable syndrome, depressive behaviors tend to disappear and are replaced by blandness of affect and denial. Yet, the clinical presence of dysphoric symptoms in even the most disoriented elderly subjects in this study was striking.

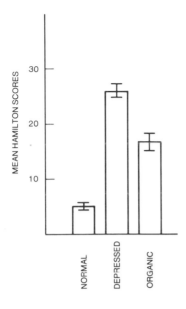

FIG. 4. Mean Hamilton Psychiatric Rating Scale for Depression scores by diagnostic group.

Admittedly, the range of severity is somewhat restricted here toward the moderate end of the organic spectrum. The difference in level of depression characterizing each of the three diagnostic groups—including the unexpectedly low scores of the normal group and the substantial depressive symptomatology in the organic group—were statistically significant at $p < 0.001$ ($F = 73.4$, d. f. $= 2,105$). Computed T-tests revealed that all three group-pairs (normal and depressed, normal and organic, and depressed and organic) were significantly different on this examiner-rated scale of depression. Though men had slightly higher scores than women on the Hamilton, and whites tended to score higher than blacks, neither difference attained statistical significance.

Measures of Affective Self-Report

While all three groups differed significantly in severity of examiner-rated depression, a somewhat different picture began to emerge when subjective reports of depression were taken into account. The data revealed that when the patients were allowed to rank themselves, the differences between psychopathologic groups disappeared. That is, scores on all self-report measures of depression consistently fail to distinguish organic from depressive subjects, in contrast to the ratings of outside examiners.

Figure 5 shows that on the Beck Depression Inventory, for example, depressives scored a mean of 11.4, while organics scored a mean of 9.7, a nonsignificant difference. Level of self-perceived dysphoria was much lower in the normal group, at 2.9. These values are in line with previous mood self-report scores collected from elderly psychiatric subjects. They appear to be somewhat lower

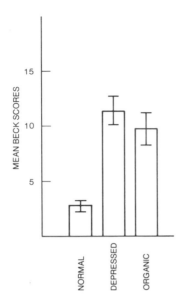

FIG. 5. Mean Beck Depression Inventory scores by diagnostic group.

on the average for a given level of symptom severity in older persons than they are in young or middle aged adults.

The F-ratios for the difference among the 3 means was significant at less than 0.001 ($F = 12.41$, d.f. $= 2,099$—the degrees of freedom here are smaller as a result of human error; data were not available for 1 subject in each of the 3 groups on the Beck Inventory. It is not probable that the results from these 3 missing cases would greatly influence these outcomes). T-tests showed that normals differed from organics and from depressed, yet the difference between depressed and organic subjects was not significant. That is, subjects with altered brain function perceived themselves to be as depressed as did those subjects with a primary diagnosis of affective disorder.

The results from both adjective checklist measures are also consistent with this self-assessment on the part of organic subjects. The grand mean on the Adjective Checklist for Vitality measure was 4.63. On this particular scale, scoring patterns are reversed, and low scores are indicative of dysphoria or absence of an *élan vital*. As would be expected, the normal group manifested the highest ratings, with mean scores of 6.85, followed by organic subjects with a mean of 4.26, and depressed subjects with a mean of 3.08 (Fig. 6). Although the range of scores was not as great on this measure as it had been on the other scales, the analysis of variance showed this difference to be significant at less than 0.001 ($F = 12.61$, d.f. $= 2,104$). Again, normals were significantly different from depressed and organic subjects, but the latter two groups did not differ significantly from each other. Neither sex nor race differences approached significance.

The grand mean for the Adjective Checklist of Depression measure was 6.27.

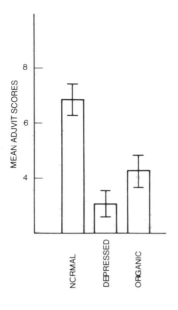

FIG. 6. Adjective mood checklist for vitality scores by diagnostic group.

Again, organic subjects earned scores between those of the depressed and normals. The latter group, in agreement with their performance throughout, and in concert with the examiner ratings, manifested very low depression self-reports ($\bar{x} = 2.67$). The depressed group yielded a mean of 8.90, and the organics followed closely with a mean of 6.66 (Fig. 7). The difference between these group means was significant at less than 0.001 ($F = 15.481$, d.f. $= 2,104$). As

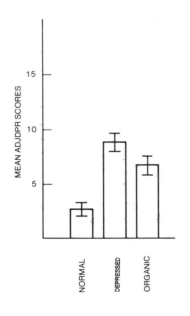

FIG. 7. Adjective mood checklist for depression scores by diagnostic group.

TABLE 2. *Correlation coefficients among demographic variables and measures of brain function and mood state across subjects*

	Whole population (N = 108)							
	AGE	ED	MSQ	FHT	ADJDPR	BECK	HAMDPR	ADJVIT
AGE	1.00							
ED	-0.15	1.00						
MSQ	0.26	-0.28	1.00					
FHT	0.21	-0.32	0.41	1.00				
ADJDPR	-0.21	-0.15	0.00	0.09	1.00			
BECK	-0.27	-0.16	0.03	0.11	0.76[a]	1.00		
HAMDPR	-0.15	-0.14	0.00	0.10	0.70[a]	0.66[a]	1.00	
ADJVIT	0.03	0.19	-0.03	-0.09	-0.63[a]	-0.62[a]	-0.60[a]	1.00

[a] $p < .001$.

was the case with the Beck and the Adjective Vitality Scale, normal subjects were found to be significantly different from depressed and organic subjects, but *t*-tests did not reveal significant differences between the depressed and organic groups. Again, there was little difference between men and women, and although black subjects scored one full point more than white subjects, this difference was not significant either.

The mean scores for all four measures of depression, including the Hamilton, the Beck, the Adjective Vitality, and the Adjective Depression Scales, are presented in Table 1, broken down by diagnostic group.

Table 2 reveals that no relationship was found between scores on measures of depression and performance on brain function tests. This holds true whether calculated across all subjects or within diagnostic groups. The table also shows that all 4 of the affect measures are significantly intercorrelated with most at probability levels less than 0.001. This suggests that there is considerable overlap in the particular factor these instruments are measuring. Across the sample as a whole, for example, the Hamilton is associated with the Beck at 0.66 ($p <$ 0.001), with the Adjective Depression checklist at 0.70 ($p <$ 0.001), and with the Adjective Vitality scale at -0.60 ($p < 0.001$). The correlation coefficient between the Adjective Depression Scale and the Beck is 0.76. When correlation coefficients were computed between examiner ratings and self-reports of depression within groups, however, some suggestive findings emerged. In the depressed group, for example, the associations attained significance but were lower than would be expected. The Hamilton Psychiatric Rating Scale for Depression correlated at 0.45 with both the Beck Depression Inventory and the Adjective Mood Checklist, respectively. On the other hand, in the organic group, the correlations were of substantially larger magnitude and significance at 0.69 and 0.75, respectively. The correlations were as high in the normal group. Performance variability on the depression scales did not differ significantly in the organic and depressed groups. Of all three diagnostic groups, the associations between examiner ratings and self reports were lowest in the depressed group.

CONCLUSION

This first systematic effort to measure affect—both objectively and subjectively—in normal, depressed, and brain-impaired elderly, has uncovered the presence of a host of potentially important, and sometimes surprising clinical phenomena. The ultimate meaning and significance of these phenomena, however, must remain in abeyance pending the collection of further empirical information. In the absence, for example, of find grained item analyses, of follow-up data at two or more points in time, and of more refined instrumentation for the measurement of mood in the presence of dementia, these findings, while suggestive cannot be viewed as definitive or conclusive.

At this juncture, keeping these caveats in mind, the study's major findings will be reviewed and placed within the context of a broader conceptual framework. Questions about the nature of what is being measured will be raised, and some practical suggestions for future research directions will be formulated.

The findings are as follows. First, results from the structured clinical assessment demonstrate the presence of significant and identifiable levels of depressive symptomatology in patients positive for organic brain syndrome. Many of these patients displayed what appeared to be genuine and sustained depressive affect over the course of the interview and testing sessions. Reports from collaterals also suggest that these dysphoric mood states often persist over the span of many months. This result is of substantial practical interest, considering that once a diagnosis of senile dementia is formulated, it is generally quite unlikely that the patient will receive symptomatic treatment or further subsidiary diagnoses. It was brought to our attention, for example, that even in the psychiatric unit where this study was carried out, where clinicians were sensitized to issues of dementia and to atypical symptomatology in the aged, none of the demented patients were subsequently treated for depressive symptoms. It is probably that their dysphoria had gone unrecognized as a potentially treatable complication of dementia. These findings suggest that both clinicians and researches alike be alert to the possible responsiveness of depressive symptoms in such patients to treatment. It should be pointed out, however, that as yet we know very little about the differential efficacy of tricyclic agents, monamine oxidase inhibitors, or electroconvulsive shock in the treatment of depressive symptoms presenting in a patient positive for dementia. Although clinical impressions and case reports are common in the literature, few systematic double-blind studies have been undertaken.

Further complicating the picture are the trends in current theory which suggest that senile dementia is associated with structural and metabolic defects in the central cholinergic system (7). If investigators are administering cholinomimetic compounds to persons with dementia in the hopes of ameliorating their cognitive deficits, then what conceivable sequelae might result from treating a patient positive for dementia with an antidepressant agent having sustained anticholinergic effects? In treating the depression it is possible that confusion might be exacerbated, and memory skills might show further decline. While it is important for the clinician to be sensitive and alert to the presence of depressive symptoms in elderly patients with altered brain function, given the high risk of suicide in this group, it is also imporant to acknowledge that, at present, recommendations for optimal treatment of mood disorder in dementia are based more often on anecdote and clinical impression than on systematic fact and empirical evidence. The need for wide-scale, carefully monitored clinical trials in this area is evident.

In addition to a lack of reliable knowledge regarding treatment effects, there remain substantial difficulties in the accurate psychiatric assessment and diagnosis of these patients. Not only are there continuing problems in distinguishing between organic and functional disorders in late life (C. E. Wells, *this volume*), but moreover, the identification of the concurrent presence of both depression and dementia within a single patient represents an issue of serious complexity which has been only minimally investigated. Yet, it is precisely this type of mixed functional/organic symptom picture which presents, in our experience, with far greater frequency than do clinically "pure" dementing states.

Certainly, greater conceptual clarity is needed to define just what it is we mean "depression" within the context of a dementing illness. In the present study, it would be more accurate to suggest that individuals with altered brain function suffered from depressive symptoms rather than from depression as a clinically recognized syndrome. But even here, we are not entirely on solid ground, since many of the usual depressive symptoms may be unreliable indicators in this population. For example, apathy, anhedonia, and social withdrawal are often associated with dementing states (33), but they could equally well be manifestations of depression. Anorexia and medically unexplained weight loss is commonly reported in elderly persons with altered brain function (21), but weight loss is also a basis vegetative marker for depression. While sleep disturbance is a common diagnostic feature in depression, sleep-awake cycles tend to be disturbed in states of diffuse, progressive cerebral disease, and the presence of insomnia as well as hypersomnia have been documented in this group (11). The large experimental literature delineating the severity of motoric slowing in senile dementia (29) can be matched by the many systematic studies showing psychomotor retardation in major affective disorder (24). Even certain psychological symptoms may not necessarily be pathognomic of depression, for at what point does hopelessness, for example, become a psychopathological rather than a realistic response to devastating losses in autonomy and cognitive function? The question then, of which symptoms and behaviors constitute reliable, objective criteria for the assessment of depression in the context of dementing illness remains to be adequately addressed.

Active clinicians with a heavy case load of older persons may view these comments with some degree of surprise and suggest that it is, in general, quite obvious and not at all hard on a day-to-day basis to reliably determine the difference between an older person who presents with depression and one who presents with chronic organic brain disease. Furthermore, the clinicians might tell us that depressive coloring in the face of a primary dementing illness can usually be elicited and identified with relative ease, once an adequate history is available. This seems quite a sensible approach on the surface, but when systematic studies of outcome are examined, the emerging picture appears decidedly less sanguine with high rates of misdiagnosis being reported. Clearly, there is as yet no experimental measure, rating scale, or research instrument that can assess as wide and heterogenous a range of clinical phenomena, or be as sensitive to the ephemeral nuances of psychopathologic symptomatology as is the skilled and observant clinician. Yet, in discussing the reliability of clinical formulations in chronic brain disease is an exhaustive recent review, Wells (37) stated, "The conclusion is inescapable that diagnostic errors, both of omission and commission, are not rare, even when patients are evaluated carefully by well-trained psychiatrists and neurologists."

The issues highlighted above, regarding the overlap in symptomatology spanning dementia and depression, constitute more than idle speculation about rarified problems in nosology. Rather, these issues raise basic questions about the qualitative nature of the diseases we are diagnosing and measuring and about the specificity of their related symptomatology. In the present study, for example, the Hamilton Psychiatric Rating Scale for Depression was used as an objective index of depressive symptomatology in all patients. The scale, while widely used in America, originated in Great Britain and reflects that country's phenomenological approach to diagnosis with its heavy emphasis on vegetative and somatic items. Given the nature of this measure, and given the difficulty of distinguishing vegetative indicators in senescent depression from those in senile dementia, is it possible that what we were rating in the demented subjects was not necessarily mood disorder at all? While this is possible, it is also true that Hamilton scores were strikingly associated with the self-report measures of mood, which focus more powerfully on subjective feeling states. While correlation does not imply causality, it appears that the multiple measures of mood are tapping a single factor in common.

More interesting, however, is that when objective and subjective report measures are compared in elderly psychiatric patients, the Hamilton Scale distinguishes the diagnostic groups clearly, but the measures of self-report do not. The Hamilton was able to make highly specific distinctions between different classes of subjects, and the results revealed that patients with cerebral brain disease were rated by clinicians as less symptomatic than patients with primary affective disorder. This is consistent with reports by Guze (15), Woodruff (38), and Weissman (36) which suggest that differing symptomatic levels are found in primary and secondary depression. The demented patients in the present study cannot be considered to have a secondary depression in the strict sense because information was not collected regarding a definitive time of onset.

Although the Hamilton distinguished the groups clearly on all self-report measures, the organic patients and patients with depressive disorder rated themselves as being equally symptomatic. The question then arises, are organic patients exaggerating or enhancing the degree of their subjective dysphoria, or alternatively, are individuals with depression minimizing or underestimating the extent of their mood impairment? A third option might be that the clinicians themselves misjudged the degree of depression in either of the psychopathologic groups. This last explanation is probably quite unlikely, considering that interrater reliability was quite high, and the odds of both independent raters sharing an identical response bias are slim. Therefore, it is probable that the locus of these discrepancies can be found in the self-ratings of the patients themselves.

The sizable magnitude of the correlations between self-report and examiner ratings in the demented group suggest that there is a high degree of consistency in the assessments of both clinicians and demented patients. While patients in the organic group manifested self-report scores relatively congruent with the level of their examiner ratings, this was not the case in the depressed group, where concordance between self-report and examiner ratings was relatively low. This would suggest that depressed patients had difficulty in accurately perceiving the degree of their own level of depression.

While the subjective accuracy of the organic group is surprising, the finding regarding depressives is consistent with other reports in the literature. For example, these results fit with Beck's (1) notion that certain forms of cognitive perceptual distortion appear to be component features of depression. Paykel and his colleagues (27) have also demonstrated that depressives exhibit disturbances in self-perception and reality testing. The discrepancies between self-ratings and psychiatric assessment of depression reported here might then be accounted for by such cognitive distortions.

In a previous study, we attempted to clarify the role of memory impairment in older persons by determining the relationship of complaint about memory to actual functioning (19). We found that aged individuals with clinical depression complained about memory as much as those with altered brain function, even though the latter showed far more severe impairment on objective tests of memory. The study suggested that there is a marked incongruity between complaint about memory and actual memory performance in clinically depressed elderly. While impairment on memory tests was strongly associated with evidence of organic brain dysfunction, complaints about memory, rather than reflecting cognitive condition, were found to be a manifestation of depression. The finding that complaint about memory (in the absence of cognitive impairment) is significantly related to depression in the elderly was recently confirmed by Barry Gurland *(personal communication)* and his colleagues in the U.S.-U.K. Cross-National Diagnostic Study.

In the study by Kahn et al. (19), good congruence between complaint and performance was shown by individuals with altered brain function (and dysphoric mood) who both did poorly on the memory tests and showed high complaint about memory. In two investigations, then, the concordance between complaint and external criteria has been found to be quite good in elderly persons with mild to moderate brain impairment. In the earlier study, there was good agreement between patient and clinician regarding level of cognitive function, and in the present study, high congruence regarding degree of mood disorder was attained. These findings were anticipated in neither study, and we are somewhat at a loss to account for them. How can it be, one might justifiably ask, that individuals who experience more than occasional difficulty finding their way home, balancing their checkbook, or following a new recipe, express perceptions about their own abilities which appear to be so accurate? Isn't one of the common criteria for ruling in dementia "impairment of personal judgment"? Could it be that these persons were not really demented in the first place? Again, that is a possibility, but it is a highly doubtful one considering that anecdotal reports over time from collaterals, performance scores on psychometric measures, ratings in experimental tests of cognition, and clinical data from structured interviews all concurred in suggesting that the observed behaviors were consistent with the presence of a diffuse, progressive dementing disorder.

From another perspective, perhaps these findings are not quite so unusual. For example, often one will interview an elderly person who, even if he cannot recall what happened yesterday, or two weeks ago, still retains a painful awareness of the fact that he is not able to remember things and an equally lucid and communicable sense of his own hopelessness and despair. It may be, then, that individuals with mild to moderate dementia are able to retain a reasonable level of judgment about subjective phenomena, about the degree of their own intellectual dysfunction, and about the nature of their personal affective status. Although their performance on objective cognitive tests may be more seriously impaired than that of depressed patients, it is possible that in the realm of subjective awareness, moderate dementia with secondary depressive coloring may not be as distorting to self-perception as in the presence of severe primary depressive disorder. While these conjectures are speculative in nature and require further experimental confirmation, they do suggest some plausible leads for future research.

In conclusion, while patient and examiner ratings of cognitive and affective function showed high concordance in both normals and in individuals with moderate levels of altered brain function, agreement was less satisfactory in patients with severe levels of depression. These are emerging results, and they are both puzzling and challenging. Much intriguing work remains to be done, and many questions answered, before we can more precisely characterize the nature of the affective component of dementing behavior. A deeper understanding of these issues may pave the way for more humane and effective treatment strategies and may yield important clues about basic mechanisms of mood and brain impairment in the latter half of life.

REFERENCES

1. Beck, A. (1967): *Depression: Clinical, Experimental and Theoretical Aspects.* Harper & Row, New York.
2. Beck, A. T., Ward, C. H., Mendelson, M., Mock, J., and Erbaugh, J. (1961): An inventory for measuring depression. *Arch. Gen. Psychiatry,* 4:561–571.
3. Bloom, P. M., and Brady, J. P. (1968): An ipsative validation of the multiple affect adjective checklist. *J. Clin. Psychol.,* 24:45–46.
4. Carroll, B. J., Fielding, J. M., and Blashki, T. G. (1973): Depression rating scales. A critical review. *Arch. Gen. Psychiatry,* 23:361–366.
5. Cawley, R. H., Whitehead, A., and Post, F. (1973): Barbiturate tolerance and psychological functioning in elderly depressed patients. *Psychol. Med.,* 3:39–52.
6. Cronholm, B., and Ottosson, J. O. (1961): Memory functions in endogenous depression: Before and after electro-convulsive therapy. *Arch. Gen. Psychiatry,* 5:193–199.
7. Davies, P. (1978): Studies on the neurochemistry of central cholinergic systems in Alzheimer's disease. In: *Alzheimer's Disease, Senile Dementia and Related Disorders,* edited by R. Katzman, R. D. Terry, and K. L. Bick. Raven Press, New York.

8. English, W. H. (1942): Alzheimer's disease: Its incidence and recognition. *Psychiatr. Q.,* 16:91–106.
9. Epstein, L. J. (1976): Depression in the elderly. *J. Gerontol.,* 31:278–282.
10. Ernst, P., Badash, D., Berzan, B., Kosovsky, R., and Kleinhauz, M. (1977): Incidence of mental illness in the aged: Unmasking the effects of a diagnosis of chronic brain syndrome. *J. Am. Geriatr. Soc.,* 25:371–375.
11. Feinberg, I., Koresko, R., and Heller, N. (1967): EEG sleep patterns as a function of normal and pathological aging in man. *J. Psychiatr. Res.,* 5:107.
12. Fink, M., Green, M. A., and Bender, M. B. (1952): The face-hand test as a diagnostic sign of organic mental syndrome. *Neurology* (Minneap.), 2:48–56.
13. Folstein, M. F., and McHugh, P. R. (1978): Demential syndrome of depression. In: *Alzheimer's Disease, Senile Dementia and Related Disorders,* edited by R. Katzman, R. D. Terry, and K. L. Bick. Raven Press, New York.
14. Gurland, B. J. (1976): The comparative frequency of depression in various adult age groups. *J. Gerontol.,* 31:283–292.
15. Guze, S. B., Woodruff, R. A., and Clayton, P. J. (1971): Secondary affective disorder: A study of 95 cases. *Psychol. Med.,* 1:426–428.
16. Hamilton, M. (1960): A rating scale for depression. *J. Neurol., Neurosurg. Psychiatry,* 23:56–62.
17. Hilbert, N. M., Niederehe, G., and Kahn, R. L. (1976): Accuracy and speed of memory in depressed and organic aged. *Educ. Gerontol.,* 1:131–146.
18. Kahn, R. L., Goldfarb, A. I., Pollack, M., and Peck, A. (1960): Brief objective measures for the determination of mental status in the aged. *Am. J. Psychiatry,* 117:326–328.
19. Kahn, R. L., Zarit, S. H., Hilbert, N. M., and Niederehe, G. (1975): Memory complaint and impairment in the aged: The effect of depression and altered brain function. *Arch. Gen. Psychiatry,* 32:1569–1573.
20. Kiloh, L. G. (1961): Pseudodementia. *Acta Psychiatr. Scand.,* 37:336–351.
21. Libow, L. S. (1978): Excess mortality and proximate causes of death. In: *Alzheimer's Disease, Senile Dementia and Related Disorders,* edited by R. Katzman, R. D. Terry, and K. L. Bick. Raven Press, New York.
22. McNair, D. M., and Lorr, M. (1964): An analysis of mood in neurotics. *J. Abnorm. Soc. Psychol.,* 69:620–627.
23. Miller, N. E. (1979): *Primary Memory in Depressed, Demented and Normal Aged.* Unpublished dissertation, University of Chicago, Chicago.
24. Miller, W. R. (1975): Psychological deficit in depression. *Psychol. Bull.,* 82:238–260.
25. Mowbray, R. M. (1972): The Hamilton Rating Scale for Depression: A factor analysis. *Psychol. Med.,* 2:272–280.
26. O'Neal, P., Robins, E., Schmidt, E. H. (1956): A psychiatric study of attempted suicide in persons over sixty years of age. *Arch. Neurol. Psychiatry,* 75:275.
27. Paykel, E. S., Myers, J. K., Dienelt, M. N., Klerman, G. L., Lindenthal, J. J., and Tepper, M. P. (1969): Life events and depression: A controlled study. *Arch. Gen. Psychiatry,* 21:753–760.
28. Post, F. (1962): *The Significance of Affective Symptoms in Old Age.* Oxford University Press, London.
29. Savage, R. P. (1973): Old age. In: *Handbook of Abnormal Psychology,* edited by H. J. Eysenck, pp. 645–688. Sir Isaac Pitman and Sons, London.
30. Schwab, J. J., Bialow, M. R., Brown, J. M., Holzer, C. E., and Stevenson, B. E. (1967): Sociocultural aspects of depression in medical patients. *Arch. Gen. Psychiatry,* 171:529–534.
31. Shapiro, M. F., Fink, M., and Bender, M. B. (1952): Exosomesthesia or displacement of cutaneous sensation into extrapersonal space. *Arch. Neurol. Psychiatry,* 68:481–490.
32. Sim, M. (1965): Alzheimer's disease: A forgotten entity. *Geriatrics,* 20:668–674.
33. Slater, E., and Roth, M. (1969): Aging and the mental diseases of the aged. In: *Clinical Psychiatry,* edited by W. Mayer-Gross, E. Slater, and M. Roth. Williams and Wilkins, Baltimore.
34. Sternberg, D. E., and Jarvik, M. E. (1976): Memory functions in depression: Improvement with antidepressant medication. *Arch. Gen. Psychiatry,* 33:219–224.
35. Terry, R. D. (1978): Aging, senile dementia and Alzheimer's disease. In: *Senile Dementia and Related Disorders,* edited by R. Katzman, R. D. Terry, and K. L. Bick. Raven Press, New York.

36. Weissman, M. M., Pottenger, M., Kleber, H., Ruben, H. L., Williams, D., and Thompson, W. D. (1977): Symptom patterns in primary and secondary depression: A comparison of primary depressives with depressed opiate addicts, alcoholics, and schizophrenics. *Arch. Gen. Psychiatry,* 34:854–862.
37. Wells, C. E. (1978): Chronic brain disease: An overview. *Am. J. Psychiatry,* 135:1–12.
38. Woodruff, R. J., Murphy, G. E., and Herjanic, M. (1967): The natural history of affective disorders. Symptoms of 72 patients at the time of index hospital admission. *J. Psychiatr. Res.,* 5:255–263.

OPEN DISCUSSION

Dr. William W. K. Zung: I think there is an alternate hypothesis to the discordant finding between the interview rating and the self-rating which you have not enumerated. The operational definition for depression in the rating scales used in your study, the Hamilton and the Beck self-rating scales, are different. Therefore you are not measuring the same things at all.

In addition, the Hamilton scale rating for depression, in addition to measuring depression, includes about five items that measure hypochondriasis, anxiety somatic, anxiety psychic; these are not part and parcel of the commonly accepted definition of depression. Therefore changes in the Hamilton score may reflect changes in anxiety symptoms rather than in depressive symptoms.

Returning to your self-rating for the Beck scale, there are items included that may not be part of a commonly accepted depressive definition. The data must be reanalyzed, with only those items considered which are common between the Hamilton and the Beck. You may find, in fact, a higher correlation and not the discordance that you found. This is one explanation.

There is an alternate hypothesis for the explanation as to why you did not find any differences using the self-ratings as opposed to finding differences in the interview ratings, and that is because of the content of the Beck rating scale. By the nature of its content and the way it is constructed, the Beck rating scale is difficult for patients to use, especially for the organic individual. He must read a number of sentences and then make a value judgment on them that is reflected in the way the test is scored. If we were to read those sentences, I think we would find, especially for organic patients, that the value judgments might be difficult to make.

You and I might read the 4 sentences that measure a particular symptom, and what Beck would consider a score of 2, I might consider a 3. When you might consider a 3, I might consider a 2. The same thing happens with organic patients. They really have difficulty comprehending the items in the forced choices. We have in fact found, in similar studies such as yours, that the self-rating inventory is really a better indicator of depression and correlates better with psychopathology in terms of global depression than does the interview rating scale.

My third point is that I would predict, if you were to reanalyze your data to account for the discordance, the Hamilton rating scale results would appear "wrong," and the Beck results would appear more "correct."

Dr. Miller: There were a number of good questions there. The first issue you raised related to substantive differences in items on the two scales, and the second related to subjective value judgments on the part of the patient. I shall try to respond to both of these. First, I do not think that we can say that the universe of items sampled by the Hamilton and Beck scales are all that different. Both of them, for example, tap information relating to somatic symptoms and dysphoric mood, and have similar items relating to appetite decline and weight loss, sleep disturbance and fatigue, work difficulties and loss of libido, guilt, suicidal ideation, worthlessness, and hopelessness, etc. While there are a few areas where overlap is minimal—for example, the Hamilton addresses paranoic behaviors and feelings of depersonalization, and the Beck asks about self-image—in general, factor analytic studies show similar factor structures for both scales. The high correlations found in the present study would also suggest that these measures may be tapping a common factor. I would agree that your suggestion to look at the concordance between similar items on the two measures is a good one, and, as I stated before, we are currently in the process of completing an item analysis. Unfortunately, the results are not yet available. On the basis of our past experience with item analyses though, I would not be overly optimistic about this approach. We found that global Hamilton scores, rather than single items or item cluster scores, were the best predictors of clinical depression in older persons. Second, it may be that the discrepancies we are finding do not have as much to do with the nature of the specific items per se, as they have to do with the distinction between self-reports and examiner-ratings. In conjunction with this, Dr. Zung's point about value judgments in dementia is well taken. It is certainly possible that demented individuals evaluate sentences on the Beck self-report inventory in ways which are qualitatively different from persons with normal brain function. It could be that there is something unusual about their approach to making decisions and weighing alternatives. While I did not have time to go into this before, I should state here that we took careful precautions in administering the Beck so as to ensure optimal test validity. The examiners, for example, were specifically trained to establish empathic rapport with respondents, to take as much time as was necessary, and to sensitively help the subject contrast one item choice with the next, until he or she could comfortably arrive at a subjective decision. It is true that sometimes this was a very long and laborious process. We found, though, that if we allowed individuals to respond in a relaxed and nondemanding environment, and if we were patient, we could elicit good cooperation. These patients appeared to be able to focus on their own feeling states and to respond to the choices offered in reliable, nonrandom ways. The variability of scores in the demented group, for example, did not significantly exceed the scatter shown by depressives. While there is a possibility that individuals with altered brain function manifest differences in value judgments from other subjects, we also should be cognizant of recent evidence suggesting that response biases may be significantly skewed in depressed patients as well. Some of Beck's studies, for instance, show that depressed patients tend to be more cautious about making responses and tend seriously to underestimate the extent of their own cognitive abilities. Dr. Zung is right in suggesting that an investigation of the nature of the subjective assessment may shed valuable light on the discrepancies reported in the present study. I would like to add that, in contrast to Dr. Zung's findings, our studies suggest that self-rating inventories do not comprise as good a measure of affective disorder as do examiner-ratings based on structured interviews. There is a good deal of evidence in the literature which suggests that, at the height of the illness, self-rating scales are not as sensitive as the Hamilton to measuring severity of clinical depression. So in that respect, our findings disagree. Certainly we need more systematic data to illuminate these issues. Before concluding, I would just like to reiterate that my major concern here is not so much focused on the question of which form of evaluation is "better," since examiner-ratings and self-reports measure different, though overlapping, experiential phenomena. But, rather, it is centered at a more basic level of investigation. Namely, what precisely are the criteria which we should be using to rule in or rule out depression? That is, do we really have pathognomonic symptom clusters for depression in the aged, or are the vegetative symptoms that older people present largely nonspecific in nature? Is it possible that what we are really measuring is severity of pathology, rather than signs and symptoms specific for disordered mood or cognitive state? These are questions which, for me, constitute the heart of the matter.

Dr. Barrett: Creeping into this discussion I hear the old controversy about whether self-report measures are better than clinician-rating measures. Hopefully by now we have progressed to where we can lay that issue to rest. Self-report measures are good for certain things, clinician ratings for other things, and there is a big area of overlap. Clinician ratings can provide information that can not be obtained from self-reports. Self-report measures are clearly very valid for measuring psychopathology, depression in particular.

However, no matter which type of measure is used, when the item pool making up each measure is different, as was the case here, you can expect different scores from each measure on that basis alone. Differences in the item pool are to me the simplest explanation for the different scale score results reported by Dr. Miller.

Dr. Miller: I think it is useful to understand the patient's psychological state, to determine the nature of his subjective feelings. That has been an area of inquiry which has been seriously neglected to date.

Dr. Zubin: I think this point, comparing self-report versus rating scales and interviews is important enough to cause us to stop for a minute and consider what are the real basic differences between them.

First of all, the patient has to know that he has the symptom before he can report it. The second point is, he has to be willing to tell about the symptom. The interviewer, if he is skilled, can overcome these two difficulties. He can find out frequently, independent of whether the patient knows or does not know that he has the symptom, whether it is present or not, by indirect subtle questioning and clinical inferences. He can also, by means of skillful strategies, overcome the reluctance to report a particular symptom.

However, with regard to the self-reporting inventories, there is something that I believe people are overlooking and which might perhaps help, namely the matter of reluctance to tell about the symptom. The signal detection theory approach seems to be one which can be applied to that. By its very nature, it separates out the sensitivity component, namely the knowledge of the presence of the particular symptom, from the reluctance or willingness to report it.

There is a very interesting way of accomplishing this by presenting each item worded in both a positive and a negative direction. You can then take the positive direction as your signal and the negative direction as your signal plus noise, and out of this combination will emerge two measures: (a) sensitivity—the presence or absence of the symptom; (b) criterion—the degree of reluctance or willingness to tell about it. I believe it is time that this technique began to be applied to the other self-reporting inventories since it would certainly improve their value.

Dr. Miller: I agree. That is a good point.

Dr. Allen Willner: When we think of people with organic troubles and people with depression there are two kinds of issues that might arise, one of them about cognitive functioning and one about depression. Depressives will sometimes say that they are less depressed than they appear to be, but complain about cognitive troubles, whereas the organic patients will deny the cognitive troubles but indicate that they are depressed. So people will sometimes tend to deny what seems to be their major problem and talk about an ancillary one.

Dr. Miller: Yes, that seems to fit with a number of the studies we have carried out, and you are essentially correct in the broadest sense. Basically, what we found was that when older people have a severe psychiatric problem, they tend to minimize it, to deny it, and to shift or displace their concern onto a less impaired aspect of their psychological functioning. For example, when older depressives came to us for treatment, they presented with complaints about their memory rather than with complaints about sadness or dysphoria. In fact, they complained as much about their memory as people positive for (moderate) senile dementia did. But when we examined the cognitive test scores of these depressives, their memories appeared to be normal in contrast to the very real performance deficits that we found in our demented subjects. So, while on the one hand the depressives exaggerated their problems in an area where they did not have any blatant difficulties, on the other hand they minimized the extent of their major problem, which was their impaired mood. That is, when they were asked to subjectively gauge the degree of their dysphoria, they seemed to underreport it. So far this agrees with your theory. We also found a similar kind of discrepant phenomenon in people who were both extremely demented and incontinent. In contrast to the depressives, who complained bitterly about their terrible memory problems, these individuals, who had the most severe cognitive impairment, informed us that they did not feel they had a memory problem at all. The place where we did find reasonable congruence between self-reports and more objective ratings was in the normal subjects. In both studies, we found that older people who had normal affect and normal brain function tended to assess their memory and mood pretty accurately. The second place where we found good agreement was in the moderately demented group. These subjects showed pretty good concordance between self-reports and examiner-ratings, both on measures of mood and on measures of memory. With them, the seriousness of their deficits seem to be evenly matched by the seriousness of their complaints. In fact, it is almost as though there is a strange continuum effect which is showing itself. The greatest discrepancies in reporting occur at the extremes of the distribution. Here we find persons with serious depressive disorders apparently minimizing the degree of their illness and, on the other hand, we find persons who are severely demented denying that they have any memory problems. But, in the middle of this distribution, there are those persons who have moderate degrees of dementia along with moderate degrees of depression. And these individuals seem to be relatively accurate in their self-assessments. It is this middle group, then, which seems to be most vulnerable to the harsh reality, to recognizing and acknowledging the extent of both their intellectual deficit and their dysphoric mood. Perhaps this suggests that we need to be very careful about the ways in which we evaluate what our patients tell us. Clearly psychopathology in older persons can be a very complicated business.

Dr. Anne S. Hardesty: I will not talk about instrumentation, but I would like to call attention to a finding from a study that we did at Bellevue about 5 years ago. Of the over 800 patients included in the study, 31 were between 65 and 84 years of age. According to the final diagnosis completed shortly before a patient was to be discharged, 4 of the 31 suffered from psychotic depressions. On 2-year follow-up there were 5 deaths among the 31 former patients over 65 years of age. Included among the 5 who died were the 4 with psychotic depression. It intrigued me that all of the 4 psychotic depressions had this outcome.

Let me also say something about the subjective nature of memory deficit. If you ask any group of college students in June about their memory, they commonly tell you, "My memory is not as good as it used to be." That is an interesting phenomenon.

Dr. Miller: The evidence is accumulating, and a number of surveys have demonstrated, that persons with depression have higher mortality rates and shorter life spans than persons without depression. If we want to spin tall tales and wildly generalize from what I have just said, we could speculate that the reason college students complain about their memory at graduation is they are really depressed about their job prospects.

We also find that sleep disorders are quite common in dementia. This harks back to what I was saying before—it is not at all clear, when we find evidence of sleep difficulties in a demented person, whether it is something which is endogenous to the disease itself, or whether it is one of a cluster of symptoms which indicate the presence of a secondary depression. How can we objectively identify the presence of a mood disorder in a demented population? That is the crux of the question.

Psychopathology in the Aged, edited by
Jonathan O. Cole and James E. Barrett.
Raven Press, New York © 1980.

The Assessment of Cognitive Dysfunction in Dementing Illness

Donna Cohen and David Dunner

*Department of Psychiatry and Behavioral Sciences, University of Washington,
Seattle, Washington 98195*

Dementing illnesses comprise a group of insidious, irreversible, life-shortening cognitive disorders among the middle aged and aged; they are characterized by a progressive decline in cognition, self-care, and adaptation to the environment and culminate in premature death. Estimates are that 10 to 20% of persons over age 65 may have an irreversible dementing illness (45); these disorders, therefore, are among the most serious health problems facing our society. A number of studies have shown that dementia in the aged is often "pseudo-senility," i.e., cognitive deterioration which is the result of medical and psychosocial factors, and which, when properly diagnosed and treated, is reversible (51,64, Keckich, Cohen, and Eisdorfer, *in preparation*).The irreversible dementias fall into three broad categories: primary neural degeneration of the Alzheimer's type, multi-infarct dementia, and other rarer variants which include Creutzfeldt-Jakob disease, Huntington's chorea, Pick's disease, and subcortical dementia. Whereas, each of these categories of dementing illness may have a similar symptom constellation at the outset, each has its own etiology, course, and response to treatment. Indeed, there may well be subgroups of Alzheimer's disease and of the multi-infarct dementias.

The most common form of dementing illness, occuring in 50 to 70% of affected individuals, is primary neuronal degeneration of the Alzheimer's type (67,68). Currently, the confirmatory neuropathologic diagnosis is made when a large concentration of neurofibrillary tangles and miliary plaques are observed in the neocortex and the hippocampus. The clinical diagnosis is presumptive and currently derived through a comprehensive medical examination and history, congruent psychological test results, supportive clinical laboratory data (blood chemistries, electrocardiogram, chest X-rays), electroencephalography (EEG), and computerized axial tomography (CT). The diagnosis is made by the elimination of all other known and testable causes of intellectual impairment such as malnutrition, drug abuse, alcoholism, depression, and cardiovascular disease (28).

Neuropathologic observations indicate that cerebrovascular alterations may be responsible for another 15 to 25% of the nonreversible disorders (67–69).

Cognitive dysfunction resulting from vascular compromise is caused primarily by the occurrence of multiple small (or larger) cerebral infarcts, i.e., multi-infarct dementia (38). The course of multi-infarct dementias is often a stepwise deterioration in contrast to the progressive, gradual decline observed in primary neuronal degeneration of the Alzheimer's type (Fig. 1). Such multiple infarcts can produce a condition of cognitive disturbance which is difficult to distinguish from Alzheimer's. The differential diagnosis of multi-infarct dementia is made on the basis of careful physical, psychiatric, psychological, and neurologic examinations, as well as clinical laboratory tests. Hachinski (37) has devised a clinical ischemic questionnaire which appears to be useful in distinguishing primary neuronal degeneration of the Alzheimer's type and multi-infarct dementia as non-overlapping groups. Focal neurologic signs and symptoms are often seen in addition to cognitive impairment, and the individual may have a history of hypertension, blackouts, cardiovascular illness, or stroke.

The increasing proportion of the aged in our population implies dramatic increases in the number of persons at risk for dementing illness who will require some form of care. Thus, the need for precise diagnosis of persons with cognitive dysfunction hardly needs to be stressed. The risk of cognitive disorders appears to double every 5 years after the age of 60 until about age 85, after which it drops off (NIHS, 1979). Furthermore, the aged are at high risk for a variety of psychiatric disorders, including depression which frequently masquerades as a dementia-like illness. The various forms of dementing illnesses and pseudodementias, then, pose important diagnostic problems. Indeed, a number of studies indicate that diagnostic errors occur with a high frequency in older patients with cognitive dysfunction (52,59).

We have argued elsewhere that one of the barriers to accurate diagnosis in the impaired aged is the lack of an adequate behavioral measure of cognitive dysfunction (12). A variety of brief mental status examinations have been used

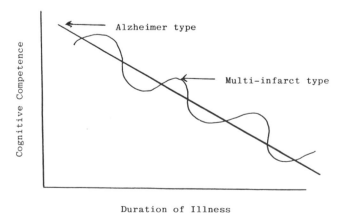

FIG. 1. Hypothetical course of dementing illness.

to assess orientation and memory in patients presenting symptoms of dementia (29,44). However, most of the existing tests for both diagnosis and assessment of change either lack reliability and validity or are conceptually limiting and misleading. For example, orientation in time, place, and person may obviously be affected in an older patient presenting with any number of medical, psychiatric, or psychosocial problems. Such a question is not a sensitive diagnostic indicator specific for the alterations in brain-behavior relationships which are characteristic of dementing illness (43). Furthermore, questions of this type provide no information regarding the aspect of cognition, i.e., the type of memory or attentional processes, that might be impaired by the destruction of central nervous system tissue.

Simply specifying that primary neuronal degeneration of the Alzheimer type affects thinking and presents as disorientation and confusion is vacuous and inadequate. It is important to elucidate specific aspects of thought, memory, attention, and perception, since our knowledge of specific deficits broadens our knowledge of the deficiency of the impaired older adult and allows us to design a reasonable program of patient management based upon what the individual can or cannot do. The development of a technology for the microanalysis of cognitive dysfunction should provide a scale to elucidate and monitor specific cognitive function/dysfunction in the individual at different stages of his or her dementing illness.

One objective of this chapter is to demonstrate that it is imperative to develop a set of clinical cognitive assessment procedures specifically for middle aged and older persons with dementing illness. Therefore, we will discuss limitations in the current clinical assessment of cognitive dysfunction, a plan for choosing appropriate tests of cognitive functioning, principles for assessment in the cognitively impaired elderly, and the research necessary before a clinical cognitive evaluation tool becomes a reality. Since it is our view that it is necessary to evaluate cognitive alterations in a way that is consistent with our present knowledge of the etiology of dementia, the next section of this chapter will briefly review what is known about biological changes in primary neuronal degeneration of the Alzheimer type.

ETIOLOGY OF COGNITIVE CHANGE IN PRIMARY NEURONAL DEGENERATION

Although the microscopic changes seen in primary neuronal degeneration of the Alzheimer's type (PND-A), including both the early and late onset types, have been reported for many years (2), it has only been in the past few decades that investigators have succeeded in correlating neuropathologic abnormalities with the type and degree of dysfunction (1,3,4,6,9,55,66). Individual brains may vary considerably in the observed frequency and location of the neuropathologic markers. One brain may present with almost nothing but plaques, whereas another individual's brain will be almost entirely neurofibrillary tangles. Marked individual differences are seen in the location of neuropathologic alterations: some brains may show the highest frequency of changes in the hippocampus, while others will have more alterations in the frontal or temporal area of the neocortex.

The regional distribution of lesions in the brain is currently an important area of investigation. Ball (4) reports that neuronal loss is greater in the hippocampus relative to the neocortex in patients with Alzheimer's compared to nondemented older patients. At the level of the reticular formation and the brain stem, neurofibrillary tangles and cell loss seem to be confined to the monoaminergic locus coeruleus (8). A greater frequency of neurofibrillary tangles have also been reported in the hippocampus and brain stem than in the neocortex (3,41,42). Granulovacuolar degeneration is also reported to be limited to the hippocampus (6). However, it is of some interest that neuritic plaques are reported to be more frequent in the amygdala and the neocortex and do not show the same regional preferences as the other neuropathologic lesions (17,25).

Kemper (47) examined brains of patients with no apparent evidence of a dementing illness and patients with neurologic and clinical evidence of dementia to evaluate the relative density of neurofibrillary tangles in different regions of the temporal lobe. Whereas both groups of patient brains showed neurofibrillary tangles in the same 4 areas, CA1 the subiculum, Pr 2, and area 35, differences were evident in the relative distribution of the lesions. Tangles were more frequent in the neocortical input zone (areas 35 and Pr 2) in the nondemented elderly, and more frequent in the limbic output or projective zone, i.e., that projecting back to the neocortex, (subiculum and CA1), in the demented elderly. The underlying reasons for these selective changes remain to be determined. However, it is known that these regions are strategic locations in cognitive and affective processes. The limbic system of the brain receives projections from association areas in the cortex, and its efferent projections are to areas described by Papez (60) in his classic paper. Therefore, limbic system lesions should be related to both memory and emotional changes observed in patients with primary neuronal degeneration.

The limbic system and especially the hippocampus have been major targets of investigation in Alzheimer's disease. Although the degree of neurofibrillary tangle formation, granulovacular degeneration, and Hirano body formation have been well quantified in the hippocampus (5), the precise histotopography of the cellular changes is just beginning to be clarified. Ball and his colleagues (5) examined the brains of cognitively and neurologically intact patients (ages 63–83) and those of patients who had died with Alzheimer's disease (ages 56–91). The gross neuropathologic examination revealed the expected greater number of tangles, plaques, and generalized cortical atrophy in the brains of the Alzheimer's patients. The total area of the hippocampal gray matter was partitioned into six zones, and the actual density of histological lesions was recorded and analyzed. All six hippocampal zones had similar relative susceptabilities to development of neurofibrillary tangles and granulovacular degeneration: the entorhinal indices showed the smallest increases, with the H_2 region followed by the subiculum; the H_1 region showed the greatest increase. By contrast, Hirano bodies had the lowest concentration in the H_2 region and the highest in the H_1 subiculum.

Although it appears that the process of primary neuronal degeneration superimposed on normal aging changes increases the density of tangles and granulovacular degneration in the H_2 zone, the largest change in Hirano body density is in the H_1 zone. This observation suggests that the extraneuronal Hirano bodies (which are seen only in the hippocampus) may be less important in the progression of cognitive dysfunction than the intraneuronal tangles and granulovacular degeneration.

Any explanation for the regional distribution of these marked microhistologic lesions must be tentative for the moment. One possibility is that regional metabolic changes or hypoxia in the hippocampus may affect the distribution of tangles, granulovacuolar changes, and/or Hirano bodies, since the microvasculature of the hippocampus has a rakelike configuration in contrast to the binary dividing pattern of terminal arterioles in the rest of the brain. Another tentative explanation proferred by Ball (5) is that alterations in a common neurotransmitter in these neurons may be related to regional lesions variations. Therefore, if memory functioning is dependent on cholinergic synapses (26,27), and if choline acetyltransferase is reduced in Alzheimer's (20) reflecting a selective vulnerability of that chemical system (8,21,61,62), then the high risk hippocampal zones may reflect areas where choline-dependent efferents are also at risk.

Current evidence suggests the possibility of multiple causal factors in primary neuronal degeneration of the Alzheimer's type. The cytotoxicity of immune factors has been reviewed by several investigators (13,14,31,58,63). The etiological role of aluminum is debatable (17,18,53,70). Evidence for transmissible viruses in dementing illnesses has been reviewed by Gajdusek (35) and Gibbs et al. (36). Furthermore, relatives of patients with Alzheimer's disease have a higher frequency of Alzheimer's (39,40,50,) as well as trisomy 21 and myeloproliferative disorders (39). The genetic hypothesis is also consistent with data on microtubular degeneration in the neurofibrillary tangles on the brain. However, in general, the amount of quantitative information which is available concerning the etiology and progression of the disease(s) is sparse, and this is what limits our current ability to develop an armamentarium of effective diagnostic, treatment, and management techniques.

It is naive to speculate that the cognitive decline occuring in primary neuronal degeneration of the Alzheimer's type involves alterations in a single transmitter and neuronal system. One of the marked changes in the aging human brain is the progressive imbalance between the dopaminergic and cholinergic systems and between the dopaminergic and GABAergic systems (25,56). A deficit in one system often results in overactivity in another. Many neurotransmitters and modulators are found in the central nervous system in addition to a very complex arrangement of neurons. In the nigrostriatal dopamine pathway, which is a relatively well-defined system in the brain, for example, at least dopamine, acetycholine (ACh), and γ-aminobutyric acid (GABA) need to be considered since they represent the minimum number of active transmitters in the pathway.

The cholinergic system is currently a target of investigation in Alzheimer's disease (20). A recent review by Davis and Yamamura (23) evaluates the evidence for decreases in the activities of both choline acetyltransferase (CAT) and acetylcholinesterase (AChE) with aging (54). The brains of patients with a diagnosis of Alzheimer's appear to have a profound loss of CAT activity (21,61). Although muscarinic receptor binding has been reported to decrease with age (71), it is not clear whether there is any significant difference between the normal aged brain and Alzheimer brains (22,23). These data, together with the finding that drugs which increase cholinergic activity may improve the Alzheimer patient's cognitive functioning, emphasize the importance of the cholinergic system in aging research. Furthermore, with the development of cognitive-acting drugs which may improve performance in the impaired elderly, it is important to develop tests with sufficient sensitivity to monitor changes in the patients' status.

Whereas the cholinergic system seems to be most affected in Alzheimer's disease, other transmitter systems and their cell types are also affected. The most marked alterations are seen in cell types modulated by the GABA system in the caudate nucleus and the frontal cortex, by the dopamine system in the caudate nucleus, and by the cholinergic system in the hippocampus (65). Thus, it will be necessary to understand the balance of neurotransmitters, both with respect to receptor density and binding activity, in these missing cell types before rational drug therapy can be offered.

CLINICAL ASSESSMENT OF COGNITION

The hypothetical course of dementing illness is a progressive decline in overall intellectual functioning over time, but our data base for plotting the pattern of cognitive change in dementing illness is practically nonexistent. If we limit assessment to gross mental status evaluation of orientation and memory alone, we would derive a simple (and questionable) index of overall performance as a function of time. Since the course of neurochemical alterations and structural damage is also progressive in the central nervous system, it seems more reasonable to examine a range of cognitive traits or processes in order to accurately evaluate changes in different brain areas as the ability to perform a specific skill, e.g., word-finding, drops out of the afflicted individual's behavioral repertoire. An innovative cognitive technology remains to be developed both to further our understanding of the nature and rate of cognitive "fallout" with brain failure, and to provide an empirical knowledge base for the care of the aged. The development of both a testable set of cognitive functions and diagnostic algorithms to scale performance changes may also provide the basis for effective treatment and rehabilitation.

Diagnosis of the presence or absence of cognitive dysfunction, as well as of the type of dysfunction in the older patient presenting with cognitive impairment should be accomplished accurately and quickly. From the clinician's perspective, the ideal measurement for use with the cognitively impaired adult should meet a number of practical criteria. It should be reasonably brief, have repeatable forms which limit practice effects, and be simple enough to facilitate administration by individuals with minimal training.

Currently, the most useful short mental status instrument in clinical use is the Mini-Mental Status Examination (34). However, the underlying assumption of current brief mental status examinations as an approach to measurement is that the intellectual deficit in the impaired older patient is a loss of knowledge or a generalized incapacity. If the goal of an effective mental status evaluation is to be a fair measure of cognitive competence, it should assess cognitive processing or the ability to manipulate information rather than test the possession of knowledge or loss of knowledge which may be manifest as confusion with respect to self, place, time, memory, and language. Primary neuronal degeneration affects the way an individual thinks and acts, and a test of the presence and/or extent of a dementing process should be a test of how well the individual can handle information across the cognitive domain.

Cognitive behavior is composed of many specific skills, e.g., the ability to focus attention without being distracted, to remember events, to perceive features in the environment. Although historically, theorists have discussed a concept of general intelligence, a framework conceptualizing specific cognitive processes or traits would be more useful both to test theories of brain deterioration and to determine the effectiveness of psychopharmacologic intervention in treating or managing the individual with dementing illness. Analyses of whole brain sections, as well as regional sections from patients with dementing illness, show that the types and frequencies of pathologic alteration vary widely from region to region in the nervous systems of different patients (5). It is entirely possible that anatomically different patients could show different clinical pictures and cognitive profiles, as well as rates and patterns of cognitive deterioration consistent with different neuropathologic profiles in cortical, subcortical, and brainstem nuclei.

The thoughtful analysis of cognition together with a comprehensive medical evaluation provide a method to differentiate and monitor neuronal destruction in dementing illness. However, at least three properties of behavior make analysis difficult (10). First, cognitive behavior is continuous, thus introducing the need for appropriate sampling and scaling. Second, behavior is complex: cognition can be fractionated into an almost unlimited number of units, and the issue of validity must be confronted. Third, cognitive behaviors are fluid; they fluctuate not only randomly, but also systematically over time in response to casual neuronal abnormalities and cell death.

How do we approach the analysis of cognitive dysfunction in a way that acknowledges the effects of biological injury and damage as well as the psychosocial determinants of test performance? What are we measuring? When? Under what circumstances? In whom? These are only a few of the questions to be asked when evaluating the selection of cognitive measures most likely to reflect parameters such as a clinical condition—e.g., dementia or depression—or the effects of pharmacologic treatment.

A PLAN FOR THE MICROANALYSIS OF BEHAVIOR

It cannot be overemphasized that there are several theoretical approaches to measuring cognitive behavior. The utility of the neuropsychological and psychometric frameworks for assessing cognitive loss in the aged have been reviewed elsewhere (14,19,30,48,49). It is our bias that the theories and methods of the cognitive information processing framework provide a particularly useful guide to develop a systematic theory of progressive cognitive dysfunction and to develop procedures for cognitive assessment which are useful both in diagnosis and assessment of change. Lengthy neuropsychological batteries such as the Halstead-Reitan could be modified and standardized for the impaired older patient; they would have limited utility as measures of change, but potentially high value as diagnostic instruments.

Cognitive processing theories describing how individuals handle information have become increasingly popular among experimental psychologists because they afford both conceptual frameworks and methodologies to define and measure discrete aspects of cognition (16,32). This approach assumes that perception, attention, and memory can be analyzed as a series of stages during which hypothetical cognitive mechanisms perform transformations on the information in the different stages of processing. Although a large number of models have been proposed, the underlying assumption has been that memory organizes information along successive stages of processing. The theories differ, however, in their assumptions about the way information is organized and about the search mechanisms that are used to locate information in the network of stages. The theories also differ in the emphasis they place upon attention as a rate-limiting process that mediates the effectiveness of a central memory processor. However, for this chapter, we need only make some minimal assumptions about how an information-processing system is organized in order to discuss our measurement problem. Another chapter would be necessary to analyze the multitude of theories that postulate mechanistic processes in information handling and their utility for assessing the cognitively impaired elderly.

A simple information-processing model assumes that information first passes through a sensory store into short- and long-term memory through a series of stages. Similarly, information in long-term memory can be passed back into short-term storage. A group of cognitive test paradigms should evaluate the various stages in this process and thereby show how efficiently a person assembles, stores, and uses information. Table 1 lists a sample set of cognitive components to be evaluated in individuals with dementing illness. In an earlier article (12), we have described sample tests that could be used to measure each of these

TABLE 1. *Processes for assessing efficiency of cognition*

Registration into sensory/perceptual store
Transfer of information from sensory/perceptual store to short-term store
Focused vs. divided attention
Memory capacity
Retrieval from short-term store
Retrieval from long-term store

processes. Degree of cognitive deficiency and environmental dependency could be defined empirically by identifying where the impaired older person is having difficulty perceiving, integrating, storing, and handling information.

It is important to recognize that deficits in both Alzheimer's disease and multi-infarct dementias often begin as focal rather than general deficits. Careful assessment of attentional versus memory deficits is essential to effective management of the patient and assistance to the family during the course of the illness. Attentional deficits affect behavior, specifically the patient's ability to perceive the difference between threatening and helpful situations, as well as his ability to recognize and use appropriate coping strategies. It is important to recognize that cognitively impaired adults often react to their cognitive loss by withdrawal, anger, irritability, aggressiveness, or denial, as well as with signs of helplessness and depression. These behaviors are secondary to the cognitive dysfunction and should be evaluated with respect to the cognitive repertoire before the initiation of symtomatic treatment of the behavioral problem. Although permanent cognitive deficits are associated with central nervous system damage, it is still very important to invest significant effort to assess what cognitive skills can and cannot be mobilized in order to develop a cognitive retraining and cognitive enhancement program. There is no reason a vigorous cognitive rehabilitation program could not be instituted analogous to physical rehabilitation.

Loss of attention and lack of motivation impose a bottleneck on cognitive processing, although we do not usually associate these abilities with central nervous system injury. If attentional abilities are affected in the impaired adult, it is useful to determine whether there is any way the deficit(s) can be remedied. For example, reaction research (57) would be most helpful in understanding the different numbers of stimulus and response alternatives to which the patient will respond appropriately as the illness progresses. Choice reaction times, but not simple reaction times, are significantly longer in the cognitively impaired aged (33); this indicates a deficit in the ability to ignore irrelevant information and respond selectively. It is possible that research evaluating the nature of preparation for a response will reveal the potential for more adaptive responses in the demented adult, at least during the earlier stages of the process. However, even in later stages of the illness, it is possible to set up expectancies in the environment to bring about appropriate responses, even though the expectancy is for an immediate event to occur.

In summary, thinking is not a solitary process. Rather, it involves a set of separate cognitive skills which allow us to react to the world around us. Prognosis for the patient with dementing illness relies heavily upon the types of cognitive losses, and it is our thesis that considerable effort should be invested in developing the technology to institute and evaluate cognitive enhancement therapies. It would be a valuable addition to our therapeutic armamentarium to be able to build cognitive strategies in impaired patients using the cognitive processing skills they do retain despite the unrelenting decline of nonreversible dementing illnesses.

REFERENCES

1. Alvord, E. C., Forno, L. S., Kusske, J. A., Kauffman, R. J., Rhodes, J. S., and Gortowski, C. B. (1974): The pathology of Parkinson's: A comparison of degeneration in cerebral cortex and brainstem. *Adv. Neurol.*, 5:175–193.
2. Alzheimer, A. (1911): Uber eigenartige krankheitsfälle des späteren Alters. *Z. Gesamte Neurol. Psychiatrie*, 4:356–385.
3. Ball, M. J. (1976): Neurofibrillary tangles and pathogenesis of dementia: A quantitative study. *Neuropathol. Appl. Neurobiol.*, 2:395–410.
4. Ball, M. J. (1977): Neuronal loss, neurofibrillary tangles and granuovacuolar degeneration in the hippocampus with aging and dementia. *Acta Neuropathol. (Berl.)*, 37:111–112.
5. Ball, M. J. (1978): Histotopography of cellular changes in Alzheimer's disease. In: *Senile Dementia: A Biomedical Approach*, edited by K. Nandy. Elsevier-North Holland, New York.
6. Ball, M. J., and Lo, P. (1944): Granulovacuolar degeneration in the aging brain and in dementia. *J. Neuropathol. Exp. Neurol.*, 36:474–487.
7. Bowen, D. M., Smith, C. B., White, P. T., and Davison, A. N. (1976): Neurotransmitter-related enzymes and indices of hypoxia in senile dementia and other bioatrophies. *Brain*, 94:459–496.
8. Brody, H., and Vijayashankar, N. (1977): Cell loss with aging. *Adv. Behav. Biol.*, 23:15–21.
9. Brun, A. and Gustafson, L. (1976): Distribution of cerebral degeneration in Alzheimer's disease. *Arch. Psychiatr. Nervenkr.*, 223:15–33.
10. Cattell, R. B. (1966): Patterns of change: Measurement in relation to state-dimension, trait change, lability, and process concepts. In: *Handbook of Multivariate Experiment Psychology*, edited by R. B. Cattell. Rand McNally, Chicago.
11. Chaffee, J., Massef, M., and Bobin, S. (1978): Cytotoxic auto-antibody to the brain. In: *Senile Dementia: A Biomedical Approach*, edited by K. Nandy. Elsevier-North Holland, New York.
12. Cohen, D., and Eisdorfer, C. (1979): Cognitive theory and the assessment of change in the elderly. In: *Psychiatric Symptoms and Cognitive Loss in the Aged*, edited by A. Raskin and L. F. Jarvik, pp. 173–282. Hemisphere, Washington.
13. Cohen, D. and Dunner, D. (1980): Assessment of cognitive dysfunction in dementing illness. In: *Psychopathology in the Aged*, edited by J. O. Cole and J. Barrett. Raven Press, New York.
14. Cohen, D., and Eisdorfer, C. (1979): Serum immunoglobulins and cognitive status in the elderly: A population study. *Br. J. Psychiatry, (in press).*
15. Cohen, D., and Wu, S. (1979): Language and cognition during aging. In: *Annual Review of Gerontology*, edited by C. Eisdorfer. Springer Verlag, New York *(in press).*
16. Corsellis, J. A. N. (1976): Aging and the dementias. In: *Greenfield's Neuropathology*, edited by W. Blackwood and J. A. N. Corsellis. E. Arnold, London.
17. Crapper, D. R., Karlik, S., and DeBoni, U. (1978): Aluminum and other metals in senile (Alzheimer) dementia. In: *Aging, Vol. 7, Alzheimer's Disease: Senile Dementia and Related Disorders*, edited by R. Katzman, R. Terry, and K. Bick. Raven Press, New York.
18. Crapper, D. R., Krishan, S. S., and Dalton, A. J. (1973): Brain aluminum distribution in Alzheimer's Disease and experimental neurofibrillary degeneration. *Science*, 180:511–513.
19. Crook, T. H. (1979): Psychometric assessment in the elderly. In: *Psychiatric Symptoms and Cognitive Loss in the Elderly*, edited by A. Raskin and L. F. Jarvik, pp. 207–220. Hemisphere, Washington.

20. Davies, P. (1978): Aging of specific neurotransmitter systems and their involvement in senile dementia. *International Congress of Neuropathology,* Washington.
21. Davies, P., and Maloney, A. J. F. (1976): Selective action of central cholinergic neurons in Alzheimer's disease. *Lancet,* 2:1403.
22. Davies, P., and Verth, A. H. (1978): Regional distribution of muscarinic acetycholine receptors in normal and Alzheimer's-type dementia brains. *Brain Res.,* 138:385–392.
23. Davies, K. L., and Yamamura, H. I. (1978): Cholinergic underactivity in human memory disorder. *Life Sci.,* 23:1729–1734.
24. Dayan, A. D. (1970): Quantitative histologic studies on the aged human brain. II. Senile plaques and neurofibrillary tangles in senile dementia. *Acta Neuropathol. (Berl.),* 16:95–102.
25. Domino, E. R., Dren, A. T., and Ciardina, W. J. (1977): Biochemical and neurotransmitter changes in the aging brain. In: *A Review of Psychopharmacology: A Second Decade of Progress,* edited by M. Lipton, A. Dimascio, and K. Killam. Raven Press, New York.
26. Drachman, D. (1978): Memory, dementia, and the cholinergic system. In: *Alzheimer's Disease: Senile Dementia and Related Disorders,* edited by R. Katzman, R. Terry, and K. Bick. Raven Press, New York.
27. Drachman, D. A. (1977): Memory and cognitive function in man: Does the cholinergic system have a specific role? *Neurology* (Minneap.), 27:783–790.
28. Eisdorfer, C., and Cohen, D. (1978): The cognitively impaired elderly: Differential diagnosis. In: *The Clinical Psychology of Aging,* edited by M. Storandt, I. Siegler, and M. Elias, pp. 7–42. Plenum Press, New York.
29. Eisdorfer, C., and Cohen, D. (1979): Dementing illness in mid and late life. In: *Geriatrics for the Primary Care Physician,* edited by F. G. Ebaugh. Addison-Wesley, Menlo Park *(in press).*
30. Eisdorfer, C., and Cohen, D. (1979): The assessment of organic impairment in the aged: In search of a new mental status examination. In: *Quantitative Techniques for the Evaluation of Psychiatric Patients,* edited by E. Burdock, A. Sudilovsky, and S. Gershon. Marcel Dekker, New York *(in press).*
31. Eisdorfer, C., Cohen, D., and Buckley, C. E., III (1978). Serum immunoglobulins and cognition in the impaired elderly. In: *Aging, Vol. 7, Alzheimer's Disease: Senile Dementia and Related Disorders,* edited by R. Katzman, R. D. Terry, and K. L. Bick, pp. 401–408. Raven Press, New York.
32. Estes, W. K. (1978): The information-processing approach to cognition: A confluence of metaphors and methods. In: *Handbook of Learning and Cognitive Processes, Vol. 5,* edited by W. K. Estes. Laurence Erlbaum, Hillside, N.J.
33. Ferris, S. H., Crook, T., Sathananthª, G., and Gershon, S. (1976): Reaction time as a diagnostic measure in senility. *J. Am. Geriatric Soc.,* 24:529–533.
34. Folstein, M. F., Folstein, S. E., and McHugh, P. A. (1975): "Mini-mental status," a practical method for grading the cognitive state of patients for the clinician. *J. Psychiatr. Res.,* 12:189–198.
35. Gajdusek, D. C. (1977): Unconventional viruses and the origin and disappearance of kuru. *Science,* 197:943–960.
36. Gibbs, C. J., Gajdusek, D. C., Asher, D. M., Alpers, M. P., Beck, E., Daniel, P. M., and Matthews, W. B. (1968): Creutzfeldt-Jakob disease (spongioform encephalopathy): Transmission to the chimpanzee. *Science,* 161:388–389.
37. Hachinski, V. (1978): Cerebral blood flow differentiation of Alzheimer's Disease from multi-infarct dementia. In: *Aging, Vol. 7, Alzheimer's Disease: Senile dementia and related disorders,* edited by R. Katzman, R. D. Terry, and K. C. Bick. Raven Press, New York.
38. Hachinski, V., Lassen, N., and Marshall, J. (1974): Multi-infarct dementia: A cause of mental deterioration in the elderly. *Lancet,* 2:207–210.
39. Heston, L. L. (1977): Alzheimer's disease, trinomy 21, and myeloproliferative disorders: Associations suggesting a genetic diathesis. *Science,* 196:322–323.
40. Heston, L. L., and Mastri, A. R. (1977): The genetics of Alzheimer's disease: Associations with myeloproliferative disorders and Down's syndrome. *Arch. Gen. Psychiatry,* 34:976–981.
41. Hirano, A., and Zimmerman, H. M. (1962): Alzheimer's neurofibrillary changes: A topographic study. *Arch. Neurol.,* 7:227–242.
42. Hooper, W. M., and Vogel, F. S.: The limbic system in Alzheimer's disease. *Am. J. Pathol.,* 85:1–13.
43. Jacobs, J. W., Bernhard, M. R., Delgado, A., and Strain, J. J. (1977): Screening for organic mental syndrome in the medically ill. *Ann. Intern. Med.,* 86:40–46.

44. Kahn, R. L., and Miller, N. E. (1978): Assessment of altered brain function in the aged. In: *The Clinical Psychology of Aging,* edited by M. Storandt, I. C. Siegler, and M. F. Elias. Plenum Press, New York.
45. Kay, D. W. K. (1977): The epidemiology of brain deficit in the aged: Problems in patient identification. In: *The Cognitively and Emotionally Impaired Elderly,* edited by C. Eisdorfer and R. O. Friedel. Yearbook Medical Publisher, Chicago.
46. Keckich, W., Cohen, D., and Eisdorfer, C. (1980): Prevalence of pseudodementia. *Arch. Gen. Psychiatry (submitted).*
47. Kemper, B. L. (1978): Senile dementia: A focal disease in the temporal lobe. In: *Senile Dementia: A Biomedical Approach,* edited by K. Nandy. North Holland, New York.
48. Klisz, D. (1978): Neuropsychological evaluation in older persons. In: *The Clinical Psychology of Aging,* edited by M. Storandt, I. C. Siegler, and M. F. Elias. Plenum Press, New York.
49. Kramer, N. A., and Jarvik, L. F. (1979): Assessment of intellectual changes in the elderly. In: *Psychiatric Symptoms and Cognitive Loss in the Elderly,* edited by A. Raskin and L. F. Jarvik, pp. 221–271. Hemisphere, Washington.
50. Larsson, T., Sjogren, T., and Jacobson, G. (1963): Senile dementia. A clinical, sociomedical and genetic study. *Acta Psychiatr. Scand.,* (Suppl.) 167:1–259.
51. Libow, L. A. (1973): "Pseudosenility": Acute and reversible organic brain syndrome. *J. Am. Geriatr. Soc.,* 21:112–115.
52. Marsden, C. D., and Harrison, M. J. G. (1972): Presenile dementia. *Br. Med. J.,* 3:50–55.
53. McDermott, J. R., Smith, A. I., Iqbal, K., and Wisniewski, H. M. (1979): Brain aluminum in aging and Alzheimer's disease. *Neurology (Minneap.),* 29:809–814.
54. McGeer, E., and McGeer, P. L. (1976): Neurotransmitter metabolism in the aging brain. In: *Neurobiology of Aging,* edited by R. D. Terry and S. Gershon. Raven Press, New York.
55. Mehraein, P., Yamada, M., and Tarnowoka-Dziduszko, E. (1975): Quantitative study on dendrites and dendritic spines in Alzheimer's disease and senile dementia. *Adv. Neurol.,* 12:453–458.
56. Meyer, J. S., Welch, K. M. A., Titus, J. L., Suzuki, M., Kim, H. S. Perez, J. J., Mathew, N. T., Gedge, J. L., and Dodson, R. F. (1976): Neurotransmitter failure in cerebral infarction and dementia. In: *Neurobiology of Aging,* edited by R. D. Terry and S. Gershon. Raven Press, New York.
57. Näätänen, R., and Merisalo, A. (1977): Expectancy and preparation in simple reaction time. In: *Attention and Performance IV,* edited by S. Dornic. Laurence Erlbaum, Hillsdale, N.J.
58. Nandy, K. (1977): Immune reactions in aging brain and senile dementia. In: *The Aging Brain and Senile Dementia,* edited by K. Nandy and I. Sherwin.
59. Nott, R. M., and Fleminger, J. J. (1975): Presenile dementia: The difficulties of early diagnosis. *Acta Psychiatr. Scand.,* 51:210–217.
60. Papez, J. W. (1937): A proposed mechanism of emotion. *Arch. Neurol. Psychiatry,* 38:725–743.
61. Perry, E. K., Perry, R. H., Blessed, G., (1977): Necropsy evidence of central cholinergic deficits in senile dementia. *Lancet,* 1:189.
62. Perry, E. K., Perry, R. H., Gibson, P. H., Blessed, G., and Tomlinson, B. E. (1977): A cholinergic connection between normal aging and senile dementia in the human hippocampus. *Neurosci. Lett.,* 6:85–89.
63. Rapport, M. M., and Karpiak, S. E. (1978): Immunological perturbation of neurological functions. In: *Senile Dementia: A Biomedical Approach,* edited by K. Nandy. Elsevier-North Holland, New York.
64. Raskind, M. (1976): Community-based evaluation and crisis intervention. A paper presented at the Workshop on Aging, New York, October, 1976.
65. Reisine, T. D., Yamamura, H. I., Bird, E., Spokes, E., and Enna, S. J. (1978): Pre- and postsynaptic neurochemical alterations in Alzheimer's disease. *Brain Res.,* 159:477–481.
66. Roth, M., Tomlinson, B. E., and Blessed, G. (1967): The relationship between measures of dementia and of degenerative changes in the cerebral gray matter of elderly subjects. *Proc. R. Soc. Med.,* 60:254–259.
67. Terry, R. D., and Wisniewski, H. (1973): Ultrastructure of senile dementia and of experimental analogs. In: *Aging and the Brain,* edited by C. Graitz. Plenum Press, New York.
68. Terry, R. D., and Wisniewski, H. (1977): Structural aspects of aging in the brain. In: *The Cognitively and Emotionally Impaired Elderly,* edited by C. Eisdorfer and R. O. Friedel. Yearbook Medical Publishers, Chicago.

69. Tomlinson, B. E., Blessed, J., and Roth, M. (1970): Observations on the brains of demented old people. *J. Neurol. Sci.,* 11:205–242.
70. Trapp, G. A., Miner, G. D., Zimmerman, R. L., Mastri, A. R., and Heston, L. L. (1978): Aluminum levels in brain in Alzheimer's disease. *Biol. Psychiatry,* 13:709–717.
71. White, P., Hiley, C. R., Goodhardt, M. J., and Keet, J. P. (1977): Neocortical cholinergic neurons in elderly people. *Lancet,* 1:668–671.

Psychopathology in the Aged, edited by
Jonathan O. Cole and James E. Barrett.
Raven Press, New York © 1980.

Psychological Dysfunction in the Elderly: Discussion

Gerald Goldstein

Veterans Administration Medical Center, Pittsburgh, Pennsylvania 15206

This discussion will not specifically provide individual critiques of the other chapters of this volume, but rather will touch on them in the context of some more general considerations. These comments will be offered as those of one who is writing primarily as a neuropsychologist. Their theme will be an analysis of the concept of dementia, and the implications of this concept for our understanding of the normal aging process. The standard medical dictionary defines dementia as "a general mental deterioration due to organic or psychological factors." A recently published psychiatric dictionary defines it as "absence or reduction of intellectual facilities in consequence of known organic brain disease," and follows this definition with a brief history of the term, indicating that it is now relatively restricted to irreversible defects associated with brain disorder. However, for scientific and clinical purposes, the term dementia is very much in need of further specification, and such specification may aid in furthering our scientific and clinical understanding of behavioral changes associated with brain damage, functional psychiatric disorders, and aging. Indeed, as Dr. Miller *(this volume)* pointed out in her paper, a major task of neuropsychology is that of finding specific relationships between altered brain function or structure and behavior.

Neuropsychologists do not like to use the term dementia in a scientific or technical sense, nor do they like to use the major alternatives: organic brain syndrome, mental deterioration, and mental signs. They have not invented a substitute term either, because the objection is not against the specific terms, but is against the idea of telescoping the rather complex and elaborate field of cognitive, perceptual, and motor changes associated with brain pathology into a single word or phrase. Thus, despite the high frequency of usage of the term dementia in this volume and elsewhere, I will nevertheless proceed with my objections.

Let us begin this examination with the example of Alzheimer's disease. As has been pointed out, there are apparently two forms of Alzheimer's disease, the presenile and senile form. However, there seems to be some controversy regarding whether or not they actually constitute the same disease. This question itself might be clarified through neuropsychological study. The point I want to raise, however, has to do with whether or not Alzheimer's disease is an appropriate model for normal aging. Is the idea that Alzheimer's disease produces premature aging a valid one? One important consideration that would weigh against its being a good model for aging relates to the matter of aphasia. Aphasia is not uncommonly seen in patients with Alzheimer's disease of both the presenile and senile types. However, aphasia does not appear to be a consequence of normal aging. Indeed, language function appears to be one of man's hardiest abilities and resists many of the ravages of age and disease. Unlike other mental abilities, vocabulary and other verbal skills may improve with age in people without brain disease (4). Thus, while there are certainly intellectual changes with normal aging, those changes may not resemble what is seen in either the presenile or senile form of Alzheimer's disease. If we call Alzheimer's disease a dementia and also describe what occurs with normal aging as progressive dementia, then we are calling what may be two entirely different phenomena by the same name. If we restrict the use of the term dementia to particular consequences of certain forms of neuropathology then we are on safer grounds, but it is important to remain aware that the different dementias such as Alzheimer's disease, Pick's disease, and multi-infarct dementia may imply very different neurobehavioral characteristics.

The definition of dementia as general mental deterioration appears to be at odds with numerous research findings that show that intellectual changes in normal aging and the various brain disorders of the aged are not general. They are often quite specific. The nature of this specificity has, however, been a controversial matter. Probably the first conceptual attempt was Wechsler's "hold" and "don't hold" abilities (17); later the distinction between "crystallized" and "fluid" intelligence became important (1). Reitan (15) and various collaborators did several neuropsychological studies of aging which led to another conceptual distinction, this time between brain- and education-related abilities. Even if none of these concepts is totally satisfactory, they all indicate that some form of selectivity does appear to exist. If so, perhaps we should develop some form of classifying terminology as an alternative to a single term, dementia, that implies general deterioration.

The argument being proposed here is not entirely a semantic one. The concept of dementia, when defined as general deterioration, suggests that the individual is impaired in all spheres. While this assumption may be true in some cases, it is generally not true, and what we find instead is some profile of impaired and preserved abilities. We would probably do better scientifically and clinically by using terminology that more specifically characterizes age-associated behavioral changes. Numerous examples could be given of how a characterization of an individual as being senile or demented can be extensively modified after a more detailed inquiry and examination. For example, what may be described as dementia or senility may in actuality be an anterograde amnesia. Amnesic disorders are sometimes independent syndromes that are unrelated to any other form of cognitive deficit. If indeed the individual does have a specific amnesic syndrome, then we at least may have some grasp of what the underlying neurological disorder may be. It may be a limbic system lesion or a frontal lobe lesion, depending on the specific characteristics of the disorder. This same analysis could be repeated for many functions such as visual-spatial abilities and abstract reasoning abilities. It may be much more useful to describe these behaviors, ideally in some systematic form such as Luria's (11) concept of "syndrome analysis," rather than to gloss over this entire realm with a more diffuse terminology.

How shall we characterize the cognitive and perceptual changes that occur in normal elderly people and in elderly people with neurological degenerative diseases? With regard to normal aging, perhaps the most popular concept at present involves the distinction between crystallized and fluid intelligence (2,7,8). In general, fluid intelligence, which supposedly reflects functioning of neurological structures, increases through adolescence and declines thereafter. Crystallized intelligence, which is thought to be based on cultural assimilation and educational influences, increases across the life span in the healthy individual. In a similar vein, the late Ward Halstead (6) and Ralph Reitan (14) developed the concept of biological or brain age. They contrasted abilities sensitive to alterations in the condition of the brain with abilities mainly influenced by educational and cultural considerations. It would appear that the normal elderly person retains crystallized intelligence or education-related abilities, but does decline in regard to brain-related or fluid intellectual abilities. The elderly individual with a degenerative disease may decline in both sets of abilities.

A major task of neuropsychology has been that of refining our analysis of cognitive, perceptual, and motor abilities, and seeking associations between those abilities and brain structure and function. Perhaps the classic example of this pursuit was the discovery by Broca that the left hemisphere of the brain is associated with speech. Since the time of Broca, a more or less standard vocabulary has developed containing the terms used by neuropsychologists and behavioral neurologists to describe the functions they study. Some of the more commonly used terms are long- and short-term memory, perception, language abilities, motor speed, psychomotor function, conceptual reasoning ability, and visual-spatial ability. Sometimes, the terminology is more neurologically oriented, and we speak of such things as frontal lobe functions, right hemisphere functions, etc. Zubin has also suggested, in regard to aging, that there is an underlying curve of physiological development and decline on which are superimposed different curves for different functions such as perception, motor functions, cognitive processes, etc. These functions develop and decline at varying rates so that while taste, for example, may begin to decline during middle age, language skills may not decline until quite late in life, if at all.

These considerations point out the difficulty neuropsychologists and developmentally oriented behavioral scientists have with the concept of dementia. A neuropsychologist may want to know, for example, if auditory comprehension is impaired in Alzheimer's disease. If it is, is there more impairment with regard to nonverbal auditory stimuli than there is to verbal auditory stimuli? In general, the idea is that of carefully determining the specific functional deficits and relating those deficit patterns to neurological or developmental variables. With regard to normal aging, this kind of inquiry appears to indicate that cognitive functions that depend more on accumulated experience rather than on some physiological substrate or sensory acuity tend to retain their integrity. Reed and Reitan (13) have shown that those functions that appear to be most sensitive to brain dysfunction in nonelderly adults are the same functions that seem to decline most dramatically with normal aging. In conceptualizing his studies of aging, Reitan (16) proposed the concept of brain age, based on the mental age notion in children's intelligence testing. Some may disagree with his formulation, but it at least represents an effort at conceptualizing what perceptual and cognitive changes occur with aging.

To the neuropsychologically oriented, the problem has structural as well as functional aspects. Aging appears to be guided by some principle of abiotrophy in which systems and organs develop and senesce at different rates. There is a body of opinion and some preliminary research which suggests that the right or minor hemisphere ages more rapidly than the left (9). Perhaps a more cautious statement of the matter would be that functions thought to be mediated by the right hemisphere decline or change with age or insult more readily than do left hemisphere functions. Parsons (12) believes that this phenomenon is seen in alcoholics who characteristically tend to show more impairment of nonverbal, visual-spatial tasks than of language-related tasks. In our own research, we have frequently made comparisons among patients with right hemisphere, left hemisphere, and diffuse brain damage. We have always found that the left hemisphere cases were readily distinguishable from the diffuse cases, but the right hemisphere cases were relatively hard to distinguish from the diffuse cases. It would therefore appear that right hemisphere functions deteriorate more readily than do left hemisphere functions in individuals with diffuse brain damage. It is quite possible that other structures in the brain age at varying rates, and that there is some systematic relationship between these changes and the behavioral changes seen in aging.

Another approach, one that is quite compatible with neuropsychology, involves an information-processing model. Is aging associated with input functions, central representation, or output? Recently, for example, Schear and Nebes *(unpublished manuscript)* looked at verbal and spatial memory from the standpoint of information processing. They conceptualized their study as an analysis of how their subjects encoded verbal and spatial information and found no evidence for a disproportionate decline with age in verbal or spatial memory. In terms of signal detection theory, a branch of information theory, one could ask whether aging is more associated with sensitivity or criterion changes. Investigations are now under way in an effort to determine whether the memory problems commonly seen in the aged are attributable simply to a failure in the memory process or to increased cautiousness in reporting memories.

While many of us are quite aware of much of this research in neuropsychology and cognitive processes, somehow this awareness has not been incorporated into clinical application. In an admittedly biased way, I would suggest that one way of incorporating this new material is through the application of neuro-psychological tests, a view shared by other contributors in this volume. These tests have the capacity to specify impaired and preserved abilities. The appropriate lexicon for these descriptions includes terms such as aphasia, gnostic abilities, perceptual abilities, long- and short-term memory, psychomotor speed, abstract reasoning, visual-spatial abilities, motor abilities, and the like. In my view, what is now described as dementia probably represents a number of syndromes associated with varying patterns of abilities of these kinds. Luria (11) has described the process of identifying these phenomena as "syndrome analysis," while Kurt Goldstein (5) described it in terms of the *"Grundstörung,"* the basic disturbance. Whether one such syndrome or basic disturbance obtains in all normal aging, or whether there are several of them, is an unanswered question.

A refined definition of the concept of dementia has several significant clinical implications. As Dr. Gershon indicated *(this volume),* one of the reasons for the lack of success of the vasodilators may be that they were frequently given to inappropriate patients. If neuropsychological assessment could aid in distinguishing behaviorally between the multi-infarct and Alzheimer-type dementias, appropriate medications could be administered on a more rational basis. Neuropsychological tests may also be helpful in distinguishing between dementia and so-called pseudodementia. Most significantly, however, neuropsychological tests have recently been used in the formulation of rehabilitation programs. Two books have already appeared on this topic, one by Luria (10) and the other by Golden (3). Both of these authors agree that rational rehabilitation planning, which may take the form of retraining or building of a prosthetic environment, requires highly detailed knowledge of the patient's abilities and deficits. For example, impairment of auditory perception in the aged may be a function of a direct loss of auditory acuity, or of a comprehension deficit associated with the speed with which incoming information is processed in the temporal lobe. Therefore, in improving oral communication with the elderly person, it is important to know whether to speak more loudly or more slowly. Considerations of this type should encourage the application of more detailed neurobehavioral analyses of normal and abnormal aging than is often the case.

REFERENCES

1. Cattel, R. B. (1963): Theory of fluid and crystallized intelligence: A critical experiment. *J. Educ. Psychol.,* 54:1–122.
2. Cunningham, W. R., Clayton, V., and Overton, W. (1975): Fluid and crystallized intelligence in young adulthood and old age. *J. Gerontol.,* 30:53–55.
3. Golden, C. J. (1978): *Diagnosis and Rehabilitation in Clinical Neuropsychology.* Charles C. Thomas, Springfield, Illinois.
4. Goldstein, G. and Shelly, C. H. (1975): Similarities and differences between psychological deficit in aging and brain damage. *J. Gerontol.* 30:448–455.

5. Goldstein, K. (1939): *The Organism.* American Book Co., New York.
6. Halsted, W. C. (1947): *Brain and Intelligence: A Quantitative Study of the Frontal Lobes.* University of Chicago Press, Chicago.
7. Horn, J. L. (1970): Organization of data on lifespan development of human abilities. In: *Lifespan Developmental Psychology,* edited by L. R. Goulet and P. B. Baltes. Academic Press, New York.
8. Horn, J. L. and Cattell, R. B. (1967): Age differences in fluid and crystallized intelligence. *Acta Psychol. (Amst.)* 26:107–129.
9. Klisz, D. (1978): Neuropsychological evaluation in older persons. In: *The Clinical Psychology of Aging,* edited by M. A. Storandt, I. C. Siegler, and M. F. Elias. Plenum, New York.
10. Luria, A. R. (1963): *Restoration of Function After Brain Injury.* MacMillan, New York.
11. Luria, A. R. (1973): *The Working Brain.* Basic Books, New York.
12. Parsons, O. A. and Prigatano, G. P. (1978): Methodological considerations in clinical neuropsychological research. *J. Consult. Clin. Psychol.* 46:608–619.
13. Reed, H. B. C., and Reitan, R. M. (1963): A comparison of the effects of the normal aging process with the effects of organic brain-damage on adaptive abilities. *J. Gerontol.* 18:177–179.
14. Reitan, R. M. (1966): A research program on the psychological effects of brain lesions in human beings. In: *International Review of Research in Mental Retardation,* edited by N. R. Ellis, Vol. I. Academic Press, New York.
15. Reitan, R. M. (1967): Psychologic changes associated with aging and with cerebral damage. *Mayo Clin. Proc.* 42:653–673.
16. Reitan, R. M. (1973): Behavioral manifestations of impaired brain functions in aging. In: J. L. Fozard (Chair), *Similarities and Differences of Brain-Behavior Relationships in Aging and Cerebral Pathology.* Symposium presented at the meeting of the American Psychological Association, Montreal.
17. Wechsler, D. (1941): *Measurement of Adult Intelligence* (2 ed.) Williams and Wilkins, Baltimore.

OPEN DISCUSSION

Dr. Alpert: I think the issues that Dr. Goldstein has raised are paramount for considering a question that has come up several times today. We are discussing phenomena on several different levels. Dr. Shagass has suggested that the uptake measures that Dr. Ingvar is investigating, measures which we think may reflect the metabolic functioning of nervous tissue, might also be reflected in processes underlying neuroelectrical activity. The question is whether Dr. Ingvar, when he investigates metabolism, is really examining the same phenomenon as Dr. Shagass when he looks at electrical activity, or whether these two different levels might somehow also reflect the measurements which other studies have considered in relation to neuropsychological activity.

Dr. Ingvar: That is a very difficult question to answer. It seems obvious that there is a dichotomy within the audience here. There are those of us who study the brain directly by blood flow studies which have revealed various patterns of activity. However, we have not completed very many studies.

There is an inherent difficulty with EEG. The electrodes only cover 25% of the surface of the brain; the rest of the brain is hidden. In addition, the generators of EEG are still not known. We do not know where the nerve cells are located which give rise to the electrical activity between two electrodes on the skull.

In evoked potentials, we have a valuable clinical method, but it is still, and I think Dr. Shagass would agree, very difficult to identify the neuronal masses and aggregates which produce the different components of such potentials, especially their later parts.

Concerning circulatory and metabolic studies, three-dimensional techniques are now being developed. They will show the total activity and circulation in the whole brain at a given time. This can never be achieved with the present electrophysiological techniques.

As I have already indicated, there appears to be a dichotomy in the audience. On our side, we study the biological substrate directly. Our friends the psychologists work more with what one might call remote indices of what is happening in the brain. They are indeed doing a very good job and have given us much knowledge about intellectual functions. We on the physiological side should use their help more in designing our studies.

Dr. Goldstein: There are two ways of studying the brain. One is by looking at the brain, and the other is by looking at what the brain does. I think Dr. Reitan has pointed this out in a very simple expression, a very telling point. The brain is the organ of behavior. One way of studying the brain, certainly, is by studying what it does in much the same manner as we investigate other organs, by examining what they do rather than how they do it.

Dr. Ingvar: Let me be more specific. In studying normal aging many of the testing techniques do not take into account the dramatic morphological changes which take place. For example, consider the cutaneous input. The number of skin receptors is reduced at the age of 50 to some 30% of what we have when we are 20 years old. Similar changes take place in the eyes and ears. I do not think that such normal morphologic changes with increasing age are taken sufficiently into account.

Dr. Max Fink: It is difficult to try to be at all critical or even to question the beautiful techniques presented by Dr. Ingvar. But when I heard him criticizing electroencephalography, I thought it was important to point out the distinct advantages and limitations of both electroencephalography and Dr. Ingvar's methodology.

Dr. Ingvar's methods are limited to a small sample in time; they are severely invasive and therefore carry inherent risks. While it is true we do not understand the origin of the EEG, we do know that it reflects the electrical activity of the brain and that small changes in physiologic functions are reflected rapidly and quantitatively. It is possible to monitor the EEG continuously as the measurements are repeatable over time. More important, the EEG is noninvasive, not dangerous, and exceptionally quantitative. It yields important information about brain function and should not be dismissed lightly, nor should its contributions have been omitted from this reivew.

Dr. Alpert: There is a definite problem in that when studies are done on individuals identified because of behavior deficits and on age-matched controls, the brains of both groups often show profound changes. One wonders why the controls had not shown equal behaviorial changes. I think these patients sought treatment because they were showing maladaptive changes in their behavior. We are pressed to understand what structural processes might underlie these changes. The issues which trigger the question are behaviorial. I think that is important.

Also, the neuropsychological assessment is an attempt, on a different level from the behavioral phenomena, to understand what components might be contributing to the maladjustment. Many different levels are interacting here, and we would like to see them relate to each other. Perhaps the most profound difficulty that we are facing is that individuals with relatively gross alterations in brain structure are *not* showing similar alterations in their adjustment.

We are all trying to converge on a common problem, and it is not at all clear that the biological explanation is more pertinent than the behavioral.

Dr. Zubin: In contrast with the state of affairs during our first symposium on aging held some years ago, we now have a much more varied armamentarium of technological developments to utilize, ranging from measures of cerebral blood flow in various brain regions to evoked potentials as well as neuropsychological and behavioral measures. It is unfortunate that each of these advances has not yet been integrated with the others so that the pattern across these techniques can be determined. It is here where the cross-disciplinary approach holds the greatest promise.

It seems to me that rather than battle about whose method is superior, we must realize that none of them is in and of itself sufficient. They must be put together in a way which is going to make sense.

Dr. Ingvar: I think you made a very good statement, Dr. Zubin, about the necessity of bringing the techniques together.

I do not want to leave you with the impression that I am advocating our flow technique as the only technique, or the best one. I have worked for 25 years with EEG, and I am fully aware of its specific capacities, especially for continuous usage. Its time resolution is fast. EEG can record events over various parts of the skull which only take milliseconds. Dr. Zubin also mentioned the economic aspect. The new emission tomographs cost about $2.3 million for a unit. These are going to remain exquisite research tools in only a few centers in the world. We will have to rely upon cheaper and noninvasive techniques. And in the future the neurophysiologists and the neuropsychologists will have to work closer together.

Psychopathology in the Aged, edited by
Jonathan O. Cole and James E. Barrett.
Raven Press, New York © 1980.

Clinical and Biological Aspects of Depression in the Elderly

George Winokur, David Behar, and Michael Schlesser

Department of Psychiatry, University of Iowa College of Medicine, Iowa City, Iowa 52240

The term "elderly" in the dictionary is defined as "approaching old age" or "somewhat old." There have been many statements about depression in the elderly, based mostly on opinion rather than on evidence. People appear strongly opinionated about what it is like to be old and what constitute the problems of the elderly. One of the prevailing opinions is that social and personal circumstances in old age are depressing affairs, and, therefore, an individual should be highly subject to depression. If this were true, the depression should be rather different from the depression which is seen in younger persons, persons who are in the middle of active and productive lives. It is possible, however, that the differences are highly overemphasized. Part of the goal of this chapter is to examine depressions in the elderly and compare them to depressions in younger people.

Statistically, it would appear that in women the incidence of depressive psychoses does not increase with increasing age (10). The rate per 100,000 population in women, age 35 to 44 is 115; age 45 to 54, 118; age 55 to 64, 112; and in women age 65 to 74, 109. Thus, one cannot say that being old is associated with any marked increase in depressive psychosis in women. It is equally true that aging does not increase the suicide rate in women. For the ages 35 to 44, the suicide rate per 100,000 population is 5.2; for the decade 45 to 54, 6.7; for 55 to 64, 6.6; and 65 to 74, 6.1. There is no consistent rise in rates after 35 to 44.

Clinical differences between elderly versus younger patients are not striking, although agitation is more frequently seen in older patients and retardation more frequently seen in younger patients (12). These data, however, are concerned with a separation between patients above and below 40 years of age. Whether this kind of difference would hold true between patients who are above and below 60 is questionable. Another finding is that those patients who are under 40 at times of index admission are less likely to have been ill for 6 months or more at the time they enter the hospital. Thus, their disturbances are somewhat more acute than those of the patients who become ill over 40.

With respect to the course of depression, chronicity is more frequently seen in older females (over 40), and recurrent episodes are more frequently seen in older males (over 40) (7). Chronicity is not age-related in males, and further episodes are not age-related in females. It would appear, then, as women become older, they are more likely to have a chronic course, and as men become older they are more likely to have multiple episodes. Whether patients who were 60 or older would have more chronicity or more episodes compared to patients who are 40 to 60 is unknown currently.

Finally, there are some interesting findings regarding treatment. Electroconvulsive therapy (ECT) is significantly more effective than either adequate or inadequate tricyclics in patients who are 50 to 60 or greater than 60. Before those ages, ECT is more efficacious than adequate or inadequate antidepressants but the differences are not significant. There is some slight suggestion that the patients over 50 do less well with adequate antidepressant treatment than they do prior to the age of 50 (1).

This background of clinical studies of depressions in the elderly raises the problem of defining a threshold age for "elderly." It may be 40 in some cases and 50 in others. It is also conceivable that patients who are over 60 will respond differently in many ways than younger patients. This chapter is another attempt to evaluate some aspects of illness in elderly patients. In one instance, we will separate patients who developed their illness prior to the age of 50 from those who developed their illness after the age of 50. This will give us an opportunity to look at age of onset as well as age at index admission, particularly if the mean age of index admission is different from the mean age of onset in both cases. In another instance, we will compare patients who are 30 to 50 at times of index admission with those who are over 50. Finally, we will look at some biological factors in depression of the elderly, including family (genetic) background and response to the dexamethasone suppression test.

Since we will be dealing with data which have been collected in different studies, the methodologies will be discussed in each of the succeeding sections.

EARLY VERSUS LATE ONSET COMPARISONS

In previous investigations, 288 female depressives were studied in three groups: (a) 104 with positive family histories of alcoholism and/or antisocial personality in the first-degree families—these were considered to have "Depression Spectrum Disease"; (b) 86 with parental histories of depression—these were considered to have "Pure Depressive Disease"; and (c) 98 with no history of depression, alcoholism or antisocial behavior—these were considered to have "Sporadic Depression Disease." The first two groups were composed of consecutive admissions to the Psychiatric Hospital of the University of Iowa between 1930 and 1975. The third group was compiled later, and was matched with the first two groups in terms of years of admission. The names of the 3 groups, Depression Spectrum Disease, Pure Depressive Disease and Sporadic Depression Disease refer to the 3 types of familial backgrounds. Otherwise, the subjects were chosen randomly. The methodology is more fully described in another publication (9).

For the purposes of the present chapter, the 288 patients were divided into 2 groups, 1 of which had an onset under the age of 50 (N-233); the other of which had an onset over age 50 (N-55). The two groups were compared with respect to a variety of symtoms, personality characteristics, treatment variables, and follow-up variables. Not all items were assessed in a reliable fashion. Interrater reliability for individual items was evaluated with the Kappa statistic (5), and items with scores of 0.7 or more were used. If the expected frequency of agreement was beyond the range of 0.3 to 0.7, a score of 0.5 was accepted. The data in Tables 1 to 4 are based on items in which there was satisfactory interrater reliability by these criteria.

Table 1 shows some clinical differences between depressive patients with an onset of illness over and under 50 years of age. What is most important to recognize is that there was also a clear and unequivocal difference in mean age at index, with the group that had an onset over 50 having a mean age at index of about 60 years. The clinical differences were not very striking. Certainly the younger and earlier-onset group had less weight loss. Also, women of that group complained more of decreased libido. Whether this was due to the fact that the elderly view sexuality (and the need for sexuality) in a different fashion is impossible to determine from the data. There were no significant differences in a number of other symptoms. Separate and previous studies of Pure Depressive Disease and Sporadic Depressive Disease have indicated that using a threshold of 40 has not made any significant difference in terms of the clinical overview (3,6). The differences are trivial at best.

Table 2 shows comparisons in terms of personality characteristics. Other than good temper, which is more frequent in the older and late-onset patients, there are no significant differences. However, a couple of personality characteristics do approach significance, i.e., nervousness and lifelong irritability. Signifi-

TABLE 1. *Clinical differences between depressive patients with onset of illness above and below 50 years of age*[a]

	Onset <50	Onset >50	p
N	233	55	
Mean age at index	40	60	
Met Feighner criteria	208 (89%)	47 (85%)	N.S.
Weight loss	129 (55%)	45 (82%)	<.0005
Early morning awaking	115 (49%)	35 (64%)	N.S.
Decreased libido	89 (38%)	6 (11%)	<.0005
Marked guilt	158 (68%)	29 (53%)	N.S.
Retardation	107 (46%)	21 (38%)	N.S.

[a] No differences in fear, anorexia, decreased energy, diurnal variation, sensorium change, hallucinations, hypochondriasis.

TABLE 2. *Personality Characteristics of depressives with onset <50 vs those with onset >50*

	Onset <50	Onset >50	p
N	233	55	
Mean age at index	40	60	
Sensitive	89 (38%)	15 (27%)	N.S.
Nervous	55 (24%)	6 (11%)	N.S. [a]
Conscientious	57 (24%)	8 (15%)	N.S.
Defaults on obligations	5 (2%)	0 (0%)	N.S.
Needs reassurance	8 (3%)	0 (0%)	N.S.
Dramatic	12 (5%)	0 (0%)	N.S.
Seductive	10 (4%)	0 (0%)	N.S.
Unreliable	2 (1%)	0 (0%)	N.S.
Worrisome	48 (21%)	9 (16%)	N.S.
Lifelong irritability	37 (16%)	3 (5%)	N.S. [a]
Good temper	61 (26%)	24 (44%)	<.025

[a] Barely misses .05 level of significance.

cantly, such personality characteristics as might be associated with stormy life patterns are more frequently seen in the younger-onset patients. However, the differences are not statistically significant. What this means is that the overlap is enormous.

Table 3 presents material related to suicide. The attempt rate is clearly higher in the younger and earlier-onset patients. Although the differences are not statistically significant for suicidal thoughts and for completed suicides in the follow-up, there is a consistency of pattern in their excess in younger patients. What is particularly interesting is the fact that there are far more completed suicides in the earlier-onset and younger women than there are in the older women.

Finally, Table 4 presents material on treatment results and follow-up. There are no clear differences between groups here. It is more likely that a younger person will have a diagnosis of reactive depression on discharge, but this does not reach significance. The effect of ECT is the same in both groups, although there is a slight tendency for the older group to fare a little better.

TABLE 3. *Suicidal behavior of depressed patients with onset <50 vs depressed patients with onset >50*

	Onset <50	Onset >50	p
N	233	55	
Mean age at index admission	40	60	
Suicide attempt	56 (24%)	6 (11%)	.05
Suicide thoughts	169 (73%)	32 (58%)	N.S. [a]
Suicide in follow-up	8 (3%)	0 (0%)	N.S.
Length of follow-up	3.5 years	2.7 years	

[a] Barely misses significance at .05 level.

TABLE 4. *Other clinical factors, treatment results, and follow-up in depressives with onset <50 vs onset >50*

	Onset <50	Onset >50	*p*
N	233	55	
Mean age at index	40	60	
Final dx of reactive depression	53 (23%)	7 (13%)	N.S.
Transferred to another hospital	15 (6%)	5 (9%)	N.S.
Total deaths in follow-up	10 (4%)	1 (2%)	N.S.
ECT: Good-Excellent effect	122/131 (89%)	36/37 (97%)	N.S.
Relapse in follow-up	72 (31%)	21 (38%)	N.S.
Length of follow-up	3.5 years	2.7 years	

CLINICALLY RELEVANT CLUSTERS AS RELATED TO AGE—"ENDOGENOUS" AND "STABLE PERSONALITY"

Clinicians think in terms of clusters rather than in terms of individual symptoms; as a consequence, we have explored a number of these clusters. First we evaluated the interrater reliability for the clusters using the intraclass correlation coefficient. Two clusters had particularly high intraclass correlation coefficients for the one-way random effects model (2). These two were the endogenous cluster and the stable personality cluster, where the intraclass correlation coefficients were .719 ($p < .001$) and .740 ($p < .001$) respectively.

Table 5 presents the endogenous symptoms. There are 11 of them, and what is clear is that if one separates the depressed women into those who are between 30 and 50 at index admission and compares them to those who are over 50, there is no significant difference in the mean number of endogenous symptoms.

If one looks at the same age breakdown in depressed women and compares them on the mean number of stable characteristics, there is likewise no significant difference between the two groups (Table 6). There are seven stable personality characteristics and these are seen equally in both groups.

There is no compelling reason then to think that age or age of onset separates the patients in any striking fashion. The clinical symptoms, though occasionally different, are not overwhelmingly different. The amount of overlap is enormous.

TABLE 5. *Endogenous symptoms[a] in depressed women aged 30–50 vs depressed women over 50*

	30–50	>50
N	127	110
Mean age at index	39	59
Mean # of endogenous symptoms	6.28	6.29

[a] Endogenous Symptoms = depressed mood, anorexia, weight loss, energy loss, terminal insomnia, decreased libido, sensorium change, retardation, self-blame, diurnal variation, hallucinations (N = 11).

TABLE 6. *Lifelong stable personality characteristics[a] in depressives aged 30–50 vs depressives over 50*

	30–50	>50
N	127	110
Mean # of stable characteristics	2.79	2.81
Mean years at index	39	59

[a] Stable personality characteristics = rigidity, meticulous, conscientious, sociable, worrisome, even tempered, hardworking (N = 7).

The reliably assessed clinical clusters—endogenous psychopathology and stable personality—do not differ in incidence between older and younger subjects. We are then confronted with the fact that such variables as age of onset, or age in a group of depressed people controlled for sex, do not lead us very far in separating autonomous illnesses. The clinical diagnosis, then, becomes more important than age.

One finding of clinical importance, however, relates to suicidal behavior: in the younger group of women, suicide is a more frequent and possibly serious problem.

BIOLOGICAL AND FAMILY DIFFERENCES

In a series of studies, we have classified depressive patients on the basis of their family histories (2,3,6,8,9,11). The family history, of course, has the advantage of not having been caused in any way by the clinical symptomatology of the patient. There is no way for a patient who is depressed currently to have caused a depression or alcoholism years before in a parent. Thus, the evaluation of the family history is clearly more independent than the evaluation of something akin to a reactive component in the illness. One can never be certain that a reactive component has not occurred as a result of the illness rather than as a cause of it.

In previous material, we have separated out three types of unipolar depressives (9). The first of these, Depression Spectrum Disease (DSD), is a depression in an individual who has a first-degree family history of alcoholism and/or antisocial personality. Thus, the spectrum refers to the family rather than to the individual herself. The diagnoses of alcoholism or antisocial personality as well as the diagnosis of depression in the proband follow ordinary research criteria. It is possible for a person with Depression Spectrum Disease to have (in addition to alcoholism or antisocial personality in the first-degree family member) the presence of depression in the first-degree family member, but it is the presence of alcoholism in the first-degree family member that is the marker. In the second type of unipolar depression, Pure Depressive Disease, familial (PDD), the index case, or patient, has a depression as does a first-degree family member. No

TABLE 7. *Clinical differences relevant to a familial breakdown of female unipolar depressive patients*

	DSD	PDD	SDD	*p*
Proportion of unipolars	17%	25%	32%	
Mean age of onset	35	33	41	<.0002
Onset over 50				
N	16	12	27	
Fear	56%	67%	26%	.03
Sensorium changes	6%	33%	4%	.02
Acute onset	19%	42%	0%	.002
Final diagnosis-reactive	31%	17%	0%	.03
Mean follow-up	2.5 yr	2.9 yr	2.4 yr	N.S.
Relapse in follow-up	13%	33%	56%	.02
Mean # of endogenous symptoms	6.0	6.1	6.5	N.S.
Mean # of stable personality features	3.1	2.6	2.8	N.S.

alcoholism or antisocial personality exists in the first-degree relationship. In the third type, Sporadic Depressive Disease (SDD), neither alcoholism nor antisocial personality nor depression exist in a first-degree family relationship. It goes without saying that in none of these families does a bipolar illness exist.

Table 7 presents material from a previous study (proportion of subtypes among unipolars and mean age of onset among subtypes) and also presents new material showing the difference between these 3 groups in patients who are over 50 years of age at onset and have a mean age at index admission of 60. (The same group appears in Tables 1 to 4.) The presence of a specific family history correlates strongly with age of onset. While there are some differences among these familially defined categories with late-onset groups, they are less significant. The sporadic depressives are less likely to be fearful, and the pure depressives are more likely to have sensorium changes. Acute onset is more frequently seen in the pure depressives and rarely seen in the sporadics. Both the pure depressives and the sporadics are more likely to have relapses in follow-up than the depression spectrum patients. The presence of endogenous symptoms does not separate the two groups, nor does the presence of a stable personality pattern. In general, clinical differences among familially defined groups are not greatly rewarding.

BIOLOGICAL FINDINGS ACCORDING TO THE FAMILIAL DIAGNOSIS

In a series of important papers, Carroll and his colleagues have investigated various aspects of the endocrinology of depression (4). He has presented the striking finding that the dexamethasone suppression test is quite frequently abnormal in "endogenous" depressive patients. Carroll found that 50% of endogenous unipolar depressives and 92% of bipolar depressives fail to suppress plasma cortisol in a normal fashion after oral administration of dexamethasone 1 to 2

TABLE 8. *Abnormal dexamethasone suppression in familially depressed groups of unipolar depressives: age of onset over 40*

Familial Diagnosis	N	N Non-Suppressors	% Non-Suppressors
Familial (PDD)	6	5	83%
Spectrum (DSD)	7	0	0%
Sporadic (SDD)	17	7	41%

$X^2 = 10.57$, d.f. $= 2$, $p < .01$

mg the night before. In addition, we have investigated 79 unipolar depressives and have separated them into the three groups, DSD, PDD, and SDD, on the basis of their first-degree family history. Sixteen bipolar depressives were also investigated (M. Schlesser, G. Winokur, and B. Sherman, *in preparation*).

The methodology, which is described more fully in another publication[1], identified individuals after hospitalization for depressive illness. All of them met Feighner's criteria for a primary depressive illness. At 11:00 p.m. they were given 1 mg of dexamethasone orally, and their blood was drawn the next morning at 8:00 a.m. Serum cortisol greater than 5 μg/100 ml was considered non-suppression, an abnormal response.

For the entire group of unipolar depressive patients, it was clear that pure depressives were most likely to fail to suppress cortisol production, while depression spectrum patients almost always showed normal suppression. The sporadics were in between the other two groups.

Data for patients who had onset over 40 is presented in Table 8. The proportions of non-suppressors for these depressive patients, which include both men and women, are similar to the total group data. The pure depressives are more likely to be non-suppressors, and the spectrum patients are more likely to be normal suppressors. If one separates the patients on the basis of being elderly, i.e., 60 years or older, at the time the test was done, the same findings and the same proportions exist (Table 9). Most familial PDD patients are non-suppressors, all DSD patients are normal suppressors, and the SDD patients are less than half non-suppressors.

TABLE 9. *Abnormal dexamethasone suppression in familially defined groups of depressives: all patients 60 or older*

Familial Diagnosis	N	Non-Suppressors N	Non-Suppressors %
Familial (PDD)	8	7	88%
Spectrum (DSD)	3	0	0%
Sporadic (SDD)	13	6	46%
Bipolar depressives	3	3	100%

[1] *Lancet* I: 739–741, April, 1979.

The appropriate way to separate depressives, therefore, may not be on the basis of age of onset or on the basis of age at index admission. The determining factor may be something that is more etiological: the family history.

DISCUSSION

We have presented evidence about the clinical appearance, personality characteristics, follow-up material, and treatment as they relate to age and age of onset. Although there are some significant differences, they are not particularly striking. The question of being elderly or not elderly may be a relatively trivial matter clinically, although it is not entirely without importance. What is most clear is that ignoring the age of the patient and looking at a familial background may predict certain kinds of biological differences between patients. Whether or not these familial subtypes and the biological differences in themselves will be particularly relevant to specific treatments is quite unknown at the present time. Presumably as treatment becomes more specific, the subtypes will come to have increasing meaning.

REFERENCES

1. Avery, D., and Winokur, G. (1976): The efficacy of electroconvulsive therapy and antidepressants in depression. *Biol. Psychiatry* 12:507–523.
2. Bartko, J. (1966): The intraclass correlation coefficient as a measure of reality. *Psychol. Rep.* 19:3–11.
3. Behar, D. (1978): Sporadic depressive disease: Symptoms, precipitants and outcome. In *Mood Disorders: The Worlds Major Public Health Problem,* edited by F. Ayd and I. Taylor., Ayd Medical Communications, Baltimore.
4. Carroll, B. (1978): Neuroendocrine procedures for the diagnosis of depression. In *Depressive Disorders.* F. K. Schattauer Verlag, Stuttgart.
5. Fleiss, J. (1973): *Statistical Methods for Rates and Proportions,* pp. 143–151. John Wiley and Sons, New York.
6. Lowry, M., VanValkenburg, C., Winokur, G., and Cadoret, R. (1978): Baseline characteristics of pure depressive disease. *Neuropsychobiology* 4:333–343.
7. Winokur, G. (1974): Genetic and clinical factors associated with course in depression. *Pharmakopsychiatr. Neuropsychopharmakol.* 7:122–126.
8. Winokur, G. (1974): The division of depressive illnesses into depression spectrum disease and pure depressive disease. *Int. Pharmacopsychiatry* 9:5–13.
9. Winokur, G., Behar, D., VanValkenburg, C., and Lowry, M. (1978): Is a familial definition of depression both feasible and valid? *J. Nerv. Ment. Dis.* 166:764–768.
10. Winokur, G., and Cadoret, R. (1975): The irrelevance of the menopause to depressive disease. In *Topics in Psychoendocrinology,* edited by E. Sachar. Grune and Stratton, New York.
11. Winokur, G., Cadoret, R., Baker, M., and Dorzab, J. (1975): Depression spectrum disease vs. pure depressive disease: Some further data. *Br. J. Psychiatry* 127:75–77.
12. Winokur, G., Morrison, J., Clancy, J. and Crowe, R. (1973): The Iowa 500: Familial and clinical families favor two kinds of depressive illness. *Comp. Psychiatry* 14:99–107.

OPEN DISCUSSION

Dr. Zubin: I would like to ask a question about your discussion of the number of symptoms present in the young and the old and your comparison of the two. You referred to this as clustering. However, clustering means a little more than that; it usually refers to the pattern across the symptoms. I wonder whether you think it might be interesting to look at the patterns that exist across the symptoms rather than the total number of symptoms.

Someone may be afraid of high places, and someone else may be drawn to them. Neither of these items by itself might be differential between contrasted groups, but the pattern of those that are drawn to high places and are also afraid of them might be differential.

Dr. Winokur: We have subjected the entire data for all ages together to a cluster analysis, as a matter of fact, and it has added nothing to what I have shown here. It does make it a little more difficult to present because it is not quite as clinical. We really have not found anything with a cluster analysis. We are also subjecting the data to a discriminate function analysis.

Our problem is that the clinical picture in the three groups really is not all that different. I think we probably have gotten to the point in depression where the percentage of advance we can expect to make on ever finer honing of the clinical picture probably will not be very great.

Dr. Robert Spitzer: Ordinarily when we define a diagnosis, we define it by the characteristics in the patient, and then we look at variables external to the diagnosis for validity, such as family history. What you have done is to include family history in the definition of some of these diagnoses, and I wonder if you can comment on what logical or conceptual problems that might impose.

Dr. Winokur: We begin by examining the clinical situation, and we assume it is not a homogeneous group. Because it is not a homogeneous group, we are looking for ways to achieve homogeneity. We have long been seeking a way to divide the depressive patients into subgroups that will cover all of the patients. If we divide them into reactive and neurotic, we do not cover all of the patients. By virtue of the tripartite separation that we presented here, we can cover 100% of the patients.

Really we are talking about a familial diagnosis rather than a necessarily clinical diagnosis. This is not the first time such methodology has been used. It has also been employed to some extent in the separation of bipolar from unipolar affective disorders.

Dr. Max Fink: You began your presentation by noting no differences in treatment response with differences in diagnosis. Did the results of the dexamethasone suppression of cortisol relate to treatment outcome?

Dr. Winokur: We have those data. But we have not yet examined that question.

155

Psychopathology in the Aged, edited by
Jonathan O. Cole and James E. Barrett.
Raven Press, New York © 1980.

The Pharmacotherapy of Depression in the Elderly: Pharmacokinetic Considerations

Robert O. Friedel

Department of Psychiatry, Medical College of Virginia, Virginia Commonwealth University, Richmond, Virginia 23298

The diagnosis of depression in the elderly presents specific problems beyond those encountered in younger patients. The pharmacological treatment of depressive disorders in aged patients is also confounded by a number of additional variables, many of which are poorly understood. These variables include the presence of concomitant medical illnesses which often also require pharmacological management, increased risk of side effects, and presumed alterations in pharmacodynamic response of aged tissues. These issues, and others, have been critically reviewed in a number of recent articles (5,6,10) and will not be dealt with in detail here. Rather, this chapter addresses the effects of age-related changes in drug absorption, distribution, metabolism, and excretion on drug plasma levels with a particular emphasis on clinical response to tricyclic antidepressants.

PHARMACOKINETIC CHANGES WITH AGING

It is generally held that CNS levels of psychotherapeutic agents which bind reversibly with their receptor sites are accurately reflected by steady state plasma levels of these substances. The level of these psychotherapeutic agents in the blood, in turn, depends on four pharmacokinetic factors: drug absorption, distribution, metabolism, and excretion (26). The qualitative relationship of these pharmacokinetic processes and drug plasma levels are shown in Fig. 1. Drugs are generally rapidly absorbed from their site of administration, usually the gastrointestinal tract, into the blood, and then rapidly distributed through a small central compartment consisting of the vascular space and the extracellular fluid of well-perfused tissue. Unbound drug is then more slowly distributed to a larger, peripheral compartment consisting of the extracellular fluid of less well-perfused tissues and all intracellular space. Most drugs have their sites of action in target tissues of the peripheral compartment where drug metabolism also takes place, mainly in the liver. Metabolites are then returned to the central compartment in a more water soluble form which permits them to be excreted, usually by the kidneys.

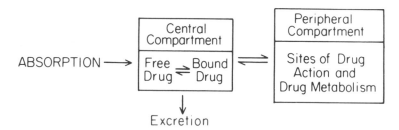

FIG. 1. Two-compartment model of drug absorption, distribution, metabolism, and excretion. (From Friedel, ref. 8.)

Quantitatively, this relationship may be expressed by the following equation which covers the condition most commonly encountered in clinical practice, i.e., a fixed dose of drug given at specific time intervals:

$$\bar{C}_\infty = 1.44 \times \frac{fD \times t_{1/2\beta}}{V_d \times \tau} \quad [1]$$

where $\bar{C}_\infty$ represents the mean steady-state concentration of the drug in the blood, fD is the absorbed dose, $t_{1/2\beta}$ is the elimination half-life, V_d is the apparent volume of distribution of the drug in the body, and τ is the dosage interval. Inspection of this equation indicates that steady state blood levels of drugs are directly proportional to the amount of drug absorbed and to the time it takes to eliminate the drug from the body, and inversely related to the volume in which the drug is distributed and to the time between doses of the same quantity. For most drugs, it is also true that, given at a fixed dose and at a dosage interval less than or equal to the elimination half-life, the steady-state condition will be achieved in approximately five half-lives ("rule of five") (11). Raising drug dosages too rapidly, therefore, may result in steady-state levels which exceed the therapeutic range and cause increased toxicity.

A number of recent articles have reviewed the age-related changes observed in the above pharmacokinetic processes (4,8,20,24). The following is a brief summary of the data available in the field at this time.

Absorption

Certain substances absorbed by active transport, such as calcium, glucose, and galactose, show a significant decline in absorption with age, while the absorption rates of other substances transported by this mechanism, such as vitamin B_{12}, thiamine, and most amino acids, are not significantly altered in older subjects. This variation is also the case with passively absorbed drugs. Diazepam and chlordiazepoxide are absorbed less well in the elderly than in the young, but paracetamol and indomethacin absorption appears to be unchanged in the elderly. Consequently, no generalization can be made regarding age-related changes in the absorption of drugs.

Distribution

Since most psychotherapeutic agents are not distributed homogeneously throughout the body (many of them are selectively concentrated in certain tissues such as brain, liver, red blood cells, fat, etc.), the two compartment, open model, shown in Fig. 1, most adequately reflects the physiological state. The relative volume of these compartments varies from one drug to another and one individual to another, and depends on the affinity of the particular drugs for the tissues involved. Therefore, changes in body composition may have significant effects on drug distribution in elderly patients. Body fat increases from 15% to 36% of body weight in men and from 33% to 48% in women as they age from 18 to 55 years (19). One would predict, then, that the volume of distribution of lipid soluble drugs in the elderly patient would be greater than in young people and that the reverse would be true for drugs with low lipid solubility. This has been found to be the case with diazepam (16) and chlordiazepoxide (21), lipid soluble drugs which show increased distribution volumes with increased age. More polar drugs, such as thyroxin and propicillin, have been shown to have age-related decreases in distribution volume (13,22). Since many drugs are also bound avidly to plasma proteins, red blood cells, and other body tissues, age-related changes affecting any of these variables may also affect drug steady-state levels (3,27).

Metabolism

The metabolism of drugs to active and inactive metabolites is generally held to be primarily under genetic control, although the effects of other drugs and exogenous substances on the enzymatic processes involved also appear to be relevant. Demethylation, oxidation, and hydroxylation, with subsequent conjugation to glucuronic acid appear to be the major metabolic conversions undergone by most psychotherapeutic agents. Clearly, age-related changes in any of these enzymatic processes might have significant effects on steady-state drug plasma levels and clinical response. For example, the well-known clinical observation that the elderly are especially sensitive to barbiturates, resulting in confusion and CNS depression, may be explained by the finding that the metabolism of amobarbital is reduced by about 50% in older subjects when compared to that of younger subjects (14). There is evidence that liver function becomes increasingly impaired over the age of 50 (23) and that elderly subjects have decreased capacities to form glucuronide and sulfate conjugates (25).

Excretion

The possible importance of altered drug metabolism on drug elimination in the elderly has already been noted. Ultimately, elimination of a drug or its metabolites from the body is achieved predominantly through the kidneys, mainly by simple glomerular filtration but also by active excretion at the tubule. Some authors contend that renal function is probably the single factor most responsible for altered drug plasma levels in an aged population (20). Renal perfusion is estimated to decrease by 40 to 50% from age 25 to 65 with a corresponding 45% drop in both glomerular filtration rate and urea clearance, and a subsequent 50% increase in blood urea nitrogen. Creatinine clearance is reduced in the elderly by about 50%, even in the absence of identifiable intrinsic renal disease. It is important to note that the impaired ability of the kidneys to excrete drugs in aged patients is not necessarily detectable by serum creatinine determinations. However, creatinine clearance may provide a more sensitive clinical indicator (17).

TRICYCLIC ANTIDEPRESSANT PLASMA LEVELS IN THE ELDERLY DEPRESSED PATIENT

With the above review serving as background, attention will now be focused on those plasma level and pharmacokinetic data which have relevance to the treatment of depression in the elderly patient.

To date, there has been only one published study correlating tricyclic antidepressant plasma levels and clinical response in elderly depressed patients (9). In this study, 15 elderly depressed patients meeting research diagnostic criteria were treated with doxepin in a single night-time dose of 50 to 300 mg. In 7 patients who demonstrated little or no improvement, the mean daily dose was 104 mg and the mean plasma concentration of doxepin and its desmethyl metabolite, desmethyldoxepin, was 60 ng/ml. In 8 patients with moderate to marked improvement, the mean daily dose was 164 mg, and the mean plasma concentration was 111 ng/ml.

This study was expanded (Table 1) to include 22 patients meeting Feighner Criteria for primary unipolar affective disorder (7) who also had at least 2 predictors of tricyclic antidepressant response (2). The age range of patients was 60 to 90, and all were living in nursing homes. Treatment began with a dose of 50 mg of doxepin at bedtime and was increased at weekly intervals until a therapeutic effect was achieved, or side effects became so severe that dosage could not be increased further, or we were hesitant to increase the dose because of the patient's age or condition in the absence of side effects, or the patient's own physician would not allow us to increase the dosage further. The patients were evaluated using Clinical Global Rating Scale and plasma levels of doxepin and its active metabolite, desmethyldoxepin, determined weekly by a mass fragmentography method (15).

There were 11 responders and 11 non-responders. In the responder group, the average daily dose of doxepin was 185 mg, and the mean plasma level was 127 ng/ml. By contrast, the non-responder group received a significantly lower mean daily dose of 80 mg ($p < 0.01$), and the mean plasma level was 49 ng/ml ($p < 0.01$). Only two patients in the non-responder group were unable

TABLE 1. *Correlation of doxepin plus desmethyldoxepin in plasma levels with clinical response in aged patients with depression*

			Unchanged or Minimal Improvement	
Patient	Sex	Age	Daily dose (mg)	Plasma conc. (ng/ml)
1.	F	82	50	36
2.	F	65	50	45
3.	F	79	50	24
4.	F	79	100	43
5.	F	67	150	47
6.	F	88	75	104
7.	F	90	50	17
8.	F	74	60	25
9.	M	72	100	77
10.	M	60	150	87
11.	M	78	50	30
		$\bar{x} = 76$	$\bar{x} = 80$	$\bar{x} = 49$

			Moderate to Marked Improvement	
Patient	Sex	Age	Daily dose (mg)	Plasma conc. (ng/ml)
12.	F	60	150	90
13.	F	65	150	131
14.	M	79	100	113
15.	F	65	150	53
16.	M	84	50	9
17.	M	68	150	124
18.	M	63	100	138
19.	F	67	300	129
20.	F	73	200	103
21.	M	68	300	168
22.	M	60	250	221
		$\bar{x} = 67$	$\bar{x} = 185$	$\bar{x} = 127$
		$t = 2.05$	$t = 3.37$	$t = 3.59$
		$p < 0.10$	$p < 0.01$	$p < 0.01$

to continue because of side effects—persistent drowsiness in both cases. Higher doses, which might have brought a response, were not used in the remaining nine patients because of our concern early in the study about causing toxic side effects. These concerns may have been age-dependent: the non-responders were on the average nine years older than the responders, and that may have resulted in increased caution by all physicians involved.

These data suggest that plasma levels of doxepin and desmethyldoxepin are related to clinical response in elderly subjects suffering from significant depression. In addition, the obvious disparity between doxepin dosage and steady-state plasma levels in a number of subjects (Table 1) indicates significant inter-patient variability in the above pharmacokinetic processes and suggests that improved clinical outcome could be achieved by monitoring drug plasma levels.

There is evidence which suggests that elderly subjects handle tricyclic antidepressants differently than younger ones. Nies et al., (18) have pointed out that depressed geriatric patients frequently exhibit toxic responses to tricyclic antidepressants such as postural hypotension, urinary retention, tachycardia, congestive heart failure, and organic confusional mental states. They report data indicating that elderly patients treated with imipramine or amitriptyline developed higher steady-state plasma levels of imipramine, desipramine, and amitriptyline than younger patients. Interestingly, elderly patients treated with amitriptyline did not achieve steady-state plasma levels of nortriptyline any higher than younger patients. This suggests that the metabolism and excretion of nortriptyline are handled differently by elderly subjects than are the metabolism and excretion of the other monomethylated tricyclic antidepressant studied, desipramine.

Further evidence that desipramine metabolism and/or excretion are impaired with aging also exists. Friedel and co-workers have recently completed a clinical trial in which plasma levels of desipramine were correlated with clinical outcome in 26 depressed outpatients (11). DMI plasma levels showed a positive correlation with age which just fell short of achieving statistical significance after week 2 ($p = 0.059$) and week 3 ($p = 0.086$). There is additional data supporting the findings of Nies et al. (18) that nortriptyline metabolism is unaffected by age (1). This suggests that in elderly depressed patients, nortriptyline may be a safer tricyclic antidepressant than amitriptyline, imipramine, or desipramine, because accumulation of toxic plasma levels of nortriptyline would be less likely.

CONCLUSION

Unfortunately, there is a paucity of data relating clinical response and plasma levels of tricyclic antidepressants in the elderly depressed patient. Moreover, there is little information regarding age-related changes in the absorption, distribution, metabolism, and excretion of tricyclic antidepressants. However, the meager data which do exist appear to support the contention that plasma levels of tricyclic antidepressants in elderly subjects are related to clinical response, and that aging affects a number of pharmacokinetic processes important in handling at least some tricyclic antidepressants. It may be concluded, then, that additional clinical studies in this field will enable us to treat with greater efficacy and less risk that very large population of geriatric patients who suffer from major depressive disorders.

REFERENCES

1. Åsberg, M., Cronholm, B., Sjöqvist, F., and Tuck, D. (1971): Relationship between plasma levels and therapeutic effect of nortriptyline, *Br. Med. J.,* 3:331–334.
2. Bielski, R. J., and Friedel, R. O. (1976): Prediction of tricyclic antidepressant response: A critical review. *Arch. Gen. Psychiatry,* 33:1479–1489.
3. Chan, K., Kendall, M. J., Mitchard, M., Wells, W. D. E., and Vickers, M. D. (1975): The effect of aging on plasma pethidine concentration. *Br. J. Clin. Pharmacol.,* 2:297–302.

4. Crooks, J., O'Malley, K., and Stevenson, I. H. (1976): Pharmacokinetics in the elderly. *Clin. Pharmacokin.*, 1:280–296.
5. Domino, E. F., Dren, A. T., and Giardina, W. J. (1978): Biochemical and neurotransmitter changes in the aging brain. In *Psychopharmacology: A Generation of Progress*, edited by M. A. Lipton, A. DiMascio, and K. F. Killam. Raven Press, New York.
6. Epstein, L. J. (1978): Anxiolytics, Antidepressants, and Neuroleptics in the Treatment of Geriatric Patients. In *Psychopharmacology: A Generation of Progress*, edited by M. A. Lipton, A. DiMascio, and K. F. Killam. Raven Press, New York.
7. Feighner, J. P., Robins, E., Guze, S. B., Woodruff, R. A., Jr., Winokur, G., and Munoz, R. (1972): Diagnostic criteria for use in psychiatric research. *Arch. Gen. Psychiatry*, 26:57–63.
8. Friedel, R. O. (1978): Pharmacokinetics in the geropsychiatric patient. In *Psychopharmacology: A Generation of Progress*, edited by M. A. Lipton, A. DiMascio, and K. F. Killam. Raven Press, New York.
9. Friedel, R. O., and Raskind, M. A. (1975): Relationship of blood levels of Sinequan to clinical effects in the treatment of depression in aged patients. In *Sinequan: A Monograph of Recent Clinical Studies*, edited by J. Mendels. Excerpta Medica, Princeton.
10. Friedel, R. O., and Raskind, M. A. (1977): Psychopharmacology of Aging. In *Special Review of Experimental Aging Research: Progress in Biology*, edited by M. F. Elias, B. E. Eleftherion, and P. K. Elias. E. A. R., Inc., Bar Harbor, Maine.
11. Friedel, R. O., Veith, R. C., Bloom, V., and Bielski, R. J. (1979): Desipramine plasma levels and clinical response in depressed outpatients. *Commun. Psychopharmacol.*, 3:81–87.
12. Greenblatt, D. J., Shader, R. I., Frank, K., and Koch-Weser, J. (1975): Pharmacokinetics of intravenous chlordiazepoxide. *Clin. Pharmacol. Ther.*, 17:235.
13. Gregerman, R. I., Gaffney, G. W., and Shock, N. W. (1962): Thyroxine turnover in enthyroid man, with special reference to changes with age. *J. Clin. Invest.*, 41:2065–2074.
14. Irvine, R. E., Grove, J., Toseland, P. A., and Trounce, J. R. (1974): The effect of age on the hydroxylation of amylobarbitone sodium in man. *Br. J. Clin. Pharmacol.*, 1:41–43.
15. Jenkins, R. G., and Friedel, R. O. (1978): Analysis of tricyclic antidepressants in human plasma by GC/CIMS with selected ion monitoring. *J. Pharm. Sci.*, 67:17–23.
16. Klotz, U., Avant, G. R., Hoyumpa, A., Schenker, S., and Wilkinson, G. R. (1975): The effects of age and liver disease on the disposition and elimination of diazepam in adult man. *J. Clin. Invest.*, 55:347–359.
17. Mølholm-Hansen, J., Kampmann, J., and Laursen, H. (1970): Renal excretion of drugs in the elderly. *Lancet*, 1:1170.
18. Nies, A., Robinson, D. S., Friedman, M. J., Green, R., Cooper, T. B., Ravaris, C. L., and Ives, J. O. (1977): Relationship between age and tricyclic antidepressant plasma levels. *Am. J. Psychiatry*, 134:790–793.
19. Novak, L. P. (1972): Aging, total body potassium, fat free mass and cell mass in males and females between the ages 18 and 85 years. *J. Gerontol.*, 27:438–443.
20. Richey, D. P., and Bender, A. D. (1977): Pharmacokinetic consequences of aging. *Annu. Rev. Pharmacol. Toxicol.*, 17:49–65.
21. Shader, R. I., Greenblatt, D. J., Harmatz, J. S., Frank, K., and Koch-Weser, J. (1977): Absorption and disposition of chlordiazepoxide in young and elderly male volunteers. *J. Clin. Pharmacol.*, 17:709–718.
22. Simon, C., Malerczyk, V., and Müller, G. (1972): Zur Pharmacokinetik von Propicillin bei Geriatrischen Patienten im Vergleich zu jungeren Erwachsenen. *Dtsch. Med. Wochenschr.*, 97:1999–2003.
23. Thompson, E. N., and Williams, R. (1965): Effect of age on liver function with particular reference to bromosulphalein excretion. *Gut*, 6:266–269.
24. Triggs, E. J., and Nation, R. L. (1975): Pharmacokinetics in the aged: A review. *J. Pharmacokinet. Biopharm.*, 3:387–418.
25. Triggs, E. J., Nation, R. L., Long, A., and Ashley, J. J. (1975): Pharmacokinetics in the elderly. *Eur. J. Clin. Pharmacol.*, 8:55–62.
26. Vesell, E. S. (1974): Factors causing interindividual variations of drug concentrations in blood. *Clin. Pharmacol. Ther.*, 16(1):135–148.
27. Wallace, S., Whiting, B., and Runcie, J. (1976): Factors affecting drug binding in plasma of elderly patients. *Br. J. Clin. Pharmacol.*, 3:327–330.

OPEN DISCUSSION

Dr. Gershon: I have a simple clinical question. I have observed it is very difficult to achieve therapeutic plasma levels in some old persons because they seem to be much more sensitive to side effects such as hypertension, or angina, or Parkinson-like tremors from depressants. Can you comment on that, please?

Dr. Friedel: The only drug that we have attempted to use in elderly patients at high dosages is doxepin. As you saw from our data, we were probably overcautious in many of those patients. We increased the dosage by 50 mg a week, which I believe minimized the frequency and severity of the side effects we observed.

Dr. William Corrier: Did you notice a particularly higher correlation between blood level and age at any age range?

Dr. Friedel: We haven't analyzed our data in this way yet. It will be interesting to see if such a correlation exists with doxepin.

Psychopathology in the Aged, edited by
Jonathan O. Cole and James E. Barrett.
Raven Press, New York © 1980.

A Placebo-Controlled Double-blind Study of Imipramine and Trazodone in Geriatric Depression

R. Gerner, W. Estabrook, J. Steuer, L. Waltuch, P. Kakkar, and
L. Jarvik

*The University of California at Los Angeles Neuropsychiatric Institute and The Brentwood
Veterans Administration Hospital, Los Angeles, California 90024*

Depression is one of the most common diagnoses in the age group above 60. Its frequency has been estimated to range from a low of 2% or 3% (30) to a high of 65% (42). Gianturco and Busse (25) reported in their 20 year study that the proportion of apparently normal elderly individuals rated depressed remained relatively constant at 20% to 25%, and yet the high risk for depressions in this age group was clearly evident, with only 30% of subjects not having had a depressive episode by the time of their last evaluation. Since there was no increase in the frequency of depression from the seventh to the tenth decade, the authors concluded that factors other than simple chronological age determine the occurrence of depressive episodes. The tricyclic antidepressants which constitute the preferred method of treatment in this age group (3,19,21,24) are generally accepted as useful for the mild and moderate depressions seen in outpatients, although their utility in the treatment of psychotic depressions is controversial for any age (13,27,44).

The literature on pharmacotherapy of depression in geriatric patients is minimal. For example, Davis' (14) review of tricyclic antidepressants summarizing 65 double-blind studies contains no age breakdown. Imipramine was judged more effective than placebo in 26 out of 38 studies and equal to or less effective than placebo in the other 12, while amitriptyline was more effective than placebo in 9 of 11 studies. In the remaining 14 studies, the tricyclic was always superior to placebo. The overall improvement on imipramine was approximately 70% compared to 39% on placebo. Although the utility of tricyclic antidepressants in the geriatric age group has not been specifically examined, imipramine has been the most widely studied tricyclic antidepressant, and, generally, the results have been favorable, albeit in open trials (49). Fryer and Timberlake (22), however, failed to find a difference between imipramine and placebo in 31 depressed inpatients with chronic physical disease. By contrast, Zung and his colleagues (53) reported that imipramine was significantly better than placebo in a study of geriatric outpatients, but not quite as effective as Gerovital, a drug which, in the hands of others, was indistinguishable from placebo in depressed older outpatients (40).

Doxepin has been reported to be useful in geriatric nursing home patients (9) and equivalent in efficacy to amitriptyline in depressed adults with an average age of 50 (29). The potency of doxepin has been questioned by Hollister (33), but Friedel's (19) preliminary data suggest efficacy in geriatric patients with memory loss. The major factors in thwarting effective treatment of depression in the geriatric age group have been the frequency and severity of side effects caused by the current antidepressant drugs and the intolerance to them displayed by the elderly.

Many of the side effects of the currently available tricyclic antidepressants fall into anticholinergic and cardiovascular categories. The former can cause or aggravate the following: sedation, acute narrow-angle glaucoma, prostatic hypertrophy, decreased bowel motility, xerostomia, and interference with visual accommodation. The latter may increase cardiac conduction time, predisposing the patient to arrhythmias, and cause both orthostatic and sustained hypotension which might precipitate falls and injuries (35,51). Since with advancing age, liver metabolism and plasma protein binding are decreased, higher tricyclic plasma levels may be reached with a given oral dose in older than in younger adults (28). Thus, older individuals may respond to relatively lower doses. Unfortunately, some side effects (such as hypotension) may not be linearly related to dose and may reach intolerable levels at doses which are therapeutically only minimally effective (Glassman, *personal communication,* 1979). Effective antidepressants with few side effects are therefore especially needed for the older age groups.

Trazodone, the first triazolo-pyridine used therapeutically, has been reported to be an effective antidepressant agent with relatively few side effects. It differs both in actions (Table 1) and in structure (Fig. 1) from the current antidepressants

TABLE 1. *Trazodone*[a] *(a triazolo-pyridine)*

—similar to chlorimipramine: inhibits fenfluramine depletion of brain 5-HT
—central serotonin agonist
—peripheral serotonin antagonist (rat stomach, bronchi); decreases response to painful stimuli.
—does not potentiate NE or L-DOPA
—lacks anti-reserpine effect
—non-anticataleptic
—no MAO inhibition
—non-cataleptogenic
—does not antagonize amphetamine or apomorphine
—no cholinergic effects

Oral LD_{50}: Rats 434–700 mg/kg
             Dogs 500 mg/kg
Half-life: Rats, 6 hrs; humans, excreted by 24 hrs

[a] Ban and Silvestrini (5).

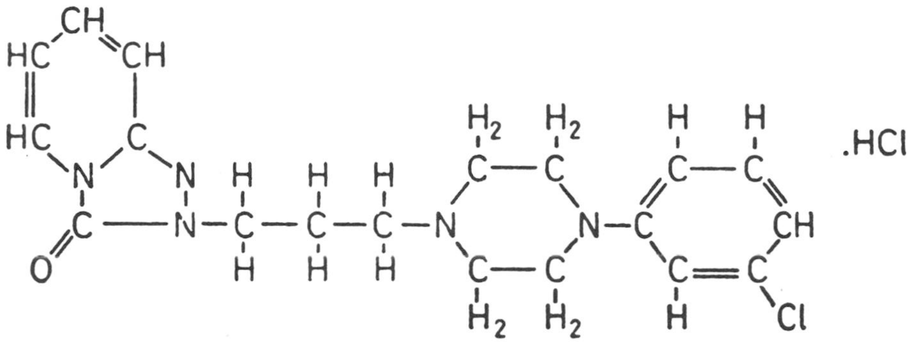

FIG. 1. Structure of trazodone.

(tricyclics, stimulants, and monoamine oxidase inhibitors) as well as the neuroleptics. Although its methods of action *in vivo* have not yet been fully elucidated, Garattini (23) proposed that trazodone, like the antidepressants currently in use, may be a presynaptic reuptake blocker which is relatively specific for serotonin. Angellucci and Bolle (2) have suggested that trazodone may either work by directly inhibiting the release of serotonin, thereby initiating positive feedback to stimulate serotonin synthesis, or it may act by stimulating the serotonin postsynaptic receptor as an agonist, with consequent increased negative feedback to the presynaptic neuron, resulting in a decreased release and turnover of serotonin. These two theories are, of course, contradictory and point to our ignorance regarding the mechanism of action of trazodone.

Trazodone has had only one previous trial in geriatric patients (39): an uncontrolled study in 10 patients with organic brain syndrome. Over the 12 weeks of that trial, depression, anxiety, and motor retardation were reported to decrease. The results of 11 double-blind studies of trazodone in adults indicate that trazodone is superior to placebo and roughly equivalent in efficacy to imipramine, amitriptyline, and desipramine (Table 2). Since many of these reports lack detailed information regarding their methodologies, the results must be viewed with caution. Interestingly, both retarded and anxious depressives have been reported to preferentially respond to trazodone compared to control medications, even though one would predict that, as a serotonergic drug, trazodone would have a preferential effect on agitated depressions, while imipramine, a relatively more noradrenergic drug would prove more beneficial in retarded depression (6,38,47).

Reported side effects of trazodone are not unlike those of the tricyclics in quality, but most authors agree that they occur less frequently. They include: drowsiness, hypersomnia, confusion, impulsiveness, anxiety, dizziness, headaches, tremor, tachycardia, hyper- and hypotension, dry mouth, nausea, constipation, and diarrhea.

The previous reports that trazodone was an effective antidepressant drug with few side effects led to the double-blind study reported below, comparing

TABLE 2. *Trials with trazodone for depression*

Reference	N	Conditions	Results
Geriatric:			
Nair et al. (38)	10 (age 65–84)	100 mg, 12 wks, open	OBS patients improved on depression, anxiety, and motor retardation
Adult:			
Ban et al. (4)	20	Traz vs AMI 25–300 mg open	equivalent
Pariante (40)	18	I.V. 100–200 mg	12 complete, 4 partial recovery
Agnoli et al. (1)	30	Traz vs DMI 500 mg 125 mg	equivalent; Traz better for symptoms of anxiety
Cassano et al. (8)	31	Traz vs IMI 350–800 mg 100–150 mg	IMI somewhat better Traz greater side effects
De Gregorio and Dionisio (15)	37	Traz vs IMI 500 mg 250 mg	equivalent, 60% improved
Vinci (49)	33	Traz vs AMI 100–600 mg	equivalent, 75% improved
Pariante (40)	17	Traz vs IMI 150–600 mg	equivalent, 70% improved
Cioffi et al. (11)	12	Traz vs IMI 150–600 mg	equivalent, 40% improved
Di Giuseppe (16)	11	Traz vs IMI 300 mg	equivalent, 80% improved
Cianchetti (10)	37	Traz vs AMI 50–400 mg	equivalent, 50% improved
Pozzi et al. (42)	17	Traz vs Placebo 300 mg	50% improved

Traz = trazodone; IMI = imipramine; AMI = amitriptyline; DMI = desipramine

trazodone with placebo and a standard tricyclic (imipramine) in depressed geriatric outpatients.

METHODS

Thirty-seven female and 23 male outpatients 60 years of age and older (mean age 68.4 years, range 60–90 years), with a diagnosis of unipolar depression by the Research Diagnostic Criteria (48) and with a Hamilton Depression Score of at least 18 were included in this study. Patients were obtained through referral from UCLA Hospital and Clinics and the medical community of the surrounding area as well as through self-referrals. The patients were largely middle- and upper-class as is the surrounding community from which they were drawn. Most of the patients were retired, and virtually all had stable living situations.

Once screened for the diagnosis and degree of depression, patients gave written, informed consent, had thorough physical examinations and were accepted into the study, if not excluded because of significant hepatic, renal, cardiovascular, neurological, or other medical problems, or use of prescribed or other drugs (including alcohol). After at least a 7 day washout period for psychotropic or CNS active medications, patients were randomly and blindly assigned to 1 of the 3 medication regimens and were rated on a series of scales prior to starting any medication, as well as at weeks 1, 2, 3, and 4 after medication began, usually by the same psychiatrist who had seen the patient initially (to eliminate inter-rater variation). Weekly ratings included the Hamilton Depression Scale, the Hamilton Anxiety Scale, the self-rated Beck Depression Scale, the Clinical Global Impression Scale, and the Treatment Emergent Symptoms Scale (TESS) (31). In order to assess treatment effects on cognition, patients were tested at week 0 and again at week 4 with the Hooper Visual Integration Test (34), the Vocabulary, Similarities, Digit Span, and Digit Symbol Substitution subtests of the Wechsler Adult Intelligence Scale (WAIS) (52), and the Guild Memory Scale (26). The Guild yields 5 subscores, while the Hooper provides a single score, as do each of the 5 WAIS subtests. Thus, 11 separate psychometric scores were obtained. All analyses were split-plot analyses of covariance, except where indicated. All medications were given in identical capsules: trazodone 50 mg, imipramine 25 mg, and placebo (lactose). Patients initially took 2 capsules at bedtime, and the dose was increased at the rate of 1 capsule per day until 8 capsules were reached, except that the dose could be adjusted depending on therapeutic response and/or side effects. In addition to being seen by a psychiatrist weekly, the patients were contacted by telephone once or twice weekly by a research nurse who answered questions and discussed side effects. Patients were also seen weekly by an internist who obtained a cardiogram as well as blood for hematological tests (complete blood count, SMA-12, SMA-6, T-3, and T-4 were obtained at baseline and at week 4). None of the patients were in psychotherapy.

RESULTS

Thirty-four (13 men and 21 women) of the original 60 patients completed the 4 week study. During the fourth week, the average dose was 145 mg per day of imipramine and 305 mg of trazodone per day. Both active medication groups received significantly fewer pills than the placebo group, suggesting that medication adjustments in the active groups reflected either therapeutic or side effects. (See Table 3 for number of pills received during the final week of study.)

Hamilton Depression Scale

Figure 2 shows the course of the Hamilton Depression ratings over the course of the study. An analysis of covariance on differences between baseline and each time interval revealed significant effects of both active drugs ($p = .0016$).

TABLE 3. *Number of pills/day during weeks 3—4*

Treatment	Pills/day	Dosage
Imipramine	5.8 ± .7	(25 mg/pill)
Trazodone	6.1 ± .5	(50 mg/pill)
Placebo	7.8 ± .2	

The average dosage during the last week of the trial was significantly greater for the placebo group (p < .01) than both active medication groups.

From baseline to end of study, trazodone and imipramine were both significantly better than placebo ($p = .0015$ and $p = .0023$, respectively). This difference was evident as early as week 1 for imipramine versus placebo ($p < .01$) and was significant for both drugs by week 2 (imipramine and trazodone, $p < .002$). There were no significant differences between imipramine and trazodone at any of the time points.

In order to determine whether there was a differential response to the two drugs in terms of the retardation–agitation axis, an analysis of covariance was done for the anxiety-somatization and retardation subscales of the Hamilton,

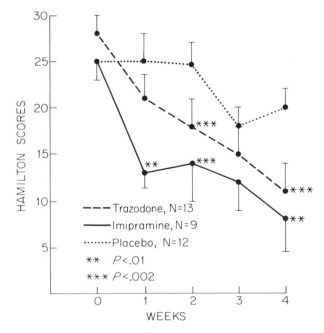

FIG. 2. Both trazodone and imipramine were significantly better than placebo over the course of the 4-week trial ($p = .0015$ and .0023, respectively). Response differences compared to placebo occurred at week 1 in the imipramine group ($p < .01$), and for both drugs at week 2 ($p < .002$).

and a ratio was calculated for those scores for each week of treatment. Addition-
ally, the total Hamilton Anxiety Scale, and its somatic and psychic subscales
were analyzed weekly. When baseline agitation scores were compared, there
was a trend for completors ($p = .07$) and women ($p = .08$) to have higher
baseline agitation scores. Over the course of the study, the agitation-retardation
and anxiety subscale scores generally paralleled the total Hamilton Depression
score.

At week 4, imipramine produced a significant reduction in the Hamilton
Agitation Subscale ($p = .023$), the total Hamilton Anxiety Scale ($p = .0043$),
and its psychic anxiety subscale ($p = .011$). No significant changes were found
for the other subscales or medication groups.

Beck Self-Rating Inventory

There was overall improvement on the Beck Depression scale for the three
treatment groups as a whole ($p < .005$) (Fig. 3). When weeks 0 and 4 were
compared by paired *t*-test, only the trazodone and imipramine groups showed
significant decreases in scores ($p < .01$ and $p < .05$, respectively).

Age and Sex Differences

There was a trend for an interaction of sex with treatment that favored men
in all conditions ($p < .10$) and was significant at week 4 ($p < .05$) in the two
active medication groups. There was no overall effect of age on outcome for

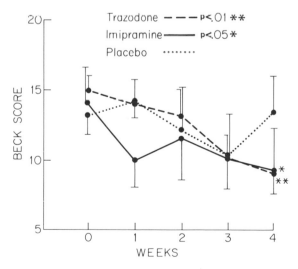

FIG. 3. Significant differences were found by paired *t*-test for Beck self ratings by comparing
weeks 0 and 4 for the trazodone ($p < .01$) and imipramine ($p < .05$) groups but not for the
placebo group.

the group as a whole, although women tended ($p < .10$) to have a positive correlation of age with outcome. When the separate treatment groups were considered, the only significant age and sex correlation found was for women on trazodone; they had a positive correlation of response with age ($p < .05$).

Psychological Tests

In the 11 separate analyses, no significant treatment effects were found. Therefore, within the limited range of depression represented in this sample, there did not appear to be any relationship between improvement of depressive symptoms (as measured by the Hamilton Depression Scale) and scores on cognitive tests, nor did it appear that cognitive performance was either enhanced or diminished by the active medications utilized in this study.

Clinical Global Impression Scale

All three groups showed significant improvement from week 0 to week 4 by paired t-test. However, no significant differences were apparent between the groups at week 4.

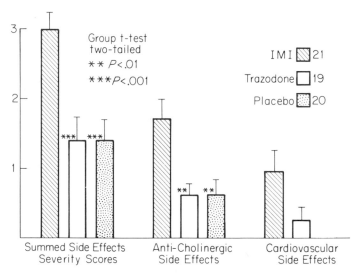

FIG. 4. Side effects were rated globally by one of the authors (R.G.) on the TESS in a blind manner for all patients. Severity scores from the TESS were rated from mild (1) to severe (3) and were summed for each patient to obtain an overall side effects score. Side effects rated as anticholinergic included tremor, impotence, dry mouth, blurred vision, and constipation; while side effects rated as cardiovascular included hypo- and hypertension, tachycardia/palpitations, syncope/dizziness, arrhythmias, and angina. Only side effects thought to have been drug related at a 50% or greater level of confidence were used. Groups were compared by t-test. Imipramine had more overall side effects ($p < .001$) than trazodone or placebo, the latter two being equivalent. Similarly, rated anticholinergic side effects were equivalent for trazodone and placebo and were significantly greater for imipramine ($p < .01$). Imipramine also had significantly more cardiovascular side effects than did placebo ($p < .01$).

Non-Completors

There was a large dropout rate in all treatment groups; 60% of the imipramine group and 30% of the placebo and trazodone groups failed to complete the study. One explanation may be found in the incidence of side effects, since imipramine had significantly more cumulative side effects than either placebo or trazodone. The last two appeared to be equivalent in terms of total side effects (Fig. 4). According to the TESS, anticholinergic effects were greater for imipramine than for placebo or trazodone, the last two being equivalent. Rated cardiovascular side effects were also significantly greater in the imipramine group than in the placebo group, the trazodone group falling in between.

Actual side effects in patients who dropped out and the number of patients affected were as follows: *trazodone*—hypotension 2, confusion 2, depression 2, pruritis 1, edema 1, drowsiness 1; *imipramine*—hypotension 6, insomnia 3, ataxia 3, constipation 2, angina 1, atrial fibrillation 1, confusion 1; *placebo*—upset stomach 4, constipation 2, edema 1. No hematological indices were significantly affected by either of the drug treatments.

DISCUSSION

It appears that trazodone was as effective an antidepressant as imipramine for our group of mild to moderately depressed, relatively healthy patients 60 years of age and over and that no significant antidepressant effect was observed for the placebo group. Although it is common clinical lore that improvement on tricyclics takes about 3 weeks (12), the marked improvement seen here on both medications in the first 2 weeks is similar to that reported by Haskell et al. (32). The suggestion that men may have responded better than women to these antidepressants is reminiscent of that made by Salzman and colleagues (46), who found that methylphenidate had preferential antidepressant effects in women but not in men. Differential response to antidepressants by sex has been reviewed by Raskin (45) who concluded that many factors might account for apparent sex differences which should be interpreted with care. We did not find that the serotonergic drug, trazodone, compared to the relatively more noradrenergic drug, imipramine, produced greater improvement in agitated as compared to retarded depressed patients. In contrast to our expectations, imipramine significantly reduced scores on agitation and anxiety scales, while trazodone had no significant effect on the agitation-retardation axis. Similarly, La Pierre and Butter (36) reported greater efficacy of the noradrenergic antidepressant, maprotiline, compared to imipramine on agitated depressives.

The improvement in the Beck Depression Scale over the course of the 4 week study, regardless of treatment condition, is consistent with the findings by Salzman et al. (46) that older patients tend to minimize negative self-report items, and it may explain the lack of significant differences on this scale between active drugs and placebo. However, the change from baseline to week 4 was significant for both active medications and not for placebo, suggesting that these self-ratings do reflect the therapeutic efficacy of the specific drugs. If a Beck Depression score of 6 or less is taken as falling within the normal range, then, 5 of the trazodone group, 4 of the imipramine group, and only 2 of the placebo group reached this level, representing 38%, 44%, and 17%, respectively, of the completors in each group (Table 4). This study demonstrates that subjective improvement does occur in response to antidepressant medication in older adults, as it does in younger adults. Similarly, 38%, 56%, and 8% of the trazodone, imipramine and placebo groups, respectively, improved sufficiently to fall within the normal range according to the psychiatrist's rating (Hamilton score of 6 or less).

A striking finding in the study was the difference in side effects among the three treatments. Imipramine, but not trazodone, showed significantly greater anticholinergic and cardiovascular side effects than did placebo, probably accounting for the relatively high dropout rate in the imipramine group and suggesting that many individuals in this age group who might respond to antidepressant treatment have no opportunity to do so when given medications with a high frequency of undesirable side effects. The difference in cardiovascular side effects has also been found in animal studies (37). This difference stands out sharply when dropouts as well as completors are considered in assessing treatment effects. Such a procedure permits generalization to the clinical population-at-large where one has to take into account patients who are unable to tolerate the full course of therapy, since these patients do not fare any better than those who fail to respond to a full course of treatment.

When improvement is defined as decrease of 30% or greater from the baseline Hamilton depression score, 45% of the patients who started on trazodone, 38% of those on imipramine, and 21% of those on placebo improved. When successful response is delineated by a Hamilton score of 6 or less, then 25%, 24%, and 5%, respectively, of those starting on trazodone, imipramine, and placebo fall into the category of successful responders. Corresponding percentages for the

TABLE 4. *Percent improved at week 4 according to various criteria of improvement for patients on trazodone (T), imipramine (I), and placebo (P)*

	Percent of starters			Percent of completors		
	T	I	P	T	I	P
Hamilton Depression ≥ 30% decrease at week 4	45	38	21	69	88	33
Hamilton Depression ≤ 6 at week 4	25	24	5	38	56	8
Beck Depression ≤ 6 at week 4	25	19	11	38	44	17

self-ratings of depression (Beck scores of 6 or less) were 25%, 19%, and 11%, respectively (Table 4).

It would appear important, therefore, to: (a) be supportive of patients and urge them to continue medication; (b) choose medications known to have the fewest dysphoric effects; and (c) when possible, systemically treat side effects, e.g., urecholine for anticholinergic (17) and propranolol for sympathomimetic symptoms (7). Great caution, however, is indicated, since many depressed patients have side effects on placebo that mimic those seen on active medication (especially anticholinergic effects) and which may be mistaken by both patients and physicians for active drug effects. Presumably, these "placebo" side effects have a significant negative influence on compliance.

Regardless of the criterion measure specifying successful treatment, a far greater proportion of patients responded successfully to the active medications than to placebo, response rates varying from 25% to 69% for trazodone, 19% to 88% for imipramine and 5% to 33% for placebo.

The lack of improvement on tests of cognitive function with either of the medications suggests that, in general, response to antidepressants by geriatric patients is unlikely to be caused by a reversal of mild organicity. Indeed, improvement, when it is seen, most likely represents effective treatment of a significant depression.

CONCLUSIONS

We conclude from this study of 60 depressed outpatients that trazodone was essentially equivalent to imipramine as an antidepressant. Trazodone was not more efficacious than imipramine in patients who were able to tolerate the latter drug, nor was it more rapid in onset, nor did it show preferential effects in agitated as compared to retarded depressions. However, trazodone was much better tolerated than imipramine because of fewer side effects and may, therefore, possess an advantage for antidepressant treatment of certain patients in the older age group.

ACKNOWLEDGMENT

The assistance of Ms. J. Turner and Ms. P. Motoike is much appreciated.

Medications were furnished by Mead-Johnson Pharmaceutical Division, Evansville, Indiana 47721.

REFERENCES

1. Agnoli, A., Piccione, M., Casacchia, M., and Fazio, C. (1974): Trazodone versus desipramine: A double-blind study on the rapidity of the antidepressant effect. In: *Trazodone: Modern Problems of Pharmacopsychiatry, Vol. IX,* edited by T. A. Ban and B. Silvestrini, pp. 190–198. S. Karger, Basel.

2. Angellucci, L., and Bolle, P. (1974): Considerations on biochemical studies with trazodone. In: *Trazodone: Modern Problems of Pharmacopsychiatry, Vol. IX*, edited by T. A. Ban and B. Silvestrini, pp. 65–75. S. Karger, Basel.
3. Ban, T. A. (1978): Treatment of depressed geriatric patients. *Am. J. Psychother.*, 27:93–104.
4. Ban, T. A., Amin, M., Nair, N., and Engelsman, F. (1974): Comprehensive clinical studies of trazodone in Canada. In: *Trazodone: Modern Problems of Pharmacopsychiatry, Vol. IX*, edited by T. A. Ban and B. Silvestrini, pp. 110–126. S. Karger, Basel.
5. Ban, T. A., and Silvestrini, B. (1974): *Trazodone: Modern Problems of Pharmacopsychiatry, Vol. IX*, edited by T. A. Ban and B. Silvestrini. S. Karger, Basel.
6. Beckman, H., and Goodwin, F. K. (1975): Antidepressant response to tricyclics and urinary MHPG in unipolar patients. *Arch. Gen. Psychiatry*, 32:17–21.
7. Benkert, O. (1978): Indikationen für Beta-Rezeptorenblocker in der Psychiatrie. *Internist*, 19:542–546.
8. Cassano, G. B., Castrogiovanni, P., and Conti, L. (1974): Clinical evaluation of trazodone in the treatment of depression. In: *Trazodone: Modern Problems of Pharmacopsychiatry, Vol. IX*, edited by T. A. Ban and B. Silvestrini, pp. 199–204. S. Karger, Basel.
9. Chien, C., Stotsky, B. A., and Cole, J. O. (1973): Psychiatric treatment for nursing home patients: Drug, alcohol, and milieu. *Am. J. Psychiatry*, 130:543–548.
10. Cianchetti, C., and Gianotti, G. (1968): Studio clinico controllato dell'attivita antidepressiva e ansiolitica di un nuovo psicofarmaco: 1'AF 1161. *Gazetta Internazionale di Medicina e chirurgia*, 73.
11. Cioffi, F., Mattioli, G., Pozzi, O., and Rinaldi, F. (1969): Ulteriori dati sull'azione antidepressiva di un nuovo psicofarmaco: 1'AF 1161. *Rassegna Internazionale di Clinica e Terapia*, 49.
12. Cole, J. O., and Davis, J. M. (1967): Antidepressant drugs. In: *Comprehensive Textbook of Psychiatry*, edited by A. M. Freedman and H. I. Kaplan, p. 267. Williams & Wilkins, Baltimore.
13. Davidson, J. R. T., McLeon, M. N., Kurland, A. A., and White, H. L. (1977): Antidepressant drug therapy in psychotic depression. *Br. J. Psychiatry*, 131:493–496.
14. Davis, J. M. (1976): Tricyclic antidepressants. In: *Drug Treatment of Mental Disorders*, edited by L. L. Simpson. Raven Press, New York.
15. DeGregorio, M., and Dionisio, A. (1971): Controlled clinical study of a new antidepressant (Trazodone). *Panminerva Med.*, 13:27–30.
16. Di Giuseppe, B., and Cesarini, F. (1969): Un nuovo psicofarmaco nella terapia delle depressioni. *La Clinica Neuropsichiatrica*, 6.
17. Everett, H. C. (1975): The use of bethanechol chloride with tricyclic antidepressants. *Am. J. Psychiatry*, 132:1202–1204.
18. Fabre, L., Mclendon, D., and Gainey, A. (1979): Trazodone efficacy in depression: a double-blind comparison with imipramine and placebo in day-hospital type patients. *Curr. Ther. Res.*, 25:827–834.
19. Fann, W. E. (1976): Pharmacotherapy in older depressed patients. *J. Gerontol.*, 31:304–310.
20. Friedel, R. O. (1975): Relationship of blood levels of sinequan to clinical effects in the treatment of depression in aged patients. In: *Sinequan: A Monograph of Recent Clinical Studies*, edited by J. Mendels, pp. 51–53.
21. Friedel, R. O. (1978): Pharmacokinetics in the geropsychiatric patient. In: *Psychopharmacology: A Generation of Progress*, edited by M. A. Lipton, A. DiMascio and K. F. Killman, pp. 1499–1506. Raven Press, New York.
22. Fryer, D. G., and Timberlake, W. H. (1963): A trial of imipramine (Tofranil) in depressed patients with chronic physical disease. *J. Chronic Dis.*, 16:173–178.
23. Garattini, S. (1974): Biochemical studies with trazodone: A new psychoactive drug. In: *Trazodone: Modern Problems of Pharmacopsychiatry, Vol. IX*, edited by T. A. Ban and B. Silvestrini, pp. 29–46. S. Karger, Basel.
24. Gerner, R. H. (1979): Depression in the elderly. In: *Psychopathology of Aging*, edited by O. Kaplan, pp. 97–148. Academic Press, New York.
25. Gianturco, D. P., and Busse, E. W. (1978): Psychiatric problems encountered during a long-term study of normal aging volunteers. In: *Studies in Geriatric Psychiatry*, edited by A. D. Isaacs and F. Post. John Wiley, New York.
26. Gilbert, J., Levee, R., and Catalano, S. (1974): Guild Memory Test Manual. Unico National Mental Health Research Foundation, Passaic, New Jersey.
27. Glassman, A. H., Kantor, S. J., and Shostak, M. (1975): Depression, delusions, and drug response. *Am. J. Psychiatry*, 132:716–719.

28. Greenblatt, D., and Shader, R. (1979): Pharmacokinetics in old age: Principles and problems of assessment. In: *Pharmacology of the Aged,* edited by L. F. Jarvik and D. Greenblatt. Raven Press, New York *(in press).*
29. Grof, P. B., Saxena, B., and Cantor, R. (1974): Doxepin versus amitriptyline in depression: A sequential double blind study. *Curr. Ther. Res.,* 16:470–476.
30. Gurland, B. J. (1976): The comparative frequency of depression in various adult age groups. *J. Gerontol.,* 31:283–292.
31. Guy, W. (1976): ECDEU Assessment Manual for Psychopharmacology. Department of HEW Publication Number 76–338, Rockville, Maryland.
32. Haskell, D. S., DiMascio, A., and Prusoff, B. (1975): Rapidity of symptom reduction in depressions treated with amitriptyline. *J. Nerv. Ment. Dis.,* 160:24–33.
33. Hollister, L., (1974): Doxepin Hydrochloride. *Ann. Intern. Med.,* 81:360–363.
34. Hooper, E. H. (1957): Hooper Visual Organization Test Protocol Booklet. Western Psychological Services, Los Angeles.
35. Jefferson, J. W. (1975): A review of the cardiovascular effects and toxicity of tricyclic antidepressants. *Psychosom. Med.,* 37:160–179.
36. La Pierre, Y. D., and Butter, H. J. (1978): Imipramine and maprotiline in agitated and retarded depression: A controlled psychiatric and psychophysical assessment. *Prog. Neuro-psychopharmacol.,* 2:207–216.
37. Lisciani, R., Campana, A., and Scorza-Barcellona, P. (1978): Comparative cardiovascular toxicity of trazodone and imipramine in the rat. *Arch. Toxocology,* [Suppl. 1], pp. 169–172.
38. Maas, J. W., Fawcett, J. A., and DeKirmenjian, H. (1972): Catecholamine metabolism, depressive illness, and drug response. *Arch. Gen. Psychiatry,* 26:252–262.
39. Nair, N., Ban, T. A., Hontela, S., and Clarke, R. (1973): Trazodone and the treatment of organic brain syndromes with special reference to psychogeriatrics. *Curr. Ther. Res.,* 15:769–775.
40. Olsen, E. J., Bank, L., and Jarvik, L. F. (1978): Gerovital-H₃: A clinical trial as an antidepressant. *J. Gerontol.,* 33:514–520.
41. Pariante, F. (1974): Clinical effects of intravenous trazodone administration in severe depression. In: *Trazodone: Modern Problems of Pharmacopsychiatry, Vol. IX,* edited by T. A. Ban and R. Silvestrini, pp. 176–180. S. Karger, Basel.
42. Pfeiffer, E., and Busse, E. W. (1973): Mental disorders in late life—affective disorders; paranoid, neurotic and situational reactions. In: *Mental Illness in Later Life,* edited by E. W. Busse and E. Pfeiffer, Chapter 7. American Psychiatric Association, Washington, D.C.
43. Pozzi, O., Margherita, G., and Rinaldi, F. (1967): Studio clinico doppio cieco cross-over sull'attivita antidepressiva dell'AF/1161. *Quaderno dell'Ospedale Psichatrico Interprovinciale Salentino,* 2.
46. Salzman, C., Shader, R. I., and Harmatz, J. S. (1975): Response of the elderly to psychotropic drugs: Predictable or idiosyncratic? In: *Aging, Vol. II,* edited by S. Gershon and A. Raskin, pp. 259–272. Raven Press, New York.
47. Schildkraut, J. J. (1973): Norepinephrine metabolites as biochemical critieria for classifying depressive disorders and predicting responses to treatment: Preliminary findings. *Am. J. Psychiatry,* 130:695–699.
48. Spitzer, R. L., Endicott, J., and Robins, E. (1975): Research diagnostic criteria (RDC) for a selected group of functional disorders, (Ed. 2). New York State Psychiatric Institute, Biometrics Research Unit, New York.
49. Stotsky, B. A. (1975): Psychoactive drugs for geriatric patients with psychiatric disorders. In: *Aging, Vol. II,* edited by S. Gershon and A. Raskin, pp. 229–258. Raven Press, New York.
50. Vinci, M. (1971): Contributo clinico alla terapia dell depressioni endogene con un derivato della triazolopiridina. *L'Ospedale Psichiatrico,* 39.
51. Vohra, J., Burrows, G., Hunt, D., and Sloman, G. (1975): The effect of toxic and therapeutic doses of tricyclic antidepressant drugs on intracardiac conduction. *Eur. J. Cardiol.,* 3:219–227.
52. Wechsler, D. (1955): Manual for the Wechsler Adult Intelligence Scale. The Psychological Corp., New York.
53. Zung, W. W. K., Gianturco, D., Pfeiffer, E., Wang, H. S., Whanger, A., Bridge, T. P., and Potkin, S. G. (1974): Pharmacology of depression in the aged: Evaluation of Gerovital-H₃ as an antidepressant drug. *Psychosom.,* 15:127–131.

OPEN DISCUSSION

Dr. Lucy King: I would like to ask Dr. Gerner how much difference there is between the actions of trazodone and the other tricyclics?

Dr. Gerner: I think an exact comparison of the differences in their effects on neurotransmitter systems has not yet been done. Some of the basic science work suggests that trazodone is a relatively specific serotonin reuptake blocker.

Dr. Fritz Henn: We are in the process at Iowa of completing a crossover study in younger patients with imipramine and trazodone. I would second your conclusions that the incidence of side effects is less serious and less severe in trazodone in all age groups. We have noted nausea with trazodone, significant enough that skilled nurses can reliably distinguish the two drugs on the basis of the nausea induced by trazodone versus the anticholinergic side effects of imipramine.

From our double-blind crossover study, it is clear that the populations which respond to imipramine and trazodone are not identical, since subjects who fail to respond to one drug will often respond to the other.

How about nausea in the elderly? Do you see much of that?

Dr. Gerner: We saw some nausea, but not an epidemic of it. Its incidence did not seem particularly different between users of trazodone and of imipramine. We did not find much nausea in any of the three groups. We also found that people who did not respond to the imipramine trial responded to trazodone in an open part of the study.

Dr. Jarvik: We had one side effect that has not yet been described, and that is edema.

Dr. Ferris: We are in the midst of a trazodone trial in geriatric patients similar to the study that has just been reported. With regard to side effects, we have seen a few cases of edema. Another side effect we have seen is sedation. I cannot comment on the outcome of the treatment since we are still in the process of running the study, but in those cases where we have had a significant side effect of sedation, it has tended to be in a patient on trazodone. It may well be that, considering the entire spectrum of side effects, trazodone is superior to imipramine. But should there be significantly more sedation with trazodone, which in the case of geriatric patients might be a more troublesome side effect, the net benefits of trazodone might not be realized.

I wonder if you could comment on the amount of sedation you found relative to the two drugs addressed.

Dr. Gerner: We did have two patients who had no bipolar history become a little hypomanic on trazodone. At this time I do not feel that sedation is a common side effect with trazodone. Of course the numbers are relatively small to determine the frequencies of side effects. It may turn out that we will have to combine findings from a number of studies.

Dr. Gershon: I would like to compliment you on your study and say that what this country needs is a good antidepressant that will not provoke mania or hypomania.

Dr. Gerner: We had no mania but no known bipolar patients either.

Dr. Cole: I have given trazodone to five patients with very mixed results. These were all patients who had failed to improve on other drugs. Two of them have shown a clear antidepressant response, one with hypomania and without side effects. One elderly patient has developed ataxia. One patient took one dose, had a headache for 18 hr, and refused further medication. She previously had failed to respond to other pharmacologic treatment and exhibited marked histrionic qualities. I think trazodone is an effective antidepressant with selected patients.

Dr. Gerner: There has been a lot of work on tricyclic plasma levels and their relationship to effectiveness, as has been presented by Dr. Friedel. To my knowledge, there are no ongoing parallel studies with trazodone.

Plasma levels were not available for this study, and that information is very important when one looks at response data. Plasma levels may answer a lot of questions about side effects as well.

Psychopathology in the Aged, edited by
Jonathan O. Cole and James E. Barrett.
Raven Press, New York © 1980.

The Therapeutic Role of Methylphenidate in Senile Organic Brain Syndrome

*Roland J. Branconnier and **Jonathan O. Cole

*Geriatric Psychopharmacology, Boston State Hospital, Boston, Massachusetts 02124; and
**Chief of Psychopharmacology, McLean Hospital, Belmont, Massachusetts 02178

Methylphenidate is an analeptic agent which produces prominent psychic stimulation. This is in contrast to other analeptics whose major action is motor stimulation (7). Pharmacologically, methylphenidate is sympathomimetic and adopts a structural conformation similar to the phenylisopropylamines such as meth- and dextro-amphetamine (13). While methylphenidate shares the central nervous system (CNS) stimulant properties of the amphetamines, it produces little effect on peripheral circulation (15).

Clinically, methylphenidate has been investigated in a wide variety of disorders. However, at the present time it is considered therapeutically effective in only two conditions: narcolepsy, a sleeping disorder, and hyperkinetic syndrome in children. Indeed, for the latter condition, it is considered the drug of choice (14,17).

Among the less well-established clinical uses of methylphenidate is the treatment of mild depression and "withdrawn or apathetic senile behavior" (7). A review by LaBrie of 18 double-blind, placebo-controlled trials in over 700 patients with mild depression has shown that methylphenidate is significantly superior to placebo in reducing presenting symptoms. Among the symptoms which were found to be improved by methylphenidate were fatigue, apathy, global rating, and self-rated depressive affect (R. LaBrie, personal communication). The available evidence would suggest, then, that this compound is effective in the treatment of mild depression.

The least compelling evidence for efficacy is in the therapy of "apathetic or withdrawn senile behavior." Of five studies reviewed by the authors, only one study, by Kaplitz, indicated any significant therapeutic superiority of methylphenidate over placebo in treating these poorly defined symptoms (10). The remaining four studies failed to demonstrate significant effects of methylphenidate in treatment of "apathetic or withdrawn senile behavior" (5,6,11,12). It is possible that the lack of significance observed in the majority of these trials may be due to patient selection criteria. "Apathetic or withdrawn senile behavior" is purely a descriptive term, and these symptoms could be interpreted as being of organic or functional origin. That is, they could represent the psychic retardation of depression, or the slowness of response attributable to organic dysfunction of the brain, or both concomitantly.

The following study was conducted in order to examine the relative therapeutic efficacy of methylphenidate in reducing psychomotor performance deficits and improving affective status in the elderly.

PROCEDURE

This 56 day study was designed as a placebo-controlled, double-blind trial. Sixty patients were randomly assigned into two groups. All patients were given single-blind placebo for an initial period of 14 days. After this run-in period, the treatment group (n = 30) received methylphenidate (Ritalin®, Ciba-Geigy) at a dosage of 10 mg b.i.d. for the next 21 days. During the last 21 days, the dosage was raised to 10 mg t.i.d. The other group (n = 30) received identical placebo tablets in such a manner as to insure that they received the same number of tablets per day. Patients were evaluated at pre-study and day 0 (pre and post run-in) and on days 21 and 42 of treatment. Patients who showed significant improvement in presenting symptoms post run-in were discontinued from further study.

Subjects

Sixty community volunteers over the age of 60, residing in Boston and surrounding suburbs, were recruited for this study by newspaper advertisement. Written consent was obtained from all patients. All patients were required to exhibit excessive fatigue. This was defined as a self-rated vigor/fatigue (V/F) ratio equal to or less than 3 on the Profile of Mood States (POMS) factors. This criterion measure was obtained by calculating the mean V/F ratio in a sample of over 300 patients with mild senile dementia. A V/F ratio of ≤ 3 represents the lower half of a normal distribution in that sample. In addition to specific fatigue levels, the patients were required to meet criteria on at least two of the following four variables: (a) score equal to or greater than 10 on the POMS Depression Factor; (b) score equal to or greater than 10 on the POMS Confusion Factor; (c) simple visual reaction time with mean in excess of 350 msec; (d) score less than 40 correct responses on the Paced Digit Symbol Substitution Test. Subjects were excluded if they had moderate depression, as defined by a score equal to or greater than 50 on the Zung Self-Rated Depression Scale, or if they had any of the following: (a) history of drug or alcohol abuse; (b) history of any other investigational drug use within 3 weeks prior to the start of the study; (c) history of any psycho-active medication within 14 days of entry into the study; (d) moderate to severe hepatic disease; (e) moderate to severe renal disease; (f) cardiac decompensation; (g) moderate to severe hypertension; (h) glaucoma; (i) severe anxiety, tension and agitation, psychoses, posttraumatic brain damage, post-infective brain disease, cerebral neoplasm, marked mental deterioration; (j) history of significant drug allergy or hypersensitivity;

(k) clinically significant abnormal electrocardiogram (EKG) reading. Of the 60 patients entered into the study, 56 completed the program.

Test Descriptions

Affective Assessment

Profile of Mood States (POMS)

The POMS is a self-administered adjective rating scale which consists of 65 items. From these items are obtained the following six dimensions of mood: (a) tension-anxiety, (b) depression-dejection, (c) anger-hostility, (d) vigor-activity, (e) fatigue-inertia, and (f) confusion-bewilderment. The POMS has been shown repeatedly to be drug sensitive to a broad spectrum of agents, e.g., the vasodilator and dopamine-blocking agent, papaverine; the stimulants, pentylene-tetrazol, and d- and l-amphetamine; the metabolic agent, naftidrofuryl; and the polypeptide, $ACTH_{4-10}$ (1,2,3,4,9).

Zung Self-Rating Depression Scale

This is a test which consists of 20 items. Ten questions are symptomatically positive, and 10 are symptomatically negative (scored reflectively). The patient is asked to rate each of the 20 items on its applicability to himself. There are four degrees of severity ranging from "none or a little of the time" to "most or all of the time." The test has been shown to be a valid and reliable assessment instrument for depression (18).

Psychomotor Assessment

Reaction Time Test

The reaction time test is of the simple visual type. Subjects are instructed to watch for a series of red lights and to depress a button as rapidly as possible when the light is presented. In this test, the stimulus is presented on a fixed interval schedule (one flash every 5 sec). The total duration for the test is 2 min, and the mean reaction time for 15 trials is determined. The apparatus is a Lafayette Model 63012 Reaction Timer with digital display of 1/1000 sec.

Digit Symbol Substitution Test (DSST)

This is a mechanized version of the DSST from the Wechsler Adult Intelligence Scale (WAIS). It consists of the digits 0 to 9 presented in random order on a digital display. The subject's task is to match the number presented against a number-symbol code card and to depress the corresponding symbol key. Each number is presented for 100 msec, and the inter-trial interval is 3 sec. Scoring is based on the number of correct responses for 50 trials.

Psychiatric Assessment

Sandoz Clinical Assessment—Geriatric (SCAG)

The SCAG is an 18 item rating scale which yields an overall score. It has been used in a variety of double-blind, placebo-controlled trials in the elderly and appears to be both sensitive and reliable (16).

Computerized Quantitative Electroencephalogram (EEG)

Bipolar resting EEG recordings were obtained from Grass E5G gold cup electrodes located sagitally at C_z and O_z. The recording instrument was a Grass Model 8 EEG with a frequency response of 1 to 60 Hz. Data obtained from these leads were stored on magnetic tape via a Vetters Model A tape recorder and were simultaneously analyzed by a Poly 88 microprocessor. The analysis program is based on a primary wave zero-cross algorithm. Data were quantified in epochs of 10 sec duration, with zero-crossings determined by AC-coupled Schmitt trigger. The following measures were selected for output: average frequency; percent time in primary wave frequency bands with upper limits of 2, 4, 7, 9, 11, 13, 20, 25, 35, and 60 Hz. Means for each of 25 epochs were calculated for each measure in the 4.5 min sampling period.

Data Analysis

Univariate Statistics

Nominal Data

Analysis by chi-square was performed. Where violations of minimal expected frequencies in chi-square analysis were encountered, Fisher exact tests were substituted. All two-category analyses were subjected to binomial tests.

Ordinal Data

These were analyzed by two-factor analysis of variance with repeated measures on one factor. Further within groups, analysis was accomplished by using distribution-free Friedman two-way analysis of variance.

Multivariate Statistics

Principle component analysis with varimax rotation was performed on pretreatment POMS and performance variables as well as on EEGs to extract a factor structure and to determine factor loadings of the individual variables.

A step-wise discriminate function analysis was conducted using data from the methylphenidate group. POMS, performance and EEG variables were used as regressors with the nominal dependent variable partitioned as treatment response versus non-response on the SCAG overall score. The program selected the independent variables in the order of the largest contribution to discrimination. Variables were included and excluded from the equation at $p < .05$.

RESULTS

Randomization of Subjects

No significant differences were noted in the random assignment of patients for either age or sex. Since patients could have been included with 11 different

TABLE 1. *Methylphenidate data: age/sex distribution of sample*

Methylphenidate			Placebo		
Subject #	Sex	Age	Subject #	Sex	Age
1	F	65	2	F	66
3	F	66	4	F	61
6	F	62	5	F	69
8	F	73	10	F	64
9	F	75	12	F	63
11	M	69	14	M	68
13	F	64	16	F	78
17	M	70	18	M	72
20	F	70	19	M	71
22	M	77	21	F	72
23	M	66	24	F	62
26	F	71	25	F	66
28	F	62	27	M	69
30	M	64	29	M	61
31	M	67	32	F	66
33	F	67	34	M	64
35	F	65	36	F	71
38	M	69	40	M	61
39	M	63	41	M	75
42	M	72	44	M	61
43	F	61	45	M	67
46	F	65	47	M	70
48	M	68	50	M	73
49	F	63	51	M	66
52	F	73	54	M	73
53	F	65	55	M	64
57	F	70	63	F	78
59	F	65			
61	F	71			

	N	$\bar{x} \pm SD$		N	$\bar{x} \pm SD$
Males	10	68.50 ± 4.03	Males	15	67.67 ± 4.72
Females	19	67.00 ± 4.20	Females	12	68.00 ± 5.75
Group	29	67.52 ± 4.14	Group	27	67.81 ± 5.10

Difference in age between groups: $t = 0.24$, df = 54, NS

	Methylphenidate	Placebo	
Males	10	15	$X^2 = 2.52$, NS
Females	19	12	

TABLE 2. *Randomization of subjects by inclusion criteria classification*

	Methylphenidate	Placebo	Group
Affect:			
Pure	1	2	3
Dominant	5	4	9
Mixed:			
Low	8	5	13
High	7	4	11
Performance:			
Pure	5	3	8
Dominant	3	9	12

	Methylphenidate	Placebo
Affect	6	6
Mixed	15	9
Performance	8	12

$X^2 = 2.23$, df $= 2$, $p =$ NS

combinations of the 4 inclusion variables, analysis of the distribution of inclusion classification was performed. No difference between the methylphenidate and placebo groups' distribution by inclusion subtype was observed. (See Tables 1 and 2.)

Factor Structure

Table 3 indicates that the principle component analysis was able to extract 2 factors and account for 61% of the variance. Factor 1 we have termed "negative affect," and the following POMS variables were all significantly loaded: depression, confusion, tension, anger, and fatigue. Reaction time, DSST, and EEG

TABLE 3. *Principal component analysis rotated factor matrix*

Variable[a]	Factor 1 (Affect)	Factor 2 (Performance)	h^2
Depression	0.809	−0.079	.798
Confusion	0.803	−0.116	.657
Fatigue	0.854	−0.091	.738
Vigor	0.412	0.544	.466
Anger	0.864	0.039	.748
Tension	0.911	−0.161	.856
Reaction time	0.327	−0.386	.256
DSST	0.206	−0.602	.405
EEG	−0.013	0.776	.603

TABLE 4. *Performance variables methylphenidate data: Analysis of variance*

Factor			Day 0	Day 21	Day 42	Non-Para-metric[a]		Para-metric[b]	
						Xr^2	p	F	p
Reaction time	Methylphenidate	$\bar{x}$	388.17	387.21	376.31	1.31	NS		
		sd	54.20	56.65	48.67			0.38	NS
	Placebo	$\bar{x}$	402.48	393.37	381.67	3.17	NS		
		sd	60.56	68.15	46.96				
DSST correct	Methylphenidate	$\bar{x}$	39.45	40.76	41.76	1.93	NS		
		sd	9.36	7.60	7.07			0.62	NS
	Placebo	$\bar{x}$	37.11	38.78	41.22	10.02	.01		
		sd	9.19	8.79	7.11				

[a] Non-parametric analysis done by Friedman two-way ANOVA
[b] Parametric analysis done by two-factor mixed design ANOVA—Drug x Trials Interaction

are significantly loaded on Factor 2 which we have termed "organic integrity." Vigor and reaction time, although more heavily loaded on Factor 2, are not orthogonal and are significantly related to both Factors 1 and 2.

Clinical Assessment

No statistically significant difference was noted in SCAG overall score as a function of treatment.

Performance Variables

Parametric analysis of variance (ANOVA) was unable to detect any significant difference between methylphenidate and placebo treatment of either reaction time or DSST. When subjected to a within-group, non-parametric analysis, the DSST showed a significant practice effect from pre-treatment in the placebo group. This effect was not observed in the methylphenidate group possibly due to the higher pre-treatment scores. (See Table 4.)

Computerized Quantitative EEG

None of the 11 EEG variables assessed evinced a significant treatment difference between methylphenidate and placebo. Within-group analysis also showed no change from pre-treatment in either group. (See Table 5.)

Affective Variables

Data from Table 6 show that neither tension, fatigue, vigor, nor anger exhibited any significant differences between methylphenidate or placebo groups. However,

TABLE 5. *EEG Bands: Methylphenidate vs placebo*

Frequency band	Drug[c]	Non-Parametric[a]		Parametric[b]	
		Xr^2	p	F	p
.5–2 Hz	M	0.93	NS	3.03	NS
	P	3.42	NS		
2–4 Hz	M	3.50	NS	2.27	NS
	P	0.42	NS		
4–7 Hz	M	1.35	NS	2.18	NS
	P	0.32	NS		
7–9 Hz	M	0.85	NS	1.14	NS
	P	2.24	NS		
9–11 Hz	M	1.84	NS	0.56	NS
	P	0.24	NS		
11–13 Hz	M	0.00	NS	1.44	NS
	P	1.86	NS		
13–20 Hz	M	2.30	NS	0.25	NS
	P	0.56	NS		
20–25 Hz	M	0.66	NS	0.21	NS
	P	2.58	NS		
25–35 Hz	M	0.07	NS	0.30	NS
	P	0.02	NS		
35–60 Hz	M	1.30	NS	1.54	NS
	P	0.86	NS		
Average	M	0.50	NS	0.33	NS
	P	1.68	NS		

[a] Non-parametric analysis done by Friedman two-way ANOVA
[b] Parametric analysis done by two-factor mixed design ANOVA—Drug x Trials interaction
[c] M = methylphenidate; P = placebo

depression and confusion both evinced a significant treatment-by-trials interaction. Depression was reduced, on the average, by 34% while confusion was reduced by 28% in the methylphenidate group. In the placebo group, the reductions in depression and confusion were only 4% and 16%, respectively.

Non-parametric ANOVA showed a significant improvement from pre-treatment in depression, fatigue, vigor, and confusion withing the methylphenidate group. No significant changes were observed in the placebo group.

Adverse Reactions

Quantitative

A 2 x 2 chi-square analysis of the incidence of reported side effects revealed a statistically significant difference between methylphenidate/placebo and low/high dose period. Specifically, there was a higher incidence of reported side

TABLE 6. *POMS factors: Methylphenidate vs placebo*

Factor	Drug[c]		Day 0	Day 21	Day 42	Non-para-metric[a]		Parametric[b]	
						Xr²	p	F	p
Depression	M	X̄	15.07	9.55	9.93	6.33	.05		
		SD	14.56	11.00	10.42				
								4.25	.025
	P	X̄	10.74	11.30	10.26	5.05	NS		
		SD	10.41	13.47	14.57				
Anger	M	X̄	8.00	5.66	6.45	2.60	NS		
		SD	9.01	6.01	7.67				
								1.30	NS
	P	X̄	7.07	7.63	7.33	1.24	NS		
		SD	8.42	10.37	10.96				
Tension	M	X̄	13.24	11.17	11.17	0.74	NS		
		SD	8.04	5.44	6.76				
								1.20	NS
	P	X̄	10.19	10.52	9.15	3.68	NS		
		SD	5.87	7.65	8.13				
Fatigue	M	X̄	12.48	9.66	9.28	6.27	.05		
		SD	6.28	4.99	5.35				
								0.16	NS
	P	X̄	12.19	10.26	9.48	2.16	NS		
		SD	6.15	7.24	6.89				
Vigor	M	X̄	11.69	13.69	15.41	7.98	.02		
		SD	5.98	5.58	5.51				
								0.81	NS
	P	X̄	11.41	13.44	13.52	3.63	NS		
		SD	5.71	6.00	6.17				
Confusion	M	X̄	11.97	8.72	8.59	7.52	.05		
		SD	7.45	5.17	5.74				
								3.37	.05
	P	X̄	9.52	9.11	7.93	5.41	NS		
		SD	4.44	6.51	6.07				

[a] Non-parametric analysis done by Friedman two-way ANOVA
[b] Parametric analysis done by two-factor mixed design ANOVA—Drug x Trials interaction
[c] M = methylphenidate; P = placebo

effects on the methylphenidate high dose than on the low dose, and significantly more side effects reported for methylphenidate than placebo.

Qualitative

Of all the side effects reported, only dry mouth was significantly associated with the administration of methylphenidate. (See Table 7.)

Discriminate Analysis

Discriminate function revealed only 1 variable which met the $p < .05$ inclusion requirement. POMS depression accounts for 23% of the variance observed in

TABLE 7. *Incidence of reported side effects of methylphenidate*

Symptom	Methylphenidate		Placebo		Binomial test
	Low	High	Low	High	
Dizziness	2	2	1	0	NS
Dry Mouth	3	3	0	0	.05
Arthritic Pain in Arms and Hands	1	1	0	0	NS
Arthritic Pain in Hip	1	0	0	0	NS
Insomnia	0	2	1	1	NS
Digestive Problems	0	0	1	0	NS
Fatigue	0	1	1	0	NS
Head Cold	0	1	3	2	NS
Fever	0	0	1	0	NS
Toothache	0	0	1	0	NS
Headache	1	1	2	0	NS
Irritability	0	0	1	0	NS
Nausea	1	1	0	1	NS
Constipation	0	0	1	0	NS
Vertigo	0	0	0	1	NS
Anxiety	0	1	0	0	NS
Jitteryness	0	1	0	0	NS
Palpitations	0	1	0	0	NS
PVC's	0	1	0	0	NS
PAC's	0	1	0	0	NS
Flushing	0	1	0	0	NS
Lightheadedness	0	0	0	1	NS
Bad Taste in Mouth	0	1	0	0	NS
Loss of Appetite	0	1	0	0	NS
Gout Attack	0	0	0	1	NS
Totals	9	20	13	7	

	Low	High	
Methylphenidate	9	20	$X^2 = 5.51$, $p < .02$
Placebo	13	7	

Binomial test

Methylphenidate		Placebo		Total		Total	
Low	High	Low	High	Low	High	M	P
9	20	13	7	22	27	29	20
$p = .019$		$p = .132$		$p = .088$		$p = .05$	

discriminating methylphenidate response by positive clinical outcome. Of the 28 patients administered methylphenidate, the regression equation was 75% correct in classifying patients in this sample. (See Table 8.)

DISCUSSION

Depression, confusion, vigor, and fatigue all showed significant improvement under methylphenidate treatment, while objective assessments of psychomotor

TABLE 8. *Discriminate analysis[a] of methylphenidate responders and non-responders[b]*

$R^2 = .232409$;   X = POMS depression score; $\beta = .51072$; $Y' = .01781(x) + .17097$

Responders (1)		Non-responders (0)	
Y (Observed)	Y' (Estimated)	Y (Observed)	Y' (Estimated)
1	.97	0	.37
1	.56	0	.38
1	.56	0	.47
1	.37	0	.65
1	.87	0	.33
1	.17	0	.37
1	.97	0	.42
1	1.06	0	.17
1	.37	0	.33
1	.38	0	.17
1	.40	0	.26
1	.24	0	.33
		0	.19
		0	.22
		0	.17
		0	.22

Percent correct classification = 75% when 0 < .50 and 1 > .50

[a] Discriminate analysis consisted of a stepwise-multiple regression program with probability limits of $p < .05$ for inclusion and exclusion of variables.

[b] Criteria for "responders" vs. "non-responders" was an improvement in clinical assessment scale rating.

impairment and EEG did not. The variables which showed improvement were significantly loaded on Factor 1 (negative affect), and the only predictor variable which discriminated treatment response was the POMS depression factor. As was suggested by Hamilton (8) "apathetic or withdrawn senile behavior" as a manifestation of mild depression in the elderly appears to be the indication for methylphenidate, not the symptoms of organic deterioration associated with senile dementia.

The observation that psychomotor test performance and EEG do not improve concomitantly with the amelioration of negative affective status may appear to be paradoxical. However, the two-factor structure derived from the variables may offer an interpretation of these findings. Factor 1, negative affect, can be referred to the activity of the subcortical limbic structures, while Factor 2, organic integrity, is referable to the higher cortical functions of the cerebral cortex. Aging and the attendant loss of neurons, alteration of cerebral blood flow, formation of lipofuscin deposits, and development of neurofibrillary tangles and plaques may reduce the capacity of the cortex to respond to methylphenidate. Limbic structures, on the other hand, may continue to be responsive. If this were true, it could explain the lability of affect and the resistance of performance deficits and EEG to alteration.

In summary, the pattern of improvement observed in affective status suggests that elderly patients with mild depression associated with psychic retardation, but not anxiety, are the best candidates for methylphenidate. While side effects occur, they are generally mild and transient and do not significantly interfere with treatment at the doses employed. Patients whose symptomatology is primarily associated with organic CNS dysfunction, in the absence of depression, are not likely to benefit from methylphenidate treatment.

REFERENCES

1. Branconnier, R. J., and Cole, J. O. (1977): The effects of chronic papaverine administration on mild senile organic brain syndrome. *J. Am. Geriatr. Soc.,* 25:458–462.
2. Branconnier, R. J. and Cole, J. O. (1978): The impairment index as a symptom-independent parameter of drug efficacy in geriatric psychopharmacology. *J. Gerontol.,* 33:217–223.
3. Branconnier, R. J., Cole, J. O., and Gardos, G. (1979): ACTH 4–10 in the amelioration of neuropsychological symptomatology associated with senile organic brain syndrome. *Psychopharmacology,* 61:161–165.
4. Cole, J. O., and Branconnier, R. J. (1977): Drugs and senile dementia. *McLean Hospital Journal,* 2:210–221.
5. Crook, T., Ferris, G., Sathananthan, G., Raskin, A., and Gershon, S. (1977): The effect of methylphenidate on test performance in the cognitively impaired elderly. *Psychopharmacologia,* 52:251–255.
6. Darvill, F. T. (1954): Double-blind evaluation of methylphenidate (Ritalin) hydrochloride. *J. Am. Med. Assoc.,* 169:1739–1741.
7. Goodman, L. S., and Gilman, A. (1975): *The Pharmacological Basis of Therapeutics,* p. 365. Macmillan Co., New York.
8. Hamilton, L. (1966): Antidepressant drugs and the organic brain syndromes. *Clin. Med.,* 73:49–52.
9. Hartmann, E. R., Orzack, M. H., and Branconnier, R. J. (1977): Sleep deprivation deficits and their reversal by d- and l-amphetamine. *Psychopharmacology,* 53:185–189.
10. Kaplitz, S. E. (1975): Withdrawn, apathetic geriatric patients responsive to methylphenidate. *J. Am. Geriatr. Soc.,* 23:271–276.
11. Lehmann, H. E., and Ban, T. A. (1967): Comparitive pharmacotherapy of the aging psychiatric patient. *Laval Med.,* 38:588–595.
12. Lehmann, H. E., and Ban, T. A. (1970): Pharmacological lead tests as predictors of pharmacotherapeutic response in geriatric patients. In: *Psychopharmacology and the Individual Patient,* edited by J. R. Wittenborn, S. C. Goldberg, and P. R. A. May. Raven, New York.
13. Maxwell, R. A., Chaplin, E., Eckhardt, S. B., Soares, J. R., and Hite, G. (1970): Conformational similarity between molecular models of phenylethylamine and of potent inhibitors of the uptake of tritiated norepinephrine by adrenergic nerves in rabbit aorta. *J. Pharmacol. Exp. Ther.,* 173:158–165.
14. Millichap, R. A. (1968): Drugs in management of hyperkinetic and perceptually handicapped children. *J. Am. Med. Assoc.,* 206:1527–1530.
15. Perel, J. M., and Dayton, P. G. (1977): Methylphenidate. In: *Psychotherapeutic Drugs, Part II—Applications,* edited by E. Usdin and I. S. Forrest, pp. 1287–1316. Marcel Dekker, Inc., New York.
16. Shader, R., Harmatz, J., and Salzman, C. (1974): A new scale for clinical assessment in geriatric populations: Sandoz clinical assessment-geriatric (SCAG). *J. Am. Geriatr. Soc.,* 22:107–113.
17. Zarcone, V. (1973): Narcolepsy. *New Eng. J. Med.,* 288:1156–1166.
18. Zung, W. W. K. (1974): The measurement of affects: depression and anxiety. In: *Psychological Measurements in Psychopharmacology Modern Problems in Pharmacopsychiatry,* edited by P. P. Paris, pp. 170–188. Karger, Basel.

OPEN DISCUSSION

Dr. John Nurnberger: You commented on side effects with methylphenidate treatment. Can you repeat the dosage used and the effects on blood pressure, pulse, and EKG changes?

Mr. Branconnier: The initial dose was 10 mg b.i.d. for 21 days. In the absence of side effects, this was raised to 10 mg t.i.d. during the second 21 days. Significant blood pressure and pulse changes were not observed. The only alterations in cardiovascular status which occurred were the development of premature ventricular contractions in one patient and premature atrial contractions in another. Both side effects occurred during the 10 mg t.i.d. dosing period.

Dr. Gerner: I appreciate your differentiation of the response by presenting symptomatology. I wonder if you could give a clinical vignette or impression of the agitated or anxious patients' reaction to methylphenidate. Do they get worse, show no effect, or respond positively?

Mr. Branconnier: In general, the conclusion regarding anxiety was strictly based on the response pattern obtained from the drug. Retardation symptoms improved significantly, while anxiety scores did not change.

We did not observe any exacerbation in anxiety in any of our patients. However, if you choose patients to treat with methylphenidate, remember that anxiety symptoms appear to be somewhat intractable. A preferable candidate for methylphenidate treatment would be a patient who is characterized by symptoms of low anxiety and high psychic retardation.

Unknown: Concerning the internal structure of your data, did you look at the correlation between reaction time and EEG frequency in this population?

Mr. Branconnier: Yes. That correlation was part of the overall factor analysis. A correlation of -0.379 was obtained for those 2 variables, and this was marginally significant at $p \leqq .05$.

Dr. Arthur Rifkin: You conclude that methylphenidate is effective on symptoms of depression and confusion in your sample. The analysis upon which you base this finding is an analysis of covariance. However, looking at your slide, I see that the end points of both groups on a rating of depression are similar, and, on the rating of confusion, the end point for the placebo group is actually better.

Your conclusion appears to be based upon a peculiarity that can occur, when analysis of covariance is used, when the groups are very different at baseline. Your methylphenidate group at baseline was quite different from the placebo group. It is difficult to conclude that one treatment is better than another when the end points are similar.

Mr. Branconnier: I tend to agree with your conclusion that it is probably the much higher initial depression level that accounts for that difference. The discriminate analysis would suggest that the break point for treatment response predicted from the equation would be a score of 18. The mean depression score for our methylphenidate group was 15. So I think that if you were to plot the equation it would indicate that you could expect a bigger response from methylphenidate the higher the initial score.

I think that the depression score level accounts for the difference overall. I think if the study were repeated with a slightly higher level of depression and with better randomization between drug and placebo groups, the effect would be more dramatic.

In terms of the "confusion" factor, it seems to go along with the depression. Overall, if you change the limits on the stepwise regression equation, confusion ceases to be an important factor. I would tend to consider the confusion aspect more organic and somewhat less amenable to treatment.

However, there was a drug effect, and it was significant even though the end points were fairly close, probably because there was a problem with randomization. I feel less confident about the confusion aspect, but I think if you take the drug response in combination with what comes out of the stepwise regression analysis, it is safe to conclude that methylphenidate is capable of reducing depression.

Psychopathology in the Aged, edited by
Jonathan O. Cole and James E. Barrett.
Raven Press, New York © 1980.

Discussion

Donald F. Klein

New York State Psychiatric Institute, New York, New York 10032

Clinical and Biological Aspects of Depression in the Elderly

Dr. Winokur's chapter presents interesting findings with regard to the question of the clinical and biological importance of the age of onset of depressive illness. He has reported that the differences between early and late onset depressives with regard to clinical presentation, personality characteristics, suicidal behavior, and endogenous symptoms are spotty, and the amount of overlap between groups is enormous.

On the other hand, Winokur et al. point out that on the basis of family history it is possible to define a tripartite nosology that correlates markedly well with differences both in clinical features and in responses to dexamethasone suppression tests. It would have been interesting if these findings had been compared with what has been, to date, the major nosological distinction within the depressions: endogenous versus nonendogenous. Here we are using the term "endogenous" with respect to symptom pattern rather than to the presence or absence of precipitation.

I have taken the stand that the most important clinical feature that distinguishes endogenous depressives is their pervasive lack of both consummatory and appetitive pleasures: These patients do not enjoy sex or food or maintain their usual interests.

Winokur points to the equivalent number of endogenous symptoms in his various groups, but he has not done a frequency distribution analysis to see if there is a subgroup in which there is a marked pile-up of endogenous symptoms. Such an analysis would be one approach to determining whether a relationship exists between the endogenous symptom pattern and his other variables and categories.

We should note that with regard to decreased libido, which I view as almost a *sine qua non* for the endogenous symptom pattern, 38% of the patients with onset below 50 reported this symptom, while only 11% of those with onset greater than 50 did. It is conceivable that the report of decreased libido in the older group is low because the base rate for libidinal interest was also low, although I am reliably informed that many 50 year olds maintain a high rate of libidinal interest and activity. However, this caveat would not apply to the younger age group. Therefore, I would estimate that only a minority (less than one-third) of the patients in this study would be likely to have the full endogenous symptom pattern. Further, in view of Winokur's description of the personality and history of his "Spectrum Disorder," it sounds as if this group would have had very few such patients.

In summary, Winokur and his colleagues have once again emphasized the utility of family history as an approach that exceeds the utility of clinical markers in the categorical analysis of the various depressive illnesses. It would be helpful if he related his schema to a stronger analysis of the clinical data.

The Pharmacotherapy of Depression in the Elderly

Dr. Friedel has chosen to emphasize the relevance of pharmacokinetics to aging. I would appreciate it if he could comment on the issue of pharmacodynamics. That is, it is conceivable that the differences in drug effects experienced by the elderly are not so much related to the metabolic and distributional issues as they are to changes in drug-receptor interaction. I realize this is a very difficult area, and perhaps there is not much known. However, it seems intuitively correct that this must be important.

Dr. Friedel presents an analysis of the relationship of plasma concentration of doxepin to therapeutic effect. Unfortunately, the dosage prescribed was determined by the clinical response of the patient. Under these circumstances, one cannot draw an inference relating the plasma level to therapeutic effect. For instance, it is conceivable that the practitioners may have pushed the dosage in those patients who were not responding. In that case, it would have been found that the plasma levels were higher in the nonresponders. In trying to determine relationship between plasma level and response, one must fix either the dosage or the plasma level without regard to the clinical status.

I was not sure I understood Dr. Friedel's point about nortriptyline metabolism in the aged. Is he suggesting that nortriptyline is more efficacious or safer?

A Placebo Controlled Double-Blind Study of Imipramine and Trazodone in Geriatric Depression

This was a study of 60 patients randomly assigned to trazodone, imipramine, or placebo. The major problem with this study is the large dropout rate. It is stated that 60% of the imipramine group and 30% of the placebo and trazodone groups failed to complete the study. There is always a difficulty with marked attrition in a drug study. For instance, it is conceivable, although not necessarily true, that imipramine simply acted as a sieve in that its side effects were tolerated poorly by the sickest people who, therefore, dropped out. Under these circumstances, for the residual group, imipramine would look better than placebo even though there was no true beneficial drug effect.

To solve this problem, the usual technique is to stipulate a minimum period, say 2 weeks, of time for a fair drug trial. Patients who dropped out before 2 weeks could be considered to have had insufficient exposure to the treatment to warrant inclusion in a comparative analysis. Then all patients who exceeded this period would be entered into the study in an end-point analysis. Analyses should be made of the initial values of the patients who have remained in the study to see if the attrition during the early phase of the study had seriously compromised the random assignment.

The authors should be complimented on the fact that not only do they speak to the issue of statistical significance, but they also speak to the issue of whether there is definite clinical significance. For instance, they define improvement as a decrease of 30% or greater from the baseline Hamilton Depression Score, and under these circumstances, less than half of the patients in any group are improved.

The Therapeutic Role of Methylphenidate in Senile Organic Brain Syndrome

The study by Branconnier and Cole attempts to deal with a crucial but neglected area of psychopharmacology, the use of stimulant medication for chronic treatment.

Their basic findings are that methylphenidate seems to be of some statistically significant value in reducing depression and confusion but that the clinical magnitude of this effect was not tremendous in that depression was reduced on the average by 34% in the methylphenidate group. It is not clear whether this represents a change that has real functional implications. Discriminant analysis using depression as a predictor of medication effect is interesting, but, without cross validation, may well overestimate predictability.

I would find it very interesting if the authors could comment on whether tolerance occurred during the chronic administration of methylphenidate. This, of course, is extremely important with regard to the chronic administration of any stimulant. I have had the personal experience of being able to maintain some depressives on low doses of stimulants indefinitely with clear benefit. This seems to go against the often repeated statement in textbooks that tolerance invariably occurs with stimulants. Naturally, this type of pharmacological intervention should only be used cautiously and in a situation where good supervision is possible.

OPEN DISCUSSION

Dr. Winokur: I will respond to two questions raised in Dr. Klein's discussion. One, would there be a subset of patients with the endogenous symptoms? We did not do a frequency distribution on endogenous symptoms and separate two groups. Why? Since so many of the patients met the Feighner criteria, and since so many of the endogenous symptoms are in the Feighner criteria, we would not have had a dichotomy of endogenous symptoms.

The question about the difference between our data and Dr. Carroll's data in terms of the nonsuppressors is answerable. Dr. Carroll did take our material and separated patients into a group he thought might be endogenous depressives and a group he thought might be neurotic depressives. He found the expected amount of nonsuppression in the group he called endogenous depressives.

It is interesting to look at our depression spectrum patients: they do in fact resemble neurotic depressives. The reason for that is simple. Our depression spectrum disease women are women with stormy past lives, including marital, sexual, and personal problems. These are people who have had an early onset of depression and who never seem to get seriously ill in the same sense that the familial "pure" depressives do in follow-up. By that I mean the depression spectrum patients have less severe depressions and require less hospitalization. They do have a chronic problem over the course of their lives. So, in fact, what we call depression spectrum illness might be very similar to what many other people call neurotic depression.

As some of you know, the Feighner criteria make no separation between neurotic and endogenous depression, and I didn't do that either.

In the dexamethasone suppression test, all three groups, comprised of not just the elderly people but the entire subsets, had exactly the same Hamilton scale rating, and all patients in the study met the Feighner criteria. The depression spectrum patients had about 12% less of the Feighner criteria symptoms than the familial pure depressives or the sporadic depressives.

Dr. Friedel: Dr. Klein made three points. Let me respond to them one at a time.

The question of pharmacodynamic response is an important one. I have not seen any extensive reviews on this subject. If anybody knows of such a review, or if anybody has a good grasp of that literature and would write one, I would certainly like to have access to that material myself.

Regarding the point made about correlating plasma levels of doxepin and clinical response in this study, Dr. Klein is quite correct. To best relate clinical response and plasma levels of any drug, it is generally accepted that a fixed dosage study yields the most meaningful data. This was a pilot study to determine what dosage range was tolerable in elderly patients and what were the resultant plasma drug and metabolite levels produced by these dosages. From these pilot data I believe that one could fix a dosage with doxepin of about 125 to 150 mg/day for this population of patients and obtain therapeutic efficacy and clinical safety. Thus, the data is hypothesis-generating rather than hypothesis-testing.

Finally, regarding the issue of nortriptyline metabolism in elderly patients, I was suggesting that if nortriptyline is metabolized by the elderly more readily than other tricyclics, it might be a safer drug to use in this group of patients since toxic levels might not be achieved as readily. I did not mean to imply that it is more efficacious.

Dr. Gerner: I appreciate Dr. Klein's comments. I can reply to a number of them. When end-point analysis was done, reflecting each patient's final week in the study, there were not any differences. These data reflect dropouts whose non-response was probably because they did not receive a high enough dose for a sufficient length of time.

I think a slower dosage increment which should diminish side effects is a viable alternative. We are doing another study in this age group and are going to increase dosage more slowly. However, it is quite possible that we may get more dropouts by slower increase because of the placebo dropout rate. I think that in this age group a placebo dropout rate of about 30% is not unusual. This population was quite depressed, and it took a lot of effort to keep people in the study.

There appears to be a strong tendency in this group of patients toward dropping out and returning to and staying in their apartments and not wanting to come in for visits. If one adds an active psychosocial treatment, then one has a factor confounding medication treatment. One cannot assume that an active social intervention is a placebo or has no effect at all.

Mr. Branconnier: To answer Dr. Klein's question, the magnitude of the response in depression, I would have to agree, is small. Again, I can point only to the regression analysis data which suggest that the best break point for treatment response would be a minimum score of 18. The methylphenidate group had a mean score of 15 on intake. So they are somewhat below an optimal response point.

Even though the methylphenidate group shows a significant reduction, the end points between the placebo and the drug are fairly close together. Again, this probably results from the fact that there is almost a 50% difference in the initial depression level. However, in the placebo group there is no effect whatever that we can see.

You questioned the use of methylphenidate on a long-term basis. Ten of the patients who were in the methylphenidate group and who responded well have been referred out for treatment. This study was completed only recently, and therefore we do not have much in the way of follow-up data. We do have one lady who continued through our clinic to be maintained on 30 mg a day of methylphenidate for the last 2 months, and she is still doing quite well at this point. There does not seem to be any tolerance.

Dr. Cole may want to speak to your question. He has used methylphenidate chronically in several patients.

Dr. Cole: I have about 20 patients taking stimulants because no other medication appears to work. My impression, like Dr. Klein's, is that the effect does not wear out, although there are two other groups.

In one patient, the first dose of methylphenidate or dextroamphetamine was effective, and then the effect disappeared. I have also had a number of patients who escalated their doses up to 80 milligrams of something a day when given access to stimulants. In these patients, the drug effect stopped. But whether they are developing tolerance or whether they are seeking pharmacological nirvana, I cannot tell. But those that do respond do so very nicely for long periods.

Dr. Frederick Quitkin: I had the impression that Dr. Winokur was suggesting that patients who met Feighner criteria for depression were a homogenous group. We do not use the Feighner criteria. We used its identical twin, the RDC criteria. I cannot exactly picture the Feighner criteria, but my guess is that the overlap is probably 95%.

Consecutive admissions to our depression clinic who meet criteria for RDC major depressive disorders are an extremely heterogeneous group of patients. This is evident from the RDC subtypes. As you all know, there are probably eight or nine subtypes: psychotic, incapacitated, precipitated, without pre-existing personality disturbance, endogenous, and so forth. It is a very heterogenous group. I am not sure what you base your conclusion on.

Dr. Winokur: I think you are right. I think they are a heterogenous group. That is the reason we separated them by familial background and attempted to work out how many possibilities there were in what is obviously a heterogenous group.

Dr. Ferris: I cannot imagine that your variables account for all the people in the group. I am sure the three groupings are based on your particular symptom picture. Whether or not that picture is valid in predicting something about cause, response, etc., remains to be seen.

Dr. Winokur: You are right. The groupings do not predict choice and response to treatment. It is possible that within those groups, instead of three, there are more. I cannot deny that possibility.

Dr. Ferris: Given what appear to be a number of clusters that I can see in your group, I cannot imagine that three groups account for all of the variance. What I would question is the suggestion that these samples are otherwise homogeneous except for these three factors.

Dr. John Straumanis: I want to make a comment about these different depressive groups. As Dr. Shagass has shown, neurotic depressives have different sedation thresholds than psychotic depressives. In our evoked potential work, psychotic depressives showed moderate reduction in potential amplitude. Neurotic depressives were basically like normals in all ways, and our neurotic depressives were close to the syndrome described by Dr. Winokur.

The suppression test also supports this. Perhaps there is some validity in keeping what we call neurotic depressions, or depression spectrum, separate from other depressions, since there are physiological parameters which seem to differentiate them.

Dr. Barrett: I want to add to that last comment about separating subgroups within depressives. The clinical description Dr. Winokur just gave is very similar to one category, labile personality disorder, in the Research Diagnostic Criteria. His data, and some of ours, support keeping that category separate from other disorders. In it are people who have stormy ups and downs. When they are down, they are very down. When they are up, they are very up. On any given day they may be one or the other or in between. As a group, they may dramatically report a lot of symptomatology even though they continue to function quite well and do not appear very ill to others. I think it likely, as Dr. Straumanis suggests, that they will differ from other depressives on various physiological parameters, and so they should be kept separate, at least at this stage of our knowledge.

Dr. Jan Loney: As a child researcher, it is refreshing to listen to a paper on methylphenidate in which minimal brain dysfunction was *not* mentioned. I suppose I should be reluctant to mention it at this point. However, I do have a morbid curiosity to ask whether responders and nonresponders in this age population look different in ways that would seem to warrant resorting to the MBD concept or anything like it.

Mr. Branconnier: While they have some degree of organic impairment as rated by the Sandoz Clinical Assessment-Geriatric, there were no patterns which suggested minimal brain dysfunction.

Dr. Friedel: I wanted to ask Dr. Winokur if Dr. Carroll looked at the family histories of his subjects who were dexamethasone suppressors?

Dr. Winokur: He was going to go back and do that. Apparently he has that kind of data and can retrieve some of it. But as far as I know, he has not done it yet.

Dr. Friedel: Right now that is the critical question. Does somebody else have data?

Dr. Winokur: I might say, parenthetically, that Dr. Carroll has published some similar data in a paper with Brian Davies in 1969. He had 25 nonsuppressors in the paper and 25 suppressors. There were, in fact, 12 people in that group who had a family history of depression, and 75% of those were nonsuppressors. Unfortunately the paper does not separate the depression spectrum patients from the pure depressives. There was nonsuppressor status, as I recall, in 9 out of 12 patients with a family history of depression. He also has a group of people who were brought up in families which were markedly disrupted because of adoption, childbeating, wifebeating, and most probably alcoholism. That group was full of normal suppressors.

Psychopathology in the Aged, edited by
Jonathan O. Cole and James E. Barrett.
Raven Press, New York © 1980.

Senile Dementia and its Borderlands[1]

Sir Martin Roth

Department of Psychiatry, University of Cambridge, Cambridge, England

The burgeoning of interest in the psychiatric problems of the aged during the past 30 years reflects growing recognition of the fact that such problems constitute the most formidable challenge posed by the aging of populations in the advanced world.

Progressive global mental decline or dementia is, for the present, the heart of the problem. After the age of 70, the prevalence of dementia increases steeply. As more of the elderly survive into their eighth and ninth decades, the growing number of those with cerebral degenerative disease inevitably causes the health and welfare services of all affluent countries to strain at the seams.

If we were to compare the contents of this volume of the American Psychopathological Association with those of a publication devoted to the psychiatric disorders of the aged 40 years ago, it would be the wide range of topics in the 1979 volume that would provide the most striking contrast. While senile and arteriosclerotic dementia and Pick's and Alzheimer's diseases might have dominated the discussions of previous publications, present volumes are concerned with the differential diagnosis of psychiatric disorders of the elderly, the epidemiology of senile dementia and depressions, and the pharmacotherapy of such depressions. A number of entirely new subjects including regional blood flow and psychopathology, psychosocial therapy, and neurochemical approaches to the treatment of dementia await rigorous evaluation.

The difference in range and outlook provide some measure of the distance we have traveled. When Hazlitt wrote that "the worst old age is that of the mind," he was implicitly assuming that all forms of mental distress in late life caused the individual to suffer progressive mental decay ending in total oblivion.

The view has the authority of deeply ingrained beliefs. In a passage from *The Anatomy of Melancholy,* Burton quotes the psalmist that "after seventy years all is trouble and sorrow." He proceeds to encompass within a few lines a wide span of the psychopathological phenomena of aging including depression, progressive cognitive decline, and subjects "suspicious of all, wayward, covetous, [or] self-conceited, braggers and admirers of themselves." The pathetic confessions often extracted from old women of changing into cats and dogs, and

---

[1] Paul Hoch Award Lecture.

rising "into the air upon a cowlstaff out of a chimney-top" are cited by famous scholars of the day as indubitable proof of witchcraft. Burton judiciously suspends judgment and quotes the compassionate verdict of Wierus: "They do no such wonders at all, only their brains are crazed."

The view that all mental maladies of old age derive from cerebral degenerative disease persisted until quite recent times. Only a few decades ago, terms such as "senile depression" and "senile paranoid psychosis" were widely used. Eugen Bleuler (2), after admitting the existence of recoverable psychoses "belonging to senility," stated:

I should not like to class "senile melancholias" with mild organic features or organic confusions and deliria, because on closer examination it is always found that after the disappearance of the striking symptoms the patient is, in the sense of dementia senilis, a weakened individual. Therefore, I conceive such storms as intercurrent manifestations of a senile brain degeneration, just as in pronounced senile dementia and analogous to the acute appearances in paresis and schizophrenia, and theoretically I place the major disease in the foreground, even though there are cases where the restoration of equilibrium has practically the significance of a cure.

One of the leading psychiatrists of the 1940s published a paper which included a report of three patients with senile and arteriosclerotic psychoses who recovered following courses of electroconvulsive treatment (53). It is almost certain that these had been depressive illnesses of senescence.

The refutation of the view that all forms of mental illness of old age are harbingers of progressive senile decay which ultimately destroy the individual's personality along with his intellect (38,44,66,70) paved the way for many lines of investigation into the management, causation, and course of psychiatric disorder in senescence. The classification which established that each phase of senescence has a number of distinct descriptive syndromes which need to be differentiated from one another provided the starting point. The demonstration of favorable outcomes in a number of common disorders widened the range and variety of psychiatric disorders that presented in clinical practice with the elderly. This paved the way for more specific treatments and improved predictions about outcome. It created opportunities for advancing knowledge through comparison and contrast of the different clinical syndromes observed and then validated by follow-up studies.

It is instructive to review briefly the new information that has emerged from comparisons of the syndromes separated from each other hypothetically on the strength of cross-sectional clinical features.

PSYCHIATRIC SYNDROMES OF OLD AGE

Examination of Fig. 1 (66) shows that the psychiatric syndromes of old age differ sharply with respect to the proportions of patients who were discharged, inpatients, or dead 2 years after admission. More than three-fourths of patients with senile and multi-infarct dementia were dead; three-fourths of those with

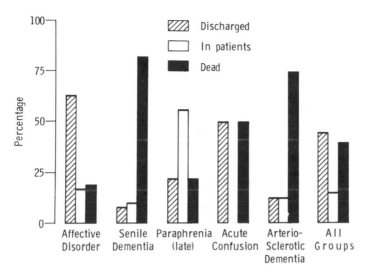

FIG. 1. Percentage of patients discharged, remaining in hospital or dead 2 years after admission to Graylingwell Psychiatric Hospital. (From Roth, ref. 66, with permission.)

depressive illnesses and late schizophrenia were alive; while those with "acute confusion" (clouded and delirious states) occupied an intermediate position. The groups differed significantly from each other with respect to performance on standardized psychological tests (35,68), the prevalence of physical illness, postmortem findings (45,69), and life expectation in comparison with normal population samples (38). It has been found that in depressions that make their first appearance in later life, hereditary factors are less important, and exogenous factors more important in causation than in the comparable affective disorders of later life (37,46,69). The depressive illnesses brought under a single heading in these early studies are now known to comprise a number of groups which differ from each other in their courses and responses to treatment.

The condition designated as "late paraphrenia" proved similar in its genetic origins to schizophrenia of early life in that the first-degree relatives showed a morbid risk for schizophrenic illness which was smaller but identical in character with that of schizophrenia of early life. The clinical features and premorbid characteristics of late paraphrenia established its close kinship with schizophrenia of earlier life (39,46). Why manifestation of the disease is postponed until late life is an important and complex question which cannot be gone into here. However, it has been shown that deafness is significantly more common and different in character from that found in other functional disorders of the aged and antedates the illness. Being found in almost half of all cases, deafness almost certainly makes some contribution to its causation (12,13,46,64).

One consequence of the differentiation of this group of disorders from senile deterioration is that they have been more widely recognized and actively treated.

With the aid of neuroleptic drugs, most patients are living in the community instead of remaining for the large part as chronic inpatients (Fig. 1).

Prior to the existence of a validated classification of psychiatric disorders in the elderly, investigators of brain pathology and the etiology of degenerative disease labored under handicaps. It was not difficult to adduce evidence that the clinical course during life and brain pathology found after death were related to one another only in loose and ill-defined ways (74). It was only after a sharp line of demarcation was drawn between the senile and arteriosclerotic disorders on the one hand and other syndromes on the other, that a strict and orderly relationship between clinical findings and the extent of neuropathological change emerged (1,14,72,73,80,81).

As far as "confusional" states are concerned, there is no theoretical reason why an attack of clouded consciousness or delirium should not be considered the first manifestation of progressive senile or multi-infarct dementia. In practice, such states of disturbed consciousness arising without warning are virtually never prodromal features of progressive cerebral disease unless there is concomitant evidence for a focal neurological lesion. The majority of cases have been found to originate from extracerebral sources, and the etiological agents responsible cover a broad span.

In addition to the common causes such as urinary or respiratory tract infection or early cardiac failure, a whole host of possibilities must be brought into consideration when the cause is not obvious. Intoxication by sedative drugs or alcohol, or drug interaction caused by imprudent polypharmacy are among the commonest. But hypothermia, atypical "silent" hyperthyroidism, cranial arteritis, pernicious anemia, tuberculosis, and subacute bacterial endocarditis, the last two being increasingly recognised as conditions which may present in occult form among the elderly, may also be etiologic agents. Wernicke's encephalopathy may produce unobtrusive physical signs, and as it is not necessarily a result of alcoholism, diagnosis ought less often to be deferred to careful neuropathological investigation post-mortem. Sudden acceleration of the rate of dementia with rapid increase in mental confusion is often caused by an associated physical illness giving rise to further clouding and delirium.

The remainder of this chapter will be devoted to recent developments in relation to the dementias of late life, and to senile dementia in particular. However, some consideration will be given to those aspects of depressive illnesses (the commonest of functional disorders of senescence) which raise problems in diagnosis and treatment.

INCIDENCE OF ILLNESS AND SOCIETAL IMPLICATIONS

A few statistics may serve to give indication of the nature and dimensions of the problems posed by diagnosis and treatment of depression and dementia in the aged.

Dementias to which a diagnosis can be confidently attached have been found in a number of surveys of community samples to have a prevalence of 5 to 6% among those in the community aged 65 and over (27,40,41). The 26 patients diagnosed as definitely demented (6.2%) in the Newcastle survey (43) had, over 2½ to 3 years, spent 255 weeks in geriatric wards (54% of the time spent by the whole sample of 449 subjects) and 57% of the total of 630 weeks spent in residential accomodation by the whole sample. As these conditions are by far the most important causes of chronic bed occupancy by the aged in institutions of every kind, a sense of urgency has entered into the investigations being undertaken into the causation of senile dementia of the Alzheimer type in particular. For this disorder accounts for the majority of cases requiring long-term institutional care.

In the community, as distinct from institutions, the depressive and related affective disorders are the most common causes of mental suffering in old age. The prevalence of definite cases has been found to be approximately 14% among those 65 and over. When milder cases are reckoned, the figures rise to 30 to 40% (40,41). There is good reason to believe that the tasks of identifying and treating this vast population have barely begun anywhere. Depression among the community aged represents a large and swelling side of human suffering. It prevents many elderly people whose personalities survive intact from making the positive contributions to life of which they are capable. It causes needless demoralization of families, friends, and neighbors, and, finally, it does something to undermine the viability of all elderly people in the community. Neglect of the depressive and related illnesses of the aged in the community reflects negatively on old age in general. On the other hand, the accurate clinical and social diagnosis of depressive illness, as well as the treatments that follow, help to keep alive the whole subject of mental disorder in the elderly. It will be apparent from the prevalence rates that even a small proportion of cases of depression misidentified as senile dementia or other organic disease could needlessly enlarge the medical and social problems of chronic mental deterioration in old age, problems which are already straining health and welfare services to the breaking point in many countries. The practical importance of differential diagnosis is therefore considerable.

THE DIAGNOSIS OF DEMENTIA

At the present time the diagnosis of dementia is made largely on the basis of clinical examination aided by psychological testing, the CAT scan, and certain laboratory procedures. The phenomenology of dementia and its differential diagnosis have been fully described in standard texts and a number of recent papers (65,71,76). Attention will be focused here on certain selected points.

Multivariate statistical methods have been applied recently to the analysis of the phenomenology of presenile dementia. Gustafson and Hagberg (30) carried out a factor analysis of the clinical ratings of 57 patients whose symptoms had commenced between 40 and 65 years of age. The 14 factors fell into 4 main groups. The first 3, designated "amnesia-apraxia," "amnesia-confusion," "amnesia-alexia," together with factor 13, "psychomotor overactivity euphoria," depicted central features of dementia. Four others described affective disturbance and personality change, while a third group of two factors depicted neurological changes and disturbances of motility. It is plain that the results cannot be generalized to the far commoner dementias of later life. But similar studies of senile and multi-infarct dementias might prove informative.

Dementia refers to a global deterioration in all aspects of mental functioning, including memory, general intellect, emotional attributes, and distinctive features of personality. The "global" nature of dementia differentiates it from the amnesic syndromes in which the defect is confined to recent memory and, to a variable extent, remote memory. The difference is important because the defect in the pure amnesic syndromes is confined to the sphere of memory throughout the patient's life. And in such patients, the prognosis for social survival is very much better than in dementia. It is noteworthy, however, that patients with multi-infarct dementias may pass through a stage when their intellectual deficit is predominantly amnesic. In the demented subject, the impairment of higher mental functioning occurs in the alert state in contrast to delirious-clouded patients in whom the level of consciousness is lowered and shows characteristic fluctuations over a period of time. The differentiation of chronic subacute delirious states from dementia can be difficult. But as the majority of cases of the former are caused by specific physical diseases, and many of these are treatable, differentiation is clearly important.

Although most cases of dementia encountered in old age are due to degenerative disease, definition of the syndrome should not include the criterion of irreversibility. When this criterion is included, the diagnosis cannot be made until the course and the response to treatment have been observed. Such a concept has the disadvantage that it may mislead the clinician into making predictions of irreversibile decline only to have these predictions refuted in some cases when it is too late for therapies that might have been effective earlier. Dementia should therefore refer to a constellation of clinical features. In the primary forms the causes are cerebral degenerative diseases, and these cases are, for the present, beyond the reach of treatment. But there is a minority of secondary cases in which therapy may prove partly or wholly effective.

Some comments on the general features of the psychopathology of dementia serve to define the origins of certain errors in diagnosis. An earlier description (71) has been adapted to illustrate a number of points.

There is a selective impairment of memory for recent events, and, in early stages, this is often the most conspicuous defect. As the dementia progresses, memory for the past suffers increasingly. Eventually, memory for recent events may be void, and those for the past restricted to a few jumbled recollections.

In intellectual functions, abstract thinking is particularly vulnerable. The patient is unable to discern common themes or essential differences. He cannot apply experience to new situations or separate the significant from the trivial.

His ideas are meager, and he is unable to grasp new ones. His inability to grasp what is happening leads to false ideas. These are technically delusions, but evidence of their falsehood is not rejected as in schizophrenia and other psychoses, but merely is not understood.

The personality becomes a caricature of its worst features, and undesirable traits such as meanness, tactlessness, impulsiveness, hypochondriasis, disinhibition of sexually deviant conduct formerly held in check may be released.

Emotional changes such as depression and, less often, elation are variable, indeed markedly so in the case of multi-infarct dementia. Special attention is merited by features reflecting fallout such as loss of the finer aspects of social tact, judgment, and sensibility. Also in this category are the fading of concern for others, the narrowing of interest, and the increasing preoccupation with self.

These pathological traits may be observed for limited periods of time in nondementing conditions including depressive and other affective disorders and chronic clouded-delirious states. Once it is clear that an organic disorder is present, the most valuable clues to the nature of the disorder are often provided not so much by positive features such as errors in reasoning and orientation, misidentification, and shifting delusional ideas, as by negative features. It is the emotional blunting, poverty of ideas, and general intellectual emptiness, the absence of insight, unawareness of illness, the random meaningless answers to questions rather than positive mistakes that are most specific for demented states. For in the depressive and neurotic pseudodementias which are to be discussed, as well as in clouded states, rapport can be established despite cognitive impairment. And clinical examination will usually reveal that emotional responsiveness is intact so as to suggest that the patient's basic personality survives relatively unimpaired.

Such negative features of intellectual and emotional deprivation and gross deterioration of personal standards also tend to be less pronounced in multi-infarct and secondary dementias than in those due to diffuse cerebral degenerative disease. As no valid or useful measures are available, the detection of such features entails subjective judgments. This does not make them any less important.

The differential diagnosis of multi-infarct from senile dementia is discussed at a later stage. The features of secondary dementia resemble those of multi-infarct forms except for the focal neurological and psychological signs and deficits, the history of strokes, and the presence of hypertension. The patchiness of cognitive impairment, the relative preservation of emotional response and personality, the slowly progressive character of the disorder as observed over a period of months, and the fluctuations in performance, behavior and in rapport are all even more striking than in the case of the dementias that stem from infarcts.

In fact, where these features are marked, the possibility should be considered that the explanation lies in a chronic subacute clouded delirious state rather than in dementia. The final feature which differentiates secondary dementias from those due to diffuse degenerative cerebral disease is the presence of some specific physical illness such as a metabolic disorder or a deficiency disease. Prevalence patterns change. Even miliary tuberculosis and subacute bacterial endocarditis with multiple emboli, regarded as very rare phenomena some years ago (76), are no longer quite such extreme rarities among the aged, and are treatable if diagnosed early.

Some Problems in Early Diagnosis

The early diagnosis of dementia has become a matter of urgent necessity for a number of reasons. Since it is rare for cases to present until the process has been ongoing for a period of some years, we know far too little about the early manifestations. Yet it is obvious that an effective attempt to treat the patient by an attack on associated etiological factors is possible only if the diagnosis is established early. Recent developments which have opened the possibility of biochemical treatment for dementia (63) have given a special urgency to the need for intervention before the process is advanced.

The earliest personality changes tend merely to bring the individual's previous character traits into sharp relief. The punctilious man of order and method becomes inflexible to a disabling degree. The man of high standards grows anxious and inefficient in relation to responsibilities and tasks he took formerly in his stride. He works longer to accomplish less, and his self-esteem is shaken. The imagination is impoverished, the capacity for creation wanes, the emotions cool and fluctuate in unaccountable ways.

The difficulty of interpreting such changes arises from the fact that similar alterations may stem from benign and treatable affective disorders and other "functional" psychiatric illnesses. While the clinician should be viligantly alert to the subtle changes that may signal early intellectual decompensation, the hypothesis that these are due to a progressive dementing process should be examined in a rigorously critical manner. Other conditions which may provide the explanation should be considered.

The most serious mistake is the erroneous diagnosis of dementia in the presence of depressive illness. The prevalence of depression is so high that even a small proportion of erroneous judgments substantially expands the assumed prevalence of dementia. Careful history-taking protects against this hazard because the majority of progressive cerebral degenerative disorders commence insidiously with a history which extends back for years, whereas depressive illnesses are usually of no more than weeks' or months' duration. Among the difficult cases are those in which a relatively protracted depression of mild or moderate severity flares up following the impact of some personal misfortune or physical illness. The clinical picture of marked withdrawal with retardation, self-neglect, and malnutrition may be complicated by constipation with impaction of feces and double incontinence, with clouding of consciousness, and disorientation. These disorders are liable to prove fatal if not diagnosed. However, persistent attempts to establish communication with the patient will bring to light some unmistakably depressive features and perhaps some glimpses of the surviving personality. Prompt medical and psychiatric treatment may prove lifesaving and reverse the prognosis.

The subject of depressive pseudodementia has been discussed by a number of authors in recent years (33,65). Post has drawn attention to the Ganser-like mistakes of an obvious and banal kind in regard to orientation and simple questions that are made by some subjects. Kendell (47), in a study of 2,000 patients first admitted to a psychiatric bed in Great Britain in 1964 and readmitted before the end of 1969, found that the original diagnosis of dementia had been changed in 8 out of 98 patients, while the change from depression to dementia had occurred in only 23 of 870 depressive patients. The misidentification of depressive illness as organic disorder caused by cerebral degenerative disease continues. The finding of Duckworth and Ross (19) that organic brain disorder was diagnosed 50% more often in New York than in Toronto or London reechoes an earlier observation that the mortality for the dementias proved substantially lower in New York State than in Great Britain (67) suggesting that the former population contained an admixture of more benign disorders.

Commoner than such psychotic or endogenous cases are the depressions of the "silent kind" with apathy, malaise, diminished energy, weakness, and hypochondriacal preoccupations. As a measure of reversible cognitive impairment occurs in some 15 to 20% of depressed patients, those with the severer and more chronic forms of neurotic depression that predominate in the elderly are liable to be misidentified as dementias. The error is particularly likely to be made where chronic depressive symptoms merge insensibly with long-standing difficulties in life adaptation. In one investigation, a combination of emotional disturbance, apathy, forgetfulness, poor intellectual performance on clinical examination, and lowered scores on a shortened form of the Wechsler Adult Intelligence Scale caused diagnostic difficulties (59). A follow-up study revealed these patients to be women drawn mainly from lower social strata in the community, handicapped by poor social skills and limited intelligence, and responding with chronic emotional disturbance to the social vicissitudes and physical limitations that old age had brought in its wake. The term "neurotic pseudodementia" seems appropriate.

A third diagnostic problem is posed by the depressive features that may color the early stages of the dementing process, particularly where this is of the multi-infarct type. The symptoms are characteristically fluctuating in character, but there may be bizarre nihilistic delusions of the "Cotard" type or a state of profound misery with concomitant pessimism and despair which carries a substantial suicide risk. The treatment of such depressive symptoms will not lead to long-lasting improvement. But even short-term remissions are well worthwhile, for after elimination of such "excess disability," patients may prove much less demented than had been initially supposed.

The results of psychological testing provide a valuable adjunct in clinical assessment of patients suspected of dementia. But no psychological measure should be allowed to override a judgment derived from careful history-taking and thorough clinical evaluation.

RELATIONSHIP OF SENILE AND PRESENILE ALZHEIMER DISEASE

The evidence that presenile Alzheimer's syndrome and senile dementia of similar pathology constitute variants of a single syndrome comes from a number of sources. On the whole, the findings from heredity are in favor of a unitary theory. Although Larsson et al. (52) concluded that Alzheimer's and senile dementias are distinct disorders, they found 10 presenile psychoses among the first-degree relatives of the senile demented as well as 60 senile dementias. Moreover, in their earlier studies of Alzheimer's disease, Sjögren et al. (75) found a number of cases of senile dementia in the presenile families. The findings of Constantinides et al. (11) were similar. The evidence is also more consistent with polygenic inheritance than with a major dominant gene. This was the hypothesis first advanced by Sjögren et al. (75) for Alzheimer's disease. In the study by Larsson et al. (52), the 43 families with secondary cases showed a two-fold increase in morbidity risk, and a sibling was much more likely to be affected when a parent was also suffering from dementia. This is more consistent with polygenic inheritance or heterogeneity than with a major gene difference. However, the evidence for a dominant type of inheritance in some pedigrees (34) suggests heterogeneity with specific major genes possibly responsible in a minority of families.

The pathological findings are most readily reconciled both with a polygenic hereditary theory and a unitary etiological basis for the majority of cases. Every one of the changes to be found in senile dementia—neuronal loss, senile plaques, neurofibrillary change, granulovacuolar degeneration, and Hirano bodies—are also to be found in Alzheimer's disease. It is generally accepted now that, even in their clearest clinical forms, the focal psychological deficits including agnosia, apraxia, and aphasia are not exclusively confined to varieties that make their appearance in middle age.

It is common for disorders caused by polygenes to show a quantitative gradation in severity of the underlying traits and also to manifest exaggerated or caricatured forms at the extremes of the distribution (20,21). Diabetes, epilepsy, and malignant hypertension provide examples of such breakaway phenomena. And many diseases manifest both in old age and early life tend to assume a more severe and malignant form when they develop precociously than when they appear in old age. This seems to be the case whether the disease in question is hypertension, schizophrenia, tuberculosis, carcinoma of the breast and other malignant disorders. The same may be true of Alzheimer's disease. If an explanation for this phenomenon were to come to light, it would probably reveal something important about aging.

It is no mere academic matter to establish or refute the unity or heterogeneity of Alzheimer's syndrome. For the early forms, with their rapid onset and progressive destruction of the mental faculties, are usually investigated in detail so that a wealth of clinical radiological, biochemical, and neuropathological observations can be collated. It is essential to determine whether one is studying a disorder *sui generis* in these cases, or a precocious form of primary senile dementia from which general inferences can be validly drawn.

RECENT DEVELOPMENTS IN THE STUDY OF SENILE DEMENTIA OF ALZHEIMER'S TYPE

This section will concentrate on those recent developments which have, through a convergence of clinical, neuropathological, neuropharmacological, and neurochemical lines of evidence, provided a promising and potentially powerful theory for the origin of Alzheimer's disease. Whether the theory is refuted, modified, or substantiated, its exploration is bound to deepen knowledge and understanding of senile and related forms of dementia. The growth of interest in neuropathology of the varying forms of mental deterioration in late life has contributed to the steep escalation of scientific inquiry into these disorders. Classical light microscopy, investigations of ultrastructure, enzyme chemistry, immunology, virology, molecular biology, and, recently, clinical trials are all being brought to bear on the problems these disorders present.

Some of the most fertile advances in the exploration into the causes of the dementias of old age have stemmed from comparisons that have been made between pathological changes that are conspicuous to light and electron microscopy in the brain of senile dements and the changes to be found in other degenerative conditions where evidence in favor of some specific causal agent is established or suggestive.

The hypothetical comparison with kuru and with Creutzfeldt-Jakob disease arises from the occurence in both of these conditions of amyloid plaques, although in the latter these lack the thickened neurites with abnormal neurofilaments of senile plaques. In the case of the plaques of scrapie induced in mice, morphological similarities closer both with respect to their abnormal fibrils and their amyloid are to be found to the human senile plaque (83).

The possible analogy with the parkinsonism-dementia syndrome of Guam is suggested by the fact that the change universally found in this condition is neurofibrillary degeneration. Granulovacuolar degeneration is also found, although it should be noted that plaques are not associated. A special interest attaches to this phenomenon, since neurofibrillary change is found as a subclinical variant in the form of limited and circumscribed pathological lesions of this nature in the brains of a substantial minority of normal subjects within the indigenous population (7,22). The search for toxic agents such as aluminum was prompted in part by the fact that neurofibrillary change can be experimentally induced in rabbits by injection of aluminum salts, although their ultrastructural morphology is quite different from that of "tangles" (49). The hypothesis that neuronal destruction seen in senile and related dementias results from decreased immuno-incompetence stems from the presence of amyloid in the senile plaque and small cerebral blood vessels. It is well-known that certain forms of amyloidosis are associated with disorders of immune function (29).

The question therefore arises as to whether the plaques, neurofibrillary change, granulovacuolar degeneration, Hirano bodies, and some of the more rare phenomena found in the brain are closely and specifically correlated with the mental deterioration.

One frequently-expressed criticism of the relevance of "senile" pathological changes is prompted by the wide range of disorders in which plaques and, to a lesser extent, other changes are to be found. Now it is true that in post-encephalitic parkinsonism, amyotrophic sclerosis, and mongolism, in which dementia is prone to develop early in life, plaques may be present. But the quantitative intensity of the change is peculiar to Alzheimer's syndrome in its senile and pre-senile forms, unless a coexistent dementia has become established as in the precocious mental decay of mongols. As we shall see, quantitative aggregation of the change is the essence of the problem because, beyond a certain point, there is reason to believe that qualitative mental changes are liable to be initiated in an abrupt manner. And the failure to heed the quantitative aspect of the pathological change was the cause for the relative neglect of the cerebral changes for many decades after their original discovery.

It is not possible to judge for the present whether the changes are directly related to the agent responsible for the destruction of neuronal tissue or whether they are epiphenomena of some other process of neuronal damage occuring at the synapses or dendrites. The latter view seems more plausible.

But the evidence strongly favors a close relationship between the "senile" changes and whatever process of cerebral degeneration gives rise to the dementia. The evidence for such an association may be summarized in a few statements. They are derived from studies (1,72,80,81) in which psychological measures of dementia applied during life at regular intervals until the preterminal stage were correlated with quantitative measures of the different pathological changes in the brain after death. The subjects included demented and functionally-ill patients (depressives, neurotics, schizophrenics) and well-preserved subjects who had been admitted to general hospital or geriatric units. The main conclusions were as follows:

(a) There is a highly significant statistical correlation between indices of dementia derived during life from psychometric assessments continued until the preterminal stage on the one hand and measures of each of the main pathological changes, plaques (Fig. 2), neurofibrillary change and granulovacuolar degeneration on the other. In the case of plaques, the correlation coefficient with dementia score in the first cohort of 90 brains was $+0.77$ ($p < 0.001$) and for tangles $+0.63$ ($p < 0.001$).

(b) Each of the pathological changes associated classically with senile demen-

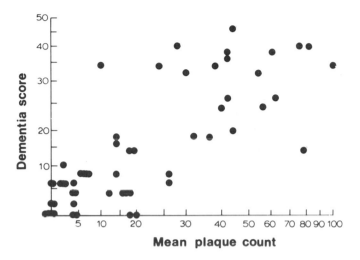

FIG. 2. The relationship ,between dementia score as computed during life and mean plaque count estimated after death in 90 patients. R = +0.077; *p* < 0.001. (From Blessed et al., ref. 1, and Roth et al., ref. 73, with permission.)

tia is present to a limited extent in the brains of mentally well-preserved subjects in old age. In other words, there is no qualitative difference; all the changes found in senile dements are present to some extent in a proportion of well-preserved old people, and these changes are augmented with increasing age.

(c) There is evidence favoring a threshold effect. In a hospital sample of mentally well-preserved, functionally-ill, and demented subjects, a plaque count of 11 and above separates most of those who had, during life, been indubitably demented from those who had been free from signs of mental deterioration. In Table 1, it is seen that 90% of affective depressive cases and 100% of paraphrenics have between 0 and 11 plaques per field, while 85% of senile dements have 12 or more. The threshold point may reflect the entry of some qualitatively distinct process. If so, this has no known neuropathological or other concomitant.

TABLE 1. *Mean plaque count for different groups of patients*

Mean plaque count	None %	None N	1–11 %	1–11 N	12–23 %	12–23 N	24–35 %	24–35 N	36–50 %	36–50 N	Total N
Physical illness	—	—	88	(7)	12	(1)	—		—		8
Confusional states	20	(3)	67	(10)	13	(2)	—		—		15
Affective-depressive	30	(3)	60	(6)	10	(1)	—		—		10
Paraphrenia	20	(1)	80	(4)	—	—	—		—		5
Senile dementia	—	—	15	(4)	50	(13)	20	(5)	15	(4)	26
Arteriosclerotic dementia	37	(7)	32	(6)	26	(5)	—		5	(1)	19
A-typical dementia	—	—	60	(3)	40	(2)	—		—		5
Dementia of known causation	100	(2)	—	—	—	—	—	—	—	—	2
	18	(16)	44	(40)	27	(24)	5	(5)	5	(5)	90

The threshold is therefore an important phenomenon which has implications for treatment, prophylaxis, and future scientific investigation.

(d) The various diagnostic groups differentiated during life are clearly separated from one another by plaque counts among other changes. The mean plaque count of all groups other than senile dementia was five per field or less. This statement can be applied to individuals with delirious or confusional states, some of which one might have expected to be cases of early dementia. They showed a mean plaque count of 2.64. In senile dements, the mean was 20.64, the difference from other groups being highly significant statistically (1).

The other morphological changes are more difficult to quantify, but the results are essentially similar. Neurofibrillary changes cannot be counted in a precise fashion. But when the change was graded "mild," "moderate," or "severe," subjects who received a "severe" grading were almost entirely confined to the senile dementia group. In fact neurofibrillary change is more specific, being very uncommon in the normal subject's cerebral cortex and also known not to occur in abundance in the pyramidal cells of the hippocampus of the normal subject (81).

If it is accepted that the morphological changes found in the brain of normal aged subjects and individuals with Alzheimer's disease are homologous, certain consequences follow. As plaques increase in number with age in the normal population (82), and neurofibrillary change is relatively rare in well-preserved subjects, the theories which postulate that neurofibrillary change in neurons represent the first stages of development of the senile plaque cannot be sustained. Although the different pathological phenomena in the brains of subjects with Alzheimer's disease are clearly correlated in some manner, the extent to which they are found independently of each other must be borne in mind. In the Guam-parkinsonism-dementia complex as also in the dementia of pugilists, neurofibrillary tangles are found without plaques, a phenomenon also true of progressive supranuclear palsy. But in this condition, granulovacuolar degeneration of the pyramidal cells of the hippocampus is found. To increase the complexity still further, while the tangles of the Guam syndrome are indistinguishable from those in Alzheimer's disease, those of supranuclear palsy prove to be quite different (79).

MULTI-INFARCT DEMENTIA AND THE "THRESHOLD PHENOMENON"

A study of patients with multi-infarct dementia together with a control population has shown that a similar quantitative principle governs the relationship between morphological change expressed as volume of softening (or infarction), as measured in 1 cm coronal section of the brain, and of dementia during life. The correlation coefficient was found to be +0.69 and highly significant statistically ($p < 0.001$). Here again a threshold phenomenon was apparent. Below a figure of 50 cc of total infarction, dementia was rare, above it almost invariable.

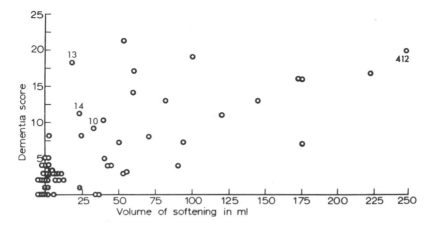

FIG. 3. Correlation between dementia score as assessed during life and volume of softening as estimated after death. $R = +0.69$; $p < .001$. The numbers above the points refer to mean plaque counts.

As shown in Fig. 3, the findings in relation to multi-infarct disorders lead to two further inferences of practical and theoretical importance:

(a) The effects of infarction are potentiated by the presence of the senile form of change. There is a minority of cases in which the two most common conditions of the aged brain overlap. This is clearly shown in the graph where it will be seen that in some patients low volumes of infarction stand in contrast with their high dementia score. But they also have relatively high plaque counts in several cases. Evidence from multiple regression analysis of multiple infarct and control cases has shown that "senile" change and softening each make independent contributions to the variance with respect to dementia. Their effects are, in other words, additive in the causation of a proportion of cases (66a).

The possibility arises that, but for added brain damage caused by infarction, some individuals might have avoided progression from the population of nondements beyond the threshold line into the ranks of those who undergo progressive dementia. This finding leads to the second inference.

(b) If plaques and the related changes were epiphenomena unconnected with dementia as had been supposed until recently—if, in other words, the correlations defined in the Newcastle study had been spurious—one would not have expected this evidence of potentiation of one sort of change by the other. We may conclude that although tangles, plaques, and other changes may not be the direct measures of the critical morphological alterations associated with dementia, they must be closely related to the processes in question. This is also shown by the size of the correlations computed. As multiple correlations for the 4 variables are near 0.8, some 63% of the variance in dementia measured during life is accounted for.

These are high correlations in the study of the biological associations of a psychiatric disorder.

The Significance of the Additive Effects of Senile and Multi-Infarct Change

The importance of potentiation of senile change by superadded change resulting from multiple infarcts resides in the fact that multi-infarct dementia may be regarded as a paradigm of the "secondary" forms of dementia. Other types of cerebral lesion or toxic damage may interact with the senile type of change in a manner similar to infarcts so as to encroach upon the brain's reserve capacity of neurons beyond the threshold point at which progressive decline of intellectual and global personality function begins. Where the source of infarction is to be found in multiple emboli emanating from a fragmenting thrombus, diagnosis and appropriate treatment may bring the production of a succession of infarcts to an end, and thus possibly avert dementia. So it may be with other kinds of cerebral injury.

For this reason, the early diagnosis of multi-infarct dementia is of crucial importance because intervention in such cases in good time may serve to decrease that quite substantial minority of cases in which softening from cerebral occlusion is the cause, or one contributory cause, of the dementing process. The main clinical criteria have been available for some time (66). Male sex, hypertension, history of strokes, marked emotional lability, or incontinence, clear fluctuations in symptomatology, the presence of focal neurological symptoms, or signs, or epileptiform convulsions, strong depressive coloring in a relatively well-preserved personality, focal psychological deficits such as dysphasia, dyspraxia, agnosia, spatial disorientation, the syndrome of pseudo-bulbar palsy in part or as a whole, and bursts of rapid deterioration after attacks of unconsciousness are the main clinical features. Hachinski et al. (31) developed an "ischemia score" which may be used clinically to differentiate multi-infarct cases from "primary degenerative dementia." When this rating scheme was applied to the patient population, frequency and distribution of patients were bimodal. Those with scores greater than seven had multi-infarct dementia, and those with under seven, dementia of the "primary" kind. In the view of the author, when prolonged confusional and amnestic syndrome follows after one or a small succession of transient or limited strokes, it should be taken as a warning signal that augmentation of the effects of preexisting senile degenerative disease is occurring. Prompt action to treat thromboembolic disease in such cases wherever possible might halt or avert dementia in a proportion of subjects.

SECONDARY DEMENTIAS

The largest single contributor to the dementias of old age is Alzheimer's disease which accounts for about 70% of the patients aged 65 and over with dementia seen in clinical psychiatric practice. A further 15 to 25% are wholly or partly accounted for by multiple infarcts (79,81).

The last few decades have seen the discovery of a growing number of dementias, the causes of which can be traced to specific events. This has provided a number of models that can be used to explore the nature and origin of Alzheimer's disease in its senile and presenile forms. Transmission of Creutzfeldt-Jakob disease and kuru to larger primates as well as to smaller animals (25,26) has substantiated the hypothesis that these disorders are caused by a virus-like organism which produces neurological disease after a long latent period and fails to provoke any of the commonly recognized neuropathological signs of viral infection of the central nervous system. The evidence that has established the similarities among the agents underlying Creutzfeldt-Jakob disease, kuru, and scrapie, the presence of cerebral amyloid in all of these disorders and of neuritic plaques in the case of murine scrapie, has generated a large body of research into the possible derivation of senile dementia from an agent of a similar kind.

Some of the rare syndromes caused by conventional viral organisms have provided additional clues. The encephalitis of herpes simplex may present as an acute psychosis. But the infection shows a predilection for the limbic system and may cause an amnestic syndrome. Progressive multifocal leucoencephalopathy which occurs in immunologically incompetent individuals in a setting of Hodgkin's disease or chronic leukemia, is now known to be caused by a Papova-like virus (84) and proves fatal within a matter of months. Subacute sclerosing panencephalitis of older children and young adults has now been established as a late consequence of infection with measles (36). But the lesions are characteristic of viral infection and have, therefore, no specific bearing on the problem presented by primary dementia. The limbic encephalitis associated with carcinoma, and the dementia of pugilists which is associated with intensive proliferation of neurofibrillary tangles in the hippocampus, both help to focus attention on the limbic system, a structure that possibly has central importance for the genesis of dementia in some forms. Sourander and Sjögren (78) describe the Klüver-Bucy syndrome as being a consistent feature of Alzheimer's disease. In the more recent investigations of Brun and Gustafson (9), there were prominent memory dysfunction and emotional and personality change, but only certain features of the Klüver-Bucy syndrome were manifest. However, the most pronounced degeneration was found in the medial-temporal region and in the lateral hemisphere within a field expanding from the posterior-inferior temporal areas to the adjoining parts of the parietal and occipital lobes. Moreover, the posterior cingulate gyrus was consistently found to be the site of severe damage (9).

In contrast, in both the senile and presenile forms of Alzheimer's disease, cerebral damage extends far beyond the realm of the limbic system, and in advanced cases very few areas of the cortex are found to be free from the characteristic pathological change. Limbic system pathology is therefore of more specific relevance for the amnestic syndrome and for those forms of dementia in which memory defect predominates for a long period (and these are mainly multi-infarct cases in old age) than for senile forms of Alzheimer's disease.

Among the other causes of "secondary" dementias are infections and inflammatory conditions such as neurosyphilis, cranial arteritis, growths and space-occupying lesions such as cerebral tumors and chronic subdural hematomas, and systemic disease that may initiate dementia by augmenting the effects of any existing subclinical degenerative change. These last include hypothyroidism, vitamin B_{12} deficiency, chronic alcoholism, and malabsorption syndrome. The dementia of boxers may not be initiated until a decade or more after cessation of pugilism, and this time lapse may therefore hold for other forms of brain damage inflicted long before senescence. Normal-pressure hydrocephalus (32) needs to be recognized from the combination of gait disturbance, mild dementia, urinary incontinence, and severe depression. The clinical picture in some cases is that of a fluctuating subacute delirious or clouded state rather than dementia.

SENILE DEMENTIA AS THE EXPRESSION OF SPECIFIC NEUROTRANSMITTER DEFICIENCY

Several lines of evidence have converged in recent years to suggest that a selective deficiency of cholinergic neurons may be the underlying basis of Alzheimer's disease or an important component of the syndrome. It has been known for some years that anticholinergic drugs such as hyoscine may produce memory impairment in human subjects (15) and that the false positive errors (56) resemble those found in patients with amnestic syndrome. In contrast, physostigmine (17) has been found to improve the memory of normal volunteers in controlled studies. There is a considerable body of evidence from learning experiments in animals which points in a similar direction. An important development was placed on record when evidence suggesting a specific deficiency of the cholinergic system in the brain in Alzheimer's disease was adduced by three groups of workers. The activity of both the enzyme that synthesizes acetylcholine, choline acetyltransferase (4,5,16,60–62) and that which breaks down acetylcholine, acetylcholinesterase (16,63) are significantly reduced in different brain regions. The selective distribution is of particular interest. The greatest decrease (to 44% of the normal figure) was found in cortical areas which have the greatest concentration of plaques and neurofibrillary change, namely the neocortex (Figs. 4, 5), and the lowest levels of all (20% of normal) were found in the hippocampus (60–63). The phenomenon also seems to be highly disease-specific. The enzymes are unchanged in Huntington's disease and in renal encephalopathy. As far as other psychiatric disorders of the elderly are concerned, depressive illness does not show the defect, and it is even more striking that multi-infarct dementia does not exhibit it. The possibility of postmortem or preterminal artifact is rendered improbable by these and other findings. The defects of the gamma-aminobutyric acid system that have been described in previous studies (60–62) are of no relevance in that the reduction is found in all clinical groups.

What is the relationship between these neurochemical effects and the morphological and other changes found in association with senile dementia and conditions with a possible kinship to it? The measure of cross-validation of evidence from different fields of observations is promising. The reduction in activity of choline acetyltransferase has a highly significant correlation ($r = +0.8$; $p < 0.005$) with plaque counts and dementia score ($r = 0.81$; $p < 0.001$) (63). Another

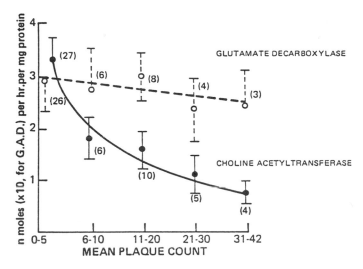

FIG. 4. Relation between choline acetyltransferase (CAT) and glutamate decarboxylase (GAD) and senile plaque formation in the cerebral cortex. Nondemented and demented individuals are grouped, irrespective of clinical diagnosis, according to the mean plaque counts (numbers of cases in parentheses). CAT activity is expressed in nmol/h/mg protein and GAD activity in nmol x 10/h/mg protein. The correlation coefficients (CAT: r = −0.82 and GAD: r = −0.21) were statistically significant for CAT ($p < 0.001$) but not for GAD ($p > 0.05$). (From Perry et al., ref. 63, with permission.)

feature of the change which parallels plaque proliferation is the augmentation in the severity of the deficiency in enzyme activity with advancing age (60).

Evidence from biopsy samples has confirmed the findings (3). As postsynaptic muscarinic cholinergic receptor activity in dements did not differ significantly from normal controls, the reduced acetylcholinesterase probably reflects a pre-

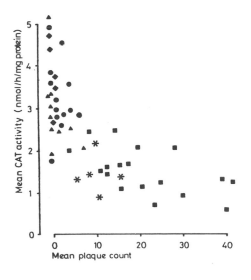

FIG. 5. Correlation between choline acetyltransferase (CAT) activity and senile plaque formation in cerebral cortex. Individual mean plaque counts plotted against mean cortical enzyme activities in 51 cases. • = Normal; ▲ = Depression; ◆ = Multi-infarct dementia; ■ = SDAT; * = Dementia of mixed pathology. (From Perry et al., ref. 63, with permission.)

synaptic abnormality, a view also substantiated by the morphological findings. This represents an impressive convergence of evidence. Psychological test performances in life, plaque counts, and specific enzyme activities all prove to be highly correlated but in senile dementia alone.

A possible connection between this body of observations and that related to the viral infection hypothesis has been established through the observations of Dickinson and his group. The choline acetyltransferase deficit is also found in some of the scrapie models (54).

Recent biochemical investigations have shed new light on the vexing question of neuronal outfall in senile dementia. Bowen et al. (3) investigated a number of biochemical indices of brain degeneration in the temporal lobes of cases of senile and senile/vascular dementia and control subjects. Senile cases showed a 58.2% reduction in choline acetyltransferase, and this was highly significant statistically. Acetylcholinesterase was not significantly altered. Taking ganglioside concentrations as a measure of changes in nerve cell membranes and cyclic nucleotide phosphohydrolase to reflect alterations in myelinated axons, the highly significant reduction in concentration of these 2 indices was construed as indicating an outfall of nerve cells of approximately 57.8% from the temporal lobes, a figure which agreed well with the direct cell counts undertaken by Colon (10). Biochemical evidence for glial proliferation was not found. In a comparison of the results obtained in senile cases with those showing mixed types of pathological change, the biochemical alterations in senile dements seemed more extensive than would have been expected from neuropathology. The authors conclude that changes in neuronal metabolism may precede slowly progressive changes in morphology in senile dementia.

These findings as also those recorded by Perry et al. (60–63) and Bowen et al. (3–5) have provided the rationale for clinical trials of precursors of acetylcholine, acetylcholine bitartrate and lecithin. With uncontrolled studies, Boyd et al. (6) and Etienne et al. (23) have reported some severe side effects arising from increased parasympathetic activity. Double-blind controlled trials have for the present registered no definite improvement in intellectual functioning in Alzheimer's disease (77), but more intensive inquiries are being undertaken with a whole range of compounds in attempts to reverse what may be, in part at any rate, a biochemical lesion. The possibility that there might be a parallel with the specific transmitter deficit in parkinsonism is one of the inspirations behind the recent endeavors. However, the distribution of lesions and the associated reductions in enzyme activity are far more diffuse than the corresponding changes in Parkinson's disease.

FUTURE PERSPECTIVES

Implications of the "Threshold" Concept

The evidence in favor of the threshold phenomenon implies that subthreshold change may be potentiated by any form of cerebral damage inflicted during the life-span of the individual to reduce his finite endowment of neurons which, being post-mitotic, are irreplaceable. The best authenticated example of such interaction is that between infarcts and senile form of neuropathological change. If the downward trend in mortality from strokes (57,58) recorded during the past 20 years in the United States is sustained, it could therefore be expected to bring about a reduction in the prevalence of dementia.

The effect would be confined to that minority of 25% of cases in which infarcts make some contribution. However any gain that accrued could be offset by trends working in an opposite direction. An increasing proportion of individuals who sustain severe cerebral injury survive to suffer the effects of "normal" senile change in senescence. Those who recover from cardiac arrest augment the number of those who enter old age with their reserve capacity of cerebral neurons already encroached upon. There is no formal scientific evidence that such a risk of dementia does indeed materialize. But there is one observation which gives substance to such predictions. It relates to the effects of head injuries at different ages. Although considerable personality change may follow severe head injury in young people, it is rare for global mental deterioration to follow. In contrast, the sequelae of comparable injuries in late life are more grave. Those people in their early 60s or later will often suffer progressive dementia after severe cerebral trauma contracted for example during traffic accidents. It would therefore be a prudent assumption to make that severe cerebral damage encountered during any stage of the life-span will enhance the chance, if only by a margin, that the individual will be likely to develop dementia when he reaches old age.

In addition to multiple infarcts, the possible contribution of a whole range of other diseases that may potentiate limited cerebral degeneration has to be studied. The role of long-standing cardiac, or respiratory disease, chronic alcoholism, and severe nutritional deficiency in the early formative years should all come under scrutiny. Chronic alcoholism is already under suspicion in this respect but needs to be investigated by much more stringent epidemiological methods than has been possible to date. Wordsworth's poetic insight that "the child is father to the man" acquires a new significance. Many infants now known to suffer cerebral damage in the course of repeated acts of child abuse are known to be more likely to suffer warping of their personality development. But perhaps the dice will also be loaded against them as far as the chance of passing through old age without dementia is concerned.

It follows that if such attempts to avert irreversible damage are to succeed, diagnosis will have to be undertaken at a much earlier stage than is usual at the present time. The majority of patients with senile dementia come under observation after some years' history of deterioration. We therefore know far too little about the early stages of the dementing process. Yet it is at this initial stage in the evolution of the disorder that the best chances present themselves of intervening to prevent the additive effects of a second form of pathology from producing irreversible damage.

Clinical Trials

It is obvious that controlled clinical trials of the effects of cholinergic drugs in dementia will constitute an important area of scientific endeavor within the next decade. With respect to the deficiency in choline acetyltransferase observed in the brains of senile dements, the use of choline by itself does not appear a logical form of treatment. The suggestion has been made by Comfort that the effects of anticholinesterases should be studied in combination with choline. Perry (63) has advanced the suggestion that guanidine ought to be tested. This is helpful in the Eaton Lambert syndrome which is also characterized by a defect of acetylcholine release.

In this area, also, early and benign cases present the best hopes of success. Here the observations of McDonald (55) may be relevant. He found that in patients with progressive dementia in old age who presented with no focal neurological symptoms or signs, the disorders could be divided into two relatively distinct groups: those with and those without evidence of impairment of parietal lobe functions. Although the former group was younger, it showed a significantly higher mortality, 26% having died within 6 months of assessment as compared with only 4% of those with intact parietal lobe function. It is possible that the benign group are related to Kral's syndrome of "benign senescent forgetfulness" (50). It would clearly be desirable to try and separate such benign and malign groups in the course of clinical trials, although in the view of the author, the contrast is too sharply drawn.

Female Preponderance in Alzheimer's Disease

There is another difference that demands attention. A preponderance of senile dementia of Alzheimer's type exists among women, while multi-infarct and mixed cases appear to predominate in men. The sex differential has been observed both in the presenile and senile cases (75). This prevalence pattern is not as yet supported by systematic epidemiological and neuropathological observations. Be this as it may, it would be wise, in clinical trials, to randomize men and women separately. If the XX cytogenetic constitution of women has any special connection with their propensity for primary dementia, the morphology of the aging brain in subjects with Kleinefelter's syndrome and those with an XYY constitution should be of special interest.

Depression and Dementia

Differentiation of depressive states from dementia must be placed on a solid foundation if spurious results from the present spate of clinical trials with cholinergic substances are to be avoided. An erroneous diagnosis of dementia will rarely be made where a careful history of the illness, evaluation of previous attacks of disorder, and assessment of the premorbid personality have been undertaken. An abrupt onset and a relatively short period of disability should always be suspect in a case of apparent dementia. Most cases of the latter in old age commence insidiously and present after a period of some years' progression. Increased mortality, compared with normal expectation, with those of old age who suffer from depression (42) may deepen the impression that an organic process is at work. There may well be some truth in this, since associated physical illness is probably the main factor in this excess mortality. But the latter also constitutes a scientific issue of some importance. The problem may be reversed, and the question then asked, does the depressive or affective disorder which often supervenes in cases of chronic physical illness increase the normal mortality rate of such illnesses? We do not know the answer to this question, but it is of general biological interest and has importance for the whole field of medicine. Does the loss of the will to live engendered by depression shorten life in those who suffer from physical illness, and would antidepressant treatment influence outcome?

Possible Causes of the Change from "Normal" Cerebral Change to the Pathology of Dementia

The fact that needs to be kept at the focus of attention is that the majority of those who survive into advanced old age die without developing any form of dementia. The problem is to define the reasons that underlie the transition from the benign state of "normal aging" into the malign state of progressive mental decay. With respect to the similarity of changes in normal and pathological cases, the human disorder most closely analogous to senile dementia is the Guam-parkinsonism dementia complex. Sufferers from this disorder, which must have specific causes, exhibit two of the changes found in senile dementia, namely neurofibrillary tangles and granulovacuolar degeneration (7,22). The theory of threshold effects advanced in relation to senile dementia does not draw support from one unique phenomenon. There are three distinct examples of a quantitatively graded pathological change in the brain which, developed beyond a defined threshold, gives rise to "breakaway" phenomena in the form of mental deterioration. Two of these, senile dementia and multi-infarct dementia, are well-substantiated. The evidence for the third is, for the present, tentative and suggestive rather than quantitative and precise.

There are a number of rival theories as to how the transmutation from normal to demented mental functioning takes place. Each of them requires separate examination; complicated theories with multiple causes rarely fare well. It is possible that the transition of pathological change from the subthreshold to the postthreshold state is under genetic control. To the extent that the familial tendency is found in Alzheimer's disease in its presenile and senile forms, the explanation may involve genetic factors or a slow virus infection or both. But the evidence in relation to a slow viral origin has to be handled with the greatest prudence and restraint. And for the present, the evidence that Alzheimer's disease in its senile or presenile form is transmissible must be regarded as negligible. Yet, premature claims might seriously impede neuropathological investigation of postmortem material.

Attention has been drawn to similarities between the plaques found in kuru and Creutzfeldt-Jakob disease on the one hand and those in Alzheimer's disease of the presenile and the senile forms on the other (8,24). The neuritic plaques that are specific for Alzheimer's disorder have not been described in the transmissible dementias of human subjects. However, the plaques of certain strains of mice infected with scrapie have been recently described as being of the neuritic variety (83).

The recent localization of immunoglobulins in the central core of the plaque with the aid of immunohistochemical methods has given substance to the possibility that some forms of amyloid have their starting points in the phagocytic breakdown of antigen-antibody complexes and in the degradation of the immunoglobulin fragments by lysozymes (28,29). It has also been suggested that the congophilic plaque may have a systemic origin and pass from serum through the walls of cerebral blood vessels. Some light has recently been shed on this possibility by the findings of Mountjoy and Tomlinson in Newcastle and Cambridge (C. Mountjoy and B. E. Tomlinson, *personal communication*). They demonstrated a significant statistical correlation between the amyloid content of the walls of cerebral vessels and the number of plaques that took up Congo red stain. However, the total plaque counts greatly exceeded the number of those identified by this method; Congophilic angiopathy does not occur in a form totally independent of neuritic plaques.

As far as neurofibrillary tangles are concerned, there is now general acceptance of the theory advanced by Kidd (48) that they are made up of paired helical filaments. They bear no structural resemblance to normal tubular protein, but recent immunohistochemical slides by Grundke-Iqbal et al. have shown that the mutant protein in paired helical filaments may have an affinity with, and may have therefore have originated from, the protein of neurotubules.

What contribution can the clinical scientist make to this field of endeavor? My view would be that there should be a determined attempt to characterize subgroups within the Alzheimer group of disorders. For, judging from the experience of the past, progress tends to occur through the separation of specific "secondary" cases in which identifiable etiologies whether of a genetical, immunological, or other etiology are in operation, from the large amorphous group of "idiopathic cases." To this end, clinical efforts should be directed toward clinical, pathological, and neurochemical comparison and contrast of familial and nonfamilial cases and cases of early onset with those that appear only at a relatively advanced age. The purpose will be plain. Cases of early onset would help to define the clinical features of the groups in which heredity, virus or a combination of etiologies might operate. Those of later onset would serve to contrast the characteristics of those most susceptible with those who are most resistant to the agents in question.

Among other considerations, manifestation in the 80s or 90s must be regarded as reflecting diminished penetrance of any genetic factors involved in causation. Through such investigations and study of their correlations with other biological parameters, more homogeneous groups of cases could be developed for purposes of scientific inquiry.

CONCLUDING REMARKS

The central purpose of scientific activity in this field is to shed light on the gap that separates the majority of people who, even in advanced age, remain mentally preserved or vigorous from that minority who suffer rapid mental decay. We must strive to narrow the gap between a Pablo Casals who conducts his last concert at 96 and dies a few weeks later, or a Bertrand Russell who works almost to the end of his 96 years on the one hand, and those who die after some years of total oblivion on the other.

Though he may hope that through one large leap in knowledge science may explain and narrow this gap, the psychiatrist working with aged and aging patients adopts a strategy that has little sanction from stringent evidence. He tries to encourage activity and interest and to discover roles and meanings in the lives of old people. He works on the assumptions that fostering relationships with others helps to keep the personality and its emotional responses intact, and that stimulus and challenge preserve the mind. These are much less clear and robust hypotheses than those that stem from virology, genetics, immunology, neurochemistry, and neuropathology. But evidence for them is not entirely lacking. Following inquiries on the effect of environmental influences upon the aging of the brain of the rat, Diamond (18) concluded that "in the absence of disease, impoverished environment, or poor nutrition, the nervous system does have the potential to oppose marked deterioration with aging." It therefore seems appropriate to end this chapter with a statement by Krech (51) which one may construe either as description or as hypothesis: "he who lives by his wits dies with his wits."

REFERENCES

1. Blessed, G., Tomlinson, B. E., and Roth, M. (1968): The association between quantitative measures of dementia and of senile change in the cerebral grey matter of elderly subjects. *Br. J. Psychiatry,* 114:797–811.
2. Bleuler, E. (1916): *Textbook of Psychiatry.* Springer, Berlin.
3. Bowen, D. M., Smith, C. B., White, P., and Davison, A. N. (1976): Neurotransmitter-related enzymes and indices of hypoxia in senile dementia and other abiotrophies. *Brain,* 99:459–496.
4. Bowen, D. M., Smith, C. B., White, P., Flack, R. H. A., Carrasco, L. H., Gedye, J. L., and Davison, O. N. (1977): Chemical pathology of the organic dementias (II), Quantitative estimation of cellular changes in post-mortem brains, *Brain,* 100: 427–453.
5. Bowen, D. M., Smith, C. B., White, P., Goodhardt, M. J., Spillane, J. A., Flack, R. H. A., and Davison, A. N. (1977): Chemical pathology of the organic dementias (I), Validity of biochemical measurements on human post-mortem brain specimens. *Brain,* 100:397–426.

6. Boyd, W. D., Graham-White, J., Blackwood, G., Glen, I., and McQueen, J. (1977): Clinical effects of choline in Alzheimer senile dementia. *Lancet,* 2:711.
7. Brody, J. A., and Kurland, L. T. (1973): Amyotrophic Lateral Sclerosis and Parkinsonism-Dementia in Guam. In: *Tropical Neurology,* edited by J. Spillane, pp. 355–375. Oxford University Press, Oxford.
8. Bruce, M. E., and Fraser, H. (1975): Amyloid plaques in the brains of mice: morphological variation and staining properties. *Neuropath. Appl. Neurobiol.,* 1:189–202.
9. Brun, A., and Gustafson, L. (1978): Limbic lobe involvement in pre-senile dementia. *Psychiat. Nervenkr.* 226:79–93.
10. Colon, E. J. (1973): The elderly brain. A quantitative analysis of the cerebral cortex in two cases. *Psychiatr. Neurol. Neurochir.* (Aust.) 75:261.
11. Constantinidis, J., Garrone, G., and de Ajuriaguerra, J. (1962): L'hérédité des démences de l'âge avancé. *Encéphale* 51:301–344.
12. Cooper, A. F., and Curry, A. R. (1976): The pathology of deafness in the paranoid and affective psychoses of later life. *J. Psychosom. Res.* 20:97–105.
13. Cooper, A. F., Curry, A. R., Kay, D. W. K., Garside, R. F. and Roth, M. (1974): Hearing loss in paranoid and affective psychoses of the elderly. *Lancet,* 2:851–854.
14. Corsellis, J. A. N. (1962): *Mental Illness and the Ageing Brain.* Oxford University Press, London.
15. Crow, T. J., and Grove-White, I. G. (1973): An analysis of the learning deficit following hyoscine administration to man. *Br. J. Pharmacol.,* 49:322–327.
16. Davies, P., and Maloney, A. J. F. (1976): Selective loss of central cholinergic neurones in Alzheimer's disease. *Lancet* 2:1403.
17. Davis, K. L., Mohs, R. C., Tinklenberg, J. R., Pfefferbaum, A., Hollister, L. E., and Kopell, B. S. (1978): Physostigmine, improvement of long-term memory processes in normal humans. *Science,* 201:272–274.
18. Diamond, M. C. (1978): The aging brain: Some enlightening and optimistic results. *Am. Sci.,* 66:66–71.
19. Duckworth, G. S., and Ross, H. (1975): Diagnostic differences in psychogeriatric patients in Toronto, New York and London, England. *Can. Med. Assoc. J.* 112:847–851.
20. Edwards, J. H. (1963): The genetic basis of common disease. *Am. J. Med.,* 34:627.
21. Edwards, J. H. (1970): The nature of familial predisposition. *Acta Diabetol. Lat.* [Suppl.] 7:1.
22. Elizan, T. S., Hirano, A., Abrams, B. M., Need, R. L., Nuis, C. V., and Kurland, L. T. (1966): Amyotrophic lateral sclerosis and parkinsonism-dementia complex of Guam. *Arch. Neurol.* 14:356–368.
23. Etienne, P., Gauthier, S., Johnson, G., Collier, B., Mendis, T., Dastoor, D., Cole, M., and Muller, H. F. (1978): Clinical effects of choline in Alzheimer's disease. *Lancet,* 1:508–509.
24. Fraser, H., and Bruce, M. E. (1973): Argyrophilic plaques in mice innoculated with scrapie from particular sources. *Lancet,* 1:981.
25. Gajdusek, D. C., Gibbs, C. J., Jr. (1975): Slow virus infections of the nervous system and the laboratories of slow, latent, and temperate virus infections. In *The Nervous System, Vol. 2, edited by D. B. Tower,* pp. 113–135. Raven Press, New York.
26. Gajdusek, D. C., Gibbs, C. J., Jr., and Alpers, M. (1966): Experimental transmission of a kuru-like syndrome to chimpanzees. *Nature,* 209:794–796.
27. Garside, R. F., Kay, D. W. K., and Roth, M. (1965): Old age mental disorders in Newcastle upon Tyne. Part III. A factorial analysis of medical, psychiatric and social characteristics. *Br. J. Psychiatry,* 111:939–946.
28. Glenner, G. G., Ein, D., and Terry, W. D. (1972): The immunoglobulin origin of amyloid. *Am. J. Med.* 52:141.
29. Glenner, G. G., Terry, W., and Isersky, C. (1973): Amyloidosis: Its nature and pathogenesis. *Semin. Hematol.,* 10:65–86.
30. Gustafson, L. and Hagberg, B. (1975): Dementia with onset in the presenile period. *Acta Psychiatr. Scand.* [Suppl.] 257:3–71.
31. Hachinski, V. C., Iliff, L. D., DuBoulay, G. H., McAllister, V. L., Marshall, J., Ross Russell, R. W., and Symon, L. (1975): Cerebral blood flow in dementia. *Arch. Neurol.,* 32:632–637.
32. Hakim, S., and Adams, R. D. (1965): The special clinical problem of symptomatic hydrocephalus with normal cerebrospinal fluid pressure—Observations on cerebrospinal fluid hydrodynamics. *J. Neurol. Sci.* 2:307.
33. Hemsi, L. K., Whitehead, A., and Post, F. (1968): Cognitive functioning and cerebral arousal in elderly depressives and dements. *J. Psychosom. Res.* 12:145–156.

34. Heston, L. L., Lowther, D. L. W., and Leventhal, C. M. (1966): Alzheimer's disease: A family study. *Arch. Neurol.*, 15:225–233.
35. Hopkins, B., and Roth, M. (1953): Psychological test performance in patients over sixty. II: Paraphrenia, arteriosclerotic psychosis and acute confusion. *J. Ment. Sci.*, 99:451–463.
36. Horta-Barbosa, L., Fuccillo, D. A., and Sever, J. E. (1969): Subacute sclerosing panencephalitis; isolation of measles virus from a brain biopsy. *Nature*, 221:974.
37. Kay, D. W. K. (1959): Observations on the natural history and genetics of old age psychoses: A Stockholm material, 1931–37. *Proc. R. Soc. Med.*, 52:791–794.
38. Kay, D. W. K. (1962): Outcome and cause of death in mental disorders of old age; a long-term follow-up of functional and organic psychoses. *Acta Psychiatr. Scand.* 38:249–276.
39. Kay, D. W. K. (1963): Late paraphrenia and its bearing on the aetiology of schizophrenia. *Acta Psychiatr. Scand.* 39:159–302.
40. Kay, D. W. K., Beamish, P., and Roth, M. (1964): Old age mental disorders in Newcastle upon Tyne. Part I. A study of prevalence. *Br. J. Psychiatry*, 110:146–158.
41. Kay, D. W. K., Beamish, P., and Roth, M. (1964): Old age mental disorders in Newcastle upon Tyne. Part II. A study of possible social and medical causes. *Br. J. Psychiatry*, 110:668–682.
42. Kay, D. W. K., and Bergmann, K. (1966): Physical disability and mental health in old age. *J. Psychosom. Res.*, 10:3.
43. Kay, D. W. K., Bergmann, K., Foster, E. M., McKechnie, A. A., and Roth, M. (1970): Mental illness and hospital usage in the elderly: A random sample followed-up. *Comp. Psychiatry*, 2:26 35.
44. Kay, D. W. K., Norris, V., and Post, F. (1956): Prognosis in psychiatric disorders of the elderly: An attempt to define indicators of early death and early recovery. *J. Ment. Sci.*, 102:129–140.
45. Kay, D. W. K. and Roth, M. (1955): Physical accompaniments of mental disorder in old age. *Lancet*, 2:740–745.
46. Kay, D. W. K. and Roth, M. (1961): Environmental and hereditary factors in the schizophrenias of old age ("late paraphrenia") and their bearing on the general problem of causation in schizophrenia. *J. Ment. Sci.*, 107:649–686.
47. Kendell, R. E. (1974): The stability of psychiatric diagnosis. *Br. J. Psychiatry*, 124:352–356.
48. Kidd, M. (1964): Alzheimer's disease—an electron microscopic study. *Brain*, 87:307.
49. Klatzo, I., Wisniewski, H., and Streicher, E. (1965): Experimental production of neurofibrillary degeneration. 1. Light microscopic observations. *J. Neuropathol. Exp. Neurol.*, 24:187.
50. Kral, V. A. (1962): Senescent forgetfulness, benign and malignant. *Can. Med. Assoc. J.*, 86:257–260.
51. Krech, D. M. R. (1978): Quoted by Diamond, M. C. *vide supra*, ref. 18.
52. Larsson, T., Sjögren, T., and Jacobson, G. (1963): Senile dementia. *Acta Psychiatr. Scand.* [Suppl.] 167:1–259.
53. Mayer-Gross, W. (1945): Electric convulsive treatment in patients over sixty. *J. Ment. Sci.*, 91:101–549.
54. McDermott, J. R., Fraser, H., and Dickinson, A. G. (1978): Reduced cholineacetyltransferase activity in scrapie mouse brain. *Lancet*, 2:318.
55. McDonald, C. (1969): Clinical heterogeneity in senile dementia. *Br. J. Psychiatry*, 115:267–271.
56. Miller, E. (1978): Retrieval from long term memory in presenile dementia: Two tests of an hypothesis. *Br. J. Soc. Clin. Psychol.*, 17:143–148.
   Mountjoy, C. and Tomlinson, B. E., "Personal communications"—to be published.
57. National Center for Health Statistics (1977): *Final Mortality Statistics, 1975,* Monthly Vital Statistics Report, Vol. 25, No. 11, DHEW Pub. No. (HRA) 77–1120.
58. National Center for Health Statistics (1975): *United States Life Tables by Cause of Death: 1969–71.* Vol. 1, No. 5, DHEW Pub. No. (HRA) 75–1150.
59. Nunn, C., Bergmann, K., Britton, P. G., Foster, E. M., Hall, E. H., and Kay, D. W. K. (1974): Intelligence and neurosis in old age. *Br. J. Psychiatry*, 124:446–452.
60. Perry, E. K., Gibson, P. H., Blessed, G., Perry, R. H., and Tomlinson, B. E. (1977): Neurotransmitter enzyme abnormalities in senile dementia. *J. Neurol. Sci.* 34:247–265.
61. Perry, E. K., Perry, R. H., Blessed, G., and Tomlinson, B. E. (1977): Necropsy evidence of central cholinergic deficits in senile dementia. *Lancet*, 1:189.

62. Perry, E. K., Perry, R. H., Gibson, P. J. (1977): A cholinergic connection between normal ageing and senile dementia in the human hippocampus. *Neuro. Sci. Lett.,* 6:85–89.
63. Perry, E. K., Tomlinson, B. E., Blessed, G., Bergmann, K., Gibson, P. H., and Perry, R. H. (1978): Correlation of cholinergic abnormalities with senile plaques and mental test scores in senile dementia. *Br. Med. J.,* 25:1457–1459.
64. Post, F. (1966): *Persistent Persecutory States of the Elderly.* Pergamon Press, London.
65. Post, F. (1975): Dementia, depression, and pseudodementia. In: Psychiatric Aspects of Neurologic Disease, edited by D. F. Benson and D. Blumer, pp. 99–120. Grune and Stratton, New York.
66. Roth, M. (1955): The natural history of mental disorders arising in the senium. *J. Ment. Sci.,* 101:281–301.
66a. Roth, M. (1971): Classification and aetiology in mental disorders of old age: Some recent developments. In: *Recent Developments in Psychogeriatrics,* edited by D. W. K. Kay and A. Walk. *Br. J. Psychiatr.,* special publication 6. Headley Brothers, Ashford, Kent.
67. Roth, M. (1959): Mental Health problems of ageing and the aged. *Bull. W.H.O.,* 21:257.
68. Roth, M., and Hopkins, B. (1953): Psychological test performance in patients over 60. I. Senile psychosis and the affective disorders of old age. *J. Ment. Sci.,* 99:439–538.
69. Roth, M. and Kay, D. W. K. (1956): Affective disorders arising in the senium. II. Physical disability as an aetiological factor. *J. Ment. Sci.,* 102:141–150.
70. Roth, M. and Morrisey, J. D. (1952): Problems in the diagnosis and classification of mental disorder in old age. *J. Ment. Sci.,* 98:66–80.
71. Roth, M. and Myers, D. H. (1969): The diagnosis of dementia. *Br. J. Hosp. Med.,* 2:705–717.
72. Roth, M., Tomlinson, B. E., and Blessed, G. (1966): Correlation between scores for dementia and counts of "senile plaques" in cerebral grey matter of elderly subjects. *Nature,* 209:109.
73. Roth, M., Tomlinson, B. E., and Blessed, G. (1967): The relationship between measures of dementia and of degenerative changes in the cerebral grey matter of elderly subjects. *Proc. R. Soc. Med.,* 60:254–259.
74. Rothschild, D. (1956): Senile psychoses and psychoses with cerebral arterio-sclerosis. In: *Mental Disorders in Later Life,* edited by O. J. Kaplan, 2nd ed. Stanford University Press, Stanford.
75. Sjögren, H. and Lindgren, A. G. H. (1952): Morbus Alzheimer and murbus Pick: Genetic, clinical and patho-anatomical study. *Acta Psychiatr. Scand., [Suppl.]* 82:611–617.
76. Slater, E., and Roth, M. (1969): *Clinical Psychiatry.* Third Edition. Revised Reprint. Baillière Tindall, London.
77. Smith, C. M., and Swash, M. (1978): Physostigmine in Alzheimer's disease. *Lancet,* 1:42.
78. Sourander, P. and Sjögren, H. (1970): The concept of Alzheimer's disease and its clinical implications. In: *Alzheimer's Disease and Related Conditions,* edited by G. E. W. Wolstenholme and M. E. O'Connor, pp. 11–32. Churchill, London.
79. Tomlinson, B. E. (1977): The pathology of dementia. In: *Dementia,* 2nd ed., edited by C. E. Wells, pp. 113–153. F. A. Davis Co., Philadelphia.
80. Tomlinson, B. E., Blessed, G., and Roth, M. (1968): Observations on the brain in non-demented old people. *J. Neurol. Sci.,* 7:331–607.
81. Tomlinson, B. E., Blessed, G., and Roth, M. (1970): Observations on the brains of demented old people. *J. Neurol. Sci.,* 11:205–242.
82. Tomlinson, B. E. (1977): Morphological changes and dementia in old age. In: *Aging and Dementia,* edited by W. L. Smith and M. Kinsbourne, pp. 25–86. Spectrum, New York.
83. Wisniewski, H. M., Bruce, M. E., and Fraser, H. (1975): Infectious etiology of neuritic (senile) plaques in mice. *Science,* 190:1108.
84. Zu Rhein, M. G., and Chou, S. M. (1965): Particles resembling papova viruses in human cerebral demyelinating disease. *Science,* 158:1477–1479.

Psychopathology in the Aged, edited by
Jonathan O. Cole and James E. Barrett.
Raven Press, New York © 1980.

Pharmacotherapy of Senile Dementia

Barry Reisberg, Steven H. Ferris, and Samuel Gershon

*Department of Psychiatry, New York University Medical Center, School of Medicine,
New York, New York 10016*

A wide variety of pharmacologic agents have been investigated in the treatment of the cognitive and behavioral symptoms which are known to accompany senile dementia. These symptoms can be quite varied. It will be of value, before beginning our comprehensive review of the many agents being used or under investigation for the symptoms of senile dementia, to review briefly the manner and frequency with which these symptoms present, particularly in Alzheimer's disease, the dominant cause of senile dementia.

In the earliest stages, there is subjective cognitive deficit only. The individual and occasionally his spouse notices that he has a tendency to forget where things are placed. Also, they notice that he has more difficulty remembering names than formerly. He may also have difficulty with appointments and find he has to write things down more frequently in order to remember them. These symptoms can be objectified utilizing a psychological test battery, but in general they do not interfere severely with employment or daily performance. The symptoms are accompanied by an increase in anxiety which is probably adaptive and in most cases does not require treatment. Pharmacologic intervention for the cognitive symptomatology may be useful at this stage.

The above state is followed by one of definite impairment in which deficit becomes evident. The cognitive deficit is classically particularly severe for memory of recent events. Orientation and concentration may be similarly affected. Memory for the past remains relatively intact. Vocabulary is largely spared; however, the individual may experience difficulty recalling appropriate words. During this stage, denial often replaces the earlier anxiety. There is often little in the way of symptomatology apart from the cognitive deficit.

In the later stages, when the senile person becomes severely disoriented and may, for example, confuse a spouse with a parent, behavioral problems may become prominent. In general, attempts at treatment of the cognitive disorder have been least successful in this group. The patient may exhibit marked anxiety despite the continuing denial. Often there is a motor restlessness which is secondary to a "cognitive abulia," i.e., the person can't carry a thought long enough to decide what to do next. Tranquilization may be necessary at this stage.

In the most severe cases, an organic brain syndrome with psychosis may develop. Symptoms such as delusions, hallucinations, paranoid ideation, and severe agitation may become manifest. The psychotic symptoms, when present, should, of course, be treated. More frequently, however, the symptoms are not truly those of psychosis but extensions of the cognitive deficit. The patient may mistake individuals or objects in the environment and respond accordingly. Often there are transient episodes in which the individual will be found "talking to himself." Anxiety and energy which cannot be channeled and therefore becomes misdirected requires treatment at this stage as well.

Depression has been said to accompany senile dementia. We do not find severe clinical depression to be a frequent concomitant of the Alzheimer's type dementia. Rather, endogenous depression, which increases in incidence with age, is a frequent cause of dementia-like symptomatology. The latter responds to treatment of the underlying depression and is therefore referred to as "pseudodementia." Treatment of this condition in the elderly will be discussed later.

Among the most important substances investigated or under investigation for the cognitive symptoms of senile dementia are hydergine, papaverine, and other cerebral vasodilators; Gerovital-H3; psychostimulants; nootropics, neuropeptides; and neurotransmitter precursors or agonists. For the behavioral symptoms of senile dementia and of "pseudodementia," the major classes of psychotropic agents have been used. The current status of treatment and research with each of these groups of substances will be reviewed, and important future research directions will be outlined.

HYDERGINE

Hydergine is a preparation consisting of three hydrogenated alkaloids of ergot. It is currently frequently employed in the treatment and management of elderly patients, particularly those in institutions. A recent study conducted among medicaid patients in the state of California revealed that hydergine was ranked second (after thioridazine) in terms of total drug expenditures among the institutionalized population (202). Hydergine accounted for 4.71% of drug expenditures among the institutionalized California Medicaid population and 1.37% of drug expenditures among the non-institutionalized California population.

Hughes et al. (92) reviewed 12 controlled studies which compared hydergine either with placebo alone, or with placebo and papaverine (13,16,47,65,100, 120,147,149,156,157,175,178). All of these studies employed similar methodologies and investigated drug treatment in elderly persons with organic brain syndrome or diagnoses indicating cerebral arteriosclerosis, cerebrovascular insufficiency, or senile mental deterioration or dementia. All of the studies lasted approximately 3 months. All but 1 (156) employed hospitalized patients, and a majority studied a population with an average age between 78 and 85 years. Thirteen of 36 behavioral variables assessed in 3 or more studies showed a statistically significant improvement with hydergine in at least 50% of the studies. The variables which improved significantly were: mental alertness, orientation, confusion, recent memory, depression, emotional lability, anxiety, fears, motivation, initiative, agitation, dizziness, vertigo, walking/mobility/locomotion, overall impression, and global therapeutic change. The magnitude of the individual effects was small, and the variable which showed the most significant change was depression. Interestingly, analysis showed continued improvement throughout the 12-week period.

The similar protocols in the 12 hydergine studies cited above had several common deficiencies. Most utilized a behavioral rating scale similar or identical to the Sandoz Clinical Assessment Geriatric (or SCAG) (166). This scale incorporates a number of measures of anxiety and depression but does not utilize any objective tests of cognitive function. Thus, the studies fail to provide objective evidence that hydergine significantly improves cognitive function. Also, there was no indication of which, if any, subgroups of the study populations were likely to respond most favorably to the medication. Finally, although individual studies employed dosages of 3.0 or 4.5 mg of hydergine daily,[1] there appears to have been no examination of differential or optimal dosage effects.

The intriguing observation of continuing improvement in behavioral measures up to 3 months was followed up more recently in a relatively long-term European study. Kugler et al. (107) conducted a double-blind, placebo-controlled trial of 4.5 mg daily hydergine treatment for a period up to 15 months. Their subjects were residents of several nursing homes in Germany. Their investigation included psychometric tests, measurements of cerebral circulation time, and electroencephalographic measures, all of which were done at the initiation of the study and repeated after 6 months and again after 15 months of treatment. After 6 months of treatment, marked differences on the performance and cognitive test measures between the hydergine and placebo groups were not observed. Performance improved for both groups, perhaps as a result of the "practice effect" and the increased general stimulation associated with the study. However, after 15 months, general intelligence as measured by the Dahl (39) version of the Wechsler Intelligence Test had increased an average of 5 to 7% in the hydergine-treated group, whereas a drop in general intelligence on this scale was observed in the placebo-treated sample. Cerebral circulation time was found to decrease significantly in the hydergine-treated group at 6 months, and this decrease remained present at 15 months. Predictably, circulation time increased progressively in the placebo-treated group. Electrophysiologic differences, which also were time dependent, were observed as well. The hydergine-treated group displayed a decrease in power range for all frequencies analyzed, which was opposite to the effect observed in the placebo-treated group.

However, the study suffered from some serious deficiencies methodologically, in regard to the proper handling of the very substantial attrition over the course of the study and statistically, in regard to the analysis of the results. Despite these flaws, the study at least raises the possibility that hydergine may be of

---

[1] One study (175) began with 6.0 mg daily for 1 month, followed by 4.5 mg daily.

some long-term benefit in the treatment of at least some patients with senile dementia. Additional long-term treatment studies may contribute further information in this regard. The introduction of an oral preparation which can be swallowed and absorbed in the gut, in addition to the sublingual tablets previously available, may serve to increase bioavailability and consistency of compliance in a confused, elderly population who may not always follow the proper procedure in ingesting the sublingual medication.

Significant questions as to precisely which senile patients are likely to be served by hydergine remain. In terms of present nosologic criteria, are they patients with multi-infarct dementia, with Alzheimer's type senile dementia, or both? Alternatively, is hydergine's effect primarily as a mood elevator, with only secondary effects on cognitive and performance measures? Finally, there is a need for dose-response studies which can lead to a more rational therapy.

PAPAVERINE AND OTHER CEREBRAL VASODILATORS

The rationale for the use of cerebral vasodilators has changed dramatically as our knowledge of the etiology and pathology of senile dementia has evolved. The original justification for their usage was based upon the assumption that arteriosclerotic narrowing was the primary pathology responsible for the syndrome and that this narrowing resulted in relative cerebral ischemia which might profitably be reversed using cerebral vasodilators. Findings of reduced cerebral blood flow in senile dementia (61,109) added further weight to this rationale. The autopsy studies of Tomlinson et al. (176) have contributed prominently towards a change in our conception of senile dementia. The latter is now generally classified into "senile dementia, Alzheimer's type" or "multi-infarct dementia" [a term originally coined by Hachinski et al. (84)], or senile dementia secondary to mixed causes including both Alzheimer's disease and multi-infarct dementia.

The implications of these new nosologic entities for studies of cerebral vasodilator therapies in senile dementia are illustrated by the recent preliminary work of Yamaguchi et al. (199). They found that a powerful endogenous vasodilatory stimulus, carbon dioxide, exerted very different effects in different types of senile dementia. They observed that in Alzheimer's dementia the capacity to increase cerebral blood flow in response to a CO_2 stimulus is well preserved and even appears to be greater than that of age-matched, non-demented, controls. In multi-infarct dementia, cerebral blood flow response to a CO_2 stimulus actually appears to be reduced. Unfortunately, the number of patients studied was small (3 Alzheimer's dementia and 5 multi-infarct dementia), and hence the full implication of these findings will have to await confirmation in larger studies. Yamaguchi et al. also confirmed previous findings (27,82,93) of differences in cerebral blood flow at rest in different kinds of presenile and senile dementia. In Alzheimer's disease, the reduction was diffuse, bilateral, and corresponded with the duration and severity of the dementia. In multi-infarct dementia, the reduction in flow was patchy and did not correlate well with either the severity or the duration of the dementia.

The actions of cerebral vasodilators cannot be explained simply on the basis of increased oxygenation in response to a vasodilatory stimulus. In their definitive double-blind study of hyperbaric oxygen treatment, Raskin et al. (148) found that a large increase in blood-oxygen levels has no effect on the cognitive and behavioral symptoms of dementia. Furthermore, when they divided outpatient senile dements into 2 groups on the basis of response or lack of response to a 5% CO_2 vasodilatory stimulus, 46 of their subjects did significantly better on cognitive tests, and 36 subjects failed to improve or did significantly worse in response to this powerful vasodilatory stimulus. Contrary to expectations, the CO_2 responders did not show a particularly good response to oxygen treatment either under hyperbaric or normobaric conditions.

Papaverine is an alkaloid which is a constituent of opium without any morphine-like activity. It is a smooth muscle relaxant which has been demonstrated repeatedly to increase cerebral blood flow (6,99,124). At least four controlled studies have found papaverine superior to placebo in alleviating at least some of the symptomatology in diverse groups of senile patients (22,23,125,153,171). Branconnier and Cole (22) have found that patients treated with papaverine for 3 months showed improvement on the depression and confusion subscales of the Profile of Mood States (POMS), whereas placebo-treated patients did not improve on these measures. However, they also found that the group treated with papaverine for 3 months was more *impaired* in their performance on the 3-second delay condition of the Peterson and Peterson test. In a more detailed report on their findings in a double-blind, placebo-controlled study of papaverine treatment for a period of 2 months in a mild to moderately impaired senile, geriatric outpatient population, Branconnier and Cole extended their findings (23). At 2 months they found improvement over baseline in the papaverine-treated patients on a Continuous Performance Test and a Paired Digit Symbol Substitution Test, as well as in the POMS. On the Peterson and Peterson test for immediate memory, the placebo group responded better than did the papaverine-treated patients. Although improvement was noted on these measures of mood, performance, and immediate recall, there was no evidence for improvement in specific "memory" areas. McQuillan et al. (125), in a double-blind, placebo-controlled study examined the effects of papaverine treatment over a period of 27 months and obtained findings which were suggestive of a dose-time relationship. Their findings suggested that definite improvement generally occurs within 16 to 24 months and that this is followed by a plateau effect and, subsequently, by a possible deterioration in mental functions. They caution that their study was of insufficient magnitude for definite conclusions. However, combined with the findings of Kugler et al. (107) on long-term treatment with hydergine, their study lends further weight to the possible value of long-term studies of both cerebral vasodilators, including papaverine, specifically, and of drugs which alter circulation in senile dementia in general.

Studies which have compared papaverine treatment with hydergine treatment on specific symptoms of diverse groups of senile patients have shown the latter to be superior (16,156), but the significance of such findings should not be overemphasized.

The electroencephalographic effects of papaverine treatment are particularly interesting and reemphasize the need for studies using current diagnostic criteria. Müller and Schwartz (131) have recently completed a clinical and autopsy study of 100 "psychogeriatric" subjects. They found that diffuse EEG slowing strongly suggests senile-Alzheimer's brain disease.[2] Intermittent lateralized slow waves strongly suggested hemodynamic problems secondary to sclerosis of cerebral arteries. Earlier studies have shown that in neuropathologically verified Alzheimer's disease, the proportion of abnormal EEGs approaches 100% (77,79,115, 133,173). In Pick's disease the EEG is usually less abnormal than in Alzheimer's disease (32,101). In multi-infarct dementia, the EEG may be abnormal in about 50% of the cases (138,164), and in many cases, a good correlation is found between the localization of the EEG changes and the vascular disturbance, especially when this is large (134,183).

McQuillan et al. (125) found that after 24 months of treatment, the EEGs of papaverine-treated patients still indicated improved or undeteriorated conditions relative to baseline. Specifically, they found 50% improved and 50% unchanged. In the placebo group, 33% of EEGs improved and 66% deteriorated. After only 2 months of treatment, they found that EEG frequencies had improved (changed in the direction of normality) in 80% of papaverine-treated patients versus 20% of placebo patients. They speculate that the EEG changes may be of value in determining the clinical utility of the drug. Supportive of these findings is the report of Branconnier and Cole (22). The latter investigators found a significant decrease in delta-theta activity and an increase in alpha activity in the quantitatively analyzed EEG, in patients treated with papaverine for 3 months.

Branconnier and Cole (23) have proposed a mechanism other than vasodilation to explain the effects of papaverine in this condition. They note that papaverine has been shown to possess dopamine receptor blocking action (54) and to antagonize the effects of L-DOPA treatment in Parkinsonian patients (51), and they postulate that this mechanism may be at least partially responsible for some of the observed clinical effects of papaverine.

Other cerebral vasodilators, apart from papaverine, have also been investigated to a somewhat lesser extent. Cyclandelate (Cyclospasmol®) has been shown to increase cerebral perfusion (135) and blood flow (12). Several double-blind, placebo-controlled studies have found cyclandelate to be superior to placebo in ameliorating various symptoms encountered in senile dementia (3,29,53,59, 88,135,200). However, one study did not find cyclandelate to be of value in the treatment of dementia (189).

---

[2] As determined by association with senile plaques and neurofibrillary tangles, ventricular dilation, and cortical atrophy.

Another vasodilator which is widely used, isoxsuprine (Vasodilan®), has also been shown to increase cerebral blood flow (91). A double-blind controlled study by Affleck et al. (5) found it superior to placebo in treating certain symptoms of organic brain syndrome. Branconnier and Cole (22), in another controlled study, found improved performance on the 9-sec delay condition of the Peterson and Peterson test in the isoxsuprine-treated group. A variety of other psychometric measures failed to distinguish between the two groups, although the drug group did show favorable EEG changes.

Another substance which deserves mention is not a primary vasodilator in the strictest sense of the term. Naftidrofuryl (Praxilene®) appears to enhance cellular metabolic processes. Fontaine et al. (60) have theorized that it activates the Krebs cycle enzyme succinic dehydrogenase and hence causes an increase in ATP stores. Others have also noted evidence for an increase in ATP stores of treated humans (167) and animals (127). Several controlled studies have found naftidrofuryl to be superior to placebo in treating certain symptoms encountered in senile dementia (19,22,26,37,66,103). Improvements have been reported in mood, cognition, and behavior. Branconnier and Cole (22) conducted a controlled study in which 60 patients were treated with 100 mg t.i.d. of naftidrofuryl or placebo. They found significant improvement on the 3-sec time-delay of the Peterson and Peterson test, reaction time, and the Perceptual Trace in the drug-treated patients compared with the placebo group. However, many other cognitive and behavioral measures, including tests of secondary short-term memory, did not reveal differences.

Carbonic anhydrase inhibitors are another group of substances which increase cerebral blood flow and therefore may prove useful in treating senile dementia. Carbonic anhydrase is the enzyme which catalyzes the hydration of carbon dioxide to form bicarbonate in the erythrocytes and in the glial cells of the choroid plexus, but not in the neurons of the brain (118). Carbonic anhydrase inhibitors cause vasodilation by much the same mechanism as an increase in the Pco_2. Acetazolamide (Diamox®) is the most widely used drug in this class. It has been shown to increase cerebral blood flow (52,78,143). However, its utility is limited because of a wide range of other physiologic effects of which perhaps the most disturbing is its diuretic effect. A more recently developed carbonic anhydrase inhibitor, UK-12,130, crosses the blood-brain barrier more readily and appears to have a more selective action on the brain. Intravenous administration produces an increase in cerebral blood flow (168). Oral tablets have also been demonstrated to increase cerebral blood flow significantly for periods up to 6 weeks (198). Investigation of this compound in the treatment of senile dementia might prove fruitful.

Yet another group of substances which are thought to improve cerebral circulation, albeit by a very different mechanism, are the anticoagulants. These would appear to have theoretical prophylactic value in the multi-infarct dementia subgroups of senile dementia; however, studies conducted to date have been in more diverse patient populations. The obvious hazards of long-term anticoagulant therapy would seem to limit the utility of such treatments from the outset.

This may be the reason why only one group of investigators has studied the effects of such agents in senile dementia. Walsh has consistently reported very favorable results in uncontrolled observations, first with bishydroxycoumarin (Dicumarol®) treatment (184–186), and recently with warfarin sodium (Coumadin®) (187). Recent reports of the prophylactic value of agents which decrease platelet aggregation, notably salicylates, in preventing strokes (28), would seem to suggest a possible role for such substances in certain forms of senile dementia.

GEROVITAL-H3

Gerovital-H3, a solution developed by Dr. Anna Aslan in Rumania, has been utilized in that country for more than a quarter of a century. Dr. Aslan has claimed a very wide range of therapeutic effects for the solution which may be said to fit within the broad category of "rejuvenation" (8-10). The composition is said to be as follows: procaine hydrochloride, 0.1000 g; benzoic acid, 0.0060 g; potassium metabisulfite, 0.0050 g; disodium phosphate, 0.0005 g. The above ingredients are mixed with 5 ml of distilled water to form a 2% procaine hydrochloride solution which may be administered orally or intramuscularly. When taken in accordance with Dr. Aslan's recommendations, 5 ml of Gerovital-H3 (G-H3) is administered intramuscularly, 3 times weekly for 4 weeks. This is followed by a 10-day period without administration, after which the 4-week, 10-day cycles are repeated indefinitely.

Although the primary active ingredient in G-H3 is said to be procaine hydrochloride (Novocain®), the solution differs both physically and chemically from a simple procaine hydrochloride mixture. Procaine has a wide range of pharmacologic properties of which the most relevant for this discussion are inhibition of the enzyme monoamine oxidase (MAO), an apparent CNS-stimulating effect; and a curare-like, anticholinergic action at the neuromuscular junction (76). The metabolites of procaine, para-amino-benzoic acid (PABA) and diethylaminoethyl (DEAE), may also contribute to its pharmacologic properties. DEAE is said to produce mild euphoria in small doses (76), and its structural similarity to the dimethylaminoethyl moiety, which is both a cholinergic agonist and a side-chain substituent of the chlorpromazine molecule, has been noted (161,165).

Monoamine oxidase activity is known to increase with age, and this has been cited as being of possible relevance to the increased incidence of depression with aging. There has also been one report of an increased MAO activity in Alzheimer's disease as compared with an age-matched control group (196). Procaine has long been known to inhibit MAO activity in animals, and several recent clinical trials have indicated the possible value of G-H3 in the treatment of geriatric depression (35,81,158,203).

The latter findings have relevance in terms of any possible value of G-H3 in the treatment of senile dementia. If G-H3 is a clinically significant MAO inhibitor, then it is likely to show value in that portion of the senile population whose cognitive dysfunction is associated with a disturbance of mood and affect.

Analogously, the "pseudo-dementia," which is secondary to depression, may be helped. Finally, the MAO inhibition should result in an increase in adrenergic activity which may, conceivably, have a positive effect on senile cognitive impairment.

Aslan has stated that she finds improvement in a majority of patients coming to her clinic with "CNS deterioration" (8). Unfortunately, "improvement" is left undefined. Specifically, Aslan has cited improved memory, concentration, orientation, and general clearing of the sensorium among numerous other therapeutic effects of G-H3. In their well-researched and comprehensive review of Gerovital-H3 treatment, Jarvik and Milne (98) call attention to the inconsistencies in Dr. Aslan's reporting of data, as well as to a lack of definition, at least in the English literature, of such improvement criteria as "capacity to work." Clearly, no objective cognitive data are cited.

The English literature contains very few studies of the value of G-H3 in senile dementia. One abstract (62) refers to an uncontrolled trial in 12 patients with organic brain syndrome, all of whom improved. A controlled study of G-H3 versus procaine in geriatric inpatients found "psychological improvement" as assessed separately by a psychiatrist, a psychologist, a relative, and a nurse, to be significantly greater in those patients treated with G-H3 as compared with procaine-treated patients (1). Studies conducted with procaine solution alone, but not G H3, on cognitive function in geriatric populations have been either negative (55,64), or only slightly positive (117).

In summary, Gerovital-H3 might have favorable effects on mood, but there exists little or no good evidence regarding its cognitive effects in senile dementia. If it does, in fact, prove to have significant antidepressant effects, it still must be determined whether these effects are clinically superior to those of existing MAO inhibitors and tricyclic antidepressants.

PSYCHOSTIMULANTS

These compounds are thought to possess properties which, on a theoretical basis, may be postulated to have positive effects on the geriatric organic brain syndromes. Some of those properties are their hypothesized value as "mood elevators," and as attention enhancers with possible positive effects on reaction time and on performance tasks. Unfortunately, these substances do not appear to have fulfilled their promise in this area, and their value in senility remains highly questionable. Some clues as to why this situation pertains may be found in the general literature evaluating psychostimulant effectiveness.

Tecce and Cole (174) administered 10 mg of dextroamphetamine to normal adults in an attempt to demonstrate a predicted increase in the amplitude of the "contingent negative variation" (CNV), an event-related electrical brain wave which is an indicator of alertness. Their results were quite different from those anticipated. They found that 13 of their 20 subjects exhibited paradoxical drowsiness accompanied by lowered electrical brain activity, as measured by the CNV, in the first hour post-drug. Seven of their subjects exhibited the expected behavioral alertness and increased CNV amplitude. Both groups of subjects did demonstrate increased alertness 2 and 3 hr after drug administration. They concluded that "amphetamine is not a simple stimulant of the central nervous system, but can also act as a depressant."

In a study of the effects of caffeine on performance on a test of verbal ability, Revelle et al. (150) found a differential in effectiveness depending upon the underlying personality of the test subject. With time pressure and 200 mg of caffeine, the performance of introverts fell considerably more than did the performance of extroverts.

In reviewing the effects of psychostimulants on the syndrome of senility, it is best to discuss some of the most carefully studied psychostimulant compounds individually.

Methylphenidate was first studied in geriatric patients with what was then called "cerebral arteriosclerosis" by Zahn (201). He concluded that 5 mg to 30 mg of methylphenidate daily, for 3 to 12 weeks, was effective in improving locomotion, initiative, and depressed mood in 50% of patients studied. Subsequently, other investigators have also found methylphenidate useful in elevating mood in geriatric patients in uncontrolled observations (11,14,15,97). Darvill in a double-blind evaluation (40) did not confirm a useful effect on depression associated with senile psychosis. Lehmann and Ban (113) did not find methylphenidate to be of therapeutic value in a mixed group of geriatric inpatients with diagnoses of schizophrenia and organic brain syndrome.

Because of the absence of any controlled study assessing the effects of methylphenidate on cognitive performance in non-psychotic, aged, cognitively-impaired outpatients, we undertook such an evaluation at New York University in cooperation with investigators from the NIMH (38). Twelve elderly subjects, 6 men and 6 women, between the ages of 65 and 80 years, were studied. The patients were all assessed as having significant memory impairment. Patients received 10 mg of methylphenidate, 30 mg of methylphenidate, and placebo in accordance with a double-blind crossover design. Results of a test battery conducted 45 min after the pill ingestion were analyzed. No significant differences at the $p < 0.05$ level were found on any of the 16 measures of cognitive function studied. An open trial of 45 mg of methylphenidate in 8 subjects failed to influence significantly performance on 15 of 16 cognitive measures. The exception, a decline on the immediate paragraph recall subtest of the Guild Memory Test, was attributed to chance. Peripheral autonomic effects were observed in some of the subjects given the 45 mg tablet. The investigators concluded that the objective of producing CNS stimulation in the elderly individual without a concomitant increase in peripheral activity may not be easily realized with methylphenidate or similar sympathomimetic amines.

Supporting these findings in impaired elderly subjects is the study of Gilbert et al. (67) in normal persons aged 60 and over. They administered methylphenidate over a 6-week period, up to a maximum of 30 mg. A control group received placebo, and testing was conducted in accordance with a double-blind design. Subjects were administered the WAIS vocabulary subtest, the Guild Memory Test, and a mood scale at the beginning of the study, at the midpoint, and at termination. No differences were found between the subjects receiving methylphenidate and those receiving placebo on any of the memory or mood variables. The only noteworthy finding was a tentative indication that methylphenidate reduced fatigue.

Another psychostimulant substance which has been evaluated in this area is pentylenetetrazol. Prien reviewed 13 controlled and comparative studies with this agent in chronic brain syndrome and noted that only 5 yielded favorable results (145). Subsequently, Lehman and Ban (144) conducted a double-blind controlled study of the effects of 300 to 600 mg of pentylenetetrazol daily over a 9-week-period in organically impaired, geriatric, psychiatric inpatients. Patients were assessed for change on a battery of psychiatric, psychometric, and electrophysiologic measures. Only one of these many measures showed any statistically significant change, and that change was in a negative direction. Specifically, patients receiving pentylenetetrazol showed a decline in "social interest," as assessed on the NOSIE scale.

The possibility remains that pentylenetetrazol may yet prove to have clinical utility if a subgroup of patients who demonstrate response can be reliably identified. Supporting this possibility are the findings of Ananth et al. (7). They observed that a subgroup of "psychogeriatric" patients treated with a combined regimen of pentylenetetrazol and nicotinic acid showed improvement, and a smaller subgroup actually showed deterioration.

Other psychostimulants with adrenergic agonist properties may prove to exert salutary effects in chronic organic brain syndrome and senility through this mechanism. The decrease in brain adrenergic activity and the increase in monoamine oxidase activity, which are well known to occur in normal aging, provide a logical rationale for such a treatment approach. Pipradol is an example of this class of psychostimulants. It is thought to be a central adrenergic activator (179) and CNS stimulant (152). One controlled study (180) and uncontrolled observations (111,119,143) support its possible utility in geriatric subjects.

In summary, psychostimulant compounds, as a group, have not fulfilled their promise in the alleviation of cognitive decline. The possibility remains that specific subgroups of patients may eventually be identified in whom one or more of these compounds may prove clinically useful. Until such groupings can be identified, clinical utility for this pharmacologic class remains unsubstantiated.

NOOTROPICS

This is a new class of pharmacologic agents. The precise definition of these substances and the common pharmacologic characteristics which can be used to define members of this class are becoming increasingly confused. The term nootropics was originally developed by Giurgea and his colleagues at the UCB-

Pharmacological Division in Brussels (68,69). It is derived from the Greek roots νοοσ, meaning "mind," and τροπειν, meaning "towards." This has resulted in some investigators' usage of the term for any drug which is postulated to enhance cognitive functioning by any mechanism. As originally developed, however, the term is considerably narrower. It refers to substances which act specifically on the associative, integrative mechanisms of the brain. The prototypical compound which formed the basis for all early work in this area is piracetam or "Nootropil."

Piracetam (2-oxo-1 pyrrolidine acetamide) is a cyclic derivative of gamma-amino-butyric acid (GABA). It has been shown to increase the threshold of central nystagmus excitability (142). In other animal models, piracetam has been shown to enhance learning in various situations (197), to delay hypoxic amnesia (70), and to alter the time course of the development of certain CNS reflexes (71). Perhaps most significantly, it increases the amplitude of the transcallosal evoked potential (72-74). The latter would seem to support the drug's postulated physiologic action, namely, the enhancement of associative cortical functioning and of the interhemispheric transfer of information.

Although piracetam possesses definite CNS activity, no peripheral effects have been demonstrated in any dosage tested, either in animals or in man (142). It differs from the known classes of compounds with CNS effects. For example, it does not possess any analgesic, sedative, or tranquillizing properties. It does not increase motor activity. It has no effect on the stereotypic behavior promoted in rats by amphetamine or the emesis provoked in dogs by apomorphine. Neither antihistaminic, anticholinergic, nor antiserotonergic properties appear to be present. It is also necessary to differentiate piracetam from the many compounds which affect cerebral circulation. Gustafson et al. (83) studied regional cerebral blood flow in eight presenile patients using the ^{133}Xe inhalation method. Patients received either placebo, 4.8 g of piracetam daily, or 9.6 g of piracetam daily. Measurements were recorded after 2 weeks and after 4 weeks. No significant effects of piracetam were obtained on regional cerebral blood flow measures. Piracetam may influence cerebral energy reserves, however. Pede et al. (139) found that the ratio of ATP to ADP in the brain was increased with drug treatment. In summary, piracetam appears to be unique in its CNS effects as well as in its lack of peripheral effects. Any other compounds to which the term "nootropic" is applied should share some of these unique features.

In the area of cognitive functioning, Dimond and Browers (46) conducted a study of the effects of piracetam on the ability of healthy college students to master a verbal memorization task. At the end of 2 weeks, students receiving 400 mg of piracetam daily performed significantly better than controls on the learning measure. Mindus et al. (129) examined the effects of 1.6 g of piracetam t.i.d. on an older group of otherwise healthy persons with subjective memory impairment. Their 19 volunteers ranged in age from 47 to 73 years. The piracetam-treated patients in their double-blind, intra-individual, cross-over designed study performed significantly better than the controls on a variety of performance, cognitive, and "global" variables. These included the ability to pair digits with symbols, to identify groupings of dots in a minimal time period, the reaction time to visual stimuli, performance on hand-tapping test, etc. Global ratings of both the psychiatrist and the psychologist were also significantly better for the subjects receiving piracetam.

Steginck (170) studied the effects of 2.4 g of piracetam daily on the behavior and performance of cognitively impaired, mostly elderly persons. They found significant positive effects on persons with mild to moderate impairment, but not on those with severe dementia. Their mild to moderate patients who were treated with piracetam improved significantly more than the placebo group on such behavior variables as fatigue, understanding, attention, concentration, irritability, agitation, and circumstantiality, as well as in terms of global improvement.

Other workers (2,177) have failed to observe significant positive effects of piracetam in severely impaired senile dements.

We may conclude at this time that piracetam is an interesting and seemingly unique substance which may be the forerunner of a new pharmacologic class of compounds. There is preliminary evidence that it may be useful in improving functioning in patients with mild to moderate senile dementia. It has not been shown to be of value in severely demented patients.

NEUROPEPTIDES

These substances have attracted considerable recent attention. They collectively serve to highlight the new-found unity of the behavioral, nervous, and endocrine systems. Some brain proteins, notably ACTH, MSH, and vasopressin, have been shown to have definite effects on the learning process, particularly in animal models.

De Wied found that removal of the pituitary decreased the ability of certain animals to acquire a conditioned avoidance behavior (191). This process could be reversed by the administration of ACTH, MSH, or vasopressin (192,193). The effect was shown to be independent of the adrenal action of ACTH. Adrenalectomy actually enhanced avoidance learning in one study, presumably because of the increase in circulating corticotropic hormone which results (188). Also MSH was as effective as ACTH in the learning model, although it lacks the peripheral effects of ACTH. Subsequent work demonstrated that a particular peptide fragment which is common to both the ACTH and MSH molecular structures was responsible for the learning effects of these compounds. It is the heptapeptide $ACTH_{4-10}$. It was even possible to further reduce these peptides to four amino acid chains while maintaining the learning properties (80,137).

Human studies with $ACTH_{4-10}$ have not as yet confirmed its clinical utility. A review of the current data suggests that the compound may act on attentional processes with both facilitatory and inhibitory results. In many ways its observed effects are analogous to those of the psychostimulants. $ACTH_{4-10}$ has been shown to improve performance of normal volunteers on such visual–attentional–performance tasks as the Benton Visual Retention test, the Visual Reproduction subscale of the Wechsler Memory test (128,162), and the Rod and Frame test (162). Other attentional tasks are either enhanced or, as is also found with the psychostimulant compounds, complex tasks may show deficits. Hence performance improved during a continuous reaction-time task (63), and declined on a bisensory memory test (48).

Three reports have appeared concerning the short-term effects of $ACTH_{4-10}$ in cognitively impaired elderly patients. Ferris et al. (143) examined the effects of single subcutaneous injections of 15 mg or 30 mg of $ACTH_{4-10}$ as compared with placebo on 13 measures of cognitive functioning. Their measures were repeated twice daily, before and after injection, over a 3-day period. The results were largely negative in that significant differences did not emerge between the placebo, 15 mg or 30 mg groups on the majority of measures. The single positive finding was improvement in the facial recognition task 24 hours following the 30 mg injection for patients with severe impairment. One other finding also emerged, a slowing of visual reaction time after the 30 mg injection as compared with the 15 mg or placebo injections. No differences were found between the groups on EEG measures.

Other investigators have also noted an absence of significant changes in impaired geriatric subjects on the great majority of cognitive measures studied following 15 mg (194) or 30 mg (24) of $ACTH_{4-10}$. Braconnier et al. did find improvement in certain behavioral measures, however. Specifically, confusion, anger, and depression were reduced in their treatment group. In contrast with the earlier results of Ferris et al. (58), they did note EEG changes with an increase in theta activity and a decrease in fast alpha activity.

The human studies in both symptomatic geriatric and normal volunteer subjects would seem to indicate non-specific CNS effects of $ACTH_{4-10}$ on arousal systems. Current evidence does not indicate clinical utility. However, studies with higher dosages or with longer periods of administration might yield somewhat different results.

Vasopressin would appear to be more promising in terms of eventual clinical utility, particularly in the light of some recent reports. We have already alluded to the ability of vasopressin to reverse the deleterious memory effects of hypophysectomy. Other animal data also implicate vasopressin activity on memory procedures, particularly on long-term memory. Rats with a congenital inability to manufacture vasopressin are unable to retain long-term memory of conditioned avoidance responses (18). This defect can be artificially reversed by exogenous administration of a vasopressin analog. Antiserum to vasopressin injected in the cerebral ventricles neutralizes the learning enhancement effect (195). A vasopressin analog, desglycinamide[9]-lysine[8]-vasopressin, known as DG-LVP, has been shown to act in reversing amnesic agents in mice. DG-LVP worked when injected either after the acquisition of a conditioned avoidance response or prior to retrieval. It reversed amnesia resulting from electroconvulsive shock, from carbon dioxide, or from puromycin treatment (108).

Clinically, two reports have appeared concerning the effects of vasopressin on cognitive processes. Oliveros et al. (136) administered vasopressin nasal spray (lysine[8]-vasopressin) to four persons with amnesia of diverse etiology. Their anecdotal reports indicated accelerated improvement in memory in each instance. Legros et al. (110) examined the effects of vasopressin spray on 23 male inpatients on a medical service between 55 and 65 years of age. Their study was conducted double-blind, with one-half of the men receiving placebo (solvent-only) spray. The patients receiving vasopressin performed better on tests involving many memory and non-memory cognitive tasks. These included general attention, concentration, motor rapidity, visual attention, recognition, and recall performance on a learning and recognition task. These effects are reminiscent of some of the actions of $ACTH_{4-10}$. Vasopressin is known to stimulate the endogenous secretion of ACTH. Hence, one question to be answered is whether the observed effects of vasopressin are direct, secondary to its stimulation of ACTH, or through some other mechanism. A trial of the effects of vasopressin spray on senile patients would seem warranted.

The enkephalins are another group of endogenous neuropeptides which may have effects on cognition. These recently identified substances have been postulated as neurotransmitters in certain central pathways. They have been particularly implicated in the mediation of analgesis such as that induced by the opiates. Rigter (151) found that the enkephalins also affected learning in rats. Methionine enkephalin reduced CO_2-induced amnesia when given either prior to acquisition or prior to retrieval. Leucine enkephalin reduced the CO_2-induced amnesia only when given prior to retrieval.

Interestingly, the pituitary hormone, β-lipotropin, contains sequences corresponding both to the peptide $ACTH_{4-10}$ and to methionine enkephalin. The significance of this interrelationship, as well as of the cognitive effects of the neuropeptides in general, should become more clear in the next several years.

NEUROTRANSMITTERS

In the previous section we referred to the unity of the behavioral, nervous, and endocrine systems and the hypothesized cognitive role of postulated neurotransmitters. In consideration of these factors, it is not surprising that the principal neurotransmitter systems, particularly the cholinergic, dopaminergic, and adrenergic, have been implicated in cognitive processes in general, and in senile dementia in particular.

The cholinergic system has recently been singled out as perhaps being a primary locus of Alzheimer's disease-related memory impairment. Since Alzheimer's disease is currently considered the cause of the majority of cases of senile dementia, the implications for the pharmacotherapy of senile dementia are quite profound. The most compelling evidence involves the enzyme choline acetyltransferase (CAT), which is involved in the synthesis of acetylcholine. Pathological studies have revealed a widespread deficiency of this enzyme in the brains of patients with Alzheimer's disease (20,41,140,190). Recently, Bowen et al. (21) studied CAT activity in the temporal lobes of human brains. They found neither atrophy nor decreased CAT activity in the brains of aged, non-demented, controls. In controls of uncertain diagnosis, CAT activity was 68% of normal values; in patients with mixed Alzheimer's disease and circulatory dementia, CAT activity was 40% of that of controls; and in patients with pure Alzheimer's dementia, CAT activity was 35% that of the normal control. They also note that since the proportionate reduction in CAT activity in Alzheimer's disease is twice as great as the loss of nerve cells from the whole temporal lobe, perhaps there is a selective loss of cholinergic neurons.

A separate series of studies has implicated the cholinergic system in memory processes. Studies performed in animals have demonstrated that the administration of cholinomimetic agents at specific times following acquisition affects recall in a reversible manner. For example, physostigmine produced retrograde amnesia for the learned response when injected 4 or 5 days following acquisition, but not when injected 1 to 3 days following acquisition (17,45,89). Intracerebral injections of cholinergic agents such as diisopropyl fluorophosphate have been found to produce amnesic patterns which are similar temporally to those produced by systemically administered physostigmine (43,44). It has been recognized for many years that anticholinergic substances which are capable of crossing the blood-brain barrier such as scopolamine are capable of producing an amnesic syndrome in man (94). More recently, Drachman and Leavitt (49) studied the effects of scopolamine on young adult volunteers. They found memory effects which are very similar to those which occur in senile dementia. Specifically, both are associated with preservation of verbal IQ, relative sparing of immediate memory, impairment of memory storage and of general cognitive functioning, and increased appearance of slow waves on the electroencephalogram, particularly in the temporal area. Other investigators have studied the effects of agents which enhance cholinergic functioning on cognition. Three studies have found that physostigmine, the acetylcholinesterase inhibitor, has a biphasic effect in normal subjects (42,130,141). That is, it improves performance and cognition in the proper dosage for an individual, but impairs them if given in too high or too low a dose.

Other cholinomimetic agents have been investigated in our laboratory. Deanol, a putative central cholinergic enhancer, was given in a 4-week open-trial to 14 outpatients with mild to moderate cognitive deficit (57). Ten of the patients improved globally, and 4 were unchanged. The drug tended to reduce behavioral symptoms such as depression, irritability, and anxiety. However, neither the clinical ratings nor an extensive pre- versus post-treatment series of cognitive tests revealed changes in memory or other cognitive functions. In a separate study (163), the effect of choline chloride up to a maximum of 20 g/day was examined. No consistent improvement in either mood or cognition was produced. We are currently conducting a placebo-controlled, double-blind crossover study in which we are examining in much greater detail the effects of choline chloride up to a maximum of 12 g daily.

The hypothesis of cholinergic deficit in Alzheimer's type senile dementia raises the question of a possible role for dietary factors and dietary supplements in the treatment of the disease. Choline is a dietary component present in many foods, notably egg yolk, meat and fish. Administration of choline orally or parenterally increases serum choline, brain choline, and brain acetylcholine in rat models (33,34). It is thought that choline accelerates the synthesis (34) and the release of brain acetylcholine (181,182). The usual source of choline in the diet is a substance called lecithin or phosphatidylcholine. Recent studies show that consumption of lecithin elevates human serum choline levels more effectively than an equivalent quantity of choline salts (90). A diet rich in choline and lecithin may cause prolonged elevations in serum choline concentrations. In contrast, a diet low in choline-containing foods produces low serum choline concentrations. The consequences of these variations for memory functioning in Alzheimer's disease and senile dementia in general remain undetermined.

Other evidence indicates a role for the catecholamines in cognition in general and senile dementia in particular. It has been found that diethyldithiocarbonic acid, a substance which inhibits the production of norepinephrine in the CNS, blocked 24-hr recall of a passive avoidance task when given to mice prior to, or immediately after, acquisition. Perhaps of even greater relevance, McEntee and Mair (121) have found a decrease in the spinal fluid concentration of the principal metabolite of norepinephrine (3-methoxy-4-hydroxyphenylglycol, or MHPG) in patients with Korsakoff's psychosis. Furthermore, they noted a correlation between the extent of decrease of MHPG in the CSF and the severity of memory impairment in individual patients.

A brief schematic review of catecholamine synthesis and metabolism will enhance our understanding of recent findings concerning the relationship between these substances and senile dementia.

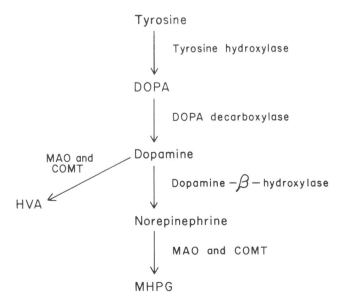

Tyrosine hydroxylase activity in certain brain areas has been shown to decrease with age (36,123), although the findings have not been consistent (155). DOPA decarboxylase activity also appears to decrease in many areas of the brain with age (181). MAO activity has been reported to increase with age in several studies (36,154,160). Given these decreases in synthesizing enzymes and increase in catabolic enzyme activity, it is not surprising that dopamine and norepinephrine levels were found to decrease with physiological aging (25).

Recently, Adolfsson et al. (4) studied MAO activity in patients with Alzheimer's disease as compared with age-matched controls. They found an increase in platelet MAO activity in the platelets of Alzheimer's patients as compared with that of age-matched controls.

The above findings have led some investigators to attempt treatment of dementia with L-DOPA and related substances. Drachman and Stahl (50) found mild parkinsonian symptoms in a group of patients with mild senile dementia and found that open treatment with L-DOPA resulted in improvement of the cognitive syndrome as well as the parkinsonian symptoms. An open, dose-ranging study was conducted in our laboratory (163). Some changes occurred in mood and cognitive test performance, but no consistent pattern of improvement was observed when 16 patients with mild to moderate dementia were treated with up to 2 g of L-DOPA for 4 weeks. Kristensen et al. (105) have published a controlled study in which they failed to differentiate between L-DOPA and placebo in presenile dementia. Using L-DOPA combined with carbidopa (dose range: L-DOPA 375 to 1,250 mg and carbidopa 37.5 to 125 mg), Adolphson et al. (4) have reported preliminary results which they consider more promising.

Other neurotransmitter systems may also interact in the genesis of the symptomatology of senile dementia. For example, brain serotonin content has been shown to decrease with aging (122), as has tryptophan hydroxylase activity (126). Perhaps, ultimately, replacement therapy will depend upon finding the proper balance among the various neurotransmitter systems. Hopefully, however, one system will ultimately be shown to play a dominant role, and therapeutic measures can be adjusted accordingly.

TRANQUILIZERS

These agents are utilized for the agitation and disturbances of thinking, mood and behavior which may occur in moderate to severe senile dementia.

Some generalizations are useful. The rule of thumb is to begin elderly patients on one-third to one-half the dose for younger adults (159). As we shall see, research has generally supported this clinical maxim. The reasons for this differential between young and old are undoubtedly many and varied. Included is the fact that the elderly are somewhat smaller than young adults. Also, their basal metabolism is lower. For the neuroleptics and other drugs which act on the central neurotransmitters, other particular sensitivities apply. As discussed previously, brain neurotransmitter levels often decrease with age. This may sensitize individuals not only to neuroleptic therapeutic effects, but also to side effects such as secondary parkinsonian symptoms. Also, in advanced Alzheimer's disease, the functioning brain tissue may be significantly reduced with concurrent lowering of receptor sites. Finally, it should be recognized that an attenuation in sensitivity for the sedative effects of all medications occurs with increased experience on the medication. For the neuroleptics, it has been shown that other side effects are also more frequent and more prominent at lower dosages in individuals who have not had as extensive exposure to these compounds (95). For patients who develop agitation and/or psychosis for the first time resulting from the effects of a senile organic process, the latter generalization may apply.

Thioridazine has been singled out among the neuroleptics as a drug of choice for the treatment of geriatric patients because of its unique combination of side effects, which are considered to be relatively benign in this particularly sensitive patient population, and its proven therapeutic efficacy (30,56,95,96, 102,104,105,112,116,122,126,159,202). The choice of this agent over other neuroleptics does not appear to be established. For example, in one relevant study conducted among geriatric patients in a nursing home, thioridazine was compared with haloperidol for efficacy in patients with chronic organic brain syndrome and senile psychosis (169). Over the 6-week period, treatment with an average dose of 2.0 mg of haloperidol or with an average dose of 106.7 mg of thioridazine proved effective on symptoms of agitation, disruptive behavior, and psychotic symptomatology. Haloperidol, in this study, actually produced consistently greater improvement on ratings of total pathology.

Other studies, although far from numerous, do support the conclusion that neuroleptics which have been proven effective in treating symptomatology in younger persons are also effective, in lower dosages, in elderly persons with behavioral disturbances secondary to senile dementia. For example, Goldstein and Dippy (75) studied mesoridazine administration in geriatric patients with organic brain syndromes. Patients were taken off their previous medications and treated with an average dose of 75 mg of mesoridazine daily. On the physicians' open ratings, 9 patients showed general improvement, 10 were unchanged, and 4 patients worsened. On the nurses' ratings, patients showed even greater improvement. Kropach (106) treated acutely agitated senile patients with trifluoperazine with good results.

For non-psychotic senile patients with agitation or anxiety, both neuroleptics and anxiolytics appear to be effective. Cervera (200) conducted a double-blind study comparing thioridazine with diazepam in the treatment of 60 nonpsychotic senile inpatients. An average dose of 79 mg of thioridazine daily (range 10 to 200 mg daily) and an average dose of 12 mg of diazepam daily (range 2 to 40 mg daily) were both 95% effective in the treatment of anxious mood, tension, insomnia, and agitation. No significant differences in efficacy were found between the two medications. However, the trend was toward more marked improvement with thioridazine.

We may conclude that the limited data from well-designed control studies conducted with senile patients available at this time support two assumptions which clinicians have traditionally followed. First, the actions of neuroleptics and anxiolytics in the elderly, in terms of efficacy and target symptomatology, are essentially the same as in younger adults. Secondly, the elderly respond to lower dosages than do younger adults. The evidence, however, does not support clinicians' prejudices in terms of choice of neuroleptic or anxiolytic medication.

ANTIDEPRESSANTS

Apart from Alzheimer's disease and vascular etiologies, depression is thought to be the most common cause of presentation with "dementia." It is also the most readily treatable common cause of dementia-like symptomatology. The incidence of depression tends to be much higher for women until age 65. After 65, depression tends to occur equally frequently in both sexes. The incidence of depression tends to be much higher for women until age 65. After 65, depression tends to occur equally frequently in both sexes. The incidence of depression in the elderly population is not precisely known. However, another study found it accounted for up to 45% of new admissions of people over 65 to voluntary and private mental hospitals (132).

Although the incidence of depression increases with age, the vast majority of controlled studies concerning the pharmacotherapy of the disorder have been conducted in persons under 65. For persons under 65, there is voluminous evidence for the utility and efficacy of tricyclics and MAO inhibitors in the treatment of the disorder. For geriatric depression *per se,* however, the literature is very limited.

One double-blind controlled study found imipramine superior to placebo on clinical rating measures in geriatric depressed patients (204). One study found the combination of an MAO inhibitor, tranylcypromine, with the neuroleptic trifluoperazine effective in aged depressed patients (172). Another study found the combination of 25 mg amitriptyline and 10 mg chlordiazepoxide to be apparently more effective than 25 mg of amitriptyline alone (86). An additional combination study found amitryptyline and perphenazine superior to placebo for the treatment of geriatric depression (87).

Balanced against these combination study results is the fact that geriatric patients may already be receiving multiple medications for various medical and psychiatric problems, and physicians should be reluctant to add unnecessarily to this list. "Polypharmacy" has encountered considerable recent criticism because of the unnecessary side effects attendant upon such treatment.

This limited information currently available regarding pharmacologic effects of antidepressants in geriatric patients is balanced somewhat by the large uncontrolled clinical experience using standard antidepressant medications in geriatric patients. At present, it is probably wise to proceed with treatment in geriatric depression in accordance with findings established more firmly in younger adults.

Dosages should be somewhat lower for the reasons discussed previously, as well as because of the sensitivity of the elderly to the anticholinergic effects of the tricyclics. Polypharmacy should be eschewed. Studies are currently being planned which should ultimately place the pharmacologic treatment of geriatric depressive illness on a firmer scientific foundation.

CONCLUSION

We may conclude that pharmacologic treatment of senile dementia remains in its infancy. However, in the last several years a body of basic information regarding this disease has been accumulating. Concurrently, a pharmacologic science of cognitive processing has begun to develop. These processes have combined to produce several logical pharmacologic treatments which have been explored to a variable extent. Some treatments, particularly hydergine and some of the other vasodilators, appear particularly efficacious, at least for certain behavioral symptoms, on the basis of current information. Others, such as the cholinomimetics, seem particularly promising. Ultimately, the real promise of medicine and pharmacology in this area must include not only symptomatic remediation, but treatment of the disease process itself, based upon a deeper understanding of its etiology and perhaps the possibility of prophylaxis.

REFERENCES

1. Abrams, A., Tobin, S. S., Gordon, P., Pechtel, C., and Hilkevitch, A. (1965): The effects of a European procaine preparation in an aged population. I. Psychological effects. *J. Gerontol.* 20:139.
2. Abuzzahab, F. S., Merwin, G. E., Zimmerman, R. L., and Sherman, M. C. (1978): A double-blind investigation of Piracetam (Nootropil) versus placebo in the memory of geriatric inpatients. *Psychopharmacol. Bull.* 14:23–25.
3. Aderman, M., Giordina, J., Korcnioski, O. (1972): Effect of cyclandelate on perception, memory and cognition in a group of geriatric subjects. *J. Am. Geriatr. Soc.* 20:268–271.
4. Adolfsson, R., Gottfried, C. G., Oreland, L., Roos, B. E., and Winblad, B. (1978): Reduced levels of catecholamines in the brain and increased activity of monoamine oxidase in platelets in Alzheimer's disease: Therapeutic implications. In: *Aging, vol. 7, Alzheimer's Disease: Senile Dementia and Related Disorders,* edited by R. Katzman, R. D. Terry and K. L. Bick. Raven Press, New York.
5. Affleck, D. C., Treptow, K. R., and Herrick, H. D. (1961): The effects of Isoxsuprine HC1 (Vasodilan) on chronic cerebral arteriosclerosis. *J. Nerv. Ment. Dis.* 132:335–338.
6. Aizawa, T., Tazaki, Y., and Gotoh, F. (1961): Cerebral circulation in cerebrovascular disease. *World Neurol.* 2:635–645.
7. Ananth, J. V., Deutsch, M., and Ban, T. A. (1971): Senilex in the treatment of geriatric patients. *Curr. Ther. Res.* 13:316–321.
8. Aslan, A. (1960): Procaine therapy in old age and other disorders (Novocain Factor H3). *Gerontol. Clin.* 3:148.
9. Aslan, A. (1962): Therapeutics of old age—the action of procaine. In: *Medical and Clinical Aspects of Aging,* pp. 279–292, edited by H. T. Blumenthal. Columbia University Press, New York.
10. Aslan, A. (1974): Theoretical and practical aspects of chemotherapeutic techniques in the retardation of the aging process. In: *Theoretical Aspects of Aging,* pp. 177–186, edited by M. Rockstein. Academic Press, New York.

11. Bachrach, S. (1959): A new stimulant supplement for the geriatric patient. *J. Am. Geriatr. Soc.* 7:408–409.
12. Ball, J. A. C., and Taylor, A. R. (1967): Effect of cyclandelate on mental function and cerebral blood flow in elderly patients. *Br. Med. J.* 3:525–578.
13. Banen, D. M. (1972): An ergot preparation (hydergine) for relief of symptoms of cerebrovascular insufficiency. *J. Am. Geriatr. Soc.* 20:22–24.
14. Bare, W. W. (1960): A stimulant for the aged. Observations on a methylphenidate-vitamin-hormone combination (Ritonic). *J. Am. Geriatr. Soc.* 8:292–297.
15. Bare, W. W., and Lin, D. Y. (1962): A stimulant for the aged. II. Long-term observations with a methylphenidate-vitamin-hormone combination (Ritonic). *J. Am. Geriatr. Soc.* 10:539–544.
16. Bazo, A. J. (1973): An ergot alkaloid preparation (hydergine) versus papaverine in treating common complaints of the aged: double-blind study. *J. Am. Geriatr. Soc.* 21:63–71.
17. Biederman, G. B. (1970): Forgetting of an operant response: physostigmine produced increase in escape latency in rats as a function of time of injection. *Q. J. Exp. Psychol.* 22:384–388.
18. Bohus, B., Wimersma Greidanus, T. B. van, and Wied, D. de (1975): Behavioral and endocrine responses of rats with hereditary hypothalamic diabetes insipidus (Brattleboro strain). *Physiol. Behav.* 14:609–615.
19. Bouvier, J. B., Passeron, O., and Chapin, M. P. (1974): Psychometric study of proxilend. *J. Int. Med. Res.* 2:59–65.
20. Bowen, D. M., Smith, C. B., White, P., and Davison, A. N. (1976): Neurotransmitter-related enzymes and indices of hypoxia in senile dementia and other abiotrophies. *Brain* 99:459–496.
21. Bowen, D. M., White, P., Spillane, J. A., Goodhardt, M. J., Curzon, G., Iwangoff, P., Meier-Ruge, W., and Davison, A. N. (1979): Accelerated aging or selective neuronal loss as an important cause of dementia? *Lancet* 1:11–14.
22. Branconnier, R., and Cole, J. O. (1977): Senile dementia and drug therapy. In: *Advances in Behavioral Biology, vol. 23, The Aging Brain and Senile Dementia*, pp. 271–283, edited by K. Nandy and I. Sherwin. Plenum Press, New York.
23. Branconnier, R. J., and Cole, J. O. (1977): Effects of chronic papaverine administration on mild senile organic brain syndrome. *J. Am. Geriatr. Soc.* 25:458–462.
24. Branconnier, R. J., Cole, J. O., and Gardos, G. (1978): ACTH$_{4-10}$ in the amelioration of neuropsychological symptomatology associated with senile organic brain syndrome. *Psychopharmacol. Bull.* 14:27–30.
25. Brody, H. (1973): Aging of the vertebrate brain. In: *Development and Aging in the Nervous System,* edited by M. Rockstein, pp. 121–133. Academic Press, New York.
26. Brodie, N. H. (1977): A double-blind trial of naftidrofuryl in treating confused elderly patients in general practice. *Practioner* 218:274–279.
27. Brun, A., Gustafson, L., and Ingvar, D. H. (1975): Neuropathological findings related to neuropsychiatric symptoms and regional cerebral blood flow in presenile dementia. In: *VIIth International Congress on Neuropathology, Budapest,* pp. 101–105. Exerpta Medica, Amsterdam.
28. Canadian Cooperative Study Group (1978): A randomized trial of aspirin and sulfinpyrazone in threatened stroke. *N. Engl. J. Med.* 299:53–59.
29. Capote, B., and Parikh, N. (1978): Cyclandelate in the treatment of senility: A controlled study. *J. Am. Geriatr. Soc.* 26:360–362.
30. Cavero, C. V. (1966): Evaluation of thioridazine in the aged. *J. Am. Geriatr. Soc.* 14:617–622.
31. Cervera, A. A. (1974): Psychoactive drug therapy in the senile patient: Controlled comparison of thioridazine and diazepam. *Psychiatry Digest* 35:15–21.
32. Christian, W. (1968): *Elektroenzephalographie Lehrbuch und Atlas.* Georg Thieme, Stuttgart.
33. Cohen, E. L., and Wurtman, R. J. (1975): Brain ACh increase after systemic choline administration. *Life Sci.* 16:1095–1102.
34. Cohen, E. L., and Wurtman, R. J. (1976): Brain ACh: Control by dietary choline. *Science* 191:561–562.
35. Cohen, S., and Ditman, K. S. (1974): Gerovital-H3 in the treatment of the depressed aging patient. *Psychosomatics* 15:15–19.
36. Cote, L. J., and Kremzner, L. T. (1974): Changes in neurotransmitter systems with increasing age in human brain. *Trans. Am. Soc. Neurochem.* 5:83.

37. Cox, J. R. (1975): Double-blind evaluation of naftidrofuryl in treating elderly confused, hospitalized patients. *Gerontol. Clin. (Basel)* 17:160–167.

38. Crook, T., Ferris, S., Sathananthan, G., Raskin, A., and Gershon, S. (1977): The effect of methylphenidate on test performance in the cognitively impaired aged. *Psychopharmacologia* 52:251–255.

39. Dahl, G. (1972): *WIP-Reduzieter Wechsler-Intelligent Test*. Meisenheim.

40. Darvill, F. T., Jr. (1954): Double-blind evaluation of methylphenidate (Ritalin) hydrochloride. *J.A.M.A.* 169:1739–1741.

41. Davies, P., and Maloney, A. J. F. (1976): Selective loss of central cholinergic neurons in Alzheimer's disease. *Lancet* 2:1403.

42. Davis, K. L., Hollister, L. E., Overall, J., Johnson, A., and Train, K. (1976): Physostigmine. Effects on cognition and affect in normal subjects. *Psychopharmacologia* 51:23–27.

43. Deutsch, J. A., Hamburg, M. D., and Dahl, H. (1966): Anticholinesterase-induced amnesia and its temporal aspects. *Science* 151:221–223.

44. Deutsch, J. A., and Lutzsky, H. (1967): Memory enhancement by anticholinesterase as a function of initial learning. *Nature* 213:742.

45. Deutsch, J. A., and Weiner, N. I. (1969): Analysis of extinction through amnesia. *J. Comp. Physiol. Psychol.* 69:179–184.

46. Dimond, S. J., and Brouwers, E. Y. M. (1976): Increase in the power of human memory in normal man through the use of drugs. *Psychopharmacologia* 49:307–309.

47. Ditch, M., Kelly, F. J., and Resnick, O. (1971): An ergot preparation (hydergine) in the treatment of cerebrovascular disorders in the geriatric patient: double-blind study. *J. Am. Geriatr. Soc.* 19:208–217.

48. Dornbush, R. L., and Nikolovski, O. (1976): ACTH$_{4-10}$ and short-term memory. *Pharmacol. Biochem. Behav.* 5, *Suppl* 1:69–72.

49. Drachman, D. A., and Leavitt, J. (1974): Human memory and the cholinergic system: A relationship to aging. *Arch. Neurol.* 30:113–121.

50. Drachman, D. A., and Stahl, S. (1975): Extrapyramidal dementia and levodopa. *Lancet* 1:809.

51. Duvoisin, R. C. (1975): Antagonism of levadopa by papaverine. *J.A.M.A.* 231:845–846.

52. Ehrenreich, D. L., Burns, R. A., Altman, R. W., and Fazekas, J. F. (1961): Influence of acetipolamide on cerebral blood flow. *Arch. Neurol.* 5:125–130.

53. Eichhorn, O. (1965): The effect of cyclandelate on cerebral circulation. *Vasc. Dis.* 2:305–315.

54. Ernst, A. M. (1962): Experiments with an O-methylated product of dopamine on cats. *Acta Physiol. Pharmacol. Neerl.* 11:48–53.

55. Fee, S. R., and Clark, A. N. G. (1961): Trial of procaine in the aged. *Br. Med. J.* 2:1680–1682.

56. Felger, H. (1966): Thioridazine in the geriatric patient. *Dis. Nerv. Syst.* 27:537–538.

57. Ferris, S. H., Sathananthan, G., Gershon, S., and Clark, C. (1977): Senile dementia. Treatment with deanol. *J. Am. Geriatr. Soc.* 25:241–244.

58. Ferris, S. H., Sathananthan, G., Gershon, S., Clark, C., and Moshinsky, J. (1976): Cognitive effects of ACTH$_{4-10}$ in the elderly. *Pharmacol. Biochem. Behav.* 5, *Suppl.* 1:73–78.

59. Fine, E. W., Lewis, D., Villa-Landa, I., and Blakemore, C. B. (1970): The effect of cyclandelate on mental function in patients with arteriosclerotic brain disease. *Br. J. Psychiatry* 117:157–161.

60. Fontaine, L., Grand, M., Chabert, J., Szavasi, E., and Bayssat, M. (1968): Pharmacology of naftidrofuryl, a new vasodilator. *Chim. Ther.* 3 (6):463–469.

61. Freyhan, F. A., Woodford, R. B., and Kety, S. S. (1951): Cerebral blood flow and metabolism in psychosis of senility. *J. Nerv. Ment. Dis.* 113:449–456.

62. Friedan, O. L. (1963): An investigation of Gerovital-H3 (procaine hydrochloride) in treatment of organic brain syndrome. *Gerontologist* 3 (3):25.

63. Gaillard, A. W. K., and Sanders, A. F. (1975): Some effects of ACTH$_{4-10}$ on performance during a serial reaction task. *Psychopharmacologia* 42:201–208.

64. Gericke, O. L., Lobb, L. G., and Pardall, D. H. (1961): An evaluation of procaine in geriatric patients in a mental hospital. *J. Clin. Exp. Psychopathol.* 22:18.

65. Gerin, J. (1969): Symptomatic treatment of cerebrovascular insufficiency with hydergine. *Curr. Ther. Res.* 11:539–546.

66. Gerin, J. (1974): Double-blind trial of naftidrofuryl in the treatment of cerebral arteriosclerosis. *Br. J. Clin. Pract.* 28:177–178.

67. Gilbert, J. G., Donnelly, K. J., Zimmer, L. E., and Kubis, J. F. (1973): Effect of magnesium pemoline and methylphenidate on memory improvement and mood in normal aging subjects. *Int. J. Aging. Hum. Dev.* 4:35–51.
68. Giurgea, C. (1972): The "Nootropic" approach to the pharmacology of the integrative activity of the brain. *Cond. Reflex* 8:108–115.
69. Giurgea, C. (1972): Vers une pharmacologie de l'activité intégrative du cerveau. Tentative du concept nootrope en psychopharmacologie. *Actual. Pharmacol.* (Paris) 25:115–156.
70. Giurgea, C., Le Fevre, D., Lescrenier, C., and David-Remacle, M. (1971): Pharmacological protection against hypoxia-induced amnesia in rats. *Psychopharmacologia* 20:160–168.
71. Girugea, C., and Mouravieff-Lesuisse, F. (1971): Pharmacological studies on an elementary model of learning. The fixation of an experience at spinal level (Part I: pharmacological reactivity of the spinal cord fixation time). *Arch. Int. Pharmacodyn. Ther.* 191/2:279–291.
72. Girugea, C., and Moyersoons, F. (1970): Differential pharmacological reactivity of three types of cortical evoked potentials. *Arch. Int. Pharmacodyn. Ther.* 188:401–404.
73. Giurgea, C., and Moyersoons, F. (1972): On the pharmacology of cortical evoked potentials. *Arch. Int. Pharmacodyn. Ther.* 199:67–78.
74. Giurgea, C., and Moyersoons, F. (1974): Contribution a l'étude électrophysiologique et pharmacologique de la transmission calleuse. *Coll. Int. Les Syndromes de Disconnexion Calleuse Chez l'Homme, Lyon,* pp. 53–72. Department de Recherches, Pharmacologiques U.C.B., Division Pharmaceutique B, Brussels.
75. Goldstein, B. J., and Dippy, W. E. (1967): A clinical evaluation of mesoridazine in geriatric patients. *Curr. Ther. Res.* 9:256–260.
76. Goodman, L. S., and Gilman, A. (1970): *The Pharmacological Basis of Therapeutics,* 4th ed., pp. 371–401. Macmillan, New York.
77. Gordon, E. B., and Sim, M. (1967): The EEG in presenile dementia. *J. Neurol. Neurosurg. Psychiatry* 30:285–291.
78. Gotoh, F., Meyer, J. S., and Tomita, M. (1966): Carbonic anhydrase inhibition and cerebral venous blood gases and ions in man. *Arch. Intern. Med.* 117:39–46.
79. Green, M. A., Stevenson, L. D., Fonseca, J. E., and Wortis, S. B. (1952): Cerebral biopsy in patients with presenile dementia. *Dis. Nerv. Syst.* 13:303–307.
80. Greven, H. M., and Wied, D. de. (1973): The influence of peptides derived from ACTH on performance structure activity studies. In: *Prog. Brain Res.* 39:429–442.
81. Gurland, M., and Hayman, M. (1974): Gerovital-H3 in the treatment of depression in a private practice population: A double-blind study. Paper presented at the annual meeting of the Academy of Psychosomatic Medicine, Scottsdale, Arizona, November 1974.
82. Gustafson, L., and Brun, A. (1976): Distribution of cerebral degeneration in Alzheimer's disease. A clinico-pathological study. *Arch. Psychiatr. Nervenkr.* 223(1):15–33.
83. Gustafson, L., Risberg, J., Johanson, M., Fransson, M., and Maximilian, V. A. (1978): Effects of Piraceton on regional cerebral blood flow and mental functions in patients with organic dementia. *Psychopharmacologia* 56:115–117.
84. Hachinski, V. C., Lassen, N. A., and Marshall, J. (1974): Multi-infarct dementia, a cause of mental deterioration in the elderly. *Lancet* 2:207–210.
85. Hadjiev, D. (1974): Impedance methods for investigation of cerebral circulation. *Brain Res.* 14:25–85.
86. Haider, I. (1967): A comparative trial of RO 4-6270 and amtriptyline in depressive illness. *Br. J. Psychiatry* 113:993–998.
87. Haider, I. (1967): Amitriptyline and perphenazine in depressive illness. A controlled trial. *Br. J. Psychiatry* 113:195–199.
88. Hall, P. (1976): Cyclandelate in the treatment of cerebral arteriosclerosis. *J. Am. Geriatr. Soc.* 24:41–45.
89. Hamburg, M. D., and Fulton, D. R. (1972): Influence of recall on an anticholinesterase induced retrograde amnesia. *Psysiol. Behav.* 9:409–418.
90. Hirsh, M. J., Growden, J. H., and Wurtman, R. J. (1978): Relations between dietary choline or lecithin intake, serum choline levels and various metabolic indices. *Metabolism* 27:953–960.
91. Horton, G. E., and Johnson, P. C. (1964): The application of radioisotopes to the study of cerebral blood flow, comparison of three methods. *Angiology* 15:70–74.
92. Hughes, J. R., Williams, J. G., and Currier, R. D. (1976): An ergot alkaloid preparation

(hydergine) in the treatment of dementia: critical review of the clinical literature. *J. Am. Geriatr. Soc.* 24:490–497.

93. Ingvar, D. H., and Gustafson, L. (1970): Regional cerebral blood flow in organic dementia with early onset. *Acta. Neurol. Scand.* [*Suppl.*] 46:42–73.

94. Innes, I. R., and Nickerson, N. (1970): Drugs inhibiting the action of acetylcholine on structures innervated by postganglionic parasympathetic nerves (antimuscarinic or atropinic drugs). In: *The Pharmacological Basis of Therapeutics,* 4th ed., pp. 524–548, edited by L. S. Goodman and A. Gilman, Macmillan, New York.

95. Itil, T. M., and Reisberg, B. (1977): Transcultural aspects of psychopharmacology. *Curr. Psychiatr. Ther.* 17:325–332.

96. Jackson, E. B. (1961): Mellaril in the treatment of the geriatric patient. *Am. J. Psychiatry* 118:543–544.

97. Jacobsen, A. (1958): The use of Ritalin in psychotherapy of depressions of the aged. *Psychiat. Quart.* 32:474–483.

98. Jarvik, L. F., and Milne, J. F. (1975): Gerovital-H3: A review of the literature. In: *Aging,* vol. 2, pp. 203–227, edited by S. Gershon and A. Raskin. Raven Press, New York.

99. Jayne, H. W., Scheinberg, P., Rich, M., and Belle, M. S. (1952): The effect of intravenous papaverine HCl on cerebral circulation. *J. Clin. Invest.* 3:111–114.

100. Jennings, W. G. (1972): An ergot alkaloid preparation (hydergine) versus placebo for treatment of symptoms of cerebrovascular insufficiency: Double-blind study. *J. Am. Geriatr. Soc.* 20:407–412.

101. Johannesson, G., Brun, A., Gustafson, I., and Ingvar, D. H. (1977): EEG in presenile dementia related to cerebral blood flow and autopsy findings. *Acta Neurol. Scand.* 56:89–103.

102. Judah, L., Murphree, O., and Seager, L. (1959): Psychiatric response of geriatric-psychiatric patients to Mellaril (TP-21, Sandoz). *Am. J. Psychiatry* 115:1118–1119.

103. Judge, T. G., and Urquhart, A. (1972): Naftidrofuryl—A double-blind cross-over study in the elderly. *Curr. Med. Res. Opin.* 1:166–172.

104. Kral, V. A. (1961): The use of thioridazine in aged people. *Can. Med. Assoc. J.* 84:152–154.

105. Kristensen, V., Olsen, M., and Theilgaard, A. (1977): Levodopa treatment of presenile dementia. *Acta Psychiatr. Scand.* 55:41–51.

106. Kropach, K. (1959): The treatment of acutely agitated senile patients with trifluoperazine (Stelazine). *Br. J. Clin. Pract.* 13:859–862.

107. Kugler, J., Oswald, W. D., Herzfeld, U., Seus, R., Pingel, J., and Welzel, D. (1978): Langzeittherapie altersbedingter insuffizienzer-scheinungen des Gehirns (Long-term treatment of the symptoms of senile cerebral insufficiency: A prospective study of hydergine). *Dtsch. Med. Wochenschr.* 103:456–462.

108. Lande, S., Flexner, J. B., and Flexner, L. B. (1972): Effect of corticotropin and desglycinamide⁹-lysine vasopressin on suppression of memory by puromycin. *Proc. Natl. Acad. Sci. U.S.A.* 69:558–560.

109. Lassen, N. A., Munch, O., and Tottey, E. R. (1957): Mental function and cerebral oxygen consumption in organic dementia. *A.M.A. Arch. Neurol. Psychiat.* 77:126–133.

110. Legros, J. J., Gilot, P., Seron, X., Claessen, J., Adam, A., Moeglen, J. M., Audibert, A., and Berchier, P. (1978): Influence of vasopressin on learning and memory. *Lancet* 1:41–42.

111. Le Hew, L. J. (1957): Pipradol (Meratran) in institutionalized geriatric patients. *J. Am. Geriatr. Soc.* 5:534–540.

112. Lehmann, H. E., and Ban, T. A. (1967): Comparative pharmacotherapy of the aging psychotic patient. *Laval. Med.* 38:588–595.

113. Lehmann, H. E., and Ban, T. A. (1970): Pharmacological lead tests as predictors of pharmacotherapeutic response in geriatric patients. In: *Psychopharmacology and the Individual Patient,* edited by J. R. W. Henborn, S. C. Goldberg, and P. R. May. Raven Press, New York.

114. Lehmann, H. E., and Ban, T. A. (1975): Central nervous system stimulants and anabolic substances in geropsychiatric therapy. In: *Aging, vol. 2.* edited by S. Gershon and A. Raskin, pp. 179–202. Raven Press, New York.

115. Letemendia, F., and Pampiglione, G. (1958): Clinical and electroencephalographic observations in Alzheimer's disease. *J. Neurol. Neurosurg. Psychiatry* 21:167–172.

116. Lifshitz, K., and Kline, N. S. (1970): Psychopharmacology in geriatrics. In: *Principles of Psychopharmacology,* edited by W. G. Clark and J. Del Giudice, pp. 695–705. Academic Press, New York.

117. Long, R. F., and Gislason, S. S. (1964): The effect of procaine on orientation, attention, memory and weight of aged psychiatric patients. *J. Neuropsychiatry* 5:186–196.
118. Maren, T. H. (1967): Carbonic anhydrase: chemistry, physiology and inhibition. *Physiol Rev.* 47:595–781.
119. Martin, K. E., Overly, G. H., and Krone, R. E. (1957): Pipradol: Combined therapy for geriatric and agitated patients. *Int. Rec. Med.* 170:33–36.
120. McConnachie, R. W. (1973): A clinical trial comparing "hydergine" with placebo in the treatment of cerebrovascular insufficiency in elderly patients. *Curr. Med. Res. Opin.* 1:463–468.
121. McEntee, W. J., and Mair, R. G. (1978): Memory impairment in Korsakoff's psychosis: A correlation with brain noradrenergic activity. *Science* 202:905–907.
122. McGeer, E. G., Fibiger, H. C., McGeer, P. L., and Wickson, V. (1971): Aging and brain enzymes. *Exp. Gerontol.* 6:391–396.
123. McGeer, E. G., and McGeer, P. L. (1976): Neurotransmitter metabolism in the aging brain. In: *Aging,* vol. 3, edited by R. D. Terry and S. Gershon, pp. 389–403. Raven Press, New York.
124. McHenry, L. C., Jaffe, M. E., West, J. W., Cooper, E. S., Kenton, E. J., Kawamura, J., Oshiro, T., and Goldberg, H. I. (1970): Regional cerebral blood flow and cardiovascular effects of hexobendine in stroke patients. *Neurology (Minneap.)* 22:217–223.
125. McQuillan, I. M., Lopec, C. A., and Vibal, J. R. (1974): Evaluation of EEG and clinical changes associated with Pavabid therapy in chronic brain syndrome. *Curr. Ther. Res.* 16:49–58.
126. Meek, J. L., Bertilsson, L., Cheney, D. L., Zsilla, G., and Costa, E. (1977): Age induced changes in acetylcholine and serotonin content of discrete brain nuclei. *J. Gerontol.* 32:129–131.
127. Meynaud, A., Grand, M., Belleville, M., and Fontaine, L. (1975): Effet du naphtidrofuryl sur le metabolisme energetique cerebral chez la souris. *Deuxieeme Part., Therapie* 30:777–788.
128. Miller, L. H., Kastin, A. J., Sandman, C. A., Fink, M., and Van Veen, W. (1974): Polypeptide influences on attention, memory and anxiety in man. *Pharmacol. Biochem. Behav.* 2:663–668.
129. Mindus, P., Cronholm, B., Levander, S. E., and Schalling, D. (1976): Piracetam-induced improvement of mental performance. A controlled study on normally aging individuals. *Acta Psychiatr. Scand.* 54:150–160.
130. Mohs, R. C., Davis, K. L., Tinklenberg, J. R., Pfefferbaum, A., Hollister, L. E., and Koppel, B. S. (1979): Cognitive effects of physostigmine and choline chloride in normal subjects. In: *Brain Acetylcholine and Neuropsychiatric Disease,* edited by K. L. Davis and P. A. Berger. Plenum Press, New York, *(in press).*
131. Müller, H. F., and Schwartz, G. (1978): Electroencephalograms and autopsy findings in geropsychiatry. *J. Gerontol.* 33:504–513.
132. Myers, J. M., Sheldon, D., and Robinson, S. S. (1963): A study of 138 elderly first admissions. *Am. J. Psychiatry* 120:244–249.
133. Nevin, S. (1967): On some aspects of cerebral degeneration in later life. *Proc. R. Soc. Med.* 60:517–526.
134. Niedermeyer, E., and Vematru, S. (1974): Electroencephalographic recordings from deep cerebellar structures in patients with uncontrolled epileptic seizures. *Electroencephalogr. Clin. Neurophysiol.* 37:355–365.
135. O'Brien, M. D., and Veall, N. (1966): Effect of cyclandelate on cerebral cortical perfusion rates in cerebrovascular disease. *Lancet* 2:729–730.
136. Oliveros, J. C., Jandali, M. K., Timsit-Berthier, M., Remy, R., Benghezal, A., Audibert, A., and Moeglen, J. M. (1978): Vasopressin in amnesia. *Lancet* 1:42.
137. Otsuka, H., and Inouye, K. (1964): Synthesis of peptides related to the N-terminal structure of corticotropin. II. The synthesis of L-histidyl-L-phenylalanyl-L-arginyl-L-tryptophan, the smallest peptide exhibiting the melanocyte stimulating and lipolytic activities. *Bull. Chem. Soc. Jap.* 37:1465–1471.
138. Paddison, R. M., and Ferris, G. S. (1961): The EEG in cerebral vascular disease. *Electroencephalogr. Clin. Neurophysiol.* 13:99–110.
139. Pede, J. P., Shimp Fessel, L., and Crokaert, R. (1971): The action of piracetam on the oxidative phospharylation. *Arch. Int. Physiol. Biochim.* 79:1036.

140. Perry, E. K., Gibson, P. H., Blessed, G., Perry, R. H., and Tomlinson, B. E. (1977): Neurotransmitter enzyme abnormalities in senile dementia. Choline acetyltransferase and glutomic and decarboxylase activities in neuropsy brain tissue. *J. Neurol. Sci.* 34:247–265.
141. Peters, B. H. and Levin, H. S. (1977): Memory enhancement after physostigmine treatment in the amnesic syndrome. *Arch. Neurol.* 34:215–219.
142. Piracetam: *Basic scientific and clinical data.* Scientific publication for the medical profession. UCB—Pharmaceutical Division, B-1060, Brussels.
143. Pomeranze, J., and Ladek, R. J. (1957): Clinical studies in geriatrics. III. The "Tonic." *J. Am. Geriatr. Soc.* 5:997–1002.
144. Posner, J. B., and Plum, F. (1960): The toxic effects of carbon dioxide and acetizolamide in hepatic encephalopathy. *J. Clin. Invest.* 39:1246–1258.
145. Prien, R. F. (1973): Chemotherapy in chronic organic brain syndrome—A review of the literature. *Psychopharmacol. Bull.* 9:5–20.
146. Randt, C. T., Quartermain, D., Goldstein, H., and Anagoste, B. (1971): Norepinephrine biosynthesis inhibition: effect on memory in mice. *Science* 176:498–499.
147. Rao, D. B., and Norris, J. R. (1972): A double-blind investigation of hydergine in the treatment of cerebrovascular insufficiency in the elderly. *Johns Hopkins Med. J.* 130:317–324.
148. Raskin, A., Gershon, S., Crook, T. H., Sathananthan, G., and Ferris, S. (1978): The effects of hyperbaric and normobaric oxygen on cognitive impairment in the elderly. *Arch. Gen. Psychiatry* 35:50–56.
149. Rehman, S. A. (1973): Two trials comparing "hydergine" with placebo in the treatment of patients suffering from cerebrovascular insufficiency. *Curr. Med. Res. Opin.* 1:456–462.
150. Revelle, W., Amaral, P., and Turriff, S. (1976): Introversion/extroversion, time stress, and caffeine: Effect on verbal performance. *Science* 192:149–150.
151. Rigter, H. (1978): Attenuation of amnesia in rats by systemically administered enkephaline. *Science* 200:83–85.
152. Rinaldi, F., and Himwich, H. E. (1955): Drugs affecting psychotic behavior and function of mesodiencephalic activating system. *Dis. Nerv. Syst.* 16:133–141.
153. Ritter, R. H., Nail, H. R., Tatum, P., and Blazi, M. (1971): The effect of papaverine on patients with cerebral arteriosclerosis. *Clin. Med.* 78:18–22.
154. Robinson, D. S., Nies, A., Davies, H. N., Bunney, W. E., Davis, J. M., Colburn, R. W., Bourne, H. R., Shaw, D. M., and Coppen, A. J. (1972): Aging, monamine and monamine oxidase levels. *Lancet* 1:290–291.
155. Robinson, D. S., Sourkes, T. L., Nies, A., Harris, L. S., Spector, S., Bartlett, D. L., and Kaye, I. S. (1977): Monamine metabolism in human brain. *Arch. Gen. Psychiatry,* 34:89–92.
156. Rosen, H. J. (1975): Mental decline in the elderly: Pharmacotherapy (ergot alkaloids versus papaverine). *J. Am. Geriatr. Soc.* 23:169–174.
157. Roubicek, J., Geiger, C., and Abt, K. (1972): An ergot alkaloid preparation (hydergine) in geriatric therapy. *J. Am. Geriatr. Soc.* 20:222–229.
158. Sakalis, G., Gershon, S., and Shopsin, B. (1974): A trial of Gerovital-H3 in depression during senility. *Curr. Ther. Res.* 16:59–63.
159. Salzman, C., Shader, R. I., and Harmatz, J. S. (1975): Response of the elderly to psychotropic drugs: Predictable or idiosyncratic? In: *Aging vol. 2,* edited by S. Gershon and A. Raskin, pp. 259–272. Raven Press, New York.
160. Samorajski, T., and Rolsten, C. (1973): Age and regional differences in the chemical composition of brains of mice, monkeys and humans. *Prog. Brain. Res.* 3:253–265.
161. Samorajski, T., Sun, A., and Rolsten, C. (1977): Effects of chronic dosage with chlorpromazine and Gerovital H3 in the aging brain. In: *Advances in Behavioral Biology, vol 23, The Aging Brain and Senile Dementia,* pp. 141–156, edited by K. Nandy and I. Sherwin. Plenum Press, New York.
162. Sandman, C. A., George, J. M., Nolan, J. D., Van Riezen, H., and Kastin, A. J. (1975): Enhancement of attention in man with $ACTH/MSH_{4-10}$, *Physiol. Behav.* 15:427–431.
163. Sathananthan, G., Ferris, S. H., Reisberg, B., and Gershon, S. (1979): Long-term choline treatment of memory impaired elderly patients. *Science* 205:4410, 1039–1040.
164. Schwab, B. S. (1955): EEG studies and their significance in cerebral vascular disease. In: *Cerebral Vascular Disease,* pp. 123–132, edited by I. S. Wright. Grune & Stratton, New York.
165. Seeman, P. (1972): The membrane actions of anesthetics and tranquilizers. *Pharmacol. Rev.* 24:583–655.
166. Shader, R. I., Harmatz, J. S., and Salzman, C. (1974): A new scale for clinical assessment

in geriatric populations: Sandoz Clinical Assessment—Geriatric (SCAG). *J. Am. Geriatr. Soc.* 22:107–113.

167. Shaw, S. W., and Johnson, R. H. (1975): Effect of naftidrofuryl on the metabolic response to exercise in man. *Acta Neurol. Scand.* 52:231–237.

168. Skinhøj, E. (1975): The effect of a new carbonic anhydrase inhibitor upon CBF and $CMRO_2$. In: *Blood Flow and Metabolism in the Brain,* edited by A. M. Harper, B. Jenne, H. D. Miller, and J. Rowan, pp. 7–8,11. Churchill Livingstone, Edinburgh.

169. Smith, G. R., Taylor, C. W., and Linkous, P. (1974): Haloperidol versus thioridazine for the treatment of psychogeriatric patients: A double-blind clinical trial. *Psychosomatics* 15:134–138.

170. Stegink, A. J. (1972): The clinical use of piracetam, a new nootropic drug. The treatment of symptoms of senile involution. *Arzneim. Forsch.* 22:975–977.

171. Stern, F. H. (1970): Management of chronic brain syndrome secondary to cerebral arteriosclerosis with special reference to papaverine hydrochloride. *J. Am. Geriatr. Soc.* 18:507–512.

172. Straker, N., and Grauer, H. (1961): Clinical study of a potent antidepressant, tranylcypramine with trifluoperazine (Parstelin) in the aged chronically ill. *Can. Med. Assoc. J.,* 85:127–130.

173. Swain, J. M. (1959): Electroencephalographic abnormalities in presenile atrophy. *Neurology* 9:722–727.

174. Teece, J. J., and Cole, J. O. (1974): Amphetamine effects in man: Paradoxical drowsiness and lowered electrical brain activity (CNV). *Science* 85:451–453.

175. Thibault, A. (1974): A double-blind evaluation of "hydergine" and placebo in the treatment of patients with organic brain syndrome and cerebral arteriosclerosis in a nursing home. *Curr. Med. Res. Opin.* 2:482–487.

176. Tomlinson, B. E., Blessed, G., and Roth, M. (1970): Observations on the brains of demented old people. *J. Neurol. Sci.* 11:205–242.

177. Trabant, R., Poljakovic, Z., and Trabant, D. (1977): Zur Wirkung von Piracetam auf das hirnorganische Psychsyndrom bei zerebrovaskulärer Insüffizienze. Ergebnis einer Doppelblindstudie bei 40 Fällen. *Ther. Ggw.* 116:1504–1521.

178. Triboletti, F., and Ferri, H. (1969): Hydergine for treatment of symptoms of cerebrovascular insufficiency. *Curr. Ther. Res.* 11:609–620.

179. Tripod, J. (1957): Caractérisation générale des effets pharmacodynamiques de substances psychotropiques. In: *Psychotropic Drugs,* edited by S. Garratini and V. Ghetti. Elsevier, Amsterdam.

180. Turek, I., Karland, A. A., Oya, K. Y., and Hanlon, R. E. (1969): Effects of pipradol hydrochloride on geriatric patients. *J. Am. Geriatr. Soc.* 17:408–413.

181. Ulus, I. H., Hirsch, M. J., and Wurtman, R. J. (1976): Transsynaptic induction of adrenomedullary tyrosine hydroxylase activity by choline: Evidence that choline administration increases cholinergic transmission. *Proc. Natl. Acad. Sci. U.S.A.* 74:798–800.

182. Ulus, I. H., and Wurtman, R. J. (1976): Choline administration: Activation of tyrosine hydroxylase in dopaminergic neurons of rat brain. *Science* 194:1060–1061.

183. Van der Drift, J. H., and Magnus, O. (1961): The EEG in cerebral ischemic lesions; correlations with clinical and pathological findings. In: *Cerebral Anoxia and the Electroencephalogram,* edited by H. Gastaut and J. S. Meyer, pp. 180–196. Charles C. Thomas, Springfield, Illinois.

184. Walsh, A. C. (1968): Senile dementia: A report on the anticoagulant treatment of thirteen patients. *Pa. Med.* 71:65–72.

185. Walsh, A. C. (1969): Preventing of senile and presenile dementia by bishydroxycoumarid (Dicumarol) therapy. *J. Am. Geriatr. Soc.* 17:477–487.

186. Walsh, A. C., and Walsh, B. H. (1972): Senile and presenile dementia: further observations on the benefits of a Dicumarol-psychotherapy regimen. *J. Am. Geriatr. Soc.* 20:127–131.

187. Walsh, A. C., Walsh, B. H., and Maloney, C. (1978): Senile-presenile dementia: Follow-up data on an effective psychotherapy-anticoagulant regimen. *J. Am. Geriatr. Soc.* 26:467–470.

188. Weiss, J. M., McEwen, B. S., Silva, M. T., and Kalkut, M. (1970): Pituitary–adrenal alterations and fear responding. *Am. J. Physiol.* 218:864–868.

189. Westreich, G., Alter, M., and Lundgren, S. (1975): Effect of cyclandelate on dementia. *Stroke* 6:535–538.

190. White, P., Hiley, C. R., Goodhardt, M. J., Carrasco, L. H., Keet, J. P., Williams, I. E. I., and Bowen, D. M. (1977): Neocortical cholinergic neurons in elderly people. *Lancet* 1:668–671.

191. Wied, D. de (1964): Influence of anterior pituitary on avoidance learning and escape behavior. *Am. J. Physiol.* 207:255–259.

192. Wied, D. de (1966): Inhibitory effect of ACTH and related peptides on extinction of conditioned avoidance behavior in rats. *Proc. Soc. Exp. Biol. Med.* 122:28–32.
193. Wied, D. de, and Bohus, B. (1966): Long-term and short-term effect on retention of a conditioned avoidance response in rats by treatment respectively with long-acting pitressin or α-MSH. *Nature* 212:1484–1486.
194. Will, J. C., Abuzzahab, F. S., and Zimmerman, R. L. (1978): The effects of ACTH$_{4-10}$ versus placebo in the memory of symptomatic geriatric volunteers. *Psychopharmacol. Bull.* 14:25–27.
195. Wimersma Greidanus, T. B. van, Dogterom, J., and Wied, D. de (1975): Intraventricular administration of anti-vasopressin serum inhibits memory consolidation in rats. *Life Sci.* 16:637–644.
196. Winblad, B., Adolfsson, R., Gottfries, C. G., Oreland, L., Ross, B. E., and Wilberg, A. (1978): Monaminergic activity in old age and in patients with dementia disorders of Alzheimer type. Resumenes—II Congreso Mundial de Psiquiatría Biologica, Barcelona, p. 59.
197. Wolthius, O. L. (1973): Farmacologische beinvloeding van leeren gehugenprocessen. *Natuur Techniek* 41:1–13.
198. Wyper, D. J., McAlpine, C. J., Jawad, K., and Jennett, B. (1976): Effects of a carbonic anhydrase inhibitor on cerebral blood flow in geriatric patients. *J. Neurol. Neurosurg. Psychiatry* 39:885–889.
199. Yamaguchi, F., Meyer, J. S., Sakai, F., Yamamoto, M., and Shaw, T. (1979): Behavioral activation testing in the dementias. *Proceedings of the 9th Salzburg Conference on Cerebral Vascular Disease.* Excrpta Medica, Amsterdam *(in press).*
200. Young, J., Hall, P., and Blakemore, C. (1974): Treatment of cerebral manifestations of arteriosclerosis with cyclandelate. *Am. J. Psychiatry* 126:177–180.
201. Zahn, L. (1955): Erfahrungen mit einem zehtralen Stimulans (Ritalin) bei cerebralen Altersveränderungen. *Berliner Gesundheitsblatt* 6:419–420.
202. Zawadski, R. T., Glazer, G. B., and Lurie, E. (1978): Psychotropic drug use among institutionalized and noninstitutionalized Medicaid aged in California. *J. Gerontol.* 33:824–834.
203. Zung, W. K., Gianturco, D., Pfeiffer, E., Wang, H. S., Whanger, A., Bridge, T. P., and Potkin, S. G. (1974): Pharmacology of depression in the aged: Evaluation of Gerovital-H3 as an antidepressant drug. *Psychosomatics* 15:127–131.
204. Zung, W. W. K., Gianturco, D., and Pfeiffer, E. (1976): Treatment of depression in the aged with Gerovital H3: Clinical efficacy and neurophysiological effects. *Psychopharmacol. Bull.* 12(2):50–51.

OPEN DISCUSSION

Dr. Goldstein: There are a small number of articles in the literature on the use of lithium with dementia. Do you have any comment on that?

Dr. Gershon: First, there is a problem in using lithium in people with organic deficits. These people do not tolerate the drug well. They are supersensitive to neurotoxicity. The claims of lithium's effectiveness are based on open studies. Again, organic deficit is only a relative and not an absolute contraindication.

Dr. Cole: A brief comment on lithium. We have had three patients at McLean who had agitated dementia, who were too agitated to place in a nursing home, who had failed on benzodiazepines, diphenhydramine, and antipsychotics, but who did well on lithium. The one I had most contact with had many hypomanic features. Whether we are dealing with secondary mania (an interesting concept), or whether the lithium slowed down her non-specific agitation is hard to tell.

Dr. Gershon: My answer to the first question was a little sweeping. Dr. Cole makes a distinction. If, in fact, we are talking about a behaviorial concomitant which is agitation or hypomania, and if we can administer the drug safely without neurotoxicity, there is no reason why these people should not respond similarly to those with the syndrome in the other age group.

Dr. Max Fink: One of the comments made in Dr. Gershon's presentation was that the patients who were given stimulants showed a lifting of their spirits, an elevation of mood, but showed no changes in memory. In studies of the treatment of depression with tricyclic antidepressants, there is some evidence that patients who have an elevation in mood also have an improvement in performance on memory tests. This is also surely true in patients who improve with ECT, usually within weeks of their treatment. Is there a lifting of mood in the patients who receive stimulants that is comparable to that seen with imipramine and amitriptyline?

Dr. Gershon: In the formal study that we published with methylphenidate, there was no significant effect. Only a small subgroup were given the whole 45 mg in one dose, and they really had an enormous response. It was an exaggerated euphoric response.

Dr. Steven Roose: Dr. Dunner and I have looked at the patient population over the age of 60 on lithium maintenance treatment in the Lithium Clinic at the New York State Psychiatric Institute. We had 31 patients. Our findings indicated that there was a statistically significant increase in the number of episodes of lithium toxicity and cardiac sinus node dysfunction in the over-60 age group, as compared to patients under 60, on lithium maintenance. Other than these two findings, there did not seem to be any specific difficulties in using lithium in the presence of the chronic illnesses and usual medications which predominate in the older patient. However, it seems prudent not to draw conclusions based on the small number of patients in this study, and we feel that the general issue of the safety of lithium in the patient over 60 years is an open question.

I wonder if you had any impressions about the complications of lithium use in your older patients.

Dr. Gershon: It was in complete accord with what you just said; there was a higher incidence of toxicity.

Dr. Peter Gruen: You did not mention anything about the cholinergic agents, lecithin, choline chloride, or deanol. Would you comment on these and also expand upon your current thinking about praxilene?

Dr. Gershon: Praxilene I mentioned very briefly. I did not discuss it in detail. Dr. Cole, Dr. Ferris, and Dr. Reisberg are conducting studies with praxilene. The results of our double-blind evaluation have not yet been analyzed. Some positive effects have been reported in other studies.

We do have data on some of the neuropeptides, such as $ACTH_{4-10}$, the injectable product, and they are disappointing. Generally the data are disappointing because they do not agree with animal data. The animal data is clearly positive on analogs of deficit, but in man we do not come up with too much. There is now available a more potent oral preparation, and we have done that study, but the answer today is that it has not been analyzed.

We have an open choline study. Again, in that study, with all the restrictions of the sampling and size of the population, we did not get any significant data.

Dr. Ralph A. O'Connell: An observation. Some years ago there was a study at St. Vincent's on magnesium pemoline, a double-blind crossover with amphetamine. Although there were no significant changes for the Wechsler Memory Scale as a whole, there was a significant change on one subtest, the one for retrieval. It was fascinating to see old people who retrieved memories stored from years ago. Magnesium pemoline was never used in the adult population.

Dr. Gershon: I gave you a very global outcome; some of the data has been analyzed on retrieval. I do not know however, whether the data is that clearcut.

Dr. Ferris: Magnesium pemoline has a fairly specific effect on dopamine. I do know of some recent animal data in primates in which a variety of stimulants were looked at in a certain memory paradigm. Pemoline, of all the stimulants, did have some positive effects on memory. It may be that it is a drug worth another look.

Psychopathology in the Aged, edited by
Jonathan O. Cole and James E. Barrett.
Raven Press, New York © 1980.

Psychosocial and Environmental Approaches to the Care of Senile Dementia Patients

M. Powell Lawton

Philadelphia Geriatric Center, Philadelphia, Pennsylvania 19141

At the outset, it is necessary to discuss briefly the residential distribution of older people with senile dementia and related conditions, since the types of care will vary greatly depending on the living conditions of the individual. The basic statistics are familiar, but should be mentioned in order to allow this reference point to be established. About 60% of the 1.1 million nursing home residents 65 and over, or 660,000 people, were designated as having some degree of apparent mental confusion by staff (50). At least another 25,000 of those in mental hospitals can be added to this total. Turning to the noninstitutionalized population, we are lacking a reliable prevalence estimate; however, a conservative median of several local-area studies reviewed by Gunner-Swenson and Jensen (25) might be around 3%, or 690,000 individuals. Thus, about half of all those with organic brain syndrome (OBS) are living somewhere in the community. We know even less about just where they live; certainly the OBS patient is probably *more* likely to live with a family member than to live alone. However, Brody (9) has reviewed evidence suggesting that there are concentrations of such people in the poorly-defined and poorly-regulated genre of residences designated as boarding homes, domiciliaries, and foster homes. Unknown numbers undoubtedly live alone in scattered community residences, including single-room-occupancy hotels and housing built for the elderly.

These data show clearly the considerable need for intervention among older OBS patients in institutions; nothing could be further from the truth, however, than the assumption that the only need for such treatment is within the institutions. Psychosocial treatment for the OBS patient in the community has had virtually no research attention. What little has been done was reviewed by Kahn and Tobin (33), together with an excellent discussion of the issues involved in dealing with the OBS patient in community programs.

This chapter will begin with the discussion of some general concepts relative to intervention, followed by separate sections on psychosocial intervention and environmental intervention.

GENERAL CONCEPTS REGARDING INTERVENTION AND THE OBS PATIENT

Therapy and Prosthesis

An enormously useful distinction between two approaches to intervention was made by Lindsley (41) in contrasting "therapy" with "prosthetics." Therapy is the traditional approach to medicine where a treatment is sought that will cure the basic cause of an illness so that, when the therapy is discontinued, the illness will not recur. By contrast, prosthesis assumes the unchangeable quality of the basic condition and seeks a measure whose *permanent* application will counteract the disability associated with the condition.

In discussing intervention programs for senile dementia, we shall usually be speaking of prosthetics, rather than therapy. That is, given the destruction of neural tissue, the reversal of this condition is not at present thought to be a realistic goal. On the other hand, the search for effective means of counteracting the functional disabilities associated with structural brain damage is, as will be seen, a potentially fruitful occupation.

Disability and Excess Disability

Anyone who has worked with OBS patients recognizes that by no means all behavioral or affective disabilities seen in this group are the direct result of brain damage. Some may be unrelated to the organic condition, while others may be more disabling than they should be. Kahn (31) used the term "excess disability" to designate either of these situations where the magnitude of the disturbance in functioning is greater than might be accounted for by basic physical illness or cerebral pathology. Thus, the functional disability may, at least theoretically, be partitioned into one component that is irreversible and one that may be reversible, the relative proportions of the two ranging from 0 to 100 and vice versa. Kahn's illustration of an excess disability is the resident who goes about with unkempt hair but who, when requested to show how one combs one's hair, will run a comb through it appropriately. A grooming disability with little "excess" component would be exhibited by someone without the use of either arm. Thus, in contrast to the disability for which only a prosthetic measure is efficacious, the excess disability *may* be susceptible to "cure."

The Possible Psychosocial Origin of OBS

For the sake of completeness, it should be noted that periodic suggestions have been made that social and psychological antecedents may be involved in the etiology of senile dementia and related conditions (54). If such factors could be identified, this fact might offer some hope that the condition could be prevented or even treated through intervention at the social or psychological level. Early work by Rothschild (54) showing a lack of complete correspondence between postmortem histological findings and the extent of behavioral disturbance was often cited as evidence that the clinical condition might be treatable. As research methods became more precise, later studies assembled impressive evidence in favor of a basic (though not perfect) concordance between brain pathology and behavior (13,53). The fact that the concordance is never complete is best explained by experimental error, variations in excess disability, and the extent to which the environment supports or discourages adequate behavior.

Clinical Confusion of OBS and Other Conditions

Throughout the short but active life of gerontology as a discipline, periodic assertions have been advanced suggesting that large numbers of impaired individuals are mistakenly diagnosed as having OBS and therefore are effectively deprived of the psychosocial treatment that is, in fact, appropriate to their nonorganic problem. In some instances the problem has been discussed as if OBS were a problem in labeling, one best approached through the study of social deviance rather than neuropathology. Certainly much evidence is available that misdiagnosis occurs. The withdrawal and unresponsiveness of depression are especially frequently taken for an organically-based disability. Some presumed consequences of institutional behavior, such as passivity, lack of motivation, intellectual listlessness, and withdrawal of interest in one's surroundings are particularly likely to be thought of as "senile" characteristics. Ernst et al. (18) made a strong case for the negative effects on behavior produced by the sensory deprivation and isolation typically imposed on the OBS patient, especially in institutional settings. While they stop short of suggesting that "organic" symptoms may be explained by such isolation, they point out many routes by which this deprived social context may exacerbate the basic symptoms. On another level, ample evidence is at hand to suggest that in many mental health contexts, merely being in the age range of 65 and over frequently has automatically entitled the individual to a diagnosis of OBS [although Slater and Lipman (56), examining staff labeling behavior in British nursing homes, found in fact that staff were relatively accurate in differentiating the symptoms of senile confusion from other behavioral symptoms]. In other instances, the symptoms may be confused in the opposite direction so that the OBS is not picked up. Suffice it to suggest here that both types of errors may be reduced greatly by the use of appropriate diagnostic and assessment measures and the training of professionals in making the diagnostic distinction. Despite these diagnostic errors, however, little comfort can be taken in the hope that better diagnosis will lead to the identification of a very large percentage of patients who are truly amenable to "therapy" in the restricted sense referred to above.

The purpose of the above discussion has been to delineate the bases for expecting that the senile dementia patient might benefit from interventive efforts, and to separate these reasonable bases from those rooted in fantasy. Illnesses of unclear etiology, especially those where true therapy has been difficult, lend themselves to the construction of wish-fulfilling fantasies that inevitably impede treatment. The wishes that organic brain damage be reversible, that psychosocial prevention can be effective, or that one's patient is not really brain-damaged, will not be confirmed. The disconfirmation must frequently be destructive to the motivation to assist such patients. All too frequently, staff move from a state of excessive expectation to one of therapeutic nihilism: if the unrealistically high goals cannot be met, then no others are seen as worth pursuing.

In this connection, the concept of minimal incremental goals is worth mentioning. As developed in greater detail elsewhere, Lawton and Nahemow (39) in their ecological model suggested that growth is more likely to occur when the external demand on the individual is metered so as to be only incrementally greater than the level of demand to which he has contemporaneously adapted. "Therapeutic" rather than prosthetic goals tend to exceed this incremental range. Thus, considerable revision of the goal-setting standards typical for therapeutic models is necessary when dealing with the OBS patient.

PSYCHOSOCIAL INTERVENTIONS

In pondering the question regarding what to include among the psychosocial therapies, I noted that no other topic included in this volume dealt with psychotherapy of any type. It is true that any attempt to discuss traditional individual or group therapy for the OBS patient would have to be completely speculative, since almost nothing appears in the literature on this topic. However, the same cannot be said of individual behavior therapy based on the principles of operant psychology. Within the past few years considerable interest in the application of behavioral reinforcement to problems of the aged has arisen (4,52). An entire conference on this topic was held at Nova University in 1978. While only a few studies have dealt explicitly with senile dementia, successful attempts have been reported in dealing with locomotion (43), participation in activities (47), social interaction (8,29), and pathological screaming (5,21). Two little-known studies singled out OBS patients for study, both in laboratory-like operant response studies (12,45). This work, with small numbers of subjects, suggested that the OBS patient was amenable to learning by contingent reinforcement, but that (a) continuous, rather than intermittent, reinforcement was more effective, and (b) that discrimination among different reinforcers was more difficult for the OBS patient. Somewhat more encouraging results were obtained by Ankus and Quarrington (1), who found their memory-disordered subjects responded to both reinforcement schedules and type of reinforcer. It seems that the power of such behavior-therapeutic approaches has not yet been adequately explored. It is especially important that studies be done to explore the limits of what can be accomplished with the OBS patient, as compared to the intact elderly. Relatively little research has singled out this group explicitly. Much more often, OBS patients are either included along with others, or undesignated groups are used in which the probability that many OBS patients were included was high. Thus, considerable use will be made of findings that are not uniquely relevant to OBS; where they are, this fact will be noted.

Milieu Therapy

A great variety of milieu therapy programs for older mental hospital and nursing home patients have been conducted over the years (see reviews in 7,9, 16,17,23,24). These programs are characterized by high participation of all levels of staff in planning and treatment, the introduction of highly structured activities, and often the use of rewards for task accomplishment (19,22,51,55). Gottesman et al. (24) described a particularly strong effect achieved by the use of paid work as an incentive, as compared to a recreational-activity-oriented program.

The "token economy" represents a ward-level application of contingency reinforcement principles, where desirable behaviors are specified and rewarded by a "generalized reinforcer," usually tokens, which can in turn "buy" privileges or direct reinforcers such as food, clothing, and so on. Several early reports on token-economy wards (2,3) indicated that a number of elderly patients were included in the groups treated. Mishara (48) appears to have reported the only token-economy evaluation done solely with organic geriatric patients. This approach was contrasted with a milieu-therapy program where rewards were delivered without regard to whether the desired behavior had been elicited. Both groups improved in somewhat differing patterns as compared to baseline; neither was clearly superior, and no untreated control comparison was available. However, even though some of these studies do describe the disorders of their subjects, few analyze results separately for the OBS patient and the "functional" or other type of disorder. Thus, we cannot conclude that they benefit the patient with senile dementia and related conditions. One wonders particularly whether those who respond to the general reinforcer include patients with significant degrees of OBS, since the capacity to generalize and to remember that there *are* behavioral contingencies may not be present among these individuals.

"Reality orientation" (RO) (20) is a cognitive training procedure designed primarily for OBS patients. It consists first of a milieu approach where staff are trained to use natural conversational situations to rehearse important orientational and informational items with patients, e.g., the date, place, identity of people, and so on. Second a classroom procedure gives formalized instruction in basic cognitive skills. RO has thousands of devoted practitioners who seem unanimous in evaluating positively what they are doing. In the hard light of experimental evaluation, RO has done less well, with negative or only marginally positive results for the most part (6,11,27,44). These studies are, like most others, also not always completely definitive in denoting their subjects as clearly suffering from senile dementia or other similar conditions. Since positive effects of RO on staff attitudes have been noted by many investigators and empirically confirmed by Smith and Barker (57), one cannot help but conclude that the quality of the milieu is improved by having such a program.

Thus we come to a very small group of studies where subjects are described clearly enough to determine that they were genuine OBS cases. They are very diverse in the approaches used. The earliest was a program of planned occupational therapy and other recreational activities offered to cognitively impaired nursing-home residents (14). Increased activity and social behavior occurred at treatment sessions but was not maintained at "off" times or in the weeks after the treatment program was discontinued. Nathanson and Reingold (49) found that a sheltered workshop activity routine was able to elicit appropriate behavior from cognitively impaired nursing home residents. The milieu approach of Pappas et al. (51) was shown to be equally effective for OBS and nonOBS patients.

The most clearly structured program offered to OBS patients was the individualized treatment program of Brody and her colleagues (10,34,35). The resources of a broad multidisciplinary treatment team were utilized, first, in the careful assessment (both formal and clinical) of the impairments and strengths of each resident. Second, specific "excess disabilities" (31) were identified as targets for treatment. Third, treatment was applied to these specific disabilities by the appropriate professional. Evaluation consisted of before-and-after assessments of functioning in a standard set of basic sectors of well-being and in the specific functions treated as excess disabilities. A significant superiority of the individualized treatment of the targeted excess disabilities was found, as compared to a randomly-assigned control group that experienced only the usual institutional routine. By contrast, no experimental effect was reflected in the generalized measures of well-being. Further, a second follow-up evaluation was done nine months after the experimental program had ceased. By this time, no advantage was discernible in the treated group.

Again, attention needs to be called to the meager number of treatment studies that have been directed toward confirmed cases of OBS, to say nothing of many deficiencies not yet noted, such as small numbers of subjects, lack of control group, lack of random assignment, and so on. On the basis of what has been presented, we have minimal, but discernible, evidence that the quality of behavior can be improved in some OBS patients: some individuals learned desired behavior in operant or behavior-therapeutic situations, occupational therapy (OT) and sheltered-workshop tasks were performed, and specific excess disabilities improved. However, some qualifications even to these small successes are necessary. It seems that to succeed a treatment must be continuously applied, whether it be contingent reinforcement, OT and recreational therapy, or individualized excess-disability treatment. Such treatments thus fall into the category of prostheses. These few studies are remarkably consistent in suggesting that improvement in one area may not generalize to another area and that gains exhibited during treatment do not persist outside of or after treatment. Is this conclusion a depressing one? Only if we persist in basing our expectations on the acute illness model. Properly applied, disseminated, and taught to caregiving staff, these conclusions should provide a *raison d'être* for the daily institutional treatment efforts that actively offer tasks to fill the resident's day, that assist the resident just enough to motivate him to perform the part of the task that he is capable of doing, and that affirm a continued sense of self. Finally, we certainly have not heard the last word on milieu therapy, remotivation, sensory training, reality motivation, or the token economy. These cannot now be included as clearly beneficial because they have not been adequately tested, not because they have been adequately tested and have failed.

ENVIRONMENTAL INTERVENTION

The case for environmental intervention rests partially on the hope that physical prostheses might be developed that would support desired behavior on a 24-hour basis even in the absence of more expensive staff. The preceding review of psychosocial treatment has shown how important is the constant application of ameliorative procedures. As an example, if privacy is seen as an important need for a given individual, the availability of a private room will gratify that need at any time with no human intervention. Few situations are this ideal, of course, and as will be seen later, the human and the physical aspects of the environment form a system whose components are so mutually interdependent that it becomes rather artificial to separate the "psychosocial" from the "physical" aspects of the treatment environment. However, physical environment has been a notably neglected aspect of the treatment system, and for this reason, if no other, some extended consideration will be given to the question of how the physical aspects of the milieu can be enlisted as a component of the assistance offered the OBS patient. The "environmental docility hypothesis" (36) suggests that as competence decreases, external environmental factors become more and more important determinants of behavior and affect. For the OBS patients, then, we might not only predict that they would be highly susceptible to the influence of the institutional environment, but that a small improvement in environmental quality would have a disproportionately favorable effect on the OBS patient as compared to a more competent individual.

In part, the neglect of the physical environment stems from the excessive intrapsychic bias of the mental health professions during their long development from the various psychodynamic perspectives of psychoanalysis, phenomenology, and existentialism. Such primacy was accorded to the individual that one frequently heard the opinion voiced that good treatment could occur in any environment. Usually this turned out to be a rationalization for delivering services in dehumanized environments, whether of old, dirty, and dingy type or the new, sterile, code-conforming type. While the aesthetic impact of an institution may be of only marginal relevance to mental health, the message conveyed by most institutional architecture is that the inhabitant is incapable of knowing or caring whether his surroundings are beautiful or ugly. While there is no research to tell us how the OBS patient perceives the institutional environment, informal observation suggests that as mental competence decreases, the aesthetic quality of the treatment environment deteriorates correspondingly.

Beyond these largely negative effects of the aesthetics of institutions, are there other ways in which the physical environment can affect the well-being of the OBS patient? For the most part, we are forced to rely on qualitative observation and theory for answers to this question, since there has been little quantitative research in this area. As in the case of the aesthetics of the institution, we usually cannot ask the OBS patient to introspect regarding his environmental experience, so we are left to direct behavior observation as the major source of information.

DeLong (15) illustrated the power of ethnographic analysis in the early stages of investigating an issue in his observation of the behavior of elderly OBS patients clustered in an institutional ward. DeLong was interested in their proxemic behavior, that is, the patients' behavioral use of space and its communicative function. He noted first their generally reduced level of sensory reception and the effect that this impairment had on communication. Touch had become, for the OBS patient, a much more important vehicle for affective communication. Touch becomes possible, of course, only when the distance between individuals is reduced; reduction of interpersonal distance also makes visual and auditory communication easier. Thus the OBS patient was observed to reach out to others and to move very close while communicating. A new set of "personal distances" were established for these mentally impaired residents, distances that did not conform to the normative personal distances accepted by staff and others who did not suffer from these impairments. Hall (26) has shown a fairly regular acceptance (in the U.S.A., at least) of different interaction distances for different purposes: Intimate distance (0–18 inches), near personal distance (18–30 inches) for close communication, far personal distance (30–48 inches) for communication "at arm's length," and public distance beyond 4 feet. From the point of view of the OBS patient, these distances were dysfunctional; each was foreshortened by the preferred distance assumed by the resident. Staff, on the other hand, were made uncomfortable by such transgressions into their "personal bubble." They withdrew physically whenever possible. When residents' personal-care needs forced staff to touch residents or to interact at very close distances, psychological distancing mechanisms occurred such as looking beyond the resident, arching the body away, handling the resident roughly, or conversing with someone other than the resident being assisted. DeLong suggested that staff could be taught to recognize their own anxieties about spatial invasion and to feel easier about actively adopting the proxemic perspective of the mentally impaired. Some suggestions included moving closer to talk, rather than shouting (which connotes aggression), touching the resident's hands or shoulder, maintaining eye contact, and orienting the body toward the subject while talking.

On the other hand, a built-in component of much institutional life is the complete denial of personal territory or privacy. Some less-impaired residents were shown by Lipman and Slater (42) to adopt and effectively to "own" the most desirable seats in the public spaces of English nursing homes. DeLong also found this territorial behavior in his OBS ward. His observations spanned the time when a small pilot architectural alteration occurred that converted two four-bed rooms to six very small private rooms plus a small social area, the latter separated by a half-wall from the main hallway. His qualitative conclusion after the remodeling was that those residents who fell heir to the private rooms showed a reduced need for territorial defense of a chair in the hallway, as compared to those who remained in multiple-bed rooms.

Lawton et al. (38) studied this architectural change quantitatively by direct behavior observation before and after the alterations. A much broader "home range" occurred afterward, that is, patients were more likely to go into the hall and other public spaces beyond their rooms; it seemed that their horizon had literally been widened by the ability to see the larger environment from their bed or the small social space. Resident-to-resident social behavior did not change absolutely. However, in the new situation about 20% of residents' time was spent alone in their rooms, an option not available previously; with this time thus deducted, a greater *rate* of social contact occurred. It had also been expected that the novelty and improved aesthetic quality of the area would attract staff and thereby increase staff-resident conduct. In fact, this type of interaction decreased. *Ex post facto,* it seemed probable that the openness of the area had made it possible for staff to perform their surveillance function from a distance, rather than having to enter the room to do so. This unanticipated finding illustrates the limitations of the "let-environment-do-it" approach. Clearly staff (and residents too) need to be taught how to use the environment.

A comparative behavioral ecology study was done among institutional wards with varying concentrations of OBS patients (37). Where intact residents generally distributed themselves among their rooms, social areas of the ward, and institutional areas away from their ward, OBS patients rarely left their floors and were typically observed in the hall or dayroom. Maxwell et al. (46) observed the spatial distinctions among the moderately-impaired and severely-impaired residents of this same ward. The most impaired were assigned rooms at the "dead" end of the hall furthest from the nurses station. Staff observed in this "most-impaired" area were lowest-level staff. Watson (58) developed at length the thesis that mental impairment is a stigma leading to the withholding of institutional favors for this group.

The segregation of the OBS resident from the more intact is regularly practiced, yet many observers remain uncomfortable with this situation. One experimental attempt to mix these residents in an activity was inconclusive in its results, the major qualitative finding being the discomfort with this arrangement experienced by staff (30). In an evaluation of a new building to be described below, a mix of those who fell into the range of moderately to severely impaired by the Kahn-Goldfarb Mental Status Questionnaire (32) was deliberately created.

Even in this restricted range, staff and relatives were overwhelmingly opposed to the inclusion of the several most-intact residents because of the discomfort experienced by them. Among the more intact who can verbalize their feelings there is no doubt that the sight of people with deteriorated personal habits, the noisy, disoriented, or wandering are very anxiety-arousing. However, if one gives any credence to the effect of modeling behavior, and of the ability of the more competent to help the less competent on occasion, these behaviors cannot take place in a segregated setting. A good illustration of the cost of segregation was provided by Harris, et al. (28). Not surprisingly, they found that in common areas inhabited by both confused and nonconfused residents, most conversation was among the nonconfused. However, when the confused did interact socially, it was usually with an intact person. Thus, in a segregated situation, the probability of interaction between impaired residents would be very low. We clearly need more research to know better what the costs and gains of such mixing might be, and the conditions under which the effect of mixing might be optimized.

An Example of Prosthetic Design and Evaluation

Focusing on the disabilities associated with senile dementia, we can think of a variety of ways in which specific environmental features might be used prosthetically. The Philadelphia Geriatric Center had a most unusual opportunity to plan and build a treatment center that incorporated these principles in its structure (40). A team composed of administrators, staff, designers, and consultants in many disciplines worked for about 8 years to evolve such a plan with features designed to aid in orientation, memory, social behavior, providing sensory variety, and in encouraging a sense of self. The major innovation was the placement of resident rooms around 3 sides of the building, leaving a 40 by 100 foot area in the center. Since the residents were highly restricted in their movement, rarely leaving their treatment area for any purpose, the intent was to centralize all activity in this large common space. Orientation to place was assisted by the full view that every resident had of all important spaces in the area from almost any vantage point. Orientation to time was indirectly assisted in this manner as well, since locations (e.g., dining area, activity space, therapeutic kitchen) that were used at different times of day could be seen and their times of use perhaps anticipated. The scheduling of most activities in the central space allowed recruitment for them to occur by making activities in progress highly visible. For those not desiring to participate, the diversion of watching was provided. Finally, the central area maximized the possibility that traffic patterns would intersect and social interaction follow. Other features included the coding of bedrooms by varying the color of both the interior and the door jambs, large three dimensional room numbers and names placed at visual height, a personal bulletin board and a full-length mirror in each room, daylight-level lighting, a mix of private and semiprivate rooms, a nurse's station with full view of the entire area, a wide variety of colors and textures in furnishings and graphics, furniture designed from anthropometric measurements (the Skandiform chair), and choice of private, small-social, and large-social informal seating.

The research was designed to evaluate the effects of the total system change from the old traditional, long double-loaded corridor building to the prosthetically-designed one. This approach thus evaluated not only the physical environment but the complex change that involved staff, their expectations, and the programs as well as the structure. Direct behavior observations, supplemented by staff ratings, were the methods used; except for a mental status measure, no other verbal data were obtained directly from residents. As judged by mental status and physical activities of daily living, the inevitable process of decline occurred over the 18 months and 5 periods of measurement; the new environment did not affect these basic functions. However, a large variety of other less basic characteristics were measured including pathological behaviors, participation in activities, observed mood, social behavior, spatial behavior, and so on. Despite the fact that most of these were highly correlated with mental status at Time 1, only 1 desirable characteristic declined following the move, 14 improved, and 39 showed no change. Thus, compared to the expected trajectory of decline, the dominant outcome was no change—a demonstration of a prosthetic effect, though there were some improvements as well. Pathological behavior decreased, several signs of interest in external surroundings increased, and meaningful non-social behavior increased. No change in social behavior occurred, and there was a decrease in amount of nursing care given. Again, one wonders whether the latter result was because the centrally-placed nursing station made both surveillance of residents and congregation among nursing staff too easy. One of the strongest findings was that amount of visiting increased in the new building; increased contact with family seems to be a highly desirable treatment goal.

Staff and relatives were also queried about their evaluations of the old and the new buildings in general and in many specific features. Overwhelmingly, both groups found the new building more functional and visually pleasing, no doubt a reason behind the relatives' more frequent visiting.

Considerably more knowledge regarding the effects of environmental characteristics on institutional residents of other types is available. However, as in the case of the psychosocial therapies, none were done with OBS patients, and one cannot tell the extent to which findings derived from the intact aged, functionally disturbed mental patients, or other groups are applicable to the OBS patient.

But in any case, one sees that the environment as an independent aspect of the treatment system has been shown to have some effect on the senile dementia patient, certainly enough to warrant the continued search for improved prosthetic features. On the negative side, the sizes of effects reported are small, and some effects appear to be variably dependent on the way people use the environment.

In conclusion, the mild evidence in favor of the plasticity of behavior in senile dementia attributable to psychosocial and environmental interventions must be viewed in relation to other types of intervention including nutritional, surgical, and pharmacologic. While it is meaningful from a scientific point of view to ask whether a single intervention has a positive effect independent of all other factors, the question is not meaningful from a clinical point of view. Where we are talking about individuals with human needs, the total armamentarium must be mobilized, and the psychosocial and environmental approaches must be considered useful components of this totality.

REFERENCES

1. Ankus, M., and Quarrington, B. (1972): Operant behavior in the mentally-disordered. *J. Gerontol.* 27:500–510.
2. Atthowe, J., and Krasner, L. (1968): Preliminary report on the application of contingent reinforcement procedures (token economy) on a chronic psychiatric ward. *J. Abnorm. Psychol.* 73:37–43.
3. Ayllon, T., and Azrin, N. H. (1965): The measurement and reinforcement of behavior of psychotics. *J. Exp. Anal. Behav.* 8:357–383.
4. Baltes, M. M., and Barton, E. M. (1977): New approaches toward aging: A case for the operant model. *Educ. Gerontol.* 2:383–405.
5. Baltes, M. M., and Lascomb, S. L. (1975): Creating a healthy institutional environment for the elderly via behavior management. *Int. J. Nurs. Stud.* 12:5–12.
6. Barnes, J. (1974): Effects of reality orientation classroom on memory loss, confusion, and disorientation in geriatric patients. *Gerontologist* 14:138–142.
7. Bennett, R., and Eisdorfer, C. (1975): The institutional environment of behavior change. In: *Long-Term Care: A Handbook for Researchers, Planners, and Providers,* edited by S. Sherwood. Spectrum Publications, New York.
8. Blackman, D. K., Howe, M., and Pinkston, E. M. (1976): Increasing participation in social interaction of the institutionalized elderly. *Gerontologist* 16:69–76.
9. Brody, E. M. (1978): The formal support network: Congregate treatment setting for residents with senescent brain function. Presented at Conference on the Clinical Aspects of Alzheimer's Disease and Senile Dementia, National Institute of Mental Health, Bethesda, MD, December 1978.
10. Brody, E. M., Kleban, M. H., Lawton, M. P., and Silverman, H. (1971): Excess disabilities of mentally impaired aged: Impact of individualized treatment. *Gerontologist* 11:124–133.
11. Citrin, R. S., and Dixon, D. N. (1977): Reality orientation: A milieu therapy used in an institution for the aged. *Gerontologist* 17:39–43.
12. Coleman, K. K. (1963): The modification of rigidity in geriatric patients through operant conditioning. *Unpublished Ph.D. dissertation,* Louisiana State University, Baton Rouge.
13. Corsellis, J. (1962): *Mental Illness and the Aging Brain.* Oxford University Press, London.
14. Cosin, L. Z., Mort, M., Post, F., Westropp, C., and Williams, M. (1958): Experimental treatment of persistent senile confusion. *Int. J. Soc. Psychiatry* 4:24–42.
15. DeLong, A. J. (1970): The microspatial structure of the older person. In: *The Spatial Behavior of Older People,* edited by L. A. Pastalan and D. H. Carson, pp. 68–87. University of Michigan Press, Ann Arbor.
16. Eisdorfer, C., Cohen, D., and Preston, C. (1978): Behavioral and psychological therapies for the older patient with cognitive impairment.
17. Eisdorfer, C., and Stotsky, B. A. (1977): Intervention, treatment, and rehabilitation of psychiatric disorders. In: *Handbook of the Psychology of Aging,* edited by J. E. Birren and K. W. Schaie. Van Nostrand, New York.
18. Ernst, P., Beran, B., Sufford, F., and Kleinhauz, M. (1978): Isolation and the symptoms of chronic brain syndrome. *Gerontologist* 18:468–474.
19. Filer, R. N., and O'Connell, D. D. (1964): Motivation of aging persons in an institutional setting. *J. Gerontol.* 19:15–22.
20. Folsom, J. C. (1968): Reality orientation therapy. *J. Geriatr. Psychiatry* 1:291–307.
21. Garfinkel, R. (1979): Brief behavior therapy with an elderly patient. *J. Geriatr. Psychiatry (in press).*

22. Gottesman, L. E. (1965): Resocialization of the geriatric mental patient. *Am. J. Public Health* 55:1964–1970.
23. Gottesman, L. E., and Brody, E. M. (1975): Psychosocial intervention programs within the institutional setting. In: *Long-Term Care: A Handbook for Researchers, Planners, and Providers,* edited by S. Sherwood. Spectrum Publications, New York.
24. Gottesman, L. E., Quarterman, C. E., and Cohn, G. M. (1973): Psychosocial treatment of the aged. In: *The Psychology of Adult Development and Aging,* edited by C. Eisdorfer and M. P. Lawton. American Psychological Association, Washington, D.C.
25. Gunner-Swenson, F., and Jensen, K. (1976): Frequency of mental disorders in old age. *Acta Psychiatr. Scand.* 53:283–297
26. Hall, E. T. (1966): *The Hidden Dimension.* Doubleday, New York.
27. Harris, C. S., and Ivory, P. (1976): An outcome evaluation of reality orientation therapy with geriatric patients in a state mental hospital. *Gerontologist* 16:496–503.
28. Harris, H., Lipman, A., and Slater, R. (1977): Architectural design: The spatial location and interactions of old people. *Gerontology* 23:390–400
29. Hoyer, W. J., Kafer, R. A., Simpson, S. C., and Hoyer, F. W. (1974): Reinstatement of verbal behavior in elderly mental patients using operant procedures. *Gerontologist* 14:149–152.
30. Kahana, E., Kahana, B., and Jacobs, K. (1970): Functionally integrated therapy programs for the elderly. *Gerontologist* 10 (3, Part 2):59 (abs).
31. Kahn, R. L. (1966): Comments. In: *Mental Impairment in the Aged,* edited by M. P. Lawton and F. G. Lawton. Philadelphia Geriatric Center, Philadelphia.
32. Kahn, R. L., Pollack, M., and Goldfarb, A. J. (1961): Factors relating to individual differences in mental status of institutionalized aged. In: *Psychopathology of Aging,* edited by P. H. Hoch and J. Zubin. Grune and Stratton, New York.
33. Kahn, R. L., and Tobin, S. S. (1978): Community treatment for aged persons with altered brain function. Presented at Conference on the Behavioral Aspects of Alzheimer's Disease and Senile Dementia, National Institute of Mental Health, Bethesda, MD, December 1978.
34. Kleban, M. H., Brody, E. M., and Lawton, M. P. (1971): Personality traits in the mentally impaired aged and their relationships to improvement in current functioning. *Gerontologist* 11:134–140.
35. Kleban, M. H., Lawton, M. P., Brody, E. M., and Moss, M. (1976): Behavioral observations of mentally impaired: Those who decline and those who do not. *J. Gerontol.* 31:333–339.
36. Lawton, M. P., and Simon, B. (1968): The ecology of social relationships in housing for the elderly. *Gerontologist* 8:108–115.
37. Lawton, M. P. (1978): Sensory deprivation and the effect of the environment on management of the senile dementia patient. Presented at the Conference on Behavioral Aspects of Alzheimer's Disease and Senile Dementia, National Institute of Mental Health, Bethesda, MD, December 1978.
38. Lawton, M. P., Liebowitz, B., and Charon, H. (1970): Physical structure and the behavior of senile patients following ward remodeling. *Int. J. Aging Hum. Dev.* 1:231–240.
39. Lawton, M. P., and Nahemow, L. (1973): Ecology and the aging process. In: *Psychology of Adult Development and Aging,* edited by C. Eisdorfer and M. P. Lawton. American Psychological Association, Washington, D.C.
40. Liebowitz, B., Lawton, M. P., and Waldman, A. (1979): Evaluation: Designing for confused elderly people. *Am. Inst. Architects J.* 68(2):59–61.
41. Lindsley, O. R. (1966): Geriatric behavioral prosthetics. In: *New Thoughts on Old Age,* edited by R. Kastenbaum. Springer, New York.
42. Lipman, A., and Slater, R. (1977): Status and spatial appropriation in eight homes for old people. *Gerontologist* 17:250–255.
43. MacDonald, M. L., and Butler, A. K. (1974): Reversal of helplessness: Producing walking behavior in nursing home wheelchair residents using behavior modification procedures. *J. Gerontol.* 29:97–101.
44. MacDonald, M. L., and Settin, J. M. (1978): Reality orientation versus sheltered workshops as treatment for the institutionalized aging. *J. Gerontol.* 33:416–421.
45. Mackay, H. A. (1965): Operant techniques applied to disorders of the senium. *Unpublished Ph.D. dissertation,* Queens University, Kingston, Ontario.
46. Maxwell, R. J., Bader, J. E., and Watson, W. H. (1972): Territory and self in a geriatric setting. *Gerontologist* 12:413–417.
47. McClannahan, L. E., and Risley, T. R. (1975): Design of living environments for nursing

home residents: Increasing participation in recreation activities. *J. Appl. Behav. Anal.* 8:261–268.

48. Mishara, B. L. (1978): Geriatric patients who improve in token economy and general milieu treatment programs: a multivariate analysis. *J. Consult. Clin. Psychol.* 46:1340–1348.

49. Nathanson, B. F., and Reingold, J. (1969): A workshop for mentally impaired aged. *Gerontologist* 9:293–295.

50. National Center for Health Statistics (1977): *Profile of Chronic Illness in Nursing Homes.* DHEW Publication No. (PHS) 78–1780, Ser. 13, No. 29. U.S. Department of Health, Education, and Welfare, Washington, D.C.

51. Pappas, W., Curtis, W. P., and Baker, J. A. (1958): A controlled study of an intensive treatment program for hospitalized geriatric patients. *J. Am. Geriatr. Soc.* 6:17–26.

52. Rebok, G. W., and Hoyer, W. J. (1977): The functional context of elderly behavior. *Gerontologist* 17:27–34.

53. Roth, M., Tomlinson, B. E., and Blessed, G. (1966): Correlation between scores for dementia and counts of "senile plaques" in cerebral grey matter of elderly subjects. *Nature* 209:219.

54. Rothschild, D. (1941): Poor correlation between pathologic and clinical findings in aged. *Dis. of the Nerv. Syst.* 2:49–54.

55. Sklar, J., and O'Neill, F. J. (1961): Experiments with intensive treatment in a geriatric ward. In: *Psychopathology of Aging,* edited by P. Hoch and J. Zubin. Grune and Stratton, New York.

56. Slater, R., and Lipman, A. (1977): Staff assessments of confusion and the situation of confused residents in homes for older people. *Gerontologist* 17:523–530.

57. Smith, B. J., and Barker, H. R. (1972): Influence of a reality orientation training program on the attitudes of trainees. *Gerontologist* 12:262–264.

58. Watson, W. H. (1970): Body image and staff-to-resident deportment in a home for the aging. *Int. J. Aging Hum. Dev.* 1:345–360.

OPEN DISCUSSION

Dr. Zubin: The psychosocial approach, which is one of the basic approaches to aging, has been underplayed in this symposium, perhaps because of the shortness of time.

We must remember that, just as in mental retardation, 75% of aging disorders are not basically biological at all. One thing that is backward about the psychosocial approach is that it does not have the kind of basic measurable parameters which, for example, genetics has in consanguinity. It is not because such parameters do not exist, but because we have not paid enough attention to these psychosocial parameters. For example, Ruth Bennett's work on isolation is a fundamental approach to the problem of how one can deal with one of the psychosocial aspects of aging, but it is not used very often.

If we began to study social networks which may perhaps play a role in the external environment parallel to that which the vascular system plays in the internal environment, we might begin to understand better what goes wrong with the majority of individuals who, upon aging, begin to have deviant situations or deviant behavior. It is high time that we began to devote some of our skill and effort to the discovery of the parameters in the psychosocial area, as we have done already in the other areas.

Dr. Lawton: Let me just say Amen. I think, however, that it really becomes imperative to define whom we are speaking of. Dr. Zubin, I think, is referring to 95% of the population 65 and over. However, our subject today was senile dementia; we have to be careful to designate the conditions in which we can produce major change and those in which we can not.

Dr. Gruenberg: I would like to add to what Dr. Zubin said. From my experience, I have to agree that there has been very little systematic research on modification of the social environment affecting behavior patterns with people who have senile dementia.

There is another way of looking at the social environment and social network different from the notion of manipulating social environment by the behavior of professionals. The first demonstrations of reduction in use of mental hospital inpatient care, done at Oxford and at Miller's place in Nottingham, were done with elderly dementia patients. What they did was to cut down radically on the use of the hospital and increase radically the bearing of the burden with the families of patients with amnestic syndrome.

While they could not cure the syndrome, they did reduced wandering and even stopped incontinence. What they did was try to define the crisis that led to rejection from the existing social system, the support system of the patient. The social support system defines the reason for asking for help in the narrowest possible way; the practitioners undertook to give it feedback and to return the patient to the system with continuing support. I do not think you mentioned this as an area of research: the prevention of collapse in social functioning.

Dr. Lawton: You are entirely right. I omitted the 800,000 or so organic brain syndrome patients who are living outside institutions; probably 60% of all such individuals are not in institutions.

I think, in relation to what Dr. Gruenberg has said, it is important to look at a couple of studies that have been made of families of relatives with dementia, those by Sainsbury and Grad in England and by others elsewhere. This research has underlined the hard choices that relatives face. Some families, through counseling and the assistance of agencies, can be helped to bear the burden of a demented relative, to work creatively to keep that relative outside an institution. For others—and I think the evidence is very clear on this—the burden on the family for dealing with dementia is far greater than the burden of dealing with a physical illness. Of course we have to take the needs of the family into account, too, no matter how much we may favor the use of noninstitutional treatment resources.

279

Dr. Ruth Bennett: I feel obliged to respond to Dr. Zubin, who mentioned our isolation studies. I am reminded that in 1961 the APPA had a meeting, at which I was a speaker, on the psychopathology of aging, and there was not a single paper on brain and behavior. I think they were almost entirely psychosocial in character. This meeting has taken the opposite approach. I do not think there was an APPA meeting on aging at any time between the two meetings I mentioned, but I may be wrong.

I feel that one is now being forced to choose between these two positions, and I am rather distressed by the sort of atmosphere in which there is on the one hand, brain, and on the other hand, psychosocial factors, and never the twain shall meet. I think these two positions can be merged fruitfully. Those of us who are gerontologists believe we do more than pay lip service to the notion that aging needs to be studied from an interdisciplinary point of view.

For example, let us look at the aforementioned isolation studies that I have been conducting. Isolation may produce a lack of stimulation and that may in turn produce cell loss. In other words, one still has to have a look at the interaction of all of these factors. Isolation may not be conducive to eating because people like to have company when they eat; thus they may suffer from malnutrition. All of these factors are still very important in the problems of the elderly. I do not think one can do studies where one completely disassociates oneself from one set of factors, soft ones, so to speak, and looks only at the hard ones. I think it is high time that all of these factors be looked at simultaneously.

Psychopathology in the Aged, edited by
Jonathan O. Cole and James E. Barrett.
Raven Press, New York © 1980.

Neurochemical Approaches to the Treatment of Senile Dementia

*John H. Growdon and **Suzanne Corkin

*Department of Neurology, Tufts-New England Medical Center, Boston, Massachusetts
02111; and **Department of Psychology, Massachusetts Institute of Technology,
Cambridge, Massachusetts 02139

The mammalian central nervous system contains an indeterminate but clearly important number of cholinergic tracts and synapses. Cholinergic neurons appear to influence a wide variety of behaviors in experimental animals (45,49); in humans, central cholinergic deficiencies occur in diseases such as Huntington's disease (6,51,66) and tardive dyskinesia (22,47). Recent evidence suggests that deficient central cholinergic tone may also contribute to the clinical manifestations of Alzheimer's disease (9,11,19,56,58,65,73), whereas cholinergic tone may be less impaired in elderly subjects without dementia.

This chapter outlines the evidence that cholinergic neurons may be selectively damaged in Alzheimer's disease and examines the possibility that these neurons influence learning and memory. It reviews ways in which availability of choline and lecithin influence acetylcholine synthesis and summarizes the preliminary attempts to treat Alzheimer's disease with these compounds.

NEUROCHEMICAL ABNORMALITIES IN ALZHEIMER'S DISEASE

Dementia refers to the progressive deterioration of a spectrum of mental functions due to diffuse or disseminated disease of the cerebral hemispheres in adult life. Presenile dementia, or Alzheimer's disease, is the most common cause of dementia in persons 45 to 65 years old; senile dementia of the Alzheimer type occurs in persons older than 65 and is one of the most common clinical syndromes among the aged. The clinical, neurologic, and neuropathologic findings in these dementias are identical (25,46), and most neurologists and neuropathologists believe that the two diseases are identical (46,68). Some decrease in brain size normally accompanies the aging process, but brain atrophy is generally more severe in patients with Alzheimer's disease (18). The histopathologic hallmarks of Alzheimer's disease include neurofibrillary tangles and neuritic or senile plaques (18,74); these occur in brains of healthy elderly subjects as well, but they are much more abundant and widespread in the brains of patients with Alzheimer's disease. Neurochemical analyses of brain tissue obtained at postmortem examination indicate that nerve cells atrophy both in healthy elderly subjects and in patients with Alzheimer's disease, but that the rate at which neurons are lost in Alzheimer's disease may exceed that in healthy elderly subjects by 5% or more per year (8). Decreased levels of enzymes and other proteins that are unaffected by the agonal state indicate that neurons are more affected than glia (8,10).

Bowen et al. (9) presented the first evidence that a specific neurotransmitter deficit occurred in Alzheimer's disease. They reported that the activity of choline acetyltransferase (CAT), the enzyme that catalyzes the conversion of choline to acetylcholine, was selectively reduced in the cortices of patients with Alzheimer's disease compared to control brains obtained at postmortem. These results were quickly confirmed by Davies and Maloney (19), who further noted that the activities of tyrosine hydroxylase, amino acid decarboxylase, dopamine-β-hydroxylase, and monoamine oxidase (enzymes important in catecholamine biosynthesis) were normal. Shortly thereafter, Perry et al. (56) reported a similar decrease in CAT activity in the parietal cortex and caudate nucleus in patients with Alzheimer's disease and made the important observation that cholinergic muscarinic receptor binding was normal. Similar data were concurrently and independently reported by White et al. (73), and subsequent studies (11,58,65) confirmed the dramatic decrease in CAT activity with preserved muscarinic binding in patients with Alzheimer's disease (Table 1). These biochemical data seem to indicate that Alzheimer's disease is a specific disease and is not necessarily the inevitable result of the normal aging process. The decrease in CAT activity in Alzheimer's disease is much greater than occurs in healthy elderly subjects without dementia (50), and it correlates very well with the regional distribution and number of senile plaques and neurofibrillary tangles (7,70). This concordance suggests that decreased CAT activity may be important in the clinical manifestations of Alzheimer's disease and provides the basis for new attempts to treat it. The distribution of CAT in the brain is limited to those neurons that synthesize acetylcholine; thus, it is the most accurate biochemical marker for cholinergic neurons. (Acetylcholine cannot be measured in human brains directly because

TABLE 1. *CAT activity in brains of patients with Alzheimer's disease: A summary of 7 series*

| | CAT activity | | Muscarinic binding |
Authors	Postmortem	Biopsy	
Bowen et al. (1976)	↓		
Davies and Maloney (1976)	↓		
Perry et al. (1977)	↓		Normal
Spillane et al. (1977)	↓	↓	
White et al. (1977)	↓		Normal
Reisine et al. (1978)	↓		Normal[a]
Bowen et al. (1979)	↓	↓	Normal

[a] Caudate nucleus, putamen and frontal cortex normal; 57% loss in hippocampus.

of rapid hydrolysis by the enzyme acetylcholinesterase.) A reduction in CAT activity probably indicates presynaptic cholinergic damage; this, in turn, might result in decreased acetylcholine synthesis and release. Since postsynaptic muscarinic receptors are preserved (11,56,58,73), it is likely that attempts to increase acetylcholine synthesis and release, or to stimulate these postsynaptic receptor sites directly, might modify some clinical aspects of Alzheimer's disease if cholinergic neurons were involved in its pathophysiology. Choline acetyltransferase activity is also reduced in brains of patients with Huntington's disease; unlike Alzheimer's disease, however, muscarinic receptor sites are also reduced, and cholinergic therapy has not suppressed chorea in these patients (34,54).

The metabolism of the biogenic amines is probably affected as well (1), and decreases in brain levels of dopamine and norepinephrine that apparently occur as part of the aging process are well known (50); however, these changes are less positively correlated with memory loss than changes in cholinergic neurons. If it were important to test the contribution of monoaminergic neurons to memory, investigators could administer precursors, such as the amino acids tyrosine or tryptophan (32).

CHOLINERGIC NEURONS AND MEMORY: PHARMACOLOGIC DATA IN HUMANS

The results of pharmacologic experiments in humans indicate that cholinergic neurons do indeed influence learning and memory. Physostigmine is a centrally active acetylcholinesterase inhibitor; its administration elevates intrasynaptic acetylcholine content and thereby stimulates postsynaptic cholinergic receptors by slowing degradation of acetylcholine released from presynaptic cholinergic neurons. Soukupova et al. (64) gave 1 mg of physostigmine to abstinent alcoholic patients and reported that it enhanced their memory quotients. In normal subjects, 1 mg of physostigmine improved long-term memory (24), and 1 to 2 mg doses reversed scopolamine-induced memory deficits (27,28,44). In similar studies, Sitaram et al. (61) found that 4 mg of arecoline, a direct-acting muscarinic agonist, improved verbal learning ability in normal subjects who had received scopolamine. Peters and Levin (57) showed that 0.8 mg of physostigmine improved long-term memory storage and retrieval in a woman with an amnesic syndrome resulting from herpes simplex encephalitis, and Smith and Swash (62) reported that 1 mg of this drug improved recall and decreased the number of intrusion errors in a single patient with Alzheimer's disease. Physostigmine and arecoline are not suitable for treating patients with Alzheimer's disease. Physostigmine must be given by injection, and its central effects last less than 1 hr. Direct-acting cholinergic agonists such as arecoline may be given by mouth but are often associated with intolerable muscarinic side effects. Deanol has also been prescribed as an acetylcholine precursor; it may be methylated to choline in the liver, but apparently it does not increase acetylcholine levels in the brain after systemic administration (79). Furthermore, deanol can also *diminish* brain acetylcholine synthesis by competing with circulating choline for transport across the blood-brain barrier (17,52). Thus, before choline had been shown to increase brain levels of acetylcholine, it was not possible to test the long-term chemical effects of increased cholinergic tone in patients with brain diseases.

PRECURSOR CONTROL OF NEUROTRANSMITTER SYNTHESIS

The synthesis of acetylcholine from choline and acetyl-coenzyme A is catalyzed by the enzyme choline acetyltransferase (CAT) (Fig. 1). Choline is the physiologic precursor of acetylcholine; some choline in the brain may be liberated by the hydrolysis of lecithin present in cell membranes (13), and a small amount may be synthesized by the methylation of ethanolamines (80). The major available source of brain choline, however, is "free" choline that is taken up from the systemic circulation at the blood-brain barrier (55). The transportation of choline into the intact brain is mediated by a low-affinity uptake system that is distinct from the high-affinity uptake system observed in synaptosomes prepared from cholinergic nerve terminals (38,78). This high-affinity uptake system may affect the distribution of choline within the brain by preferentially shunting it to loci of acetylcholine synthesis; it may also allow neurons to capture and reuse choline formed from the hydrolysis of acetylcholine released in the synapses. The K_m of the low-affinity system that transports choline into the intact brain is 0.22 mM (55). Since plasma choline levels normally fall below this concentration (16,59), the uptake system is highly unsaturated. Hence, any significant variation in plasma choline levels should generate corresponding changes in brain uptake and ultimately in brain choline levels. This has been shown to be the case: Brain choline levels normally bear a linear relationship to plasma choline concentrations throughout their dynamic range (16). The K_ms of choline acetyltransferase for choline (0.4 mM) and for acetyl-coenzyme A (18 μM) are both well above the normal brain concentrations of these substances which are 30 to 50 μM and 7 to 11 μM, respectively. Therefore, changes in the brain levels of either of the precursors for acetylcholine might be expected to modify the rates at which the neurotransmitter is synthesized. This expectation

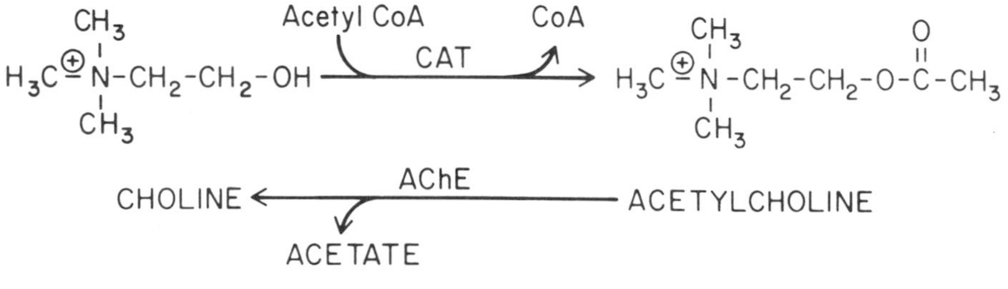

FIG. 1. Synthesis of acetylcholine. Acetylcholine is synthesized from choline and acetylcoenzyme A in a reaction catalyzed by the enzyme choline acetyltransferase (CAT).

was realized when Cohen and Wurtman (15,16) showed that the administration of choline by injection or in the diet increased blood choline, brain choline, and brain acetylcholine levels in rats (Fig. 2). Concurrently and independently, Haubrich and his collaborators (39,40) drew similar conclusions from studies in which they gave rats intracarotid, intraventricular, and parenteral choline injections. Choline administration elevated acetylcholine levels within all brain regions examined, including the cerebral cortex, the caudate nucleus, and in cholinergic nerve terminals within the hippocampus (41).

The increase in acetylcholine levels induced by choline administration apparently results from increased *de novo* synthesis. Cohen and Wurtman (16) gave rats physostigmine, an acetylcholinesterase inhibitor that is active in the central nervous system, in conjunction with choline injections. The resulting increase in brain acetylcholine levels was equal to the sum of the effects of either agent alone, and indicated that choline acts by increasing acetylcholine synthesis and not by slowing its degradation. The increase in neuronal acetylcholine levels induced by choline administration probably causes increased acetylcholine *release* as well. In order to examine the relationship between precursor-induced increases in acetylcholine levels and the amounts of transmitter released into synapses, Ulus and Wurtman (71) used indirect experimental approaches that involved measuring biochemical changes in cells that are postsynaptic to the cholinergic neurons. Two such cells are the dopaminergic neurons that terminate in the caudate nucleus and chromaffin cells of the adrenal medulla. Both contain tyrosine hydroxylase, the rate-limiting enzyme that converts tyrosine to DOPA. Tyrosine hydroxylase in the caudate nucleus undergoes a rapid and short-lived

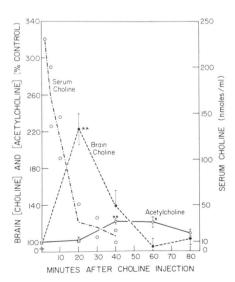

FIG. 2. Time-course of the response of serum Ch, brain Ch, and brain ACh to Ch administered by injection. Groups of 5 to 9 150 to 200 g male rats received Ch chloride (60 mg/kg, i.p.) in saline (0.9% NaCl) or the diluent alone. The animals were killed at various intervals after the injection by microwave irradiation of the head, and whole brain Ch and ACh concentrations were measured. Data for brain Ch and ACh levels are expressed as percents of control means. Bars, SEM. Groups of 2 or 3 rats were injected as described above and killed by decapitation at various intervals after injection. Blood was collected from the cervical wound, and serum Ch levels are expressed as nmoles/ml. Open circles, range of values for serum Ch levels at each point; *$p < 0.01$, **$p < 0.001$, differs from corresponding concentrations in rats injected with saline alone. (From Wurtman et al., ref. 75, with permission.)

activation when the neuron containing it is depolarized (53); the enzyme in chromaffin cells apparently does not exhibit short-term activation, but it is induced 24 to 48 hr after the cells are subjected to prolonged cholinergic stimulation (69). Choline administration increased striatal tyrosine hydroxylase activity by approximately 25% within 2 hr of injection; this effect was dose-related and was blocked by pretreatment with the muscarinic antagonist atropine (72). Choline administration also caused a parallel acceleration in the accumulation of DOPA, the product of this enzyme, in animals treated with an inhibitor of DOPA decarboxylase. When large doses of choline were given to animals by stomach tube, the levels of choline and acetylcholine in the adrenal medulla rose markedly; acetylcholine levels returned to normal 16 hr after intubation. Tyrosine hydroxylase activity did not change significantly for the initial 12 to 16 hr, but did increase by 30% 24 hr after choline intubation, and by 50% after daily intubation for 4 days (71). This increase was not simply a nonspecific response to stress since it did not occur in animals intubated with saline or ammonium chloride; furthermore, it was blocked by pretreatment with cyclohex-imide, an inhibitor of protein synthesis, and by prior adrenal denervation. Choline administration similarly elevated urinary epinephrine levels in intact animals but not in rats subjected previously to bilateral adrenal denervation. Physiologic studies with isolated chicken and cat hearts have demonstrated that choline administration increased acetylcholine release (26,48). In other experiments, choline administration also increased the amount of acetylcholine released from the stimulated rat diaphragm-phrenic nerve preparation (5). These observations are all compatible with the view that choline administration accelerates acetyl-

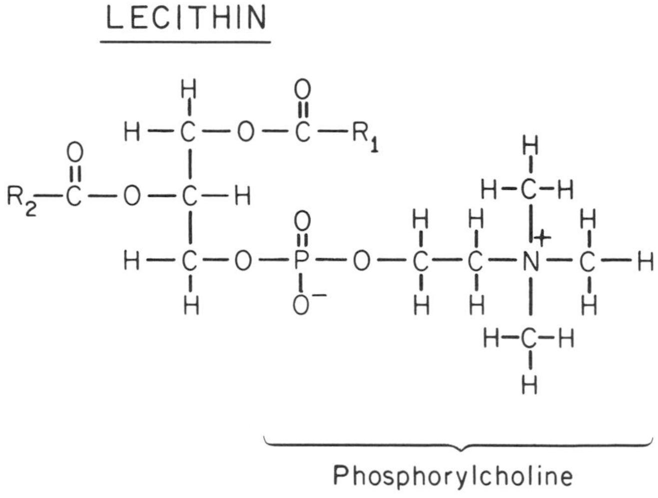

FIG. 3. Chemical structure of phosphatidylcholine (lecithin). Lecithin contains choline attached to a glycerol molecule. The side chain fatty acids R_1 and R_2 are unsaturated in soya lecithin and more saturated in egg lecithin.

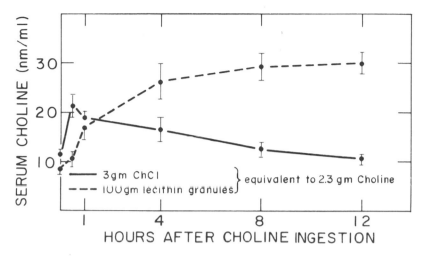

FIG. 4. Effects on serum choline concentrations of consuming choline chloride or lecithin. Ten healthy subjects consumed either 3 g of choline chloride or 100 g of lecithin granules in a single meal; both meals contained 2.3 g of choline. Subjects fasted for the following 12 hours. (From Wurtman et al., ref. 76, with permission.)

choline synthesis, increases acetylcholine levels, and stimulates acetylcholine release. Since the catalytic enzyme CAT is normally unsaturated, choline or lecithin administration should increase the rate of acetylcholine synthesis in surviving cholinergic neurons, even though many cholinergic neurons apparently degenerate in Alzheimer's disease.

Food contains very little free choline; most occurs covalently bound to glycerol and fatty acids in the form of lecithin (phosphatidylcholine) (Fig. 3). Since this is the major source of choline in the diet, Wurtman et al. (42,76) compared the effects of consuming equimolar amounts of choline as a chloride salt or as lecithin on neuronal acetylcholine levels in rats and on plasma choline levels in humans. Choline ingested as lecithin increased brain and adrenal acetylcholine levels in rats (43), and produced greater and more prolonged elevations in plasma choline levels than choline chloride (76) (Fig. 4). Most patients prefer lecithin, since it is tasteless and does not produce the fishy odor commonly associated with choline chloride ingestion (36).

CLINICAL USES OF CHOLINE AND LECITHIN IN TREATING PATIENTS WITH ALZHEIMER'S DISEASE

The demonstration that choline and lecithin can increase blood choline, brain choline, and brain acetylcholine levels in rats, and plasma and CSF levels in humans suggested that these compounds may be useful in treating human diseases such as Huntington's disease, tardive dyskinesia, and Alzheimer's disease, in which cholinergic deficiencies have been postulated (22,35). Shortly after the publication of the initial animal data, Davis et al. (20) reported that 16 g of choline per day suppressed buccal-lingual movements in a single patient with tardive dyskinesia. They subsequently found that choline ingestion improved four of four patients with tardive dyskinesia and two of four patients with Huntington's disease (21). Growdon et al. (37) gave 8 to 20 g of choline chloride per day to 20 patients with permanent tardive dyskinesia according to a double-blind crossover protocol. They found that choline ingestion increased plasma choline levels in all patients and decreased choreic movements in 9 of 20. Tamminga et al. (67) also demonstrated choline's efficacy in treating patients with tardive dyskinesia, and this has been confirmed by other investigators (4,31,77). Growdon et al. (36) also gave lecithin to patients with tardive dyskinesia; its administration increased plasma choline levels and suppressed the choreiform movements as effectively as choline chloride. In addition, lecithin may reduce the symptoms of Friedreich's ataxia, or at least slow the progression of this disease (3). Choline administration has also been used to treat patients with Huntington's disease. It produced a dose-related increase in plasma choline levels (2,33) and raised CSF choline content as well (33). In one series, chorea was suppressed in 3 of the 8 patients (23), but in two other studies, none of the 15 patients was helped (2,34). The clinical improvement during choline ingestion, especially in tardive dyskinesia, is consistent with increased acetylcholine synthesis and release. These experiments encouraged investigators to test the effects of administering precursors of acetylcholine to patients with Alzheimer's disease.

There are seven published studies that report the effects of physostigmine, choline, or lecithin administration on selected cognitive tasks used to assess behavior in demented patients (Table 2). Most investigators studied the memory system primarily, since loss of recent memory capacities is often the initial clinical symptom of Alzheimer's disease, and it had been demonstrated previously that cholinergic mechanisms could affect learning and memory in healthy young adults. Boyd et al. (12) reported the first treatment study, in which they gave 5 g of choline chloride per day for 2 weeks and then 10 g per day for the next 2 weeks to 7 severely demented patients. Choline administration did not improve cognitive function, although some of the patients were less irritable and more aware of their surroundings. These changes in social behavior could have resulted from choline administration; alternatively, stimulation from greater staff attention might also explain these benefits. The authors speculated that patients with less severe dementia would be better candidates for choline treatment. This idea received some support from the finding of Etienne et al. (30) that the 3 least demented of 5 patients with Alzheimer's disease reproduced the easiest design of the Wechsler Block Design subtest while taking 8 g of choline per day for 4 weeks, but were unable to perform this test before or after choline ingestion; the other 2 more severely demented patients did not improve. In a third study, Smith et al. (63) administered 9 g of choline per day for 2 weeks and also gave a placebo for 2 weeks to 10 patients with Alzhei-

TABLE 2. *Preliminary reports of cholinergic treatment in patients with Alzheimer's disease*

Author	Number of patients	Age of patients	Severity of Alzheimer's	Treatment	Results
Boyd et al. (1977)	7	70–80	Severe	Choline 5–10g/D	Less irritable
Etienne et al. (1978)	3	76–88	Severe	Choline 10g/D	No benefit
Smith et al. (1978)	10	$\bar{x}=77$		Choline 9g/D	No benefit
Signoret et al. (1978)	8	59–78	Mild	Choline 9g/D	Slightly improved memory
Smith and Swash (1979)	1	42	Moderate	Physostigmine 1mg	Decreased intrusion errors
Etienne et al. (1979)	7	42–81	Moderate	Lecithin 25–100g/D	Improved associate learning
Christie et al. (1979)	10	<65	Mild-Severe	Choline 5g/D and Lecithin 28–100g/D	No improvement; Deterioration possibly slowed

mer's disease. They tested the effects of these treatments on the Raven's Progressive Matrices Test, a verbal fluency test (saying boys' names), and on memory tasks that assessed the patients' capacity to recall or recognize verbal and nonverbal material immediately after presentation and following a delay. This dose of choline bitartrate did not change patients' performance on any task. Signoret et al. (60) also administered an extensive battery of cognitive tasks to 8 patients with mild Alzheimer's disease who received 9 g of choline chloride per day. After 3 weeks of treatment, 3 patients younger than 65 years old with dementia of short duration were slightly more efficient on tests of delayed learning and delayed recall of 30 pictures. Unfortunately, testing was not repeated after choline withdrawal, so there was no control for a practice effect. These patients and their relatives also reported an improvement in "everyday" memory, but these reports are difficult to evaluate without a placebo condition.

There are two other studies in which lecithin has been used to treat patients with Alzheimer's disease. Etienne et al. (29) gave 25 g of lecithin (20% phosphatidylcholine content) per day for 4 weeks to 7 patients, and reported that 3 of them performed the Associate Learning subtest of the Wechsler Memory Scale and the Benton Visual Retention Test with fewer errors when plasma choline levels were at their peak than they did before or after lecithin ingestion. In another investigation, Christie et al. (14) found that 5 g of choline chloride per day and 100 g of lecithin per day (20% phosphatidylcholine) were equally effective in raising the serum and CSF choline levels in 10 patients with Alzheimer's disease. In addition, pretreatment behavioral test results for 8 patients were compared with scores obtained after 4 weeks and 3 months of lecithin treatment. There were no changes in measures of orientation, digit span, immediate recall of short prose passages, or naming visual, auditory, and tactual stimuli. However, 5 patients seemed to improve on constructional and other complex sensorimotor tasks, whereas 2 declined in this respect. More qualitative observations suggested that lecithin treatment may have slowed the progression of the disease.

Physostigmine administration can also increase brain acetylcholine levels, but its short duration of action, muscarinic side effects, and requisite mode of administration limit its clinical applications. Physostigmine injections have theoretical utility, however; positive responses to physostigmine infusions would implicate cholinergic neurons in a specific behavior or disease, and might also predict the effects of more chronic cholinergic stimulation with choline or lecithin (22). Smith and Swash (62) gave 1 mg of physostigmine or a placebo injection to a single patient with Alzheimer's disease. A comparison of behavioral test results under the two conditions revealed significantly fewer inappropriate responses on two verbal memory tests and a verbal fluency task with physostigmine; there were no differences between drug and placebo on seven other memory tests, however. These are all preliminary reports in which known cholinergic drugs were given for short periods of time without placebo controls. Nevertheless, these studies will probably encourage more rigorously controlled trials of choline or lecithin administration to patients with Alzheimer's disease.

CONCLUSION

There is universal agreement on the biochemical abnormality in Alzheimer's disease: CAT activity is decreased, and muscarinic receptor binding sites are apparently preserved. Similar changes may occur in healthy elderly subjects, although the decrease in CAT activity is more variable and much less severe. CAT is the enzyme that catalyzes the conversion of choline to acetylcholine; it is the best marker for cholinergic neurons in the brain. Since its activity is decreased in the cortices of patients with Alzheimer's disease, it is likely that levels of acetylcholine are also reduced, and this deficiency may contribute to the symptoms of Alzheimer's disease much as reduced levels of dopamine contribute to the symptoms of Parkinson's disease. Treatments that increase striatal levels of dopamine, such as levodopa administration, often suppress the signs and symptoms of Parkinson's disease. By analogy, it might be possible to improve cognitive or behavioral deficits in patients with Alzheimer's disease by treatments that increase central cholinergic tone. Most of the currently available cholinergic agonists, including physostigmine, arecoline, and deanol, have serious limitations. In contrast, choline administration, either as the salt or as lecithin (phosphatidylcholine), is an effective way to increase central cholinergic tone and is also remarkably free of serious side effects. Choline and lecithin have already been used to treat one brain disease successfully—tardive dyskinesia—and should be thoroughly tested in patients with Alzheimer's disease as well as in healthy elderly subjects with only slight memory loss. Precursor therapy does require intact presynaptic terminals, and choline administration would not be expected to increase acetylcholine levels if all cholinergic neurons had been destroyed. This should not restrict precursor therapy, however, since some CAT activity is preserved even in severe cases of Alzheimer's disease. This enzyme is normally unsaturated, and treatments that increase the availability of its substrate, choline, within cholinergic neurons would be expected to enhance acetylcholine synthesis, levels, and release. Future studies should determine the optimal dose of choline and also test pure lecithins (100% phosphatidylcholine) with known fatty acid compositions. In addition, neuropsychologic evaluations should use cognitive tests that are sensitive to cholinergic manipulations and also employ a placebo-controlled protocol.

ACKNOWLEDGMENTS

Some of the studies described in this chapter were supported, in part, by grants from NIMH (MH-28783) and from the Ford Foundation.

REFERENCES

1. Adolfsson, R., Gottfries, C. G., Oreland, L., Roos, B. E., and Winblad, B. (1978): Reduced levels of catecholamines in the brain and increased activity of monoamine oxidase in platelets in Alzheimer's disease: Therapeutic implications. In: *Alzheimer's Disease: Senile Dementia and Related Disorders,* edited by R. Katzman, R. D. Terry and K. L. Bick, pp. 441–451. Raven Press, New York.
2. Aquilonious, S. M., and Eckernas, S.-A. (1977): Choline therapy in Huntington's chorea. *Neurology,* 27:877.
3. Barbeau, A. (1978): Friedreich's ataxia 1978—an overview. *Can. J. Neurol. Sci.* 5:161–165.
4. Barbeau, A. (1978): Lecithin in neurologic disorders. *N. Engl. J. Med.,* 299:200.
5. Bierkamper, G. G., and Goldberg, A. M. (1979): The effect of choline on the release of acetylcholine from the neuromuscular junction. In: *Choline and Lecithin in Brain Diseases,* edited by A. Barbeau, J. Growdon, and R. J. Wurtman, pp. 243–251. Raven Press, New York.
6. Bird, E. D., and Iverson, L. L. (1974): Huntington's chorea: Post-mortem measurement of glutamic acid decarboxylase, choline acetyltransferase, and dopamine in basal ganglia. *Brain,* 97:457–472.
7. Blessed, G., Tomlinson, B. E., and Roth, M. (1968): The association between quantitative measures of dementia and of senile change in the cerebral grey matter of elderly subjects. *Br. J. Psychiatry* 114:797–811.
8. Bowen, D. M., and Davison, A. N. (1978): Changes in brain lysosomal activity, neurotransmitter and related enzymes, and other proteins in senile dementia. In: *Alzheimer's Disease: Senile Dementia and Related Disorders,* edited by R. Katzman, R. D. Terry and K. L. Bick, pp. 421–424. Raven Press, New York.
9. Bowen, D. M., Smith, C. B., White, P., and Davison, A. N. (1976): Neurotransmitter-related enzymes and indices of hypoxia in senile dementia and other abiotrophies. *Brain* 99:459–496.
10. Bowen, D. M., Smith, C. B., White, P., Goodhardt, M. J., Spillane, J. A., Flack, R. H. A., and Davis, A. N. (1977): Chemical pathology of the organic dementias. I. Validity of biochemical measurements on human post-mortem brain specimens. *Brain* 100:397–426.
11. Bowen, D. M., Spillane, J. A., Curzon, G., Meier-Ruge, W., White, P., Goodhardt, M. J., Iwangoff, P., and Davison, A. N. (1979): Accelerated aging or selective neuronal loss as an important cause of dementia? *Lancet* 1:11–14.
12. Boyd, W. D., Graham-White, J., Blackwood, G., Glen, I., and McQueen, J. (1977): Clinical effects of choline in Alzheimer senile dementia. *Lancet* 1:711.
13. Browning, E. T., and Schulman, M. P. (1968): (^{14}C) acetylcholine synthesis by cortex slices of rat brain. *J. Neurochem.* 15:1391.

14. Christie, J. E., Blackburn, I. M., Glen, A. I. M., Zeisel, S., Sherring, A., and Yates, C. M. (1979): Effects of choline and lecithin on CSF choline levels and on cognitive function in patients with presenile dementia of the Alzheimer type. In: *Choline and Lecithin in Brain Diseases,* edited by A. Barbeau, J. H. Growdon, and R. J. Wurtman, pp. 377–387. Raven Press, New York.

15. Cohen, E. L., and Wurtman, R. J. (1975): Brain acetylcholine: Increase after systemic choline administration. *Life Sci.* 16:1095.

16. Cohen, E. L., and Wurtman, R. J. (1976): Brain acetylcholine: Control by dietary choline. *Science* 191:561–562.

17. Cornford, E. M., Braun, L. D., and Oldendorf, W. H. (1978): Carrier mediated blood-brain barrier transport of choline and certain choline analogies. *J. Neurochem.* 30:299–308.

18. Corsellis, J. A. N. (1976): Aging and the dementias. In: *Greenfield's Neuropathology,* edited by W. Blackwood and J. A. N. Corsellis, 3rd ed. Edward Arnold, London.

19. Davies, P., and Maloney, A. J. F. (1976): Selective loss of central cholinergic neurons in Alzheimer's disease. *Lancet* 2:1403.

20. Davis, K. L., Berger, P. A., and Hollister, L. E. (1975): Choline for tardive dyskinesia. *N. Eng. J. Med.* 293:152.

21. Davis, K. L., Hollister, L. E., Barchas, J. D., and Berger, P. A. (1976): Choline in tardive dyskinesia and Huntington's disease. *Life Sci.* 19:507–516.

22. Davis, K. L., Hollister, L. E., Berger, P. A., and Barchas, P. A. (1975): Cholinergic imbalance hypotheses of psychoses and movement disorders. *Psychopharmacol. Commun.* 1:533–547.

23. Davis, K. L., Hollister, L. E., Berger, P. A., and Vento, A. L. (1978): Studies on choline chloride in neuropsychiatric disease: Human and animal data. *Psychopharmacol. Bull.* 14:56–58.

24. Davis, K. L., Mohs, R. C., Tinklenberg, J. R., Pfefferbaum, A., Hollister, L. E., and Kopell, B. S. (1978): Physostigmine: Improvement of long-term memory processes in normal humans. *Science* 201:272–274.

25. DeJong, R. N., and Pope, A. (1975): Dementia. In: *The Nervous System,* edited by D. B. Tower. Raven Press, New York.

26. Dieterich, H. A., Lindmar, R., and Loffelholz, K. (1978): The role of choline in the release of acetylcholine in isolated hearts. *Naunyn Schmiedebergs Arch. Pharmacol.* 301:207–215.

27. Drachman, D. A. (1977): Memory and cognitive function in man: Does the cholinergic system have a specific role? *Neurology* 27:783–790.

28. Drachman, D. A., and Leavitt, J. (1974): Human memory and the cholinergic system. *Arch. Neurol.* 30:113–121.

29. Etienne, P., Gauthier, S., Dastoor, D., Collier, B., and Ratner, J. (1979): Alzheimer's disease: Clinical effect of lecithin treatment. In: *Choline and Lecithin in Brain Disorders,* edited by A. Barbeau, J. H. Growdon, and R. J. Wurtman, pp. 389–396. Raven Press, New York.

30. Etienne, P., Gauthier, S., Johnson, G., Collier, B., Mendis, T., Dastoor, D., Cole, M., and Muller, H. F. (1978): Clinical effects of choline in Alzheimer's disease. *Lancet* 1:508–509.

31. Gelenberg, A. J., Wojcik, J. D., and Growdon, J. H. (1979): Lecithin for the treatment of tardive dyskinesia. In: *Choline and Lecithin in Brain Diseases,* edited by A. Barbeau, J. H. Growdon, and R. J. Wurtman, pp. 285–303. Raven Press, New York.

32. Growdon, J. H. (1979): Neurotransmitter precursors in the diet: Their use in the treatment of brain diseases. In: *Nutrition and the Brain, vol. 3,* edited by R. J. Wurtman and J. J. Wurtman, pp. 117–181. Raven Press, New York.

33. Growdon, J. H., Cohen, E. L., and Wurtman, R. J. (1977): Effects of oral choline administration on serum and CSF choline levels in patients with Huntington's disease. *J. Neurochem.* 28:229–231.

34. Growdon, J. H., Cohen, E. L., and Wurtman, R. J. (1977): Huntington's disease: Clinical chemical effects of choline administration. *Ann. Neurol.* 5:418–422.

35. Growdon, J. H., Cohen, E. L., and Wurtman, R. J. (1977): Treatment of brain disease with dietary precursors of neurotransmitters. *Ann. Intern. Med.* 86:337–339.

36. Growdon, J. H., Gelenberg, A. J., Dollar, J., Hirsch, M. J., and Wurtman, R. J. (1978): Lecithin can suppress tardive dyskinesia. *N. Engl. J. Med.* 298:1029–1030.

37. Growdon, J. H., Hirsch, M. J., Wurtman, R. J., and Weiner, W. (1977): Oral choline administration to patients with tardive dyskinesia. *N. Engl. J. Med.* 297:524–527.

38. Haga, T., and Noda, H. (1973): Choline uptake systems of rat brain synaptosomes. *Biochim. Biophys. Acta* 291:564.

39. Haubrich, D. R., Wang, P. F. L., Clody, D. E., and Wedeking, P. W. (1975): Increase in rat brain acetylcholine induced by choline or deanol. *Life Sci.* 17:975–980.
40. Haubrich, D. R., Wang, P. F. L., and Wedeking, P. (1974): Role of choline in biosynthesis of acetylcholine. *Fed. Proc.* 33:477.
41. Hirsch, M. J., Growdon, J. H., and Wurtman, R. J. (1977): Increase in hippocampal acetylcholine after choline administration. *Brain Res.* 125:383–385.
42. Hirsch, M. J., Growdon, J. H., and Wurtman, R. J. (1978): Relations between dietary choline intake, serum choline levels, and various metabolic indices. *Metabolism* 27:953–960.
43. Hirsch, M. J., and Wurtman, R. J. (1978): Lecithin consumption elevates acetylcholine concentrations in rat brain and adrenal gland. *Science* 202:223–225.
44. Hrbek, J., Komenda, S., Sirokam, A. and Macakova, J. (1971): On the interaction of scopolamine and physostigmine in man. *Act. Nerv. Super. (Praha)* 13:200–201.
45. Karczmar, A. G. (1977): Exploitable aspects of central cholinergic functions, particularly with respect to the EEG, motor, analgesic and mental functions. In: *Cholinergic Mechanisms and Psychopharmacology,* edited by D. J. Jenden, pp. 679–708. Raven Press, New York.
46. Katzman, R., Terry, R. D., and Bick, K. L. (1978): Recommendations of the nosology, epidemiology, and etiology and pathophysiology commissions of the workshop-conference on Alzheimer's disease—senile dementia and related disorders. In: *Alzheimer's Disease: Senile Dementia and Related Disorders,* edited by R. Katzman, R. D. Terry, and K. L. Bick, pp. 579–585. Raven Press, New York.
47. Klawans, H. L., and Rubovits, R. (1974): Effect of cholinergic and anticholinergic agents on tardive dyskinesia. *J. Neurol. Neurosurg. Psychiatry* 27:941–947.
48. Loffelholz, K., Lindmar, R., and Weide, W. (1979): Relationship between choline and acetylcholine release in the autonomic nervous system. In: *Choline and Lecithin in Brain Diseases,* edited by A. Barbeau, J. H. Growdon, and R. J. Wurtman, pp. 233–241. Raven Press, New York.
49. Matthies, H., Ott, T., and Kammerer, E. L. (1975): Cholinergic influences on learning. In: *Cholinergic Mechanisms,* edited by P. G. Waser. Raven Press, New York.
50. McGeer, E., and McGeer, P. L. (1976): Neurotransmitter metabolism in the aging brain. In: *Neurobiology of Aging,* edited by R. D. Terry and S. Gershen, pp. 389–403. Raven Press, New York.
51. McGeer, P. L., McGeer, E. G., and Fibiger, H. C. (1973): Choline acetylase and glutamic acid decarboxylase in Huntington's choreas. *Neurology* 23:912–917.
52. Millington, W. R., McCall, A. L., and Wurtman, R. J. (1978): Deanol acetamidobenzoate inhibits the blood-brain barrier transport of choline. *Ann. Neurol.* 4:302–306.
53. Murrin, C. L., Morgenroth, V. H., and Roth, R. H. (1976): Dopaminergic neurons: Effects of electrical stimulation on tyrosine hydroxylase. *Mol. Pharmacol.* 12:9170.
54. Nutt, J. G., Rosin, A., and Chase, T. N. (1978): Treatment of Huntington's disease with a direct cholinergic agonist. *Neurology* 28:358.
55. Pardridge, W. M., and Oldendorf, W. H. (1977): Transport of metabolic substrates through the blood-brain barrier. *J. Neurochem.* 28:5.
56. Perry, E. K., Perry, R. H., Blessed, G., and Tomlinson, B. E. (1977): Necropsy evidence of central cholinergic deficits in senile dementia. *Lancet* 1:189.
57. Peters, B. H., and Levin, H. S. (1977): Memory enhancement after physostigmine treatment in the amnesic syndrome. *Arch. Neurol.* 34:215–219.
58. Reisine, T. D., Yamamura, H. I., Bird, E. D., Spokes, E., and Enna, S. J. (1977): Pre- and postsynaptic neurochemical alterations in Alzheimer's disease. *Brain Res.* 159:477–481.
59. Schuberth, J., and Jenden, D. J. (1975): Transport of choline from plasma to cerebrospinal fluid in the rabbit, with reference to the origin of choline and acetylcholine metabolism in the brain. *Brain Res.* 84:245.
60. Signoret, J. L., Whiteley, A., and Lhermitte, F. (1978): Influence of choline on amnesia in early Alzheimer's disease. *Lancet* 2:837.
61. Sitaram, N., Weingartner, J., and Gillin, J. C. (1978): Human serial learning: Enhancement with arecoline and choline and impairment with scopolamine. *Science* 201:274–276.
62. Smith, C. M., and Swash, M. (1979): Physostigmine in Alzheimer's disease. *Lancet* 1:42.
63. Smith, C. M., Swash, M., Exton-Smith, A. N., Phillips, M. H., Overstall, P. W., Piper, M. E., and Bailey, M. R. (1978): Choline therapy in Alzheimer's disease. *Lancet* 2:318.
64. Soukupova, B., Vojtechovsky, M., and Safratova, V. (1970): Drugs influencing the cholinergic system and the process of learning and memory in man. *Act. Nerv. Super. (Praha)* 12:91–93.

65. Spillane, J. A., White, P., Goodhardt, M. J., Flack, R. H. A., Bowen, D. M., and Davison, A. N. (1977): Selective vulnerability of neurones in organic dementia. *Nature* 7:558–559.
66. Stahl, W. L., and Sawnson, P. D. (1974): Biochemical abnormalities in Huntington's chorea brains. *Neurology* 24:813–819.
67. Tamminga, C. A., Smith, R. C., Ericksen, S. E., Chang, S., and Davis, J. M. (1977): Cholinergic influences in tardive dyskinesia. *Am. J. Psychiatry* 134:796.
68. Terry, R. D. (1978): Aging, senile dementia, and Alzheimer's disease. In: *Alzheimer's Disease: Senile Dementia and Related Disorders,* edited by R. Katzman, R. D. Terry, and K. L. Bick. Raven Press, New York.
69. Thoenen, H. (1974): Trans-synaptic enzyme induction. *Life Sci.* 14:223.
70. Tomlinson, B. E., Blessed, G., and Roth, M. (1970): Observations on the brains of demented old people. *J. Neurol. Sci.* 11:205–242.
71. Ulus, I. H., Hirsch, M. J., and Wurtman, R. J. (1977): Trans-synaptic induction of adrenomedullary tyrosine hydroxylase activity by choline: Evidence that choline adminstration increases cholinergic transmission. *Proc. Natl. Acad. Sci. USA* 74:788–790.
72. Ulus, I. H., and Wurtman, R. J. (1976): Choline administration: Activation of tyrosine hydroxylase in dopaminergic neurons of rat brain. *Science* 194:1060–1061.
73. White, P., Hiley, C. R., Goodhardt, M. J., Carrasco, L. H., Keet, J. P., Williams, I. E. I., and Bowen, D. M. (1977): Neocortical cholinergic neurons in elderly people. *Lancet* 1:668–671.
74. Wisniewski, H. M., and Terry, R. D. (1976): Neuropathology of the aging brain. In: *Neurobiology of Aging,* edited by R. D. Terry and S. Gershon. Raven Press, New York.
75. Wurtman, R. J., Cohen, E. L., and Fernstrom, J. D. (1977): Control of brain neurotransmitter synthesis by precursor availability and food consumption. In: *Neuro-regular and Psychiatric Disorders,* edited by E. Usdin, D. A. Hamburg, and J. D. Barchas, pp. 103–121. Oxford University Press, New York.
76. Wurtman, R. J., Hirsch, M. J., and Growdon, J. H. (1977): Lecithin consumption raises serum-free-choline levels. *Lancet* 1:68–69.
77. Yahr, M. D. (1979): Discussion of paper by Growdon and Gelenberg. *Trans. Am. Neurol. Assoc. (in press).*
78. Yamamura, H. I., and Snyder, S. H. (1973): High affinity transport of choline into synaptosomes of rat brain. *J. Neurochem.* 21:3155.
79. Zahniser, N. R., Chou, D., and Hanin, I. (1977): Is 2-dimethylaminoethanol (deanol) indeed a precursor of brain acetylcholine? *J. Pharmacol. Exp. Ther.* 200:545.
80. Ziesel, S., Blusztajn, J. K., and Wurtman, R. J. (1979): Brain lecithin biosynthesis; Evidence that bovine brain can make choline molecules. In: *Choline and Lecithin in Brain Disorders,* edited by A. Barbeau, J. H. Growdon, and R. J. Wurtman, pp. 47–57. Raven Press, New York.

OPEN DISCUSSION

Dr. Francis: In using lecithin, do you need blood plasma level, or do you give a set dose to any person?

Dr. Growdon: As you probably know, there is some evidence to suggest a biphasic cholinergic effect on memory, in which a little bit of cholinergic stimulation might improve memory, but too much impairs it. Your question therefore is an important one: how much choline or lecithin should be prescribed? To my knowledge, there are no published data that relate plasma choline levels to clinical effects. It may be necessary to double plasma choline level before you get an effect; it is equally likely, however, that such a dose might be on the downside of the curve and actually impair memory.

Dr. Gerner: Is there a great deal of individual variation of percent increase in plasma choline levels by dosage? You have a figure which indicated about a 200% increase. Were they all on similar doses?

Dr. Growdon: We gave 200 mg per kg per day of choline. Random plasma choline levels range between 5 to 15 nmole/ml but can normally vary over a 2- to 3-fold range depending on the composition of the diet. Foods such as liver and eggs that have a relatively high choline content can produce a twofold increase in plasma choline levels which does not occur with a diet consisting primarily of carbohydrates. Choline is still detected in the plasma, however, despite low choline intake since the liver is able to synthesize it from serine.

Dr. Goldstein: I have two related questions about Huntington's disease. Do you see any point in using lecithin prophylactically? Is there anything to support or to contraindicate the use of lecithin in people who have already developed the illness?

Dr. Growdon: Huntington's disease is even more difficult to treat than Alzheimer's disease. Cholinergic neurons are apparently involved in both diseases, but muscarinic receptors are destroyed in Huntington's disease whereas they are preserved in Alzheimer's disease. Furthermore, other neuronal populations, including those that employ GABA and substance P as neurotransmitters, are also damaged in Huntington's disease. It is not surprising therefore that we, and others, have not had much success treating Huntington's disease with choline administration. Thus, I doubt that choline or lecithin administration could prevent Huntington's disease.

Unknown: I have two questions. The first is: are the benefits from choline therapy sustained over time? In tardive dyskinesia, for example, such therapy has been successful acutely but failed with longer usage.

The other question concerns competitive transport of amino acids into the brain. In rats you can give a favorable stabilized diet and consistently get results that relate blood levels and brain levels. In humans, is it not true that the brain levels depend on whether or not there are other substances in the diet competing for transport? Is there information available whether or not competitive transport is a problem in humans?

Dr. Growdon: Yes, competitive transport could be a problem. Two drugs, deanol and lithium, share a common uptake system at the blood-brain barrier with choline; high plasma levels of either drug can impair choline's entry into the brain. Lithium blocks choline's transport out of the brain even more than its entry; thus, a combination of lithium plus lecithin increases brain choline levels more than either treatment alone. This combination may have therapeutic utility for patients with mania and studies are under way at several centers to test this hypothesis.

To answer your first question, I believe that the benefits from choline therapy will be sustained. We gave choline for only 2 weeks in our initial study. In our current one, we have several patients who have been taking lecithin for a year and have sustained continued benefit. These are small numbers, however, and more data are needed.

Dr. Ferris: You interestingly mentioned the possible problems with biphasic response, namely that perhaps giving too much choline might impair the transmitting function. As far as I know, that type of situation has not been shown to apply to presynaptic situations, but it does apply to postsynaptic activity. Do you know of any data which indicate a presynaptic biphasic situation?

I also wonder whether you have any plasma level data suggesting that the elevation produced by dietary changes is maintained over a long period of time, several months or longer, since there is the possibility that there might be some regulatory mechanisms that would offset a major dietary change in choline intake.

Dr. Growdon: Choline is a naturally occurring dietary constituent, but we are using choline and lecithin as drugs. We prescribe doses that are two or three times the amount of choline that one might ordinarily choose to consume in his diet. Plasma choline levels rise after each dose and then fall within several hours; this sequence repeats itself after each dose. There is no evidence to suggest either a feedback regulatory mechanism or the development of tolerance. We measure plasma choline levels in our patients every month, and they are always elevated. Plasma choline levels are also a good way to check compliance.

Psychopathology in the Aged, edited by
Jonathan O. Cole and James E. Barrett.
Raven Press, New York © 1980.

Discussion

Robert Terry

Department of Pathology, Albert Einstein College of Medicine, Bronx, New York 10461

It is nice to see psychiatrists talking about neuropathology. It is rare in this country, happening only when Sir Martin visits.

A major point here is that Alzheimer's disease is by far the most important cause of senile dementia. But there are numerous other causes, and without a very careful application by all available diagnostic means, including clinical, neurophysiologic, cerebral blood flow, electroencephalographic, and so on, much of the strength of pharmacologic and neurophysiological studies is vitiated. There seems to me little point in grouping various diseases into a single treatment study and then saying that the treatment helps in 10% of cases. This must be avoided whenever possible. Not only must all existing diagnostic criteria be applied, but ultimately follow-up by autopsy would be extremely useful. With the best of efforts, diagnostic truth is not achieved in more than 80% or so of cases.

The difference between Alzheimer's disease of the senile type and of the presenile type, it seems to me, has most to do with the duration of the disorder. The older patients are very short-lived. Ninety-five percent of them are dead in 5 years, whereas most of the preseniles go on for about 10 years and therefore develop much more severe Alzheimer's disease. They are less susceptible to all the other problems of aging which are associated with senile Alzheimer's disease.

We have been taught a great deal about Alzheimer's disease among the senile that now seems not to be true. For example, when we had a series of 18 normal patients, normal clinically and normal histologically, between ages 70 and 90, whom we compared to 20 demented patients, demented clinically and with lots of plaques and tangles, we found that the brain weights were not significantly different. We found that the ventricles were not significantly different; some of the tomographers found this also. One cannot rely on ventricular dilatation or gyral atrophy to differentiate normals from seniles. This was not true for the preseniles who went on to much more severe disease.

Similarly we found that the cortical thickness, specifically of the midfrontal and superior temporal cortex, were not different on the average. We have done extensive cell counts in these two areas, midfrontal and superior temporal, and again we found only small differences in terms of neurons. These counts and measurements were done by an image analyzer without foreknowledge of clinical diagnosis, and then later correlated.

In the mid frontal area, it looked as if there were a small, but perhaps critical, loss of neurons; these may correspond to that small percentage of neurons which in the human cortex are cholinergic.

I had intended to talk about transmitters, but since Dr. Davies is here and was the first to report these deficiencies, I would prefer him to do so. I can only say that I think it is a very slim hope that the administration of a precursor in the almost total absence of the synthetic enzyme will do much good. I do not think that that is the approach which is most likely to produce therapeutic benefit.

Dr. David Dunner: Before you leave, could you discuss for a minute whether there was any evidence for changes in cerebral blood flow as pointed out by Dr. Ingvar yeasterday.

Dr. Terry: Dr. Ingvar presented his results in splendid fashion, and I think his observations were undoubtedly correct. Our patients were not studied with regard to cerebral blood flow. They were studied clinically, neuropsychologically, and pathologically. The abnormalities that we found were particularly in the temporal, frontal, and parietal areas, the same areas in which he showed marked deficiency of blood flow in the senile dements of the Alzheimer's type.

May I add one other point with regard to the diagnostic features exemplified in many other studies. In these, the authors simply indicated they were treating patients with organic brain syndrome and made no attempt to differentiate Alzheimer type of dementia from multiple infarct type or from any of the other possible types. To me this presents a very real problem in interpretation of any results.

OPEN DISCUSSION

Dr. Gershon: Dr. Terry's point is crucial. In other areas of psychopharmacology we are better able to deal with the issue of diagnostic heterogeneity. Here we have not dealt with it very well, for whatever reason. We have patients here with multiple types of dementia, and we are throwing treatments at them which may be of limited value anyway. This was the question that was raised, that treatments show very little effect. Maybe we need more sensitive scales.

Moreover, we have diagnostic heterogeneity, and it may be that Treatment A might be very good in the ordinary Alzheimer's disease, may be less useful in the vascular one, and vice versa. We are clearly lumping them together without significant distinction.

So there is no question but that there is a problem in design quite apart from the drug. But it isn't sensitivity of instruments. That is the least of our problems.

Dr. Alpert: I would appreciate Dr. Davies commenting on the usefulness of L-DOPA in Parkinson's disease. One might not have tried L-DOPA since the cells are shown to be lacking. It is noted that enzymes have to function within those cells. How could L-DOPA be useful?

Dr. Davies: This is a very interesting point that has cropped up in the past. Choline does not work in Alzheimer's disease because the cholinergic neurons are dead; why does L-DOPA work in Parkinson's disease? There is a trick here that is often missed. A good scientist, I think, would not have used L-DOPA initially in Parkinson's disease.

The reason why L-DOPA works is that the rate-limiting step for DOPA is tyrosine hydroxylase. The logical therapy for Parkinson's disease might equally well be tyrosine. Tyrosine is converted to dopamine. We use L-DOPA because L-DOPA gets in around the rate-limiting step. There is a lot of DOPA decarboxylase present, not only in dopaminergic neurons, but in neurons that make 5-HT and in cerebral capillaries. L-DOPA can get in around the rate-limiting step and produce dopamine not only in neurons but in other sites.

This is not possible with acetylcholine production. We have to go through the one enzyme step we have. If the enzyme is not good, there is no alternative route. I think this is the basic problem. Whatever dopamine neurons survive in Parkinson's disease will have an increased capacity to produce dopamine if we supply them with L-DOPA because they have plenty of DOPA decarboxylase. Neurons do not have much choline acetyltransferase (CAT).

If the precursor therapy idea worked in general, then tyrosine would be as good a therapy for Parkinson's disease as L-DOPA. It is not. There are some subtleties that have to be appreciated here.

Dr. Cole: Does Dr. Davies have any ideas as to available cholinergic agonists? I think arecoline is a possible agonist, but I am not sure it is a true cholinergic agonist. It has been used by Gillin at NIMH in young adults and by Pfeiffer in catatonic schizophrenics years ago. I planned to use it in senile dementia, but I am not sure it is a true agonist.

Dr. Davies: I am not sure about that either. I had hoped, as I do at every meeting in which psychiatrists are involved, that somebody would stand up and say, "I used it in senile dementia cases, and here is the lady who has been treated." She would then walk on the stage and exhibit a marvelous response to the treatment.

I do not know if arecoline is the right drug at all. There is an enormous amount of literature, mostly buried in the chemical literature, on agonists and antagonists. There may be a group of isolated scattered workers who have produced these agonists for years. They have not been investigated in any physiological sense other than as pure agonists. I think it will be a fascinating area over the next 10 years.

Dr. John Nurnberger: We have used arecoline in sleep studies of bipolar patients in remission with results on REM latency that are significantly different between bipolars and controls. This data will be presented by Dr. Sitaram at the APA this year. We have not experienced any difficulty in the use of arecoline with methscopolamine pretreatment. I cannot speak to the issue of Alzheimer's disease.

Dr. Growdon: I should like to respond to the criticism of precursor strategy. Certainly precursor loading would not work if all cholinergic cells were destroyed. This is not the case, however; 25 to 50% of them still survive in Alzheimer's disease. Since the enzyme CAT is normally unsaturated with its substrate (choline), treatments that increase the availability of choline would be expected to increase the rate of acetylcholine synthesis and thereby amplify cholinergic transmission from the surviving cells. Dr. Joseph Coyle at Johns Hopkins has recently reported experimental data in rats that confirm this prediction. We also know that neurons become more precursor dependent when they are firing rapidly. This may be the case in Alzheimer's disease, as surviving neurons may be working overtime.

Dr. Max Fink: In the 1950s there was an interest in the mechanism of the effects of seizures on brain function. Studies done at that time showed that spontaneous seizures or experimentally-induced seizures produced elevations in cholinesterase. The studies I am referring to are those of Tower and McEachern published in the early 50s (*Can. J. Res.,* Sect. E *27:* 105–119, 132–145, 1949). In one of their reports, subsequently verified in my laboratory, ECT produced an elevation of cholinesterase which persisted for 48 hr. After the first treatment, the elevation was transitory. But after the sixth to eighth treatment, the elevation was persistent.

Among the substances that Dr. Gershon and others have listed, piracetam seems to be omitted. Many claim this compound to be a memory enhancer. Also, recent letters in *Lancet* suggest that the peptide DGAVP has specific effects in improving memory in humans. Does anybody have any experience with either DGAVP or piracetam in memory studies?

Dr. Cole: I have one patient who tried some vasopressin and said he remembered better.

Dr. Wagner Bridger: It was interesting that Professor Roth, after surveying all the biological mechanisms in senile dementia, concluded his remarks by stating "If you use your wits you will die with your wits." This suggests a social etiology for senility.

I was struck by the experiment on stimulated versus spontaneous release of acetylcholine showing that stimulation had more of an effect. Kretch and Rosenzweig's study showed that rats, brought up in an enriched environment, had a more active cholinergic system. I was wondering whether anybody has information related to that, in terms of using one's wits, and also controlling for genetic variables. Perhaps Dr. Terry, or somebody in epidemiology, would have some information in terms of retirement versus "using one's wits."

Dr. Terry: All of us have seen many patients who have had advanced educations, who have been in highly responsible positions where they were indeed using their wits, and yet who have deteriorated over a period of months or years with Alzheimer's disease of the presenile or senile type. I am afraid that living by one's wits is not much protection, although it may raise the threshold beyond which symptoms appear.

Sir Martin Roth: I should like to respond to Professor Terry's remarks. I would hold that one has to draw a distinction between the attitude one adopts to a problem as a scientist and that which one uses for the purpose of clinical practice. I agree that one does see individuals of intellectual distinction who have developed dementia. But they are very uncommon. It is rare to find judges, experimental scientists, professors of philosophy or medicine with advanced deterioration spending their last months or years in institutions. I should like to add that in the course of our community studies we found that there was no difference in the prevalence of dementia in different social classes. But far fewer are admitted from the classes of the relatively privileged, and the difference does not arise merely from more favorable home circumstances. As far as those who live by their intellect is concerned, deterioration when it appears in advanced age seems to have less global effects. The damage tends to be patchy, and more of the personality survives. These comments stem from clinical observation, but no facts are available from stringent studies. The problem is of great interest and in need of investigation.

In short, it may be that to say "if you live by your wits, you die by your wits" is to whistle in the dark. But I would unashamedly continue to adopt the philosophy implied in this in clinical practice and preventive work.

I should like to ask a question on a quite different subject. The data in relation to cholinergic mechanisms in the brain are particularly impressive because of their specificity. It is a striking fact that one does not find diminished choline acetyltransferase activity in Huntington's chorea and, even more unexpectedly, it is not found in multi-infarct dementia. Nor does it occur in depressed patients or normal subjects, although the latter might have had to be admitted to hospital for treatment of physical disease. Only such "normals" have been available as controls in the relevant investigations.

It would be interesting to study the correlation of the regional distribution of the deficiency with what is known about the localization of lesions. Some recent evidence relating to lesions comes from the studies of Brun and Gustafson. These were confined to cases of Alzheimer's commencing in middle life, and they should not therefore be applied without qualification to classical "senile" cases. But they found the distribution of lesions to be most severe in the posterior part of the cingulate gyrus and the temporal parietal and occipital lobes. It would be interesting to determine therefore whether the pattern of diminished CAT activity matches the distribution of these lesions.

Dr. Davies: On the points about regional distribution, it is something of a problem in examining the cholinergic system. In that kind of morphological way, we have no idea how many or what cholinergic neurons there are in the cerebral cortex. We lack a method of specifically visualizing cholinergic neurons. It could be 2%, which is one estimate I heard, or it could be 25%, another I have encountered.

As to the lesions, whether the neurofibrillary tangles and plaques match the distribution of cholinergic neurons, they certainly do not. This is a very interesting point.

Dr. Terry: Neurons, of course, have their major function as neurotransmitters. They are synthesizers of chemical neurotransmitters, but they also have major vegetative functions having to do with keeping themselves alive. These other functions may well determine their lifespan, and that is probably determined also by their own genetic inheritance. Each type of neuron, because of its individual inheritance and metabolism, may well have a different susceptibility to viral infection, and to all sorts of other disorders. The spectrum of susceptibility might explain the regional distribution of the lesions rather than simply what in this sense is a gross mapping by neurotransmitter function.

In normal aging, there is apparently a significant loss of neocortical neurons. However, in many brain stem nuclei there is no such loss, whereas in locus coeruleus there is a decrement. These things differ.

This other aspect of normal lifespan of neurons undoubtedly is added to the cholinergic problem in determining the particular signs in a particular disease or even in a particular patient with that disease.

Dr. Peter Gruen: A couple of comments and questions. I am addressing myself principally to neurochemists or neuropathologists.

Would you speculate as to which neurochemical system is post-synaptic to the cholinergic fibers?

And a related question, are there any further thoughts about receptor hypersensitivity? If you follow the dopamine acetylcholine balance hypothesis, we might guess that if you used a choline antagonist, you might see hypersensitivity similar to that produced by dopamine blockade.

Also, I did want to address one other issue. Dr. Growdon made a point that I think is very important and not widely appreciated. That is that the cholinergic input to the adrenal medulla causes the release of catecholamines. I wonder if there is any data available as to how important that is quantitatively or physiologically.

Dr. Davies: With regard to your first question, we have no idea, except what attaches to cholinergic neurons in the basal ganglia; there it would be dopamine. Anywhere else in the brain, we have no clues.

Receptor hypersensitivity in the muscarinic system is what I would predict when I look at Alzheimer's cases. In fact, there is no evidence for that. In the rat, we can remove the cholinergic input to the hippocampus by making a lesion. We follow that rat up to 6 months afterwards and can look at the receptors. They remain absolutely constant, with no change whatsoever. It does not seem that hypersensitivity is necessarily a general phenomenon.

Dr. Zubin: I want to go back to the statement "those who live by their wits die with their wits" if I may. In this area there is no solid information, so one can be free to speculate. I would like to speculate for a few moments. No one is destined to develop dementia. No one is destined to develop schizophrenia. All we have are vulnerable individuals. Sixty percent of monozygotic twins who have a schizophrenic co-twin do not develop schizophrenia. There must be something environmental necessary to trigger an episode in the vulnerable individual.

From that point of view, it seems to me that one can adopt a very hopeful attitude toward the problems of dementia. There must be something that we can do to intervene, because not everybody who is vulnerable to dementia develops it. It is this particular fact, that nothing is really destined irrevocably, that makes it necessary for us to consider other than the biological and the genetic components in old age.

Dr. Goldstein: What I have to say was in reference to Dr. Lawton's talk. I think he gave a very nice survey of the field. However, it seems to me that he left out one entire area of psychosocial intervention which is educational in nature. I refer to the work of Diller, Weinberg, and others at the N.Y.U. Institute of Rehabilitation Medicine. These investigators are doing retraining of stroke patients, using a neuropsychological-educational model.

I wanted to point that out that there have been several books written about this aspect of rehabilitation, one by Charles Golden on rehabilitative assessment and the other by Luria on recovery of function. I suspect this may be a promising area, independently, or in conjunction with behavior modification and other methods.

Dr. David Dunner: We have physical therapists who do rehabilitation work, with some success, with accident victims who have paralysis. I wonder what the representation of that model would be in terms of people who have brain disease and have confusional problems rather than problems with paralysis. Maybe we could combine pyschosocial techniques, such as educational programs, to help some of our patients.

Dr. Powell Lawton: Let me be the first to say that this type of intervention has been omitted from my presentation today. I suspect that the behavioral manifestations of dementia are different from cognitive functions that need to be trained. But the point is that such educational approaches have been ignored. If some of you are interested in a provocative bit of ideology, about a year ago in one of our journals *(The Gerontologist)*, Harold Wershaw advocated benign vegetative care for the OBS patient because society's resources were better needed in places that could do some good.

That point of view is what has produced the inability to specify what can help, in what kind of increments, and in what kind of person. We lump together all kinds of disorders in a much more gross way than just mixing Alzheimer's and other brain disorders. The kind of grouping I am talking about puts all institutionalized persons 65 years or over into the same program and does not differentiate among them.

We are suffering from abysmal ignorance. My own interpretation of the available research on intervention with dementia is that the gains are minimally perceptible—incremental, but still measurable. What is needed is a treatment technology that will focus on the details of speech, thinking, and very explicit memory and orientational functions in order to know what are the limits of behavior therapy or educational treatment or any other kind of therapy.

Dr. Ruth Bennett: I will be very brief. I would like to say that in our current study, as Dr. Gurland mentioned, we are finding more demented and disabled and otherwise deteriorated people outside institutions than in. They are surviving. I feel it is our obligation to document what exactly it is they are doing, whether they die before their institutional counterparts, what they are doing to survive, who is helping them to survive, and how it is that they are able to function in the community whereas their counterparts in institutions cannot do so.

Clearly something is happening to them. Many of them are living out in the community and are getting along. This has been documented since the early 1960s studies of Goldfarb conducted in housing projects. I really feel we are obligated to study these people, as my colleagues and I are doing, in order to learn what is keeping them going.

Dr. Jarvik: I should like to underscore the point that functional disorders are *not* necessarily easier to reverse than organic ones. As an example, we can take treatable or preventable forms of mental retardation, and the one that comes to mind immediately is phenylketonuria, a genetically-determined organic form. I believe that the situation will be similar in the organic brain syndromes—a specific identifiable organic derangement will lead us to methods of treatment and/or prevention.

My second point concerns the survival of demented patients. It is a general experience now that they survive longer. I believe that in the second follow-up in the Swedish study, unlike the first, the average lifespan remaining, after the diagnosis of senile dementia was made, was somewhat in excess of 8 years, compared to 2 years during the first follow-up 10 years earlier. The speculation has been that environmental factors, such as better care, improved nutrition, antibiotics, and other changes contributed to that.

The third point is I am curious about the sex distribution of those individuals in the community who are surviving alone with dementia. Not only couples are surviving. In couples, I think it is very often the male who has dementia and who receives support and total care from his wife. We have had many such cases from the community now that it is known that we are interested in senile dementia patients.

Dr. Gurland: There were three cases of diagnosed pervasive dementia living alone in New York; all were females. Male dements in New York were all living in a household with a related person. The primary provider was in four cases the spouse, and in two the daughter.

Subject Index

Acetazolamide, 239
Acetylcholine, synthesis of, 284–287
Acetylcholinesterase, dementia levels
of, 222–224
Adjective Mood Checklist, 101–102,
108–111
Adrenocorticotropic hormone, dementia
therapy with, 245–247
Aging
attitudes toward, 8–14, 17–18
behavioral changes in, 3
of brain, 127–128, 140
cellular theory of, 3
intelligence in, 2, 4–6, 17, 138
memory changes in, 6–7, 138, 140
normative data base for study of, 1–2,
39–40, 139–140
pathology risks of, 1, 2–7, 10, 17
pharmacokinetic changes with, 157–
160
physical changes in, 21–22
sleep patterns in, 10–11, 17–18
social aspects of, 7–9, 14, 17
stress theory of, 4–5
Agoraphobia, 58
Alcoholism
brain changes in, 140
dementia related to, 225
depression related to familial, 150–151
Aluminum, in Alzheimer's disease, 71,
127, 215
Alzheimer's disease
aluminum in, 71, 127, 215
brain degeneration in, 3, 66, 123,
125–128, 215
cerebral blood flow in, 74–75, 79,
80, 123–124, 298
choline administration for, 284–291,
295–296, 300
cholinergic deterioration in, 247, 249,
281–283
cognitive dysfunction in, 123–125,
128–132
depression with, 105–116

diagnosis of, 99–103, 112, 128–132,
297–298
Down's syndrome and, 66–68, 127
forms of, 63, 68, 137, 214
gender factors in, 226
hematologic cancer and risk of,
67, 221
intelligence standards for, 131, 139
memory in, 93, 104, 115, 288
neurotransmitter levels in, 127–128,
222–224, 247–250, 282–283
onset of, 66, 72
prevalence of, 220
regional distribution of brain lesions
in, 126–127
senile dementia compared with, 63, 68,
214–215
viral cause of, 71, 220, 224
Amitriptyline
effectiveness of, 167, 252
metabolism of in elderly, 162
Amnesia, 138–139, 210
Amobarbital interview, 27
Amyloidosis, 216
Anticoagulants, in dementia therapy,
239–240
Antidepressants
in dementia therapy, 252–253
in depression therapy, 160–162
Antisocial behavior, 150–151
Anxiety, cognitive performance response
to, 4–5
Arecoline, 283, 299
Arteriosclerosis, memory disturbance
from, 59
Aphasia, 138
Attitude toward aging, 8–14, 17–18
Automated Behavioral Assessment
System, 85–90, 91, 93, 94

Beck Depression Inventory, 101–102,
107, 110, 111, 119–120, 173,
175–176